Quantitative Research Methods

Applied CQRM Book Series

Volume I

Applying Monte Carlo Risk Simulation, Machine Learning, Artificial Intelligence, Strategic Real Options, Stochastic Forecasting, Portfolio Optimization, Data Science, and Decision Analytics

IIPER Press

Third Edition

IIPER
Press

Johnathan Mun, Ph.D.

California, USA

Risk Simulator

RQV BizStats

Printed in the United States of America

For Jayden, Emma, and Penny.

In a world where risk and uncertainty abound, you are the only constants in my life.

Dedicated in loving memory of my mom.

Delight yourself in the Lord and He will give you the desires of your heart.

Psalm 37:4

The Applied CQRM Book Series showcases how the advanced analytics covered in the Certified in Quantitative Risk Management (CQRM) certification program can be applied to real-life business problems. In Volume I, we show how Risk Simulator and ROV BizStats can be used to perform quantitative analysis in graduate and postgraduate research.

Pragmatic applications are emphasized in order to demystify the many elements inherent in quantitative analysis. A statistical black box will remain a black box if no one can understand the concepts despite its power and applicability. It is only when the black box methods become transparent so that researchers can understand, apply, and convince others of their results, value-add, and applicability, that the approaches will receive widespread attention. This transparency is achieved through step-by-step applications of quantitative modeling as well as presenting multiple cases and discussing real-life applications.

This book is targeted at those individuals who have completed the CQRM certification program but can also be used by anyone familiar with basic quantitative research methods—there is something for everyone. It is also applicable for use as a second-year MBA/MS-level or introductory Ph.D. quick reference. The examples in the book assume some prior knowledge of the subject matter. Additional information on the CQRM program can be obtained at:

www.iiper.org

www.realoptionsvaluation.com

www.rovusa.com

Dr. Johnathan C. Mun is the founder, chairman, and CEO of Real Options Valuation, Inc. (ROV), a consulting, training, and software development firm specializing in strategic real options, financial valuation, Monte Carlo risk simulation, stochastic forecasting, optimization, decision analytics, business intelligence, healthcare analytics, enterprise risk management, project risk management, quantitative research methods, and risk analysis located in northern Silicon Valley, California. ROV has partners around the world including Argentina, Beijing, Chicago, China, Colombia, Ghana, Hong Kong, India, Italy, Japan, Malaysia, Mexico City, New York, Nigeria, Peru, Puerto Rico, Russia, Saudi Arabia, Shanghai, Singapore, Slovenia, South Africa, South Korea, Spain, United Kingdom, Venezuela, Zurich, and others. ROV also has a local office in Shanghai.

Dr. Mun is also the chairman of the International Institute of Professional Education and Research (IIPER), an accredited global organization staffed by professors from named universities from around the world that provides the Certified in Quantitative Risk Management (CQRM) and Certified in Risk Management (CRM) designations, among others. He is the creator of many powerful software tools including Risk Simulator, Real Options SLS Super Lattice Solver, Modeling Toolkit, Project Economics Analysis Tool (PEAT), Credit Market Operational Liquidity Risk (CMOL), Employee Stock Options Valuation, ROV BizStats, ROV Modeler Suite (Basel Credit Modeler, Risk Modeler, Optimizer, and Valuator), ROV Compiler, ROV Extractor and Evaluator, ROV Dashboard, ROV Quantitative Data Miner, and other software applications, as well as the risk-analysis training DVD. He holds public seminars on risk analysis and CQRM programs. He has over 21 registered patents and patents pending globally. He has authored over 23 books published by John Wiley & Sons, Elsevier Science, IIPER Press, and ROV Press, including multiple volumes of the Applied CQRM Series (IIPER Press, 2019-2020); *Modeling Risk: Applying Monte Carlo Simulation, Strategic Real Options, Stochastic Forecasting, Portfolio Optimization, Data Analytics, Business Intelligence, and Decision Modeling,* First Edition (Wiley, 2006), Second Edition (Wiley, 2010), and Third Edition

(ROV Press, 2015); *The Banker's Handbook on Credit Risk* (2008); *Advanced Analytical Models: 250 Applications from Basel II Accord to Wall Street and Beyond* (2008); *Real Options Analysis: Tools and Techniques,* First Edition (2003) and Second Edition (2005); *Real Options Analysis Course: Business Cases* (2003); *Applied Risk Analysis: Moving Beyond Uncertainty* (2003); and *Valuing Employee Stock Options* (2004). His books and software are being used at over 350 top universities around the world, including the Bern Institute in Germany, Chung-Ang University in South Korea, Georgetown University, ITESM in Mexico, Massachusetts Institute of Technology, U.S. Naval Postgraduate School, New York University, Stockholm University in Sweden, University of the Andes in Chile, University of Chile, University of Hull, University of Pennsylvania Wharton School, University of York in the United Kingdom, and Edinburgh University in Scotland, among others.

Currently a risk, finance, and economics professor, Dr. Mun has taught courses in financial management, investments, real options, economics, and statistics at the undergraduate and graduate MS, MBA, and Ph.D. levels. He teaches and has taught at universities all over the world, from the U.S. Naval Postgraduate School (Monterey, California) and University of Applied Sciences (Switzerland and Germany) as full professor, to Golden Gate University (California) and St. Mary's College (California), and has chaired many graduate research MBA thesis and Ph.D. dissertation committees. He also teaches weeklong Risk Analysis, Real Options Analysis, and Risk Analysis for Managers public courses where participants can obtain the CRM and CQRM designations on completion. He is a senior fellow at the Magellan Center and sits on the board of standards at the American Academy of Financial Management.

He was formerly the Vice President of Analytics at Decisioneering, Inc., where he headed the development of options and financial analytics software products, analytical consulting, training, and technical support, and where he was the creator of the Real Options Analysis Toolkit software, the older and much less powerful predecessor of the Real Options Super Lattice software. Prior to joining Decisioneering, he was a Consulting Manager and Financial Economist in the Valuation Services and Global Financial Services practice of KPMG Consulting and a Manager with the Economic Consulting Services practice at KPMG LLP.

He has extensive experience in econometric modeling, financial analysis, real options, economic analysis, and statistics. During his tenure at Real Options Valuation, Inc., Decisioneering, and KPMG Consulting, he taught and consulted on a variety of real options, risk analysis, financial forecasting, project management, and financial valuation issues for more than 100 multinational firms (current and former clients include 3M, Airbus, Boeing, BP, Chevron Texaco, Financial Accounting Standards Board, Fujitsu, GE, Goodyear, Microsoft, Motorola, Northrop Grumman, Pfizer, Timken, U.S. Department of Defense, U.S. Navy, Veritas, and many others). His experience prior to joining KPMG included being department head of financial planning and analysis at Viking Inc. of FedEx, performing financial forecasting, economic analysis, and market research. Prior to that, he did financial planning and freelance financial consulting work.

Dr. Mun received a Ph.D. in finance and economics from Lehigh University, where his research and academic interests were in the areas of investment finance, econometric modeling, financial options, corporate finance, and microeconomic theory. He also has an MBA in business administration, an MS in management science, and a BS in biology and physics. He is Certified in Financial Risk Management, Certified in Financial Consulting, and Certified in Quantitative Risk Management. He is a member of the American Mensa, Phi Beta Kappa Honor Society, and Golden Key Honor Society as well as several other professional organizations, including the Eastern and Southern Finance Associations, American Economic Association, and Global Association of Risk Professionals.

In addition, he has written many academic articles published in the *Journal of Expert Systems with Applications; Defense Acquisition Research Journal; American Institute of Physics Proceedings; Acquisitions Research (U.S. Department of Defense); Journal of the Advances in Quantitative Accounting and Finance; Global Finance Journal; International Financial Review; Journal of Financial Analysis; Journal of Applied Financial Economics; Journal of International Financial Markets, Institutions and Money; Financial Engineering News;* and *Journal of the Society of Petroleum Engineers.* Finally, he has contributed chapters in dozens of books and written over a hundred technical whitepapers, newsletters, case studies, and research papers for Real Options Valuation, Inc.

JohnathanMun@cs.com

San Francisco, California

ACCOLADES FOR DR. MUN'S BOOKS

...powerful toolset for portfolio/program managers to make rational choices among alternatives...
    Rear Admiral James Greene (Ret.), Acquisitions Chair
    Naval Postgraduate School (USA)

...unavoidable for any professional...logical, concrete, and conclusive approach...
    Jean Louis Vaysse, Vice President, Airbus (France)

...proven, revolutionary approach to quantifying risks and opportunities in an uncertain world...
    Mike Twyman, President, Mission Solutions,
    Cubic Global Defense, Inc. (USA)

...must read for anyone running investment economics...best way to quantify risk and strategic options...
    Mubarak A. Alkhater, Executive Director, New Business,
    Saudi Electric Co. (Saudi Arabia)

... pragmatic powerful risk techniques, valuable theoretical insights and analytics useful in any industry...
    Dr. Robert S. Finocchiaro, Director,
    Corporate R&D Services, 3M (USA)

...most important risk tools in one volume, definitive source on risk management with vivid examples...
    Dr. Ricardo Valerdi, Engineering Systems,
    Massachusetts Institute of Technology (USA)

...step-by-step complex concepts with unmatched ease and clarity... a "must read" for all professionals...
    Dr. Hans Weber, Product Development Leader,
    Syngenta AG (Switzerland)

...clear step-by-step approach...latest technology in decision making for real-world business...
    Dr. Paul W. Finnegan, Vice President, Alexion Pharmaceuticals (USA)

...clear roadmap and breadth of topics to create dynamic risk-adjusted strategies and options...
    Jeffrey A. Clark, Vice President Strategic Planning,
    The Timken Company (USA)

…clearly organized and tool-supported exploration of real-life business risks, options, strategy…

> Robert Mack, Vice President, Distinguished Analyst,
> Gartner Group (USA)

…full range of methodologies for quantifying and mitigating risk for effective enterprise management…

> Raymond Heika, Director of Strategic Planning,
> Northrop Grumman Corporation (USA)

…a must-read for product portfolio managers…captures risk exposure of strategic investments…

> Rafael Gutierrez, Executive Director Strategic Marketing Planning,
> Seagate Technologies (USA)

…complex topics exceptionally explained…
can understand and practice…

> Agustín Velázquez, Senior Economist,
> Venezuela Central Bank (Venezuela)

…constant source of practical applications with risk management theory…simply excellent!

> Alfredo Roisenzvit, Executive Director/Professor,
> Risk-Business Latin America (Argentina)

…the best risk modeling book is now better…
required reading by all executives…

> David Mercier, Vice President Corporate Dev.,
> Bonanza Creek Energy [Oil & Gas] (USA)

…bridge of theory and practice, intuitive,
understandable interpretations…

> Luis Melo, Senior Econometrician,
> Colombia Central Bank (Colombia)

…valuable tools for corporations to deliver value to shareholders and society even in rough times…

> Dr. Markus Götz Junginger, Lead Partner,
> Gallup (Germany)

CONTENTS

QUANTITATIVE RESEARCH METHODS IN A NUTSHELL

The fields of statistics and quantitative methods are very closely related, and they collectively refer to the compilation, presentation, analysis, and utilization of numerical data to make inferences and decisions in the face of uncertainty. Statistics is used mainly to describe the behavior of certain variables and to make inferences about the true nature of these variables. Descriptive statistics summarize data and inferential statistics generalize the population through a small sample set to make predictions. Quantitative analysis can be seen as the application of statistics to help managers make informed decisions. A simple example illustrates how statistics can be applied to collect information on the average income level of the population in a particular city. A sample of the city's population is surveyed, and the average income is tabulated. Then, statistical sampling techniques are used to infer the population's true average income levels. Quantitative analysis is then applied to make decisions as to whether a local shopping mall should be built in the city center based on the wealth distribution of the local residents.

In general, most statistical methods employed in quantitative and mixed methods research require designing the experiment, collecting sample data, analyzing the collected data using basic descriptive statistics, hypothesis testing on the data, estimating or predicting, running goodness-of-fit, and making strategic and tactical decisions. The remainder of this book covers both descriptive statistics and inferential statistics. This chapter provides a quick overview of these methods.

The term *variable* refers to the item of interest being studied, such as income, weight, age, and so forth. The term *sample* refers to the subset of the population being measured, and its tabulated results are collectively referred to as *statistics*. The ultimate goal of statistics is to infer the actual and true nature of the entire *population*, which includes all the observations of interest of a variable, whose tabulated results are collectively known as *parameters*.

DESCRIPTIVE STATISTICS AND DISTRIBUTIONAL MOMENTS

Descriptive statistics are generally applied to collected research data. With descriptive statistics, we are simply describing what is or what the collected data show. Descriptive statistics are used to present quantitative descriptions in a manageable and simplified form. The analysis may include graphical representations of the data in the form of bar charts, line charts, cumulative charts, and probability histograms. In addition, basic statistical computations can be employed to determine a dataset's mean, median, mode, standard deviation, variance, volatility, coefficient of variation, percentiles, confidence intervals, and so forth. Figure 1.1 provides an overview of the methods.

PROBABILITY THEORY AND PROBABILITY DISTRIBUTIONS

An area between descriptive statistics and inferential statistics is the application of probability theory and probability distribution. Sometimes, data that is collected can come in the form of proportions, or chances that certain events occur, in other words, the probability of an event. These probabilities can then be generalized to infer about the entire population. For example, relative frequencies can be used to generate a probability histogram to describe the data collected. Basic probability rules and Bayes' Theorem are shown in Figure 1.2, while discrete probability distributions, followed by an explanation of continuous probability distributions are shown in Figure 1.3.

Hypothesis tests are based on various underlying probability distributions (Figure 1.3). With hypothesis testing (Figure 1.4), we enter the area of inferential statistics, where the researcher is trying to reach conclusions that extend beyond the immediate data alone. Inferential statistics allows the researcher to make judgments of the probability or chances that observed differences between two or more groups are dependable and reliable or are ones that might have happened by random chance.

Hypothesis testing is a statistical method used to test whether a sample dataset is close enough to some hypothesized value, or if two or more datasets are statistically similar or statistically different. For instance, suppose you run a simple linear correlation using collected data on daily sunspot activity and stock market returns for the last 10 years. Theoretically, it would be almost impossible to obtain a perfect zero correlation (i.e., 0.0000...) when a large dataset exists. Suppose the correlation calculated is 0.02. Is this correlation close enough to zero to unequivocally state that the actual correlation is really zero and that any slight variation is due to random chance? What if the correlation was 0.03, or 0.05, or 0.20? At what point can we state that the correlation is far enough from zero and that is it no longer zero, or statistically significant?

STATISTICAL METHODS
FOR ONE VARIABLE

Figure 1.5 provides an overview of the basics of hypothesis testing on one variable. This includes statistical hypothesis testing, where an assumption is made about a population parameter and tested using the data collected. This assumption may or may not be true and can be statistically tested if sample statistics are available. The technical term *hypothesis testing* refers to the formal statistical and mathematical procedures used by statisticians to either accept or reject a certain hypothesis. Clearly, the best way to determine with absolute certainty whether a hypothesis is true would be to examine the entire population. This is usually impractical, so, researchers examine a smaller but random sample from the population. If the sample data's calculated statistics are not consistent with the statistical hypothesis, the hypothesis is rejected. Sometimes, a one-variable hypothesis test is done to determine if a certain variable's mean or standard deviation is some predetermined value (e.g., whether a correlation coefficient is statistically significant).

STATISTICAL METHODS FOR TWO OR MORE VARIABLES

Figures 1.6 and 1.7 cover additional hypothesis testing on two or more variables. The two-variables test, as its name suggests, compares two sample datasets against each other to determine if there is a statistically significant difference between their population means, in other words, if a certain event or experiment has an effect. Additional variables can be added, and these variables can be tested against each other simultaneously. See Chapter 6 for a detailed list of all the methods available in the ROV BizStats software. The overview also dives into the most commonly used methodologies, starting with paired t-tests, paired F-tests, and ANOVA, and continues with multiple regression and nonparametric analysis.

SIMULATION, PREDICTIVE MODELING, AND OPTIMIZATION

This book also covers the basics of additional advanced techniques that will assist in your ongoing research efforts. For additional detailed information, please see Dr. Johnathan Mun's *Quantitative Research Methods* and *Modeling Risk* (Third Edition) books. For instance, these books provide details into forecasting and predictive modeling, where collected historical or contemporaneous data can be used to forecast and predict future outcomes. Modeling techniques applying multivariate regression are also addressed, where you can model the interactions and statistical effects of multiple independent variables on the dependent variable, and statistically quantify the effect levels. These books include data simulation and data generation using probability distributions. Using limited sample data, the population's distribution can be generated empirically using simulation techniques. In the event of limited data, simulation can be used to perform nonparametric resampling to generate a larger dataset for analysis.

SAMPLE MEASURES OF RISK

Beta (β)
Coefficient of Variation (CV)
Probability of Failure
Risk Adjusted Return on Capital ($RAROC$)
Standard Deviation (σ)
Value at Risk (VaR)
Variance (σ^2)
Volatility (σ)

HYPOTHESIS TESTS OF MOMENTS

The first moment has many types of theoretical hypothesis tests such as t-test, z-test, F-test, and other parametric tests of significance or tests of differences. The second moment has limited theoretical tests of significance and differences such as χ^2 tests. The third and fourth moments require solely nonparametric empirical tests such as bootstrap simulations, which can also be used to test the first and second moments on their confidence intervals, precision levels, and statistical significance.

MOMENTS

First Moment

Mean, median, 50th percentile
Measures central tendency
Measures central location
Expected value and expected returns

Second Moment

Standard deviation, variance, range, confidence interval, interquartile range, volatility, coefficient of variation
Measures the distributional spread and width
Accounts for risk and uncertainty of the variable

Third Moment

Coefficient of Skew
Skew means Mean $\neq$ Median
Skew of 0 implies symmetry
Normal implies skew is 0
Skew > 0 if Mean > Median
Skew < 0 if Median > Mean
Skew is 0 if Mean = Median and the distribution is deemed as symmetrical

Fourth Moment

Coefficient of Kurtosis
Excess kurtosis of 0 implies regular or normal tails (mesokurtic)
Leptokurtic (fat tails) with high positive excess kurtosis implies higher expected chances of extreme events occurring
Distributions with no tails (e.g., uniform distribution has a min and max) are platykurtic with negative excess kurtosis

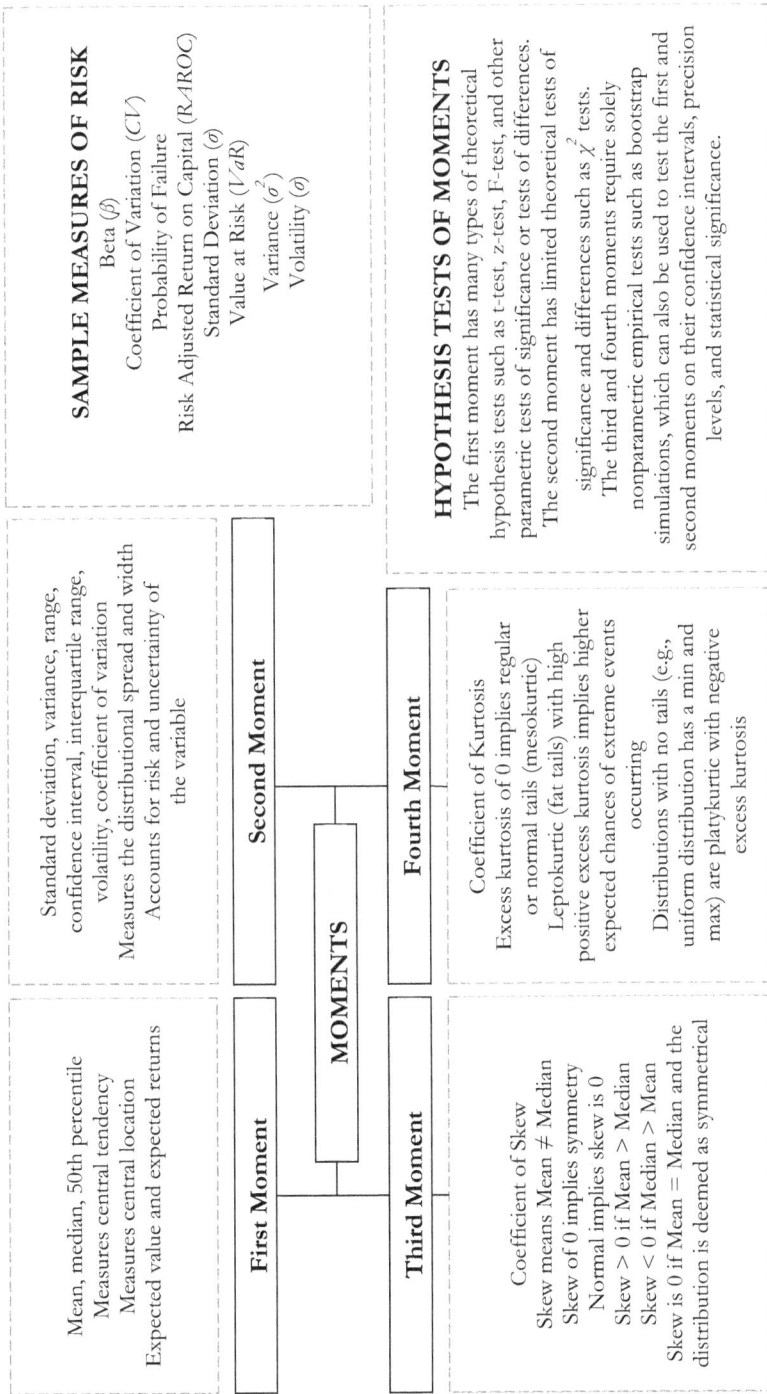

Figure 1.1: Distributional Moments and Descriptive Statistics

Bayes' Theorem

$$P(A|M) = \frac{P(A \cap M)}{P(M)} = \frac{P(A)P(M|A)}{P(M)} = \frac{P(A)P(M|A)}{P(A \cap M) + P(B \cap M) + P(C \cap M)} = \frac{P(A)P(M|A)}{P(A)P(M|A) + P(B)P(M|B) + P(C)P(M|C)}$$

$$P(X_1|M) = \frac{P(X_1)P(M|X_1)}{P(X_1)P(M|X_1) + P(X_2)P(M|X_2) + P(X_3)P(M|X_3) + \ldots + P(X_n)P(M|X_n)}$$

Combinations and Permutations

$$C_x^n = \frac{n!}{x!(n-x)!} \qquad P_x^n = \frac{n!}{(n-x)!}$$

Binomial Distribution

$$P(x) = \frac{n!}{x!(n-x)!} p^x (1-p)^{(n-x)} \quad for\ n > 0;\ x = 0,\ 1,\ 2,\ \ldots\ n;\ and\ 0 < p < 1$$

For each trial, only two outcomes are possible that are mutually exclusive. The trials are independent—what happens in the first trial does not affect the next trial. The probability of an event occuring remains the same from trial to trial.

Poisson Distribution

$$P(x) = \frac{e^{-\lambda} \lambda^x}{x!}$$

The number of possible occurrences in any interval is unlimited. The occurrences are independent. The number of occurrences in one interval does not affect the number of occurrences in other intervals. The average number of occurrences must remain the same from interval to interval. The values x and $\lambda > 0$.

Hypergeometric Distribution

$$P(x) = \frac{\dfrac{(N_x)!}{x!(N_x - x)!} \dfrac{(N - N_x)!}{(n-x)!(N - N_x - n + x)!}}{\dfrac{N!}{n!(N-n)!}} \quad for\ x = Max(n - (N - N_x), 0), \ldots, Min(n, N_x)$$

The total number of items or elements (the population size) is a fixed number, a finite population. The population size must be less than or equal to 1,750. The sample size is the number of trials and represents a portion of the population. The known initial probability of success in the population changes after each trial.

Normal Distribution

$$f(x) = \frac{1}{\sqrt{2\pi}\sigma} e^{\frac{-(x-\mu)^2}{2\sigma^2}} \quad for\ all\ values\ of\ x$$

Some value of the uncertain variable is the most likely (the mean of the distribution). The uncertain variable could as likely be above the mean as it could be below the mean (symmetrical about the mean). The uncertain variable is more likely in the vicinity of the mean than further away.

Figure 1.2: Probability Theory and Probability Distributions

COMMONLY USED

NORMAL
Continuous bell curve, a.k.a. Gaussian distribution, infinite tails on both ends, requires mean and standard deviation as inputs. Symmetrical with zero skew and zero excess kurtosis. Ex.: stock returns, height, weight, IQ (truncated normal with limits).

UNIFORM
Flat continuous area with equal probability of occurrence at any point between the minimum and maximum. Symmetrical with zero skew and negative excess kurtosis (fixed end points). Examples: business forecasts and economic forecasts.

TRIANGULAR
Looks like a triangle, continuous values, tails end at min and max with most likely as its peak. Can be skewed or symmetrical, with negative excess kurtosis (truncated tails). Examples: sales forecasts, subject matter estimates, management assumptions.

POISSON
Discrete events occurring independently with the same average rate of repetition and measured in time or space (area). Examples: sales forecasts, subject matter estimates, management assumptions. Approaches normal with high average rates.

CUSTOM
Empirically fitted discrete distribution when little data is available or when other theoretical distributions fail. Suitable for Delphi methods, can be multimodal or irregular. Examples: subject matter estimates, management assumptions, and qualitative estimates that are converted numerically.

BINOMIAL
Discrete events with two mutually exclusive and independent outcomes with fixed probability of success at each successive trial. Symmetrical and approaches normal distribution with high number of trials. Example: tossing a coin multiple times.

LESS COMMONLY USED BUT IMPORTANT DISTRIBUTIONS

BETA 4
Highly flexible continuous distribution capable of taking on multiple shapes and scales.

DISCRETE UNIFORM
Range of discrete events with equal probability of occurrence (e.g., rolling a six-sided die).

EXPONENTIAL 2
High probably of low values, low probability of continuous high values (e.g., wait time).

BERNOULLI
Single discrete trial version of Binomial (e.g., simulating success or failure of projects).

LOGNORMAL
Variables with continuous non-negative and non-zero values (e.g., stock prices).

STUDENT'S T
Continuous-normal with fat tails or higher probability of extremes (e.g., risky returns).

WEIBULL 3
Continuous mean time before failure and reliability estimates (e.g., MTBF of an engine).

GUMBEL
Tail-end extreme value simulations of continuous outcomes (e.g., market crashes).

OTHER DISTRIBUTIONS: Arcsine, Beta, Beta 3, Cauchy, Chi-square, Cosine, Double Log, Erlang, Exponential, F, Fréchet, Gamma, Geometric, Gumbel Min, Gumbel Max, Hypergeometric, Laplace, Logistic, Lognormal 3, Negative Binomial, Parabolic, Generalized Pareto, Pareto, Pascal, Pearson V, Pearson VI, Pert, Power, Power 3, Rayleigh, Standard-Normal, Standard-T, Weibull

Figure 1.3: Most Common Probability Distributions

The hypotheses tested are typically:

$H_0: \mu_1 = \mu_2$, that is, the two samples' means are statistically similar

$H_a: \mu_1 \neq \mu_2$, that is, the two samples' means are statistically significantly different

The null hypothesis (H_0) generally has the equivalence sign (i.e., $=$, $\geq$, $\leq$), whereas the alternate hypothesis (H_a) has its complement (i.e., $\neq$, $<$, $>$). The sign of the alternate hypothesis points to whether the test is a two-tailed test ($\neq$) or a one-tailed test (right tail is denoted with $>$, whereas a left tail test uses $<$). As an example, to get started in a two-sample hypothesis test, a dataset with some number of data points for two variables (with n_1 and n_2 sample sizes) are put side by side. Then, their respective sample averages $\bar{x}_1$ and $\bar{x}_2$ and sample standard deviations s_1 and s_2 are computed. The t-statistic is then calculated using the various formulae and compared against the critical t-values. In most situations, the p-values of this calculated t-statistic are calculated and compared against some predefined level of significance (i.e., the standard α significance levels of 0.10, 0.05, and 0.01 will be assumed throughout) using the t-distribution with a certain degree of freedom (df). If the p-value is below these α significance levels, we reject the null hypothesis and accept the alternate hypothesis.

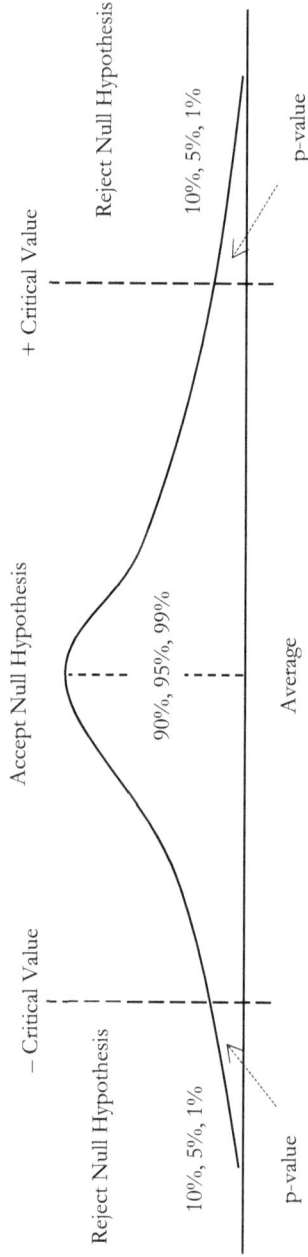

Figure 1.4: Hypothesis Testing Basics

1-Variable Tests

Testing Population Mean μ

Known σ:
- Normality Assumed → Z-Test: $Z = \dfrac{\bar{x} - \mu_{\bar{X}}}{\sigma_{\bar{X}}} = \dfrac{\bar{x} - \mu_{\bar{X}}}{\frac{\sigma}{\sqrt{n}}}$ $\quad \sigma_{\bar{X}} = \dfrac{\sigma}{\sqrt{n}}\left(\sqrt{\dfrac{N - n}{N - 1}}\right)$
- Data is Not Normal:
  - $n \geq 30$ → Z-Test
  - $n < 30$ → Wilcoxon Signed-Rank Test for 1 Variable $\quad W = \Sigma\,(R+)$

Unknown σ:
- Normality Assumed or $n \geq 30$ → T-Test $\quad t = \dfrac{\bar{x} - \mu}{s_{\bar{X}}} = \dfrac{\bar{x} - \mu}{\frac{s}{\sqrt{n}}}$
- Data is Not Normal or $n < 30$ → Wilcoxon Signed-Rank Test for 1 Variable $\quad W = \Sigma\,(R+)$ $\quad$ Testing Medians

Testing Population Proportion π

$n\pi \geq 5$ or $n(1 - \pi) \geq 5$ → Z-Test for Proportions $\quad Z = \dfrac{p - \pi}{\sigma_P}$ $\quad \sigma_P = \sqrt{\dfrac{\pi(1 - \pi)}{n}}$

Testing Normality $\Phi(N)$

- $n \geq 30$ → Kolmogorov-Smirnov, Anderson-Darling, Akaike, Bayes' Criterion $\quad KS = \max_{1 \leq i \leq N}\left|F(Y_i) - \dfrac{i}{N}\right|$ $\quad \chi^2 = \sum_{i=1}^{k}(O_i - E_i)^2 / E_i$
- $n < 30$ → Lilliefors Test $\quad D = max\,|O_i - CDF_i|$

Testing Randomness → Runs Test $\quad z = \dfrac{T - \left(\dfrac{2n_1 n_2}{n_1 + n_2} + 1\right)}{\sqrt{\dfrac{2n_1 n_2(2n_1 n_2 - n_1 - n_2)}{(n_1 + n_2)^2\,(n_1 + n_2 - 1)}}}$

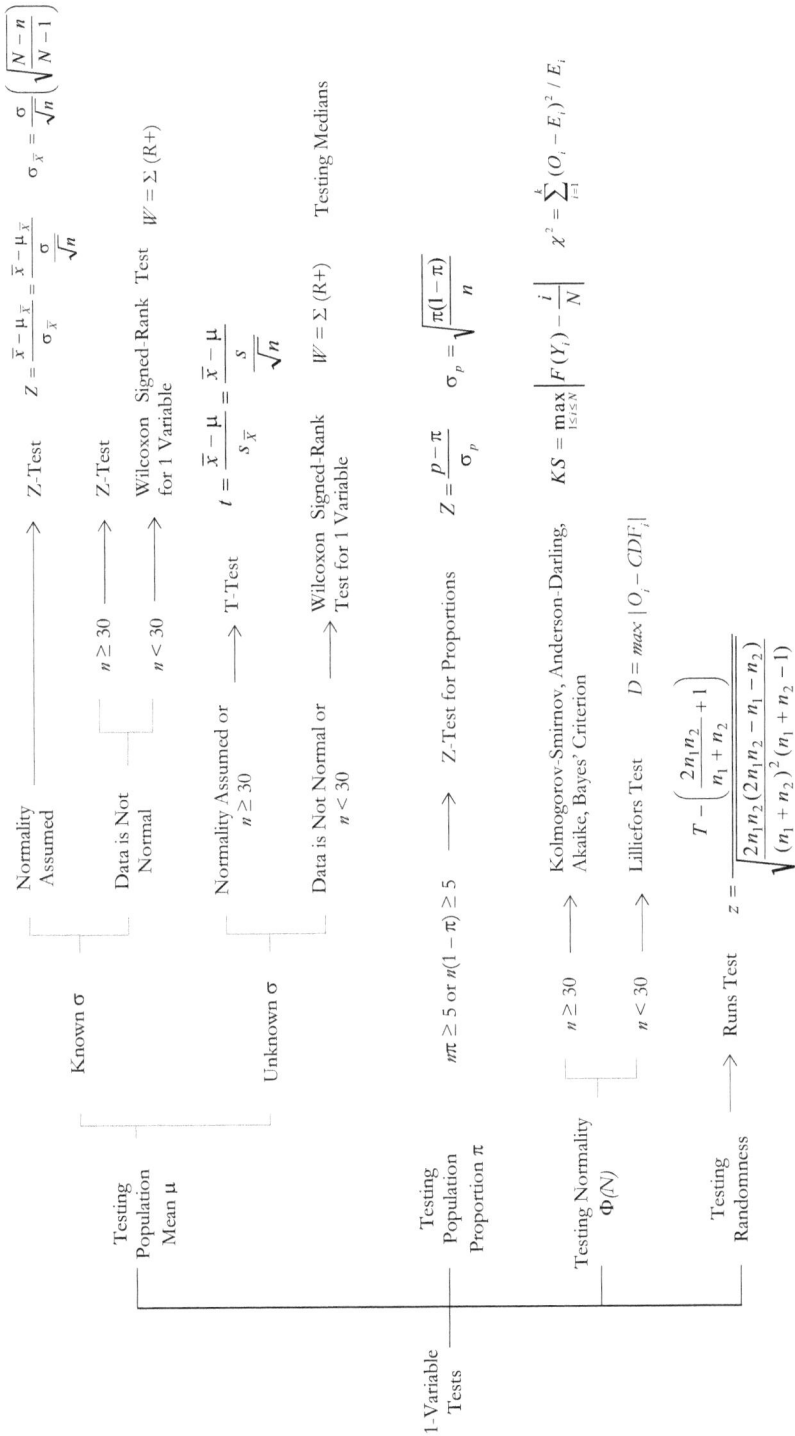

Figure 1.5: Statistical Methods for One Variable

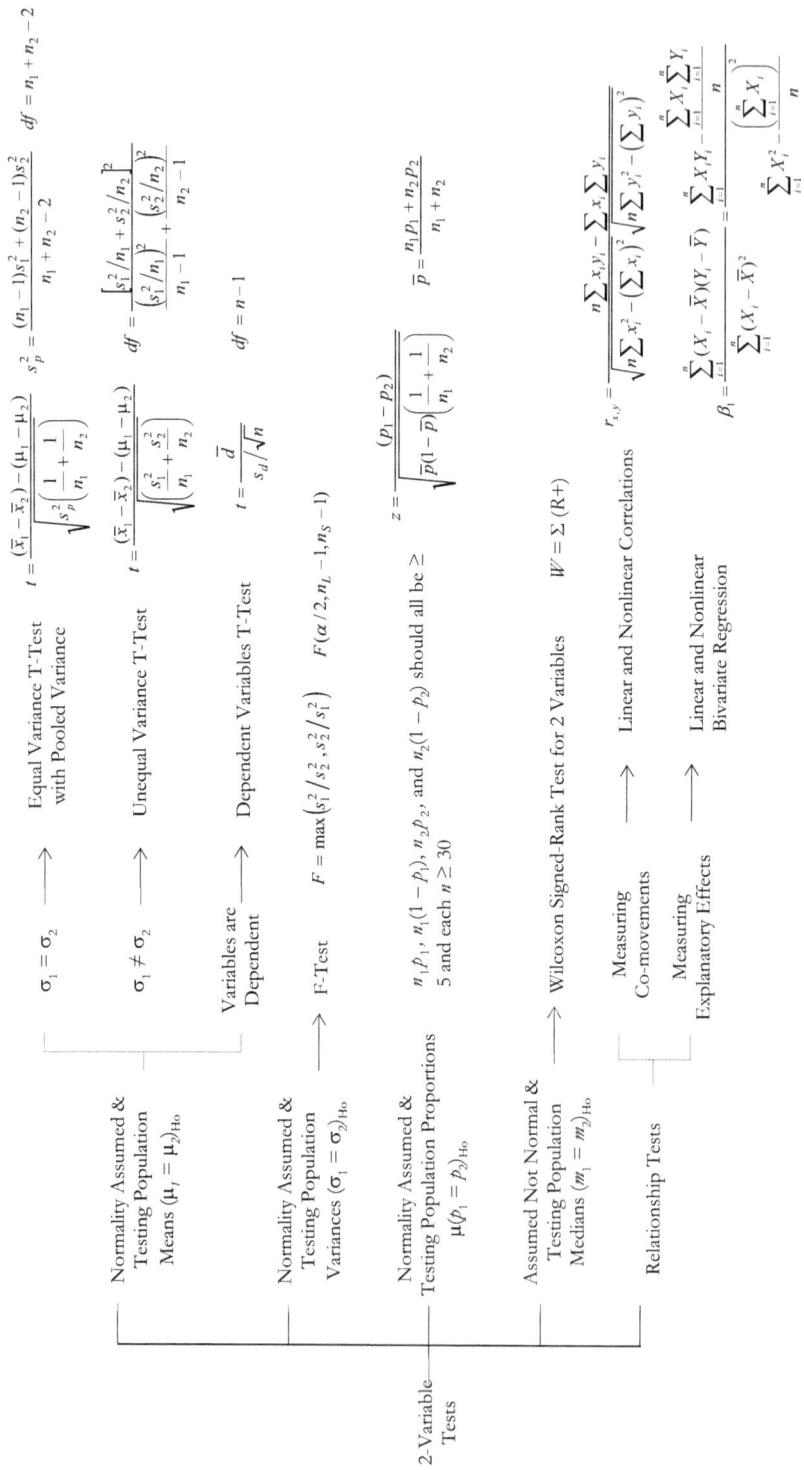

2-Variable Tests

Normality Assumed & Testing Population Means $(\mu_1 = \mu_2)_{Ho}$

- $\sigma_1 = \sigma_2 \longrightarrow$ Equal Variance T-Test with Pooled Variance

$$t = \frac{(\bar{x}_1 - \bar{x}_2) - (\mu_1 - \mu_2)}{\sqrt{s_p^2\left(\dfrac{1}{n_1} + \dfrac{1}{n_2}\right)}} \qquad s_p^2 = \frac{(n_1-1)s_1^2 + (n_2-1)s_2^2}{n_1 + n_2 - 2} \qquad df = n_1 + n_2 - 2$$

- $\sigma_1 \neq \sigma_2 \longrightarrow$ Unequal Variance T-Test

$$t = \frac{(\bar{x}_1 - \bar{x}_2) - (\mu_1 - \mu_2)}{\sqrt{\dfrac{s_1^2}{n_1} + \dfrac{s_2^2}{n_2}}} \qquad df = \frac{\left[s_1^2/n_1 + s_2^2/n_2\right]^2}{\dfrac{\left[s_1^2/n_1\right]^2}{n_1-1} + \dfrac{\left[s_2^2/n_2\right]^2}{n_2-1}}$$

- Variables are Dependent $\longrightarrow$ Dependent Variables T-Test

$$t = \frac{\bar{d}}{s_d/\sqrt{n}} \qquad df = n-1$$

Normality Assumed & Testing Population Variances $(\sigma_1 = \sigma_2)_{Ho}$ $\longrightarrow$ F-Test

$$F = \max\left(s_1^2/s_2^2, s_2^2/s_1^2\right) \qquad F(\alpha/2, n_L - 1, n_S - 1)$$

Normality Assumed & Testing Population Proportions $\mu(p_1 = p_2)_{Ho}$

$n_1 p_1, n_1(1-p_1), n_2 p_2,$ and $n_2(1-p_2)$ should all be $\geq$ 5 and each $n \geq 30$

$$z = \frac{(p_1 - p_2)}{\sqrt{\bar{p}(1-\bar{p})\left(\dfrac{1}{n_1} + \dfrac{1}{n_2}\right)}} \qquad \bar{p} = \frac{n_1 p_1 + n_2 p_2}{n_1 + n_2}$$

Assumed Not Normal & Testing Population Medians $(m_1 = m_2)_{Ho}$ $\longrightarrow$ Wilcoxon Signed-Rank Test for 2 Variables $\qquad W = \Sigma\,(R+)$

Relationship Tests

- Measuring Co-movements $\longrightarrow$ Linear and Nonlinear Correlations

$$r_{x,y} = \frac{n\sum x_i y_i - \sum x_i \sum y_i}{\sqrt{n\sum x_i^2 - (\sum x_i)^2}\,\sqrt{n\sum y_i^2 - (\sum y_i)^2}}$$

- Measuring Explanatory Effects $\longrightarrow$ Linear and Nonlinear Bivariate Regression

$$\beta_1 = \frac{\sum_{i=1}^n (X_i - \bar{X})(Y_i - \bar{Y})}{\sum_{i=1}^n (X_i - \bar{X})^2} = \frac{\sum_{i=1}^n X_i Y_i - \dfrac{\sum_{i=1}^n X_i \sum_{i=1}^n Y_i}{n}}{\sum_{i=1}^n X_i^2 - \dfrac{\left(\sum_{i=1}^n X_i\right)^2}{n}}$$

$$\beta_0 = \bar{Y} - \beta_1 \bar{X}$$

Figure 1.6: Statistical Methods for Two Variables

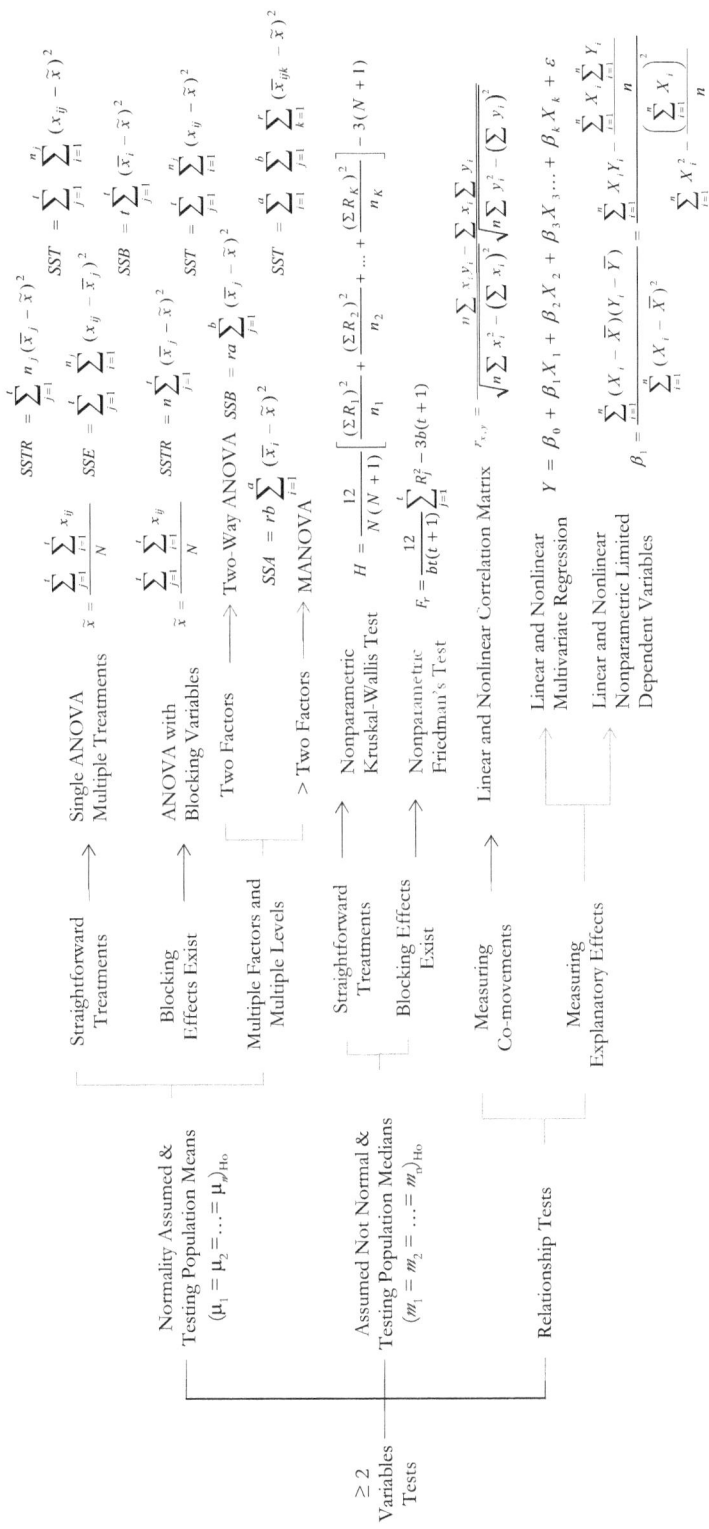

≥2 Variables Tests

Normality Assumed & Testing Population Means $(\mu_1 = \mu_2 = ... = \mu_a)_{H_0}$

- Straightforward Treatments → **Single ANOVA Multiple Treatments**

$$\tilde{x} = \frac{\sum_{j=1}^{t}\sum_{i=1}^{t} x_{ij}}{N}$$

$$SSTR = \sum_{j=1}^{t} n_j (\bar{x}_j - \tilde{x})^2$$

$$SSE = \sum_{j=1}^{t}\sum_{i=1}^{n_j} (x_{ij} - \bar{x}_j)^2$$

$$SST = \sum_{j=1}^{t}\sum_{i=1}^{n_j} (x_{ij} - \tilde{x})^2$$

- Blocking Effects Exist → **ANOVA with Blocking Variables**

$$\tilde{x} = \frac{\sum_{j=1}^{t}\sum_{i=1}^{t} x_{ij}}{N}$$

$$SSTR = n \sum_{j=1}^{t} (\bar{x}_j - \tilde{x})^2$$

$$SSB = t \sum_{j=1}^{t} (\bar{x}_j - \tilde{x})^2$$

$$SST = \sum_{j=1}^{t}\sum_{i=1}^{n_j} (x_{ij} - \tilde{x})^2$$

- Multiple Factors and Multiple Levels
  - Two Factors → **Two-Way ANOVA**

$$SSA = rb \sum_{i=1}^{a} (\bar{x}_i - \tilde{x})^2$$

$$SSB = ra \sum_{j=1}^{b} (\bar{x}_j - \tilde{x})^2$$

$$SST = \sum_{i=1}^{a}\sum_{j=1}^{b}\sum_{k=1}^{r} (\bar{x}_{ijk} - \tilde{x})^2$$

  - > Two Factors → **MANOVA**

Assumed Not Normal & Testing Population Medians $(m_1 = m_2 = ... = m_a)_{H_0}$

- Straightforward Treatments → **Nonparametric Kruskal-Wallis Test**

$$H = \frac{12}{N(N+1)}\left[\frac{(\Sigma R_1)^2}{n_1} + \frac{(\Sigma R_2)^2}{n_2} + ... + \frac{(\Sigma R_K)^2}{n_K}\right] - 3(N+1)$$

- Blocking Effects Exist → **Nonparametric Friedman's Test**

$$F_r = \frac{12}{bt(t+1)}\sum_{j=1}^{t} R_j^2 - 3b(t+1)$$

Relationship Tests

- Measuring Co-movements → **Linear and Nonlinear Correlation Matrix**

$$r_{x,y} = \frac{n\sum x_i y_i - \sum x_i \sum y_i}{\sqrt{n\sum x_i^2 - (\sum x_i)^2}\sqrt{n\sum y_i^2 - (\sum y_i)^2}}$$

- Measuring Explanatory Effects
  - **Linear and Nonlinear Multivariate Regression**

$$Y = \beta_0 + \beta_1 X_1 + \beta_2 X_2 + \beta_3 X_3 ... + \beta_k X_k + \varepsilon$$

$$\beta_1 = \frac{\sum_{i=1}^{n}(X_i - \bar{X})(Y_i - \bar{Y})}{\sum_{i=1}^{n}(X_i - \bar{X})^2} = \frac{\sum_{i=1}^{n} X_i Y_i - \dfrac{\sum_{i=1}^{n} X_i \sum_{i=1}^{n} Y_i}{n}}{\sum_{i=1}^{n} X_i^2 - \dfrac{\left(\sum_{1}^{n} X_i\right)^2}{n}}$$

$$\beta_0 = \bar{Y} - \beta_1 \bar{X}$$

  - **Linear and Nonlinear Nonparametric Limited Dependent Variables**

Figure 1.7: Statistical Methods for Two or More Variables

DISTRIBUTIONAL MOMENTS

The study of statistics refers to the collection, presentation, analysis, and utilization of numerical data to infer and make decisions in the face of uncertainty, where the actual population data is unknown. There are two branches in the study of statistics: descriptive statistics, where data is summarized and described, and inferential statistics, where the population is generalized through a small random sample, making it useful for making predictions or decisions when the population characteristics are unknown.

A *sample* can be defined as a subset of the population being measured, while the *population* can be defined as all possible observations of interest of a variable. For instance, if one is interested in the voting practices of all U.S. registered voters, the entire pool of a hundred million registered voters is considered the population while a small survey of one thousand registered voters taken from several small towns across the nation is the sample. The calculated characteristics of the sample (e.g., mean, median, standard deviation) are termed *statistics*, while *parameters* imply that the entire population has been surveyed and the results tabulated. Thus, in research, the statistic is of vital importance considering that sometimes the entire population is yet unknown (e.g., who are all your customers, what is the total market share, and so forth) or it is very difficult to obtain all relevant information on the population because it would be too time- or resource-consuming.

In inferential statistics, the following are the usual steps in conducting research:

- Designing the experiment—this phase includes designing the ways to collect all possible and relevant data.

    o Collection of sample data—data is gathered and tabulated

    o Analysis of data—statistical analysis is performed

    o Estimation or prediction—inferences are made based on the statistics obtained

    o Hypothesis testing—decisions are tested against the data to see the outcomes

- Determining goodness-of-fit—actual data is compared to historical data to see how accurate, valid, and reliable the inference may be.

- Decision making—decisions are made based on the outcome of the inference.

MEASURING THE CENTER OF THE DISTRIBUTION— THE FIRST MOMENT

The first moments of a distribution of outcomes measure the expected rate of return on a particular project. They measure the location of the project's scenarios and possible outcomes on average. The common statistics for the first moment include the *mean* (average), *median* (center of a distribution), and *mode* (most commonly occurring value). Figure 2.1 illustrates the first moment—where in this case, the first moment of this distribution is measured by the mean (μ) or average value.

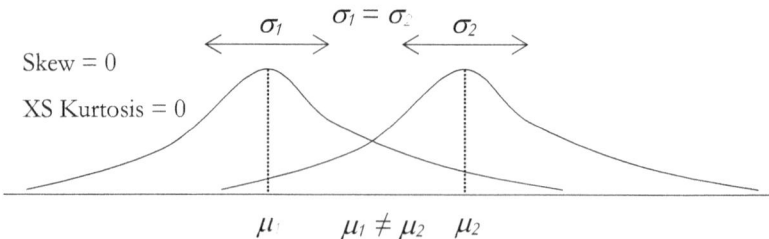

Figure 2.1: First Moment

The second moment measures the spread of a distribution, which is a measure of risk. The spread or width of a distribution indicates the variability of a variable, that is, the potentiality that the variable can fall into different regions of the distribution—in other words, the potential scenarios of outcomes. Figure 2.2 illustrates two distributions with identical first moments (identical means) but very different second moments or risks. The visualization is clearer in Figure 2.3. As an example, suppose there are two stocks and the first stock's movements (the solid line) with the smaller fluctuation is compared against the second stock's movements (the dotted line) with a much higher price fluctuation. Clearly, an investor would view the stock with the wilder fluctuation as riskier because the outcomes of the riskier stock are relatively more unknown than the less risky stock. The vertical axis in Figure 2.3 measures the stock prices; thus, the riskier stock has a wider range of potential outcomes. This range is translated into a distribution's width (the horizontal axis) in Figure 2.2, where the wider distribution represents the riskier asset. Hence, the width or spread of a distribution measures a variable's risks. Notice that in Figure 2.2, both distributions have identical first moments or central tendencies but clearly, the distributions are very different. This difference in the distributional width is measurable. Mathematically and statistically, the width or risk of a variable can be measured through several different statistics, including the range, standard deviation (σ), variance, coefficient of variation, percentile, interquartile range, confidence interval, volatility, beta, Value at Risk, and others.

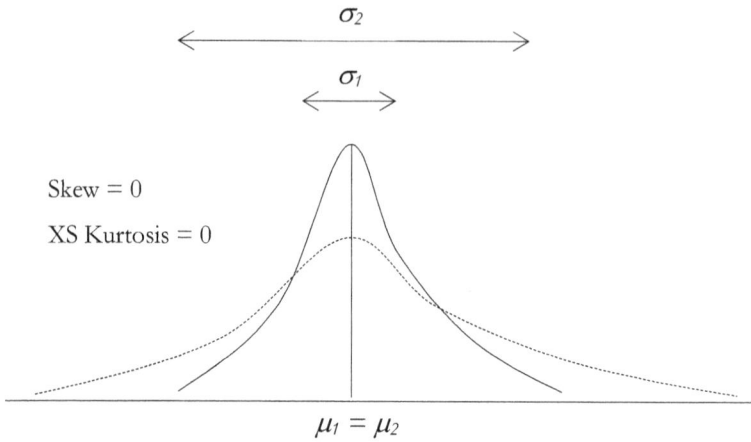

Figure 2.2: Second Moment

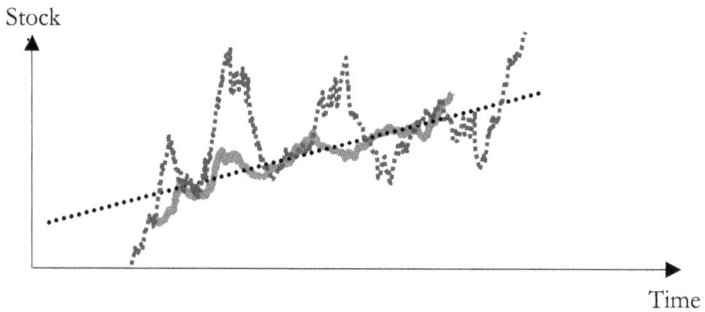

Figure 2.3: Stock Price Fluctuations

Variance and Standard Deviation

Variance and standard deviation are two common measures of the second moment. Variance is the average of the squared deviations about their means, in squared units:

$$\sigma^2 = \sum_{i=1}^{N} \frac{(x_i - \mu)^2}{N} \ and \ s^2 = \sum_{i=1}^{n} \frac{(x_i - \bar{x})^2}{n-1}$$

Standard deviation is in original units and, thus, useful as a direct means of comparison of dispersion and variability measured in the same units:

$$\sigma = \sqrt{\sum_{i=1}^{N} \frac{(x_i - \mu)^2}{N}} \quad and \quad s = \sqrt{\sum_{i=1}^{n} \frac{(x_i - \bar{x})^2}{n-1}}$$

Although standard deviation and variances have many uses, those uses are limited because their measurements are in the same units and, hence, are considered absolute values of risk, uncertainty, or spread. Greek letters (μ, σ) and upper-case letters (N) represent the population whereas standard Latin alphabets and lower-case letters (s, n, x) represent the sample.

Coefficient of Variation

The coefficient of variation (CV) is unitless and measures relative variability. It thus allows the comparison of two datasets to see which has more variability without worrying about the units. In comparison, standard deviations are absolute measures of variability and depend heavily on the data's unit of measure.

$$CV = \frac{s}{\bar{x}} \quad or \quad CV = \frac{\sigma}{\mu}$$

EXAMPLE

Statistic	# in family	Food expenditure ($)
$\bar{x}$	3.23	$110.5
s	1.34	$25.25

Which has more variation, the number of family members or the food expenditure?

CV in family = 1.34/3.23 = 0.415

CV in expenditures = 25.25/110.25 = 0.229

The calculations show that there is more variation in the number of family members.

The third moment measures a distribution's skewness, that is, how the distribution is pulled to one side or the other. Figure 2.4 illustrates a negative or left skew (the tail of the distribution points to the left), and Figure 2.5 illustrates a positive or right skew (the tail of the distribution points to the right). The mean is always skewed towards the tail of the distribution, while the median remains constant. Another way of seeing this is that the mean moves but the standard deviation, variance, or width may still remain constant. If the third moment is not considered, then looking only at the expected returns (mean) and risk (standard deviation), a positively skewed project might be incorrectly chosen! For example, if the horizontal axis represents the net revenues of a project, then clearly a left- or negatively-skewed distribution might be preferred as there is a higher probability of greater returns (Figure 2.4) as compared to a higher probability for a lower level of returns (Figure 2.5). Thus, in a skewed distribution, the median is a better measure of returns, as the medians for both Figures 2.4 and 2.5 are identical, risks are identical, and, hence, a project with a negatively skewed distribution of net profits is a better choice. Failure to account for a project's distributional skewness may mean that the incorrect project may be chosen (e.g., two projects may have identical first and second moments, that is, they both have identical returns and risk profiles, but their distributional skews may be very different). Skew is calculated by:

$$Skew = \frac{n}{(n-1)(n-2)} \sum_{i=1}^{n} \left(\frac{x_i - \bar{x}}{s}\right)^3$$

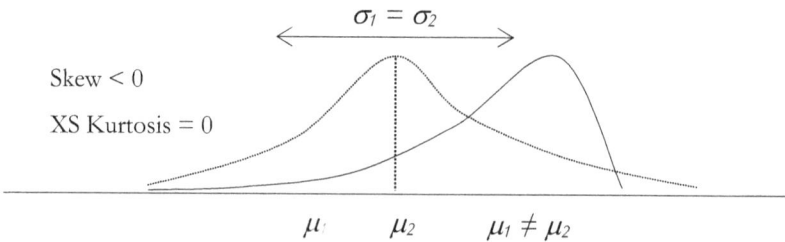

Figure 2.4: Third Moment (Left Skew)

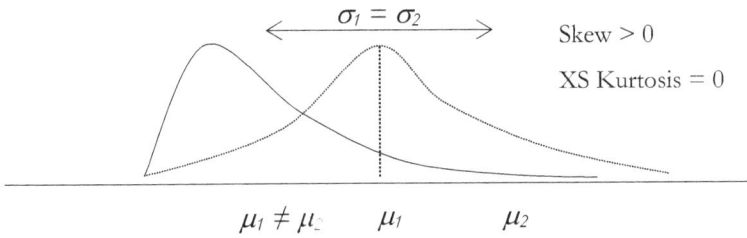

Figure 2.5: Third Moment (Right Skew)

MEASURING THE CATASTROPHIC TAIL EVENTS IN A DISTRIBUTION— THE FOURTH MOMENT

The fourth moment, or kurtosis, measures the peakedness of a distribution. Figure 2.6 illustrates this effect. The background is a normal distribution with a kurtosis of 3.0 or an excess kurtosis of 0 (XS kurtosis is defined as the kurtosis difference from a normal distribution). The new distribution has a higher kurtosis, thus the area under the curve is thicker at the tails with less area in the central body. This condition has major impacts on uncertainty analysis because, for the two distributions in Figure 2.6, the first three moments (mean, standard deviation, and skewness) can be identical but the fourth moment (kurtosis) is different. This means that although the expected returns and uncertainties are identical, the probabilities of extreme and catastrophic events (potential large losses or large gains) occurring are higher for a high kurtosis distribution (e.g., stock market returns are leptokurtic or have high kurtosis). Ignoring a project's return's kurtosis may be detrimental. Fortunately, the calculations for these four moments are automatically done for you using the Risk Simulator and ROV BizStats software as will be seen in later chapters. Kurtosis is defined as:

$$Kurtosis = \frac{n(n+1)}{(n-1)(n-2)(n-3)} \sum_{i=1}^{n} \left(\frac{x_i - \bar{x}}{s}\right)^4 - \frac{3(n-1)^2}{(n-2)(n-3)}$$

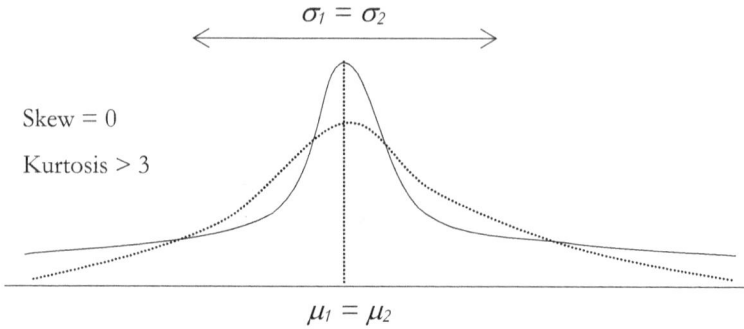

$$\sigma_1 = \sigma_2$$

Skew = 0

Kurtosis > 3

$$\mu_1 = \mu_2$$

Figure 2.6: Fourth Moment

Most distributions can be defined by up to four moments. The first moment describes a distribution's location or central tendency (expected value); the second moment describes its width or spread (uncertainty); the third moment, its directional skew (most probable events); and the fourth moment, its peakedness or thickness in the tails (catastrophic extreme tail events). All four moments should be calculated and interpreted to provide a more comprehensive view of the project under analysis. Finally, the term moment refers to the highest power of x in each of the statistics' equations.

HYPOTHESIS TESTING

A statistical hypothesis is an assumption we make about a population parameter. This assumption may or may not be true and can be statistically tested if sample statistics are available. The term *hypothesis testing* refers to the formal statistical and mathematical procedures used by statisticians to either accept or reject a certain hypothesis or research question. Clearly, the best way to determine with absolute certainty whether a hypothesis is true would be to examine the entire population. This is usually impractical; therefore, researchers examine a smaller, but random, sample from the population. If the sample data's calculated statistics are not consistent with the statistical hypothesis, the hypothesis is rejected. There are two types of statistical hypotheses. The Null Hypothesis, usually denoted by H_0, is typically the hypothesis that the sample observations result purely from chance. The competing or Alternative Hypothesis, usually denoted by H_1 or H_a, is the hypothesis that the sample observations are influenced by some nonrandom cause.

To summarize, hypothesis testing is:

- An educated guess of how the world looks or doesn't look.

- A test of an assumption using samples to infer to the population.

- Can be solved using four different but related methods:
    o Classical Method
    o Standardized Method
    o P-Value Method
    o Confidence Interval Method

This chapter assumes that the reader already has some passing familiarity and knowledge of basic statistics and hypothesis testing. For instance, the next few examples will jump right into the midst of hypothesis tests with a standard normal Z and student's t-distribution.

Example: You are a cereal manufacturer of 20 oz. boxes of Muesli, Nut 'N Honey, and Count Chocolate. Quality control is on your mind, and you wish to test the hypothesis that these cereal boxes are filled at 20 oz. on average. So, you take a sample of 100 boxes and find its average $\bar{x}$ to be 20.15 oz. with some variation, where its sample standard deviation s is 0.2 oz., is the population of boxes on average μ equivalent to 20 oz.? Test this assumption using a 5% significance α level. The question, then, is: Is 20.15 oz. far enough from 20 oz. to say that it is statistically different, or could it be that, by random chance, 20.15 oz. is close enough to be proclaimed as statistically identical to 20 oz.?

- Step 1: Identify the hypotheses—H_0: $\mu = 20$ and H_a: $\mu \neq 20$. So, this is a two-tailed test.

- Step 2: Use $\bar{x}$ as the test statistic, with $\alpha = 0.05$. Hence, a two-tailed test is called for. Decision rule: if $\bar{x} > x_U$ upper limit, or when $\bar{x} < x_L$ lower limit, reject H_0 and accept H_a; otherwise, accept H_0 and reject H_a.

- Step 3: Calculate the limits:

  We know that $n = 100$, so we can assume normality and we can use a Z-score (standard normal distribution). The equation for confidence limits is

  $$\mu \pm Z\left(\frac{\sigma}{\sqrt{n}}\right)$$

  As we assume normality when $n > 30$, the limits are

  $20 \pm 1.96\left(\frac{0.2}{\sqrt{100}}\right)$ returns 19.96 and 20.04.

  Consequently, reject H_0 and accept H_a. The conclusion is that there is a statistically significant difference.

Note that in this example, we use the Z statistic or Z-score, which is another name for the standard normal distribution, i.e., a normal distribution with a mean of zero and a standard deviation of one, denoted as $N(0,1)$. In addition, with a 5% significance α level for a two-tailed confidence interval, the 5% is divided into two tail ends, or 2.5% in each tail. We can draw this three different but equivalent ways. In the following illustration, A1 should be 47.5%, A2 should be 97.5%, and A3 is 95%, leaving the tail ends $\alpha/2$ or 2.5%. Using the partial area standard normal table at the end of this book, we look up the A1 area of 0.4750, which yields a Z score of 1.96. We can likewise use the cumulative standard normal distribution and look for 0.9750, which also yields a Z-value of 1.96. Similarly, using Excel, one can input the function "=NORMSINV(0.975)", the inverse cumulative distribution function for a standard normal distribution (i.e., area A2), which will also yield 1.96. Using a similar approach, one can easily find the relevant Z score for any significant α level. When $n < 30$, we would use a t-distribution instead, as will be seen in future examples. The only added care we need for a t-distribution is the number of degrees of freedom.

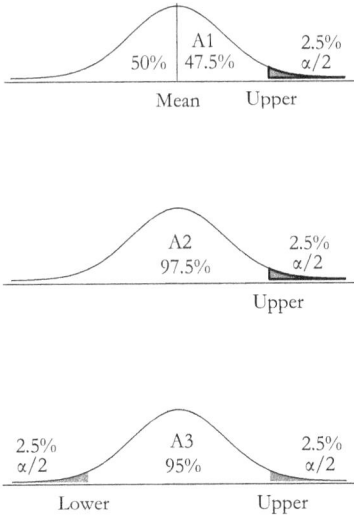

Classical Method

1. Set up the null hypothesis (H₀) and the alternate hypothesis (Hₐ).

    a. Always set up the alternate hypothesis first, then the null hypothesis.

    b. The alternate hypothesis will always be either > or < or ≠ .

    c. The null hypothesis will always be either ≥ or ≤ or =.

    d. If the alternate hypothesis is ≠, then it is a two-tailed test; if <, then a left (one) tail; and if >, then a right (one) tailed test.

    e. The sign of the alternate hypothesis always points to the limits.

2. Draw the normal curve and draw in the limits—the tail ends are the *rejection* areas, i.e., set up the Decision Rules: if $\bar{x} > x_U$ upper limit, or when $\bar{x} < x_L$ lower limit, reject H₀ and accept Hₐ; otherwise, accept H₀ and reject Hₐ.

3. Calculate these limits when $n > 30$ or normal, but use

    $$\mu \pm t\left(\frac{\sigma}{\sqrt{n}}\right)$$

    when $n < 30$ where Z and t values are obtained from the statistical tables at the end of this book. Due to the smaller sample size assumption in the t-distribution, use a finite sample correction factor (see the Central Limit Theorem section for additional details on this correction factor) with a degree of freedom correction where $df = n - 1$.

4. If $\bar{x}$ is in the rejection area, reject H₀; if in the acceptance area, accept H₀.

Two Tails

Reject H$_0$
$\alpha/2$
Accept H$_0$
Reject H$_0$
$\alpha/2$

Lower   Mean   Upper

One Right-Tail

Accept H$_0$
Reject H$_0$
α

Mean   Upper

One Left-Tail

Reject H$_0$
α
Accept H$_0$

Lower   Mean

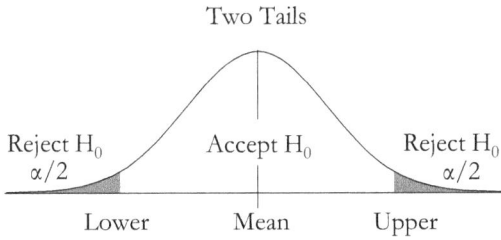

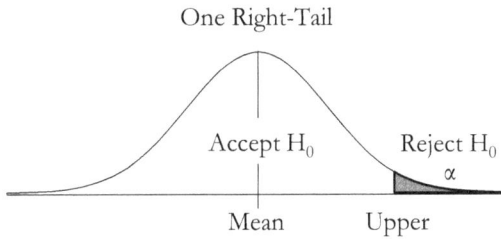

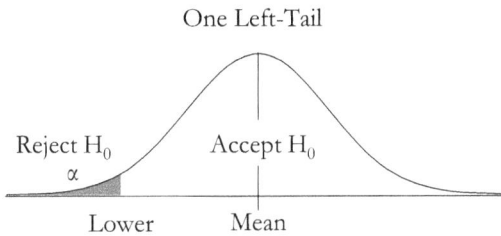

Standardized Method

Instead of changing the Z values into upper and lower limits by using

$$\mu \pm Z\left(\frac{\sigma}{\sqrt{n}}\right) \text{ or } \mu \pm t\left(\frac{\sigma}{\sqrt{n}}\right)$$

we may also simply leave the standardized $\pm Z$ units as the critical limits.

Convert the $\bar{x}$ units into standardized units and use the same decision rules, i.e., if Z calculated $> Z_U$ upper limit, or when Z calculated $< Z_L$ lower limit, reject H$_0$ and accept H$_a$; otherwise, accept (fail to reject) H$_0$ and reject H$_a$.

P-Value Method

- Calculate the Z values as usual, then obtain the approximate p-value from the tables. If there are no exact matches, use an interval.

- If the one-tail p-value calculated is $< \alpha$ for a one-tail test or $2 \times$ one-tail p-value $< \alpha$ for a two-tailed test, reject H_0 and accept H_a.

Confidence Interval Method

- C.I. $= 1 - \alpha$ or for an $\alpha = 0.05$, one C.I. $= 95\%$, and if the value $\bar{x}$ lies within the limits of the interval, accept H_0 and reject H_a.

- For a two-tailed test, double the p-value calculated, halve the α level for each tail area, and use the statistical tables.

Examples: Hypothesis Testing

$$Z = \frac{\bar{x} - \mu_{\bar{x}}}{\sigma_{\bar{x}}} = \frac{\bar{x} - \mu_{\bar{x}}}{\frac{\sigma}{\sqrt{n}}}$$

$$FPC = \sigma_{\bar{x}} = \frac{\sigma}{\sqrt{n}} \sqrt{\frac{N-n}{N-1}} \text{ for } \frac{n}{N} \geq 5\%$$

Example 1: A light bulb manufacturing company wants to test the hypothesis that its bulbs can last, on average, 1,000 burning hours. It employs a student who is currently taking statistics and bribed the instructor to allow this student to perform this project for them in lieu of a final exam. So, for an A– in the class (since it is an easy problem): If the manager randomly selects 100 sample bulbs, and finds that the sample's mean is 980 hours and the standard deviation is 80 hours, at a 5% significance level, what is the conclusion?

H_0: $\mu = 1000$ and H_a: $\mu \neq 1000$

Since $n > 30$, we can assume normality and we can estimate σ.

For $\alpha = 0.05$ level, $Z = \pm 1.96$ for a two-tailed test or $\alpha/2 = 0.025$. Use the standard normal table at the back of this book or =NORMSINV(0.975) in Excel to obtain the 1.96 value.

If the calculated values lie in the tails beyond the critical, reject H_0.

Classical—Critical limits:

$x_{critical} = \mu \pm Z\left(\frac{s}{\sqrt{n}}\right) = 1000 \pm 1.96\left(\frac{80}{\sqrt{100}}\right)$ we have

$X_{upper} = 1015.68$ and $X_{lower} = 984.32$.

So, $980 < X_{lower}$ and we reject H_0.

Standardized:

$$Z = \frac{\bar{x} - \mu_{\bar{x}}}{\frac{s}{\sqrt{n}}} = \frac{980 - 1000}{\frac{80}{\sqrt{100}}} = -2.5$$

$-2.5 < -1.96$ means it lies in the tail and we reject H_0.

P-Value: For the calculated Z value of -2.5, we have p-value $= 0.5 - 0.4938$ yielding p-value 0.0062, which is less than α of 0.05, and so we reject H_0. Use the standard normal table at the end of this book or =NORMSDIST(-2.5) in Excel to obtain this 0.0062 value.

Confidence Interval: The confidence interval has already been calculated above using the classical method. Hence, C.I. ranges from 984.32 to 1015.68, and since the measured sample $\bar{x} = 980$ does not fall within this region, we reject H_0.

In all cases, the approaches might be slightly different but yield similar conclusions, that is, reject H_0. Hence, we accept H_a stating that the population mean is significantly different from 1000.

Example 2: A firm wants to know with a 95% level of confidence (α=0.05) if it can claim that the boxes of detergent it sells contain more than 500g of detergent. From past experience, the firm knows that the amount of detergent in the boxes is normally distributed. Taking a random sample of $n = 25$, the average was found to be 520g and the standard deviation, 75g. Perform a hypothesis test.

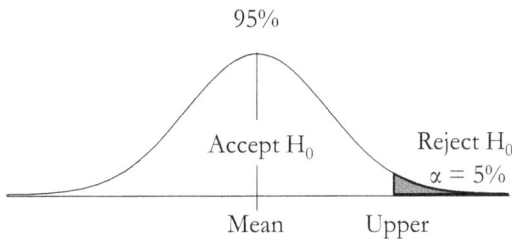

95%

Accept H_0

Reject H_0
$\alpha = 5\%$

Mean   Upper

$H_0: \mu \leq 500$ and $H_a: \mu > 500$

Since $n = 25$, we use a t-distribution.

Critical t for $df = n - 1 = 25 - 1 = 24$ is 1.711 at $\alpha = 0.05$ for a one-tail test. Use the t-table at the end of this book or Excel's =TINV(0.05*2,24) to obtain this 1.711 value (table returns an approximate 1.709 compared to Excel's exact value of 1.711).

Classical:

$$x_{critical} = \mu \pm t\left(\frac{s}{\sqrt{n}}\right) = 500 \pm 1.711\left(\frac{75}{\sqrt{25}}\right) = 525.66$$

Since 520 < critical level 525.66, we accept H_0.

Standardized:

$$t = \frac{\bar{x} - \mu_{\bar{x}}}{\frac{s}{\sqrt{n}}} = \frac{520 - 500}{\frac{75}{\sqrt{25}}} = 1.33$$

which falls within the acceptance region; so, accept H_0.

P-Value: With the calculated t-value as 1.33, for df = 24, the p-value is between 0.05 and 0.10, which means we will accept the H_0 since it is above α of 0.05. The relevant Excel function is =TDIST(1.33,24,1), yielding an exact p-value of 0.0980.

Confidence Interval: Using the results from the classical method, C.I. ranges from 0.00 to 525.66, and since 520 falls within this C.I. region, we accept H_0.

CENTRAL LIMIT THEOREM

Since attempting to measure a whole population is oftentimes very costly, time-consuming, and difficult, we usually take a sample and use it to infer about the population. For example, trying to figure out the percentage of voters who like a certain politician would consist of polling every voter (N), up to several million of them; hence, we use a small sample (n) of, say, a thousand instead. Then we need a way to quantify these samples, and this is where sampling theory comes in. As an example, assume there exists a population with a uniform distribution, we then sample $n = 2$ on $N = 4$.

X	$1	2	3	4
P(x)	0.25	0.25	0.25	0.25

P(x)

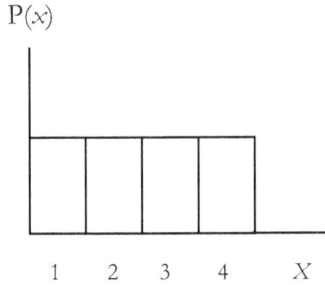

Here, the population $\mu = \Sigma x P(x) = 1(.25) + 2(.25) + 3(.25) + 4(.25) = \$2.50$.

Also, the population $\sigma^2 = \Sigma(x - \mu)^2 P(x) = \$1.25$.

If we take samples of $n = 2$, the following shows all the possible sets of samples we can take:

$$
\begin{array}{cccc}
1,1 & 1,2 & 1,3 & 1,4 \\
2,2 & 2,2 & 2,3 & 2,4 \\
3,1 & 3,2 & 3,3 & 3,4 \\
4,1 & 4,2 & 4,3 & 4,4
\end{array}
$$

Hence, all the $\bar{x}$ average sample values possible in a probability distribution are:

X	$1	1.5	2	2.5	3	3.5	4
P(x)	1/16	2/16	3/16	4/16	3/16	2/16	1/16

The sampling distribution looks nothing like the original uniform distribution. In fact, according to the Central Limit Theorem, all sampling distributions given will tend toward a normal distribution, thereby justifying the times we assume normality if our sample size is large enough, typically when $n > 30$.

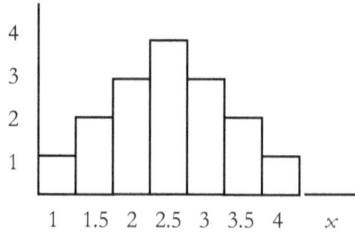

In fact, here the sampling distribution's $\mu_{\bar{x}} = \sum \bar{x}P(\bar{x}) = 1(1/16) + 1.5(2/16) + \ldots = \$2.50$, which is the same as the population mean of $\mu = \$2.50$ So, the sample mean is an unbiased estimator of the population mean.

Next, the sampling distribution's $\sigma_{\bar{x}}^2 = \sum(\bar{x} - \mu_{\bar{x}})P(\bar{x}) = (1-0.25)^2(1/16) + (1.5-0.25)^2(2/16) + \ldots = 0.625$ compared to $\sigma^2 = 1.25$, which is twice that. In general, for sampling distributions, $\sigma_{\bar{x}}^2 = \frac{\sigma^2}{n}$ or similarly, $\sigma_{\bar{x}} = \frac{\sigma}{\sqrt{n}}$, which always holds. Since here $n = 2$, therefore, $1.25/2 = 0.625$.

According to the Central Limit Theorem, even if the population itself is not normal, for large enough n, the random variable's mean or $\bar{x}$ is approximately normal with mean μ and $\sigma_{\bar{x}} = \frac{\sigma}{\sqrt{n}}$.

In other words, we have:

$$Z = \frac{\bar{x} - \mu_{\bar{x}}}{\sigma_{\bar{x}}} = \frac{\bar{x} - \mu_{\bar{x}}}{\frac{\sigma}{\sqrt{n}}}$$

In addition, according to the Finite Population Correction Factor (FPC), when the population is too small, and the sample is too large, then when n is small, the FPC approaches unity. This FPC factor increases the accuracy of the estimates.

$$FPC = \sigma_{\bar{x}} = \frac{\sigma}{\sqrt{n}}\sqrt{\frac{N-n}{N-1}} \text{ for } \frac{n}{N} \geq 5\%$$

Example 1: From a population of 550,000 in the area, we randomly select 100 people to survey their income. From economic theory, we know that incomes are not necessarily normally distributed, depending on the income stratification of the population. The sample reveals a mean of $35,000 and a standard deviation of $5,000. What is the probability that a randomly selected individual in the area has an income above $40,000?

$Z = (40 - 35)/(5/\sqrt{100}) = 10$, so, the $P(x \geq 40,000) = 0.0$. Do not use the simple Z score where $Z = (40 - 35)/5 = 1.0$ with $P(x) = .5 - .3413 = 0.1587$.

Example 2: Suppose a virulent strain of the Ebola virus kills all but 1,000 of the aforementioned population. Being such staunch statisticians, ignore the threats to your own life and continue to survey a sample of 100 people. The new sample income mean is $5,000 and the standard deviation is $1,000 (deadly viruses tend to mess up business). What is the probability that a randomly selected individual has an income above $5,500?

We must use the finite population correction factor (FPC):

FPC corrected $\sigma_{\bar{x}} = (1000/\sqrt{100})([1000 - 100]/[1000 - 1]) = 94.915$ and, hence, $Z = (5500 - 5000)/94.915 = 5.26$, and we have $P(x \geq 5500) = 0\%$. Note: We should *not* be calculating regular $Z = (5500 - 5000)/(1000) = 0.5$ with a corresponding $P(x \geq 5500) = 0.5 - 0.1915 = 0.3085$, which is incorrect.

Example 3: Suppose we take a single die with 6 sides and throw it 100,000 times. We see that the resulting mean and standard deviation are theoretically 3.50 and 1.71, respectively. We know that the theoretical mean for a discrete uniform distribution is $rank\left[\frac{n+1}{2}\right] = 3.5th\,rank = 3.5$ and the standard deviation is $rank\sqrt{\frac{(n-1)(n+1)}{12}} = rank\sqrt{\frac{(6-1)(6+1)}{12}} = rank(1.71) = 1.71$. In fact, a computational Monte Carlo simulation was run, and we see the simulated empirical results (3.50 and 1.71, rounded) match our theoretical results (see Figure 3.1).

Now, suppose instead of tossing a single die 100,000 times, we now toss 4 dice at once, for 25,000 times. This is similar to throwing the single die 100,000 times because we would record a total of 100,000 outcomes. The results are shown in Figure 3.2. We see the same 3.50 mean, but the standard deviation is now 0.85. This case is a sampling distribution problem, where the sample size each time is 4. We just empirically proved that $\frac{1.71}{\sqrt{4}}$ = 0.85 (rounded).

Similarly, if we tossed 10 dice simultaneously for 10,000 times, we obtain the results shown in Figure 3.3, where the mean is still 3.50 and the standard deviation is 0.54 (rounded). We can empirically prove that $\frac{1.71}{\sqrt{10}}$ = 0.54 (rounded).

Examples 1, 2, and 3 show the power of the Central Limit Theorem and statistical sampling. The mean of the sample approaches the population mean, and the sampling standard deviation approaches the population standard deviation divided by the square root of the sample size.

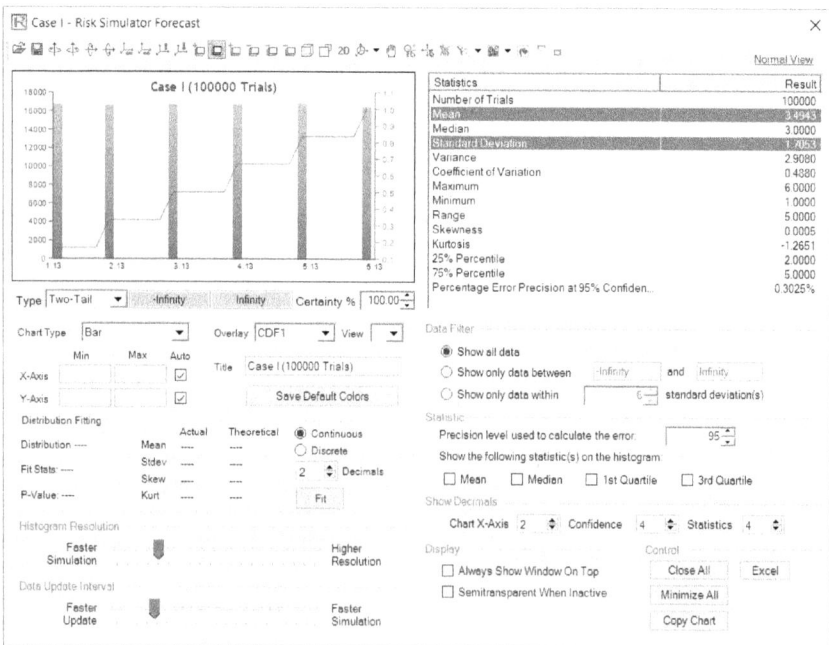

Figure 3.1: Tossing a Single Die 100,000 Times

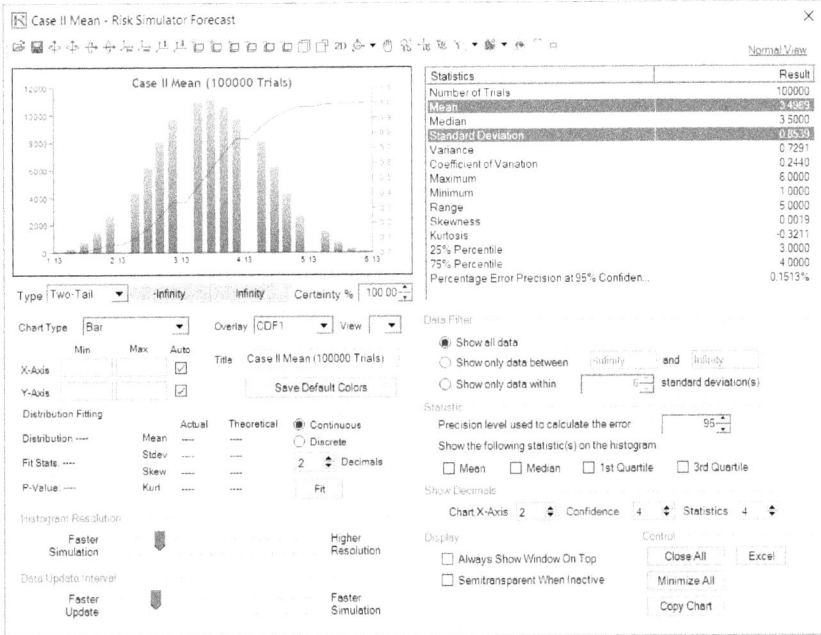

Figure 3.2: Tossing 4 Dice 25,000 Times

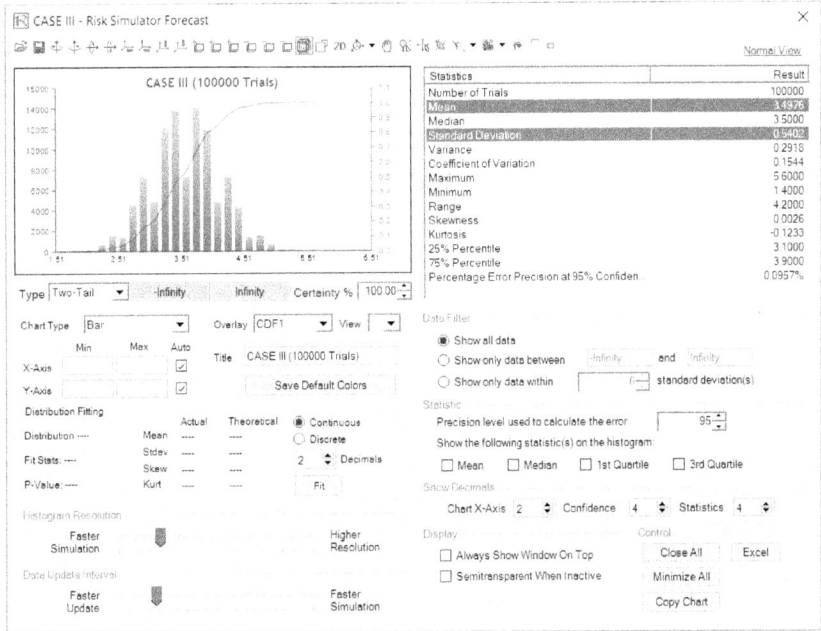

Figure 3.3: Tossing 10 Dice 10,000 Times

As previously discussed, there are single-tailed directional and two-tailed nondirectional hypotheses. We would reject the null hypothesis when the calculated p-value is less than or equal to some prespecified significance level α, typically set at 0.01, 0.05, or 0.10. But a little more discussion is required on this simple rule.

The question is, why do we use these rules for rejecting the null hypothesis? Why not set a rule to accept the null hypothesis instead? The issue is a key question in the philosophy of science. For instance, say we wish to test for alien life (extraterrestrial microorganisms, not the green superbeings with advanced interstellar spacecraft). The null hypothesis would be that there is zero alien life outside of Earth, and the alternate hypothesis would be that there is life outside of Earth. In order to reject the null hypothesis, all one has to do is to find a single occurrence or evidence of life outside of Earth. However, to truly and completely "accept" the null hypothesis, we would have to scour every nook and cranny in the entire known universe for life and prove that no life exists. It is, therefore, almost always simpler to reject a null hypothesis than to accept it, and we usually say that we "fail to reject the null," rather than accept the null outright. The failure to reject does not mean we automatically accept it as fact, but that the empirical evidence from the sample thus far has shown that it is more probable that an acceptance of the null is correct, rather than a rejection. Another simple example would be that we receive a delivery box of 1,000 sealed cartons of eggs. Each carton has a dozen eggs. We open several of these cartons and find that all the eggs are unbroken. Given that we open enough cartons to test (sufficient sample size) and all eggs are unbroken, we can probabilistically state that the chances are all 1,000 cartons have no broken eggs (the null hypothesis). Clearly, this cannot be confirmed with 100% certainty (i.e., hard to "accept" the null hypothesis with complete certainty) unless all cartons are opened, and all eggs are accounted for.

Another related issue to consider is that of Types I–IV errors. The significance level α actually controls for the Type I error, also known as *alpha error* or *false positives*. Type I error is the probability that you will *reject the null hypothesis when it is true*. We want this to be set low, of course. This error is committed when we reject the null when it is actually true and should not be rejected. Stated another way, we say that there is an effect when in fact no effect exists at all. A simple analogy might better explain this concept. We can all agree that for a civilized society, it is better to let a guilty man go free rather than incarcerate an innocent man. Hence, if we assume that innocence is true, the null hypothesis is innocence or that there is zero guilt. So, if we reject this null hypothesis, we reject innocence and zero guilt, which means you throw an innocent person in jail. This creates a false positive (*false* because he is innocent, but we say he is guilty; and *positive* because we found him guilty). Therefore, in this situation, you would want that false-positive error to be small, that is, a low alpha, which traditionally is set at 1%, 5%, or 10%.

Type II errors occur when we *accept a null hypothesis that is false*. We use the term "accept" here interchangeably with "failure to reject," as discussed above. This error is also known as a *beta error* or *false negative*. Accepting or failing to reject the null hypothesis when it is false means that we miss or ignore an effect when that effect actually exists. A simple analogy would be that of a fire alarm in your home. Let us assume a binary condition where the alarm could either go off or not go off. Further, this binary state also includes whether there is a house fire or there is no fire. The null hypothesis is that there is zero instance of a fire. In this case, a Type I error means that you reject when the null hypothesis is true (i.e., the alarm goes off when there is no fire, no big deal, it just wakes you up and you get annoyed). However, a Type II error is a much bigger deal because it means that you accept the null hypothesis when it is false (i.e., the alarm does not go off when there really is a fire). In this example, we would want to minimize beta error or maximize $1 - \beta$, its complement. Another name for this complement is the *power of the test* (Power $= 1 - \beta$).

The following matrix summarizes the first two types of errors.

Null Hypothesis	True	False
Accept	True Negative $(1 - \alpha)$	Type II (β) False Negative
Reject	Type I (α) False Positive	Power $(1 - \beta)$ True Positive

There are also less commonly known Type III and Type IV errors. A Type III error occurs when the correct conclusion is made but for the wrong reason. For instance, you incorrectly used a one-tailed hypothesis instead of a two-tailed hypothesis, or vice versa, a wrong question was posed, or the hypothesis is incorrectly formulated. A Type IV error occurs when there is data aggregation bias, mistakes interpreting the results, or you correctly reject the null hypothesis, but the dataset has multicollinearity issues or data collection biases.

Type IV errors are more difficult to quantitatively measure. The chapter on regression modeling and data diagnostics covers how to test for some of these biases, whereas the chapter on hypothesis testing covers some examples of using the Shannon Diversity Index model, Grubbs Outliers test, Runs model for randomness, and others. The following is a list of the most common self-explanatory examples of data and sampling biases that can cause a Type IV error.

Attrition Bias	Confirmation Bias
Confounding Variables Bias	Cultural Bias
Exclusion Bias	Friendliness Bias
Habituation Bias	Inclusion Bias
Maturation Bias	Measurement Bias
Nonresponse Bias	Observer Bias
Outlier Bias	Over- and Underfitting Bias
Question Order Bias	Prejudice Bias
Recall Bias	Reporting Bias
Researcher Bias	Respondent Bias
Response Bias	Sampling Bias
Selection Bias	Self-Selection Bias
Social Desirability Bias	Sponsor Bias
Survivorship Bias	

GETTING STARTED WITH ROV BIZSTATS

ROV BizStats tool is a very powerful and fast module in Risk Simulator software that is used for running more than 200 business statistics and analytical models on your data. The following provides a few quick getting started steps on running the module and details on each of the elements in the software. Follow these steps for running ROV BizStats (see Figures 4.1–4.4 for screenshots and locations of certain elements), assuming you have already installed either Risk Simulator or ROV BizStats.

- Start ROV BizStats inside Risk Simulator at *Risk Simulator | ROV BizStats* or start the stand-alone ROV BizStats software directly from the desktop icon, and then follow the steps below:

  o Step 1. To get started learning the tool, click on the *Example* button [A] to load the default sample data and model profile or type in your data or *Copy/Paste* your own data into the data grid [B] from Excel or another software (Figure 4.1). You can add your own notes or variable names in the first *Notes* row [C].

  o Step 2. Select the relevant model [D] to run and enter in the appropriate variables [G]. See area [F] for some example inputs of the selected model as well as short descriptions. Separate variables for the same parameter using semicolons and use a new line (hit *Enter* to create a new line) for different parameters. (Click on any one of the saved models in

Step 4 [J] to see some examples of predefined models and their user inputs.)

- Step 3. Click *Run* [K] to compute the results [L]. You can view any relevant analytical *Statistical Results* or *Charts* from the two tabs [M].

- Step 4. If required, you can provide a model name [H] to *Add* [I] the model into the profile. Multiple models [J] can be saved in the same single profile. Existing models can be edited or deleted [I] and rearranged in order of appearance [N], and all the changes can be saved into a single profile with the file name extension *.bizstats. The profile can be saved using the menu *File | Save* or *File | Save As* [O].

Additional Notes and Reminders

- Saving. Note that the *File | Save* menu [O] command saves the entire dataset, settings, notes, and created models and computations into a single *.bizstats file. As an example, this is similar to saving an Excel *.xlsx file. However, there is also the *Add*, *Edit*, and *Delete* functionality [I] in Step 4 of the user interface to save individual models, input variables, notes, and settings. Think of these saved models [J] as different worksheet tabs in Microsoft Excel. So, you will still need to save the entire *.bizstats file when you are done adding all these models. That is, adding multiple worksheets in Excel is fine but you need to remember to save the entire *.xlsx file when done.

- Maximizing User Interface. You can maximize the user interface for larger views of the data grid, results, and charts or use the standard-sized view for easier manipulation of the software. Change between maximized or standardized views by clicking on the relevant Windows form buttons on the top right corner of the software.

- Pasting Data. When copying and pasting your data into the data grid [B] in ROV BizStats, make sure to click on and select the correct single-cell location before pasting (click on and select the location, then *CTRL+V* or right-click and select *Paste Data*). Make sure to select a cell in the data grid (this is the top left corner of the data to paste) either starting from the data rows (ROW 1) or from the NOTES row if your copied data has headers.

- Grid Size. The data grid size can be set in the menu, where the grid can accommodate up to 1,000 variable columns with 1 million rows of data per variable. The menu also allows you to change the language settings and decimal settings for your data. Finally, the *Data | Auto Fit Columns* [O] allows you to auto-fit the entire data grid at once.

- Load Example. To get started, it is always a good idea to load the example file [A] that comes complete with some data and precreated models [J]. You can double-click on any of these models to run them and the results are shown in the report area [L], which sometimes can be a chart or model statistics [M or U]. Using this example file, you can now see how the input parameters [G] are entered based on the model description [F], and you can proceed to create your own custom models.

- Auto Fit. If a cell has a large value that is not completely displayed, click on and hover your mouse over that cell and you will see a pop-up comment showing the entire value, or simply resize the variable column (drag the column to make it wider, double-click on the column's edge to auto fit the column or right-click on the column header and select auto fit). You can also use the *Data | Auto Fit Columns* menu [O] item to auto-fit the entire data grid at once.

- Navigation. Use the up, down, left, and right keys to move around the grid, or use the *Home* and *End* keys on the keyboard to move to the far left and far right of a row. You can also use a combination of keys such as *Ctrl+Home* to jump to the top-left cell, *Ctrl+End* to the bottom-right cell, *Shift+Up/Down* to select a specific area, and so forth.

- Adding Notes. You can enter short notes for each variable on the *Notes* [C] row. Remember to make your notes brief and simple.

- Chart Icons. Try out the various chart icons on the *Visualize* tab [S] to change the look and feel of the charts (e.g., rotate, shift, zoom, change colors, add legend, and so forth).

- **Copy Button.** The *Copy* button [R] is used to copy the *Results*, *Charts*, and *Statistics* tabs in *Step 3* after a model is run. If no models are run, then the copy function will only copy a blank page.

- **Report Button.** The *Report* button [R] will only run if there are saved models in *Step 4* or if there are data in the grid, else the report generated will be empty. You will also need Microsoft Excel to be installed to run the data extraction and results reports, and Microsoft PowerPoint available to run the chart reports. If you have a large number of saved models, it may take a few minutes for the report to finish.

- **Load Example Button.** When in doubt about how to run a specific model or statistical method, start the *Example* [A] profile and review how the data is set up in *Step 1* or how the input parameters are entered in *Step 2*. You can use these as getting started guides and templates for your own data and models.

- **Languages.** The language can be changed in the *Language* menu [O]. Note that currently there are 12 languages available in the software with more to be added later. However, sometimes certain limited results will still be shown in English.

- **View Models List.** You can change how the list of models in *Step 2* is shown by changing the *View* droplist [E]. You can list the models alphabetically, by various model categories, and by data input requirements—note that in certain Unicode languages (e.g., Chinese, Japanese, and Korean), there is no alphabetical arrangement and, therefore, the first option will be unavailable.

- **Decimals.** The software can handle different regional decimal and numerical settings (e.g., one thousand dollars and fifty cents can be written as 1,000.50 or 1.000,50 or 1'000,50 and so forth). The decimal settings can be set in ROV Biz-Stats' menu *Data | Decimal Settings* [O]. However, when in doubt, please change the computer's regional settings to English USA and keep the default North America 1,000.50 in ROV BizStats (this setting is guaranteed to work with ROV BizStats and the default examples).

- Column Headers. Click on the data grid's column header(s) to select the entire column(s) or variable(s), and once selected, you can right-click on the header to *Auto Fit* the column, *Cut*, *Copy*, *Delete*, or *Paste* data. You can also click on and select multiple column headers to select multiple variables and right-click and select *Visualize* to chart the data or click the *Visualize* button [Q] (Figure 4.2). You can also change the different chart types using the chart droplist [T].

- Data Length. If you need to run models with different data lengths of the same dataset, we recommend simply creating additional data variable columns. This helps simplify tracking and auditing your results. Alternatively, you can use the data row controls between [K] and [M].

- Visualize Data. Click on the variable headers [P] to select one or multiple variables at once, and then right-click to add, delete, copy, paste, or visualize [Q] the variables selected. You can then click on the *Visualize* tab [S] to see the chart.

- Command. Models can also be entered using a *Command* console [V/W/X] (Figure 4.3). To see how this works, double-click to run a model [J] and go to the *Command* console [V]. You can replicate the model or create your own and click *Run Command* [X] when ready. Each line in the console represents a model and its relevant parameters. Here, you can run all or one selected command, save existing commands as a separate file, or open previously saved commands. Commands allow you to quickly run multiple models at once without the need for clicking around the user interface. Results can also be appended to the bottom, where multiple models are run in sequence, and all the results will be created as a single lengthy report (see the two radio buttons below area M).

- XML Editor. The entire *.bizstats profile (where data and multiple models are created and saved) can be edited directly in XML [Z] by opening the *XML Editor* from the *File* menu [Y]. Changes to the profile can be programmatically made here and take effect once the file is saved (Figure 4.4).

Figure 4.1: ROV BizStats (Statistical Analysis)

[EXAMPLE] - ROV Biz Stats

File Data Language Help

STEP 1 Data — Manually enter your data, paste from another application, or load an example dataset with analysis

STEP 2 Analysis

Choose analysis and enter parameters required (see example inputs below)

Example
Visualize

Dataset   Visualize   Command

View   All Methods

VAR28
VAR29-VAR33

N	VAR1 Group1 X1	VAR2 Group1 X2	VAR3 Group1 X3	VAR4 Group1 X4	VAR5 Group2 X1	VAR6 Group2 X2	VAR7 Group2 X3	
NOTES								
1	12	45	20	12	17.5	70.8	71.4	3
2	39	37	42	10	104.6	45.9	55	3
3	36	13	31	19	64.7	47.5	54	3
4	17	50	24	18	47	77.8	27.9	4
5	25	35	15	14	22	70.9	40.6	2
6	15	40	13	8	12.4	84.8	33	3

ANCOVA (Single Factor Multiple Treatments)
ANCOVA (MANOVA General Linear Model)
ANOVA (Randomized Blocks Multiple Treatments)
ANOVA (Single Factor Multiple Treatments)
ANOVA (Two-Way Analysis)
Auto ARIMA
ARIMA
Auto Econometrics (Detailed)
Auto Econometrics (Quick)
Autocorrelation and Partial Autocorrelation
Autocorrelation Durbin-Watson AR(1) Test
Bonferroni Test (Single Variable with Repetition)
Bonferroni Test (Two Variables with Repetition)
Box's Test for Homogeneity of Covariance
Box-Cox Normal Transformation
Charts: 2D Area
Charts: 2D Bar
Charts: 2D Line
Charts: 2D Pareto

Dependent Variable Independent Variables, P-Value Threshold (Optional:0.1), Time-Series Lags (Optional:0), Autoregressive AR(p) (Optional:0):
> Var1
> Var2; Var3; Var4
> 0.1
> 0
> 0

Tests multiple combinations of models that provide the best fit for your data (linear, nonlinear, logarithmic, and interaction models).

STEP 4 Save (Optional)
You can save multiple analyses and notes in the profile for future retrieval

Name
Notes

Auto Econometrics (Quick)

ADD
EDIT
DEL
Save
Exit

Chart: 3D Point
Chart: 3D Scatter
Chart: Box-Whiskers
Chart: QQ Normal
Coefficient of Variation Homogeneity Test
Cointegration Test (Engle-Granger)
Combinatorial Fuzzy Logic
Control Chart: C
Control Chart: NP
Control Chart: P
Control Chart: R

STEP 3 Run

Run   Run the current analysis in Step 2 or the selected saved analysis in Step 4, view the results, charts and statistics, copy the results and charts to clipboard or generate reports

Use All Data
Use Rows   20

Copy
Report

Results   Charts

Show New Results Only   Append Results at the End

	Coeff	Std. Error	T-stat	P-value	Lower 5%	Upper 95%
Intercept	3664.81960	805.12137	4.55188	0.00006	2028.61616	5301.02305
LN(VAR1)	-321.07588	83.62231	-3.83960	0.00051	-491.01655	-151.13490
DIFF(VAR1)	-0.00469	0.00144	-3.26953	0.00247	-0.00761	-0.00178
LN(RATE(VAR1))	138.26285	31.97150	4.35696	0.00012	74.09217	203.63352
DIFF(VAR2)	0.93499	0.36471	2.25944	0.02839	0.09380	1.57617
RATE(VAR2)	-137.48661	77.44510	-1.77528	0.08480	-294.87399	19.90076
LN(VAR3)	286.43034	66.04043	4.33720	0.00012	152.22005	420.64063
DIFF(VAR4)	-0.35191	0.05970	-5.89427	0.00000	-0.47325	-0.23058
RATE(VAR5)	-497.73236	156.06627	-3.18924	0.00306	-814.89716	-180.56756
LN(RATE(VAR5))	431.68094	163.34071	2.64283	0.01234	99.73269	763.62920
VAR1*VAR4	0.00004	0.00001	3.46983	0.00143	0.00002	0.00006
VAR1*VAR5	-0.00193	0.00007	-2.49557	0.01759	-0.00350	-0.00036
VAR3*VAR4	-0.15513	0.04131	-3.75557	0.00065	-0.23908	-0.07119
VAR3*VAR5	8.92027	2.57281	3.46713	0.00145	3.69169	14.14884
VAR4*VAR5	0.03743	0.01553	2.40975	0.02152	0.00586	0.06900

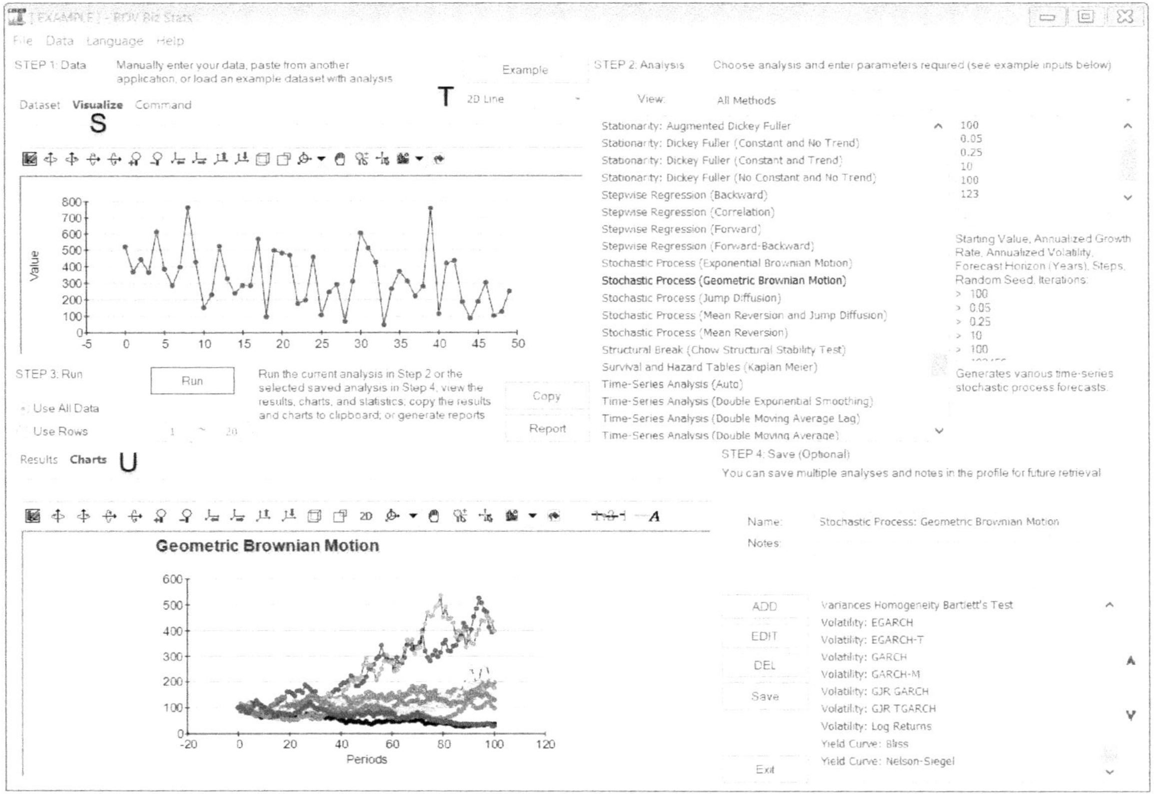

Figure 4.2: Data Visualization and Results Charts

File Data Language Help

STEP 1 Data Manually enter your data, paste from another application, or load an example dataset with analysis   Example

STEP 2 Analysis Choose analysis and enter parameters required (see example inputs below)

Dataset: Visualize **Command** ∨

View   All Methods   VAR29:VAR33

Run All Commands | Run Current Command Line | Save Commands | Open Commands File

1 AutoEconometricsQuick (VAR28 # VAR30, VAR31, VAR32, VAR33)
2 AutoEconometricsDetailed (VAR28 # VAR29, VAR30, VAR31, VAR32, VAR33)
3 AutoEconometricsDetailed (VAR28 # VAR29, VAR30, VAR31, VAR32, VAR33)
4 AutoEconometricsQuick (VAR28 # VAR29, VAR30, VAR31, VAR32, VAR33)
5 ANOVAMANOVAGeneralLinearModel ()
6 ANOVARandomizedBlocksMultipleTreatments (VAR14, VAR15, VAR16, VAR17)
7 PrincipalComponentAnalysis (VAR29, VAR30, VAR31, VAR32, VAR33)
8

Nonparametric: Mood's Multivariate Median Test
Nonparametric: Runs Test for Randomness
Nonparametric: Shapiro-Wilk-Royston Normality Test
Nonparametric: Wilcoxon Signed-Rank Test (One Var)
Nonparametric: Wilcoxon Signed-Rank Test (Two Var)
Parametric: One Variable (T) Mean
Parametric: One Variable (Z) Mean
Parametric: One Variable (Z) Proportion
Parametric: Power Curve for T Test
Parametric: Two Variable (F) Variances
Parametric: Two Variable (T) Dependent Means
Parametric: Two Variable (T) Independent Equal Variance
Parametric: Two Variable (T) Independent Unequal Variance
Parametric: Two Variable (Z) Independent Means
Parametric: Two Variable (Z) Independent Proportions
Partial Correlations (Using Correlation Matrix)
Partial Correlations (Using Raw Data)
Principal Component Analysis
Quick Statistic: Absolute Values (ABS)

Data
> Var1, Var2, Var3

Runs a principal component analysis on multiple variables

STEP 4 Save (Optional)
You can save multiple analyses and notes in the profile for future retrieval

Name
Notes   Principal Component Analysis

ADD
EDIT
DEL
Save
Exit

Markov Chain Transition Matrix
Multiple Poisson Regression (Population and Freq)
Multiple Regression (Deming Regression Known Var)
Multiple Regression (Linear)
Multiple Regression (Nonlinear)
Multiple Regression (Ordinal Logistic)
Multiple Regression (Through Origin)
Multiple Regression (2VAR Functional Forms)
Multiple Ridge Regression (High VIF Bias)
Multiple Weighted Regression (Heteroskedasticity)
Nominal Contingency Table 'Ncdemar's Homogeneity)

STEP 3 Run   Run the current analysis in Step 2, view the selected saved analyses in Step 4, view the results, charts, and statistics, copy the results and charts to clipboard, or generate reports

Copy
Report

W

STEP 3 Run
Run   1 ~ 20
Use All Data
Use Rows

Results Charts

● Show New Results Only   ○ Append Results at the End

Eigenvalues: 2.4180   1.0760   0.8665   0.6003
Proportions: 48.36%   21.52%   17.33%   12.01%
Cum. Proportions: 48.36%   69.88%   87.21%   99.21%

Eigenvectors:

0.5820	-0.3560	-0.1169	0.1485
0.3759	0.1935	-0.6364	-0.5911
0.5770	-0.3868	-0.1066	0.0858
0.3228	0.6453	0.2073	0.6563
0.2878	0.5157	-0.6789	0.4364

Eigenvalues (Arranged and Ranked):
2.4180   1.0760   0.8665   0.6003
Proportions Ranked:
48.36%   21.52%   17.33%   12.01%

Figure 4.3: Command Console

Y

Example   [ ] [□] [✕]

File Data Language Help

STEP 1 Data   Manually enter your data, paste from another application, or load an example dataset with analysis

STEP 2 Analysis   Choose analysis and enter parameters required (see example inputs below)

Dataset Visualize **Command**

View   All Methods   ‹ VAR29:VAR33

Grubbs Test for Outliers
Heteroskedasticity Test (Breusch-Pagan-Godfrey)
Heteroskedasticity Test (Lagrange Multiplier)
Heteroskedasticity Test (Wald's on Individual Variables)
Heteroskedasticity Test (Wald Glesjer)
Hotelling T-Square: 1 VAR with Related Measures
Hotelling T-Square: 2 VAR Dependent Pair with Related Meas...
Hotelling T-Square: 2 VAR Indep. Equal Variance with Related...
Hotelling T-Square: 2 VAR Indep. Unequal Variance with Relat...
Inter-rater Reliability: Cohen's Kappa
Inter-rater Reliability: Inter Class Correlation (ICC)
Inter-rater Reliability: Kendall's W (No Ties)
Inter-rater Reliability: Kendall's W (With Ties)
Internal Consistency Reliability; Cronbach's Alpha (Dichotomou...
Internal Consistency Reliability; Guttman's Lambda and Split H...
Kendall's Tau Correlation (No Ties)
Kendall's Tau Correlation (With Ties)
Linear Interpolation
Logistic Curve

Data
> Var1 Var2 Var3

Runs a principal component analysis on multiple variables

Propel Component Analysis

STEP 4 Save (Optional)
You can save multiple analyses and notes in the profile for future retrieval

Name
Notes

ADD   Distributional Fitting (Kuiper's Statistic)
    Distributional Fitting (Schwarz/Bayes Criterion)
    Distributional Fitting (Chi-Square)
EDIT   Diversity Index
    Eigenvalues and Eigenvectors
DEL   Endogeneity Test 2SLS Durbin-Wu-Hausman
    Endogenous Model IV and 2SLS
Save   Error Corrector Model Engle-Granger
    Exponential J Curve
    Factor Analysis (PCA Varimax Rotation)
Exit   Expected Accuracy (Akaike, Bayes, Schwarz, RMSE...

0.6003   12.21%
99.21%
0.1495
0.5911
0.0359
0.6663
0.4364
0.6003   12.21%

Z

XML Editor   [ ] [□] [✕]

```
405 VAR290
406 VAR291
407 VAR292: VAR293: VAR294: VAR295"/>
408    <model name="Endogenous Model IV and 2SLS" notes="" id="237" parameter=="VAR289
409 VAR290
410 VAR291: VAR292: VAR293"/>
411    <model name="Error Correction Model Engle-Granger" notes="" id="229" parameter==
       "VAR10"/>
412 VAR104"/>
413    <model name="Exponential J Curve" notes="" id="20" parameter=="400
414 3
415 100"/>
416    <model name="Factor Analysis (PCA Varimax Rotation)" notes="" id="242" parameter==
       "VAR105:VAR113"/>
417    <model name="Forecast Accuracy (Akaike, Bayes, Schwarz, RMSE)" notes="" i="220"
       parameter="VAR114
418 6"/>
419    <model name="Forecast Accuracy (Diebold Mariano Competing Forecast)" notes="" id=
       "186" parameter="VAR115
420 VAR116: VAR117"/>
421    <model name="Forecast Accuracy (Pesaran Timmermann Direction)" notes="" id="187"
       parameter="VAR118
422 VAR119"/>
423    <model name="GLM Logit with Binary Outcomes" notes="" i="94" parameter="VAR120
424 VAR121:VAR129"/>
425    <model name="GLM Logit with Bivariate Outcomes" notes="" i="246" parameter=
       "VAR129: VAR130
426 VAR131
427 VAR132"/>
```

Hide basic XML tags

Save   OK   Cancel

Eigenvalues (Arranged and Ranked):
2.4550   1.0760   0.2665
Proportions Ranked:
45.18%   21.52%   17.33%
Cum Proportions Ranked:

Figure 4.4: XML Editor

MOST COMMON ANALYTICS

This chapter is the heart of the quantitative portion of the book in that it covers the most commonly used analytical methodologies. As in most research projects, whenever data is collected, it will need to be analyzed. Typically, the researcher is attempting to test some theory or hypothesis whereby if a certain situation or condition is applied in an experiment, the data is collected prior to and after said experiment and analyzed to see if the hypothesis is validated or debunked.

For example, if a bank is trying to test whether a new check deposit scanning system and associated training will reduce its operational risks (i.e., making mistakes during deposits), it could start collecting data prior to implementing the new system in a single branch, and continue to collect the same data after the system proof of concept implementation at that single branch. Then, using statistical hypothesis tests, determine whether the differences seen in the before and after data can be attributed to randomness or are a clear indication that the new system is working, and, hence, make a decision about implementing the same system in all its other branches.

Other examples could include the U.S. military testing the effectiveness of implementing a series of equipment and support services to increase the mean time between failures (MTBF); a pharmaceutical company assessing the efficacy of its new experimental drug; a vehicle manufacturer testing a new engineering design that improves engine life compared to a conventional design; and the like.

The chapter begins with simple t-, F-, and z-tests where two variables are tested simultaneously to determine if their means and variances are statistically significantly different or similar. The chapter continues with the application of ANOVA or analysis of variance, where multiple variables are tested at once. Other nonparametric tests are introduced, where normality and large datasets do not have to be assumed, as they are required in standard t- and z-tests. Tests of normality, multicollinearity, and heteroskedasticity are introduced, together with the basic concepts of multivariate linear and nonlinear regression models.

TWO-SAMPLE EQUAL VARIANCE T-TEST

The two-sample equal variance t-test, as its name suggests, compares two sample datasets against each other to determine if there is a statistically significant difference between their population means (μ). In other words, the test can identify if a certain event or experiment has an effect. This t-test assumes that the unknown population standard deviations (σ) of both samples are roughly equal, and the populations are roughly normally distributed. The t-distribution is appropriate here as the true standard deviations of the populations are unknown, and when smaller sample sizes are available (typically < 30). This test is also known as the pooled-variances t-test because it takes the standard deviations of both samples and pools them into a single parameter in the model.

The hypotheses tested are typically:

H_0: $\mu_1 = \mu_2$, the samples' means are statistically similar

H_a: $\mu_1 \neq \mu_2$, the samples' means are statistically significantly different

As a reminder, the null hypothesis (H_0) generally has the equivalence sign (i.e., =, ≥, ≤), whereas the alternate hypothesis (H_a) has its complement (i.e., ≠, <, >). The sign of the alternate hypothesis points to whether the test is a two-tailed test (≠) or a one-tailed test (right tail is denoted with >, whereas a left tail test uses <).

To get started, two datasets with a number of data points (with n_1 and n_2 sample sizes) are put side by side (see Figure 5.2). Then, their respective sample averages ($\bar{x}_1$ and $\bar{x}_2$) and sample standard deviations (s_1 and s_2) are computed. The t-statistic is then calculated using the formula below and compared against the critical t-values. In most situations, the p-values of this calculated t-statistic are calculated and compared against some predefined level of significance (i.e., the standard α significance levels of 0.10, 0.05, and 0.01 will be assumed throughout these examples) using the t-distribution with a certain degree of freedom (*df*). If the p-value is below these α significance levels, we reject the null hypothesis and accept the alternate hypothesis (Figure 5.1).

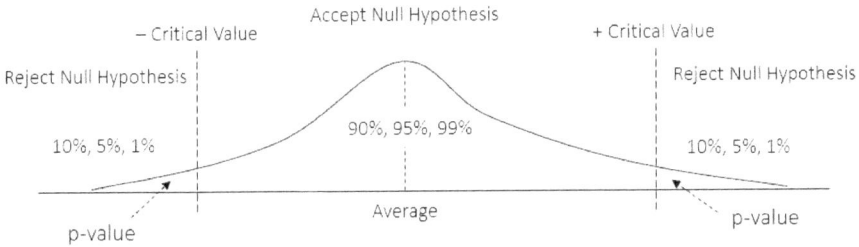

Accept Null Hypothesis

− Critical Value   + Critical Value

Reject Null Hypothesis   Reject Null Hypothesis

10%, 5%, 1%   90%, 95%, 99%   10%, 5%, 1%

Average

p-value   p-value

Figure 5.1: Visual Representation of Acceptance/Rejection Regions

The formal specification of the two-sample equal variance test is:

$$t = \frac{(\bar{x}_1 - \bar{x}_2) - (\mu_1 - \mu_2)}{\sqrt{s_p^2\left(\frac{1}{n_1} + \frac{1}{n_2}\right)}} \text{ with } s_p^2 = \frac{(n_1 - 1)s_1^2 + (n_2 - 1)s_2^2}{n_1 + n_2 - 2} \text{ and}$$

$$df = n_1 + n_2 - 2$$

As seen in Figure 5.2, the model was run in Microsoft Excel's Data Analysis Toolkit. The t-statistic was computed as −1.2273, and the two-tail p-value is 0.2355, corresponding to a two-tailed critical t-value of ±2.1009. As explained in previous chapters, if the calculated t-statistic exceeds these critical t-values, we reject the null hypothesis, otherwise, we will fail to reject the null and summarily *accept* the alternate hypothesis. An alternate, and perhaps a simpler, approach is to compare the computed p-value against the α significance level. If the p-value is $\leq \alpha$, then we reject the null hypothesis.

VAR 1	VAR 2
11	10
8	11
8	9
3	7
7	2
5	11
9	12
5	3
1	6
3	7

t-Test: Two-Sample Assuming Equal Variances
Results from Excel's Data Analysis Toolpak

	Variable 1	Variable 2
Mean	6.0000	7.8000
Variance	9.7778	11.7333
Observations	10.0000	10.0000
Pooled Variance	10.7556	
Hypothesized Mean Difference	0.0000	
df	18.0000	
t Stat	-1.2273	
P(T<=t) one-tail	0.1178	
t Critical one-tail	1.7341	
P(T<=t) two-tail	0.2355	
t Critical two-tail	2.1009	

Figure 5.2: Two-Sample Equal Variance T-Test

Based on the calculations above, the p-value exceeds the standard 0.10, 0.05, 0.01 thresholds, which means we fail to reject the null hypothesis and conclude that the two sample datasets are statistically not different from one another and that whatever experiment or treatment was applied was ineffective.

The analysis can be done manually (Figure 5.3 shows the manual computations performed in Excel and you can see the corresponding cell equations) using the model specification provided above, or by using the ROV BizStats software (Figure 5.4).

	A	B	C	D	E	F	G	H	I	J	K	L	M	N	O
1															
2		VAR 1	VAR 2												
3		11	10		Average 1		6.0000	=AVERAGE(B3:B12)							
4		8	11		Average 2		7.8000	=AVERAGE(C3:C12)							
5		8	9		Sample Variance 1		9.7778	=VAR(B3:B12)							
6		3	7		Sample Variance 2		11.7333	=VAR(C3:C12)							
7		7	2		Pooled Variance		10.7556	=((COUNT(B3:B12)-1)*G5+(COUNT(C3:C12)-1)*G6)/(COUNT(B3:B12)+COUNT(C3:C12)-2)							
8		5	11		Paired T Statistic		-1.2273	=(G3-G4)/SQRT(G7*(1/COUNT(B3:B12)+1/(COUNT(C3:C12))))							
9		9	12		P-value One Tail		0.1178	=TDIST(-G8,COUNT(B3:B12)+COUNT(C3:C12)-2,1)							
10		5	3		P-value Two Tail		0.2355	=TDIST(-G8,COUNT(B3:B12)+COUNT(C3:C12)-2,2)							
11		1	6												
12		3	7												
13															

Figure 5.3: Manual Computations

EXAMPLE - ROV Biz Stat

File Data Language Help

STEP 1 Data   Manually ente STEP 2 Analysis   Choose analysis and enter parameters required (see example inputs below)

            application, or

                               View   All Methods

Dataset Visualize Command

			Parametric: One Variable (T) Mean	VAR261; VAR262
			Parametric: One Variable (Z) Mean	0
N	VAR261	VAR262	Parametric: One Variable (Z) Proportion	
NOTES	Similar A	Similar B	Parametric: Power Curve for T Test	
1	11	10	Parametric: Two Variable (F) Variances	
2	8	11	Parametric: Two Variable (T) Dependent Means	
3	8	9	**Parametric: Two Variable (T) Independent Equal Variance**	Data (=2) Hypothesized Mean
4	3	7	Parametric: Two Variable (T) Independent Unequal Variance	> Var1, Var2
5	7	2	Parametric: Two Variable (Z) Independent Means	> 5
6	5	11	Parametric: Two Variable (Z) Independent Proportions	

Parametric: Two Variable (Z) Independent Proportions
Partial Correlations (Using Correlation Matrix)
Partial Correlations (Using Raw Data)
Principal Component Analysis
Quick Statistic: Absolute Values (ABS)
Quick Statistic: Average (AVG)

STEP 3 Run   R   Quick Statistic: Count
                 Quick Statistic: Difference
- Use All Data   Quick Statistic: Lag
- Use Rows   1   Quick Statistic: Lead

Tests if the means are equal for two independent+equal variance variables (Null: the two variables means are equal)

Results Charts

◉ Show New Results Only   ◯ Append Results at the End

```
Column 2 Observations : 10
Column 2 Sample Mean : 7.800000
Column 2 Sample Standard Deviation : 3.425395
Sample Mean Difference : -1.800000
t-Statistic : -1.227273
Hypothesized Mean : 0.000000

p-Value Left Tailed : 0.117765
not significant at any of the following significance levels: 1%, 5%, and 10%
not rejected
not significantly less than the hypothesized mean difference.

p-Value Right Tailed : 0.882235
not significant at any of the following significance levels: 1%, 5%, and 10%
not rejected
not significantly greater than the hypothesized mean difference.

p-Value Two Tailed : 0.235530
not significant at any of the following significance levels: 1%, 5%, and 10%
```

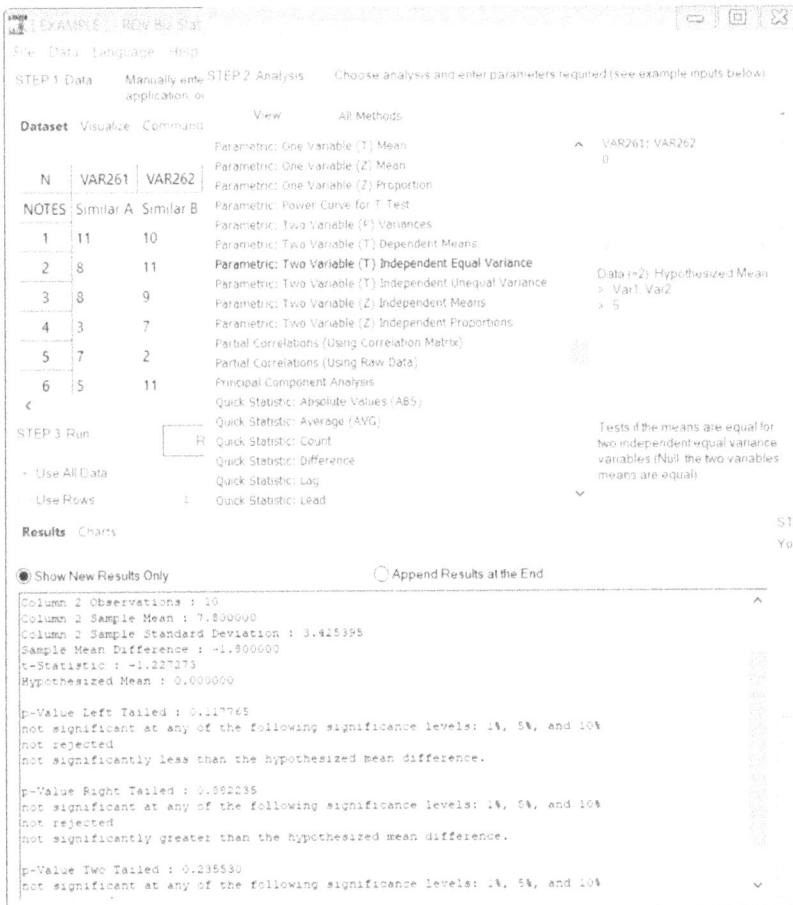

Figure 5.4: ROV BizStats Calculations

To use the ROV BizStats tool, make sure that ROV Risk Simulator is installed on your computer. Then, start Excel, click on the *Risk Simulator* menu and select *ROV BizStats* from the icon ribbon. You will see a user interface similar to Figure 5.4. In Step 1's data grid, you can now manually enter the two datasets or copy and paste from another source such as Microsoft Excel or another database or text file. Next, select the relevant analysis in Step 2. In this specific example, the *Parametric Two Variable (T) with Independent and Equal Variances* should be selected. When this item is selected, you will see the sample data requirements (e.g., Data = 2 Variables, Hypothesized Mean, and examples VAR1, VAR2). Next, either manually type in *VAR1; VAR2* separated by a semicolon, then hit enter and type *0* into the input box in Step 2 for the hypothesized difference, or simply double-click the variable header (e.g., VAR1 and then VAR2) to add these variables automatically. Next, just hit *Run* to perform the calculations. You can see that the results confirm both the manual computations and Excel Data Analysis Toolkit results (e.g., t-statistic is –1.2273 and p-value is 0.2355).

TWO-SAMPLE UNEQUAL VARIANCE T-TEST

If the standard deviations of the two sample datasets are still unknown but assumed to be different, combining them into a single pooled estimate as done previously would be inappropriate. Therefore, the sample standard deviations (s) will be used independently to estimate the population standard deviations (σ). Nonetheless, normality of the underlying dataset is assumed, although this assumption becomes less important with larger datasets. The two-sample unequal variance t-test would be needed, and its specifications are described below:

$$t = \frac{(\bar{x}_1 - \bar{x}_2) - (\mu_1 - \mu_2)}{\sqrt{\left(\frac{s_1^2}{n_1} + \frac{s_2^2}{n_2}\right)}} \text{ and } df = \frac{\left[s_1^2/n_1 + s_2^2/n_2\right]^2}{\frac{\left(s_1^2/n_1\right)^2}{n_1 - 1} + \frac{\left(s_2^2/n_2\right)^2}{n_2 - 1}}$$

As an example, suppose that a chemical manufacturer is testing a new engine oil additive to see if there is a significant difference in fuel efficiency. The manufacturer randomly selects 70 cars in a city and tests its additive on half of these cars selected randomly, leaving the other half without the additive. Figure 5.5 shows the mean and standard deviation of the two sample datasets. The hypotheses tested are the typical two-tail test:

H_0: $\mu_1 = \mu_2$, the two samples' means are statistically similar

H_a: $\mu_1 \neq \mu_2$, the two means are statistically significantly different

The calculations are shown in Figures 5.5 and 5.6. The two-tail p-value is 0.0212, which is less than the standard alpha significance levels ($\alpha = 0.10, 0.05$), so we can conclude that the engine oil additive has statistically significantly different miles per gallon fuel efficiency. Because the types of cars were not stratified and preselected, we do not know if the variances of the two sample datasets are identical. Therefore, the unequal variance t-test is used in this case.

In situations when the two datasets are dependent on each other, the two-sample t-test with dependent means is used. This test is also known as the paired observations test, which means that the number of observations in each of the two datasets has to be the same ($n = n_1 = n_2$). For example, if the researcher is interested in testing the before and after-effects on productivity of the same sample of employees after a change in work hours, the data is obtained from the same dataset (i.e., the same employees are tested).

The dependent means test uses:

$$t = \frac{\bar{d}}{s_d / \sqrt{n}} \text{ and } df = n - 1$$

where $\bar{d}$ is the average of each difference between two test units, and $d = (x_1 - x_2)$.

Figure 5.7 provides an example of the productivity study where X_1 measured after the change in work hours, compared to the before-change measured in X_2. The numbers indicate the total hours it takes to complete a certain activity, and each row of the dataset represents an individual. The hypotheses tested are the typical one-tail test:

H_0: $\mu_1 \geq \mu_2$, the samples' means are statistically similar

H_a: $\mu_1 < \mu_2$, sample 1's mean is statistically significantly less than

sample 2's mean

As the one-tail p-value calculated is 0.0141, we reject the null hypothesis and accept the alternate hypothesis and conclude that the change in work hours will result in a higher productivity (measured by lower total hours required to complete some prespecified task). Figure 5.8 illustrates the implementation of the problem in ROV Biz-Stats.

	B	C	D	E F G H I J
3	Mean 1	18.2229		
4	Stdev 1	2.6319		
5	Count 1	35		
6	Mean 2	20.1000		
7	Stdev 2	3.8865		
8	Count 2	35		
10	Calculated T	-2.3659		=((C3-C6)-0)/SQRT((C4^2/C5)+(C7^2/C8))
11	Calculated DF	60		=ROUND(((((C4^2/C5)+(C7^2/C8))^2/(((C4^2/C5)^2/(C5-1))+((C7^2/C8)^2/(C8-1)))),0)
12	P-Value	0.0212	2 Tails	=TDIST(C10,C11,2)
13	Critical T @ 0.10	1.6706	2 Tails	=TINV(0.1,C11)
14	Critical T @ 0.05	2.0003	2 Tails	=TINV(0.05,C11)
15	Critical T @ 0.01	2.6603	2 Tails	=TINV(0.01,C11)
16	P-Value	0.0106	1 Tail	=TDIST(C10,C11,1)
17	Critical T @ 0.10	1.2958	1 Tail	=TINV(0.1*2,C11)
18	Critical T @ 0.05	1.6706	1 Tail	=TINV(0.05*2,C11)
19	Critical T @ 0.01	2.3901	1 Tail	=TINV(0.01*2,C11)

Figure 5.5: Example Calculations for Unequal Variance T-Test

EXAMPLE 1 - ROV BizStats

File   Data   Language   Help

STEP 1 Data   Manually enter yo STEP 2 Analysis   Choose analysis and enter parameters required (see example inputs below)
               application, or loa

Dataset Visualize Command

View   All Methods

N	VAR263	VAR264
NOTES	Different A	Different B
1	22.5	21.6
2	24.6	16.8
3	17.5	16.4
4	16.2	20.5
5	14.5	20.5
6	16.3	16.2

Parametric: One Variable (T) Mean
Parametric: One Variable (Z) Mean
Parametric: One Variable (Z) Proportion
Parametric: Power Curve for T Test
Parametric: Two Variable (F) Variances
Parametric: Two Variable (T) Dependent Means
Parametric: Two Variable (T) Independent Equal Variance
Parametric: Two Variable (T) Independent Unequal Variance
Parametric: Two Variable (Z) Independent Means
Parametric: Two Variable (Z) Independent Proportions
Partial Correlations (Using Correlation Matrix)
Partial Correlations (Using Raw Data)
Principal Component Analysis
Quick Statistic: Absolute Values (ABS)
Quick Statistic: Average (AVG)
Quick Statistic: Count
Quick Statistic: Difference
Quick Statistic: Lag
Quick Statistic: Lead

VAR263; VAR264
0

Data (=2) Hypothesized Mean
> Var1, Var2
> 5

Tests if the means are equal for
two independent unequal variance
variables (Null: the two variables
means are equal)

STEP 3 Run   Run

· Use All Data

Use Rows   1

Results Charts

STEP 4
You can

◉ Show New Results Only   ○ Append Results at the End

```
Column 2 Observations : 35
Column 2 Sample Mean : 20.100000
Column 2 Sample Standard Deviation : 3.986477
Sample Mean Difference : -1.877143
t-Statistic : -2.365954
Hypothesized Mean : 0.000000

p-Value Left Tailed : 0.010616
significant at 10% and 5%
rejected
significantly less than the hypothesized mean difference.

p-Value Right Tailed : 0.989384
not significant at any of the following significance levels: 1%, 5%, and 10%
not rejected
not significantly greater than the hypothesized mean difference.

p-Value Two Tailed : 0.021231
significant at 10% and 5%
```

Figure 5.6: Unequal Variance T-Test in ROV BizStats

	A	B	C	D	E	F	G	H
1								
2		X1	X2	Difference (d)				
3		25.5	43.6	-18.10				
4		59.2	69.9	-10.70				
5		38.4	39.8	-1.40				
6		66.8	73.4	-6.60				
7		44.9	50.2	-5.30				
8		47.4	53.9	-6.50				
9		41.6	40.3	1.30				
10		48.9	58.0	-9.10				
11		60.7	66.9	-6.20				
12		41.0	66.5	-25.50				
13		36.1	27.4	8.70				
14		34.4	33.7	0.70				
15								
16			Average	-6.5583	=AVERAGE(D3:D14)			
17			Stdev	9.0010	=STDEV(D3:D14)			
18			Calculated T	-2.5240	=D16/(D17/SQRT(COUNT(D3:D14)))			
19			DF	11	=COUNT(D3:D14)-1			
20			P-value (2 Tail)	0.0283	=TDIST(ABS(D18),COUNT(D3:D14)-1,2)			
21			P-value (1 Tail)	0.0141	=TDIST(ABS(D18),COUNT(D3:D14)-1,1)			

Figure 5.7: Calculations for Dependent Paired Observations T-Test

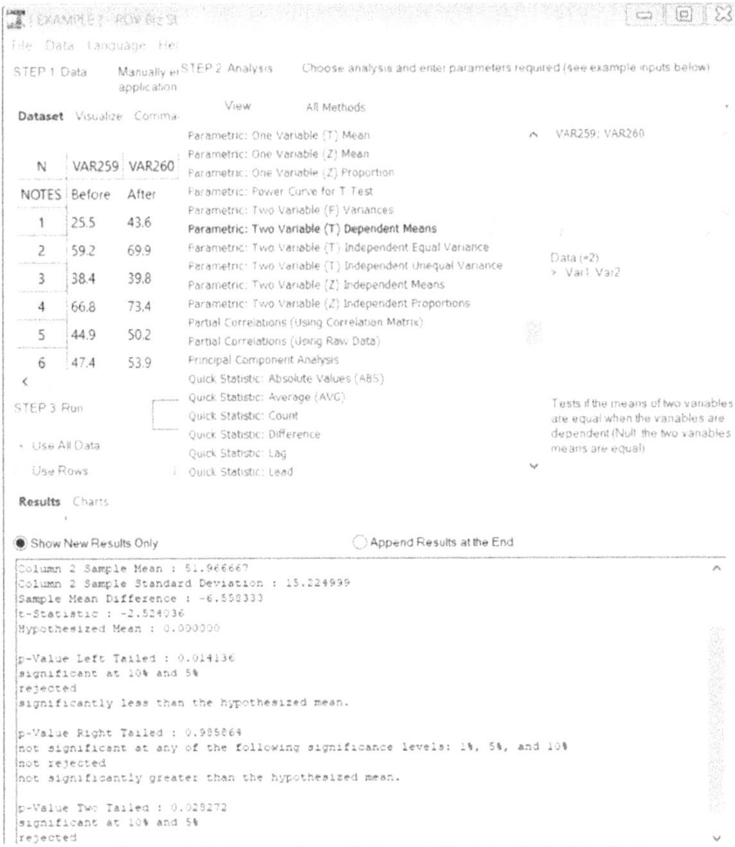

Figure 5.8: Dependent Paired T-Test in ROV BizStats

On occasion, we may need to compare the variances of two independent sample sets. For instance, when comparing the mean time between failure (MTBF) of two different equipment setups and measuring the amount of variation that exists, we can determine if the variation of MTBF of the old or new equipment is greater. The F-test is used in this instance, where we test the following hypotheses:

H_0: $\sigma_1^2 = \sigma_2^2$, there is no difference in variation between the samples

H_a: $\sigma_1^2 \neq \sigma_2^2$, there is a difference in variation between the samples

The test employs the following specifications:

$$F = \max\left(s_1^2/s_2^2, s_2^2/s_1^2\right) \text{ and critical value is } F(\alpha/2, n_L - 1, n_S - 1)$$

where $n - 1$ values are the degrees of freedom, n_L is the sample with the larger variance, and n_S is the sample with the smaller variance.

Example: Suppose two equipment sets were each implemented in seven different locations and their respective MTBF in months were collected. As shown in Figure 5.9, the sample standard deviations were calculated as 0.7091 and 0.5350 for these two equipment sets (see Figure 5.9). The F statistic is computed as 1.7571 with a corresponding p-value of 0.2552 (one-tail) and 0.5104 (two-tail), which means we do not reject the null hypothesis and conclude that there is no statistically significant difference in variation of the MTBF. Figure 5.10 shows how to implement the computation in ROV BizStats.

	A	B	C	D	E	F	G
1							
2		X1	X2				
3		2.5	5.2				
4		2.6	5.6				
5		3.4	5.4				
6		2.9	5.9				
7		4.3	5.9				
8		4.1	6.2				
9		3.6	6.8				
10							
11	Mean	3.3429	5.8571	=AVERAGE(B3:B9) and =AVERAGE(C3:C9)			
12	Stdev	0.7091	0.5350	=STDEV(B3:B9) and =STDEV(C3:C9)			
13	Count	7	7	=COUNT(B3:B9) and =COUNT(C3:C9)			
14	F Statistic	1.7571	One Tail	=MAX(B12^2/C12^2,C12^2/B12^2)			
15	P-value	0.2552	One Tail	=FDIST(B14,B13-1,C13-1)			

Figure 5.9: F-Test for Variances

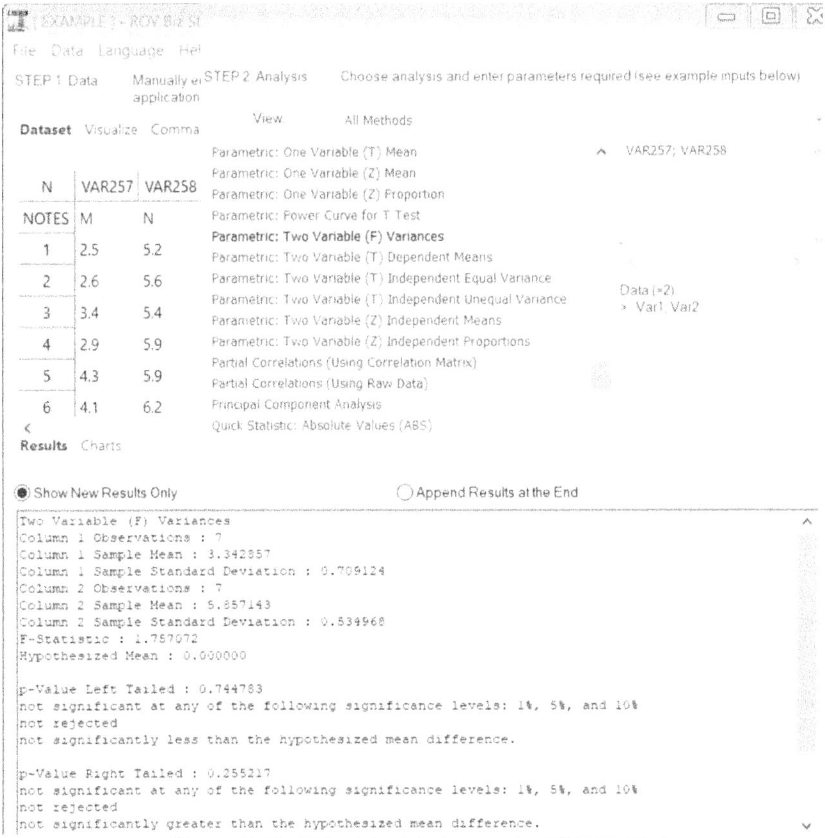

EXAMPLE) - ROV Biz St

File Data Language Hel

STEP 1 Data   Manually e STEP 2 Analysis   Choose analysis and enter parameters required (see example inputs below)
application

Dataset Visualize Comma

View   All Methods

N	VAR257	VAR258
NOTES	M	N
1	2.5	5.2
2	2.6	5.6
3	3.4	5.4
4	2.9	5.9
5	4.3	5.9
6	4.1	6.2

Parametric: One Variable (T) Mean
Parametric: One Variable (Z) Mean
Parametric: One Variable (Z) Proportion
Parametric: Power Curve for T Test
Parametric: Two Variable (F) Variances
Parametric: Two Variable (T) Dependent Means
Parametric: Two Variable (T) Independent Equal Variance
Parametric: Two Variable (T) Independent Unequal Variance
Parametric: Two Variable (Z) Independent Means
Parametric: Two Variable (Z) Independent Proportions
Partial Correlations (Using Correlation Matrix)
Partial Correlations (Using Raw Data)
Principal Component Analysis
Quick Statistic: Absolute Values (ABS)

VAR257; VAR258

Data (×2)
> Var1 Var2

Results Charts

⦿ Show New Results Only   ◯ Append Results at the End

```
Two Variable (F) Variances
Column 1 Observations : 7
Column 1 Sample Mean : 3.342857
Column 1 Sample Standard Deviation : 0.709124
Column 2 Observations : 7
Column 2 Sample Mean : 5.857143
Column 2 Sample Standard Deviation : 0.534968
F-Statistic : 1.757072
Hypothesized Mean : 0.000000

p-Value Left Tailed : 0.744783
not significant at any of the following significance levels: 1%, 5%, and 10%
not rejected
not significantly less than the hypothesized mean difference.

p-Value Right Tailed : 0.255217
not significant at any of the following significance levels: 1%, 5%, and 10%
not rejected
not significantly greater than the hypothesized mean difference.
```

Figure 5.10: F-Test for Variances in ROV BizStats

In certain situations, proportions (p) are used instead of raw values. In such situations, when there are two sets of data, the two proportions can be tested using the following hypotheses:

H_0: $\mu(p_1 - p_2) = 0$, there is no difference between the two datasets

H_a: $\mu(p_1 - p_2) \neq 0$, there is a difference between the two datasets

The z-test for two independent proportions is used, with the following specifications:

$$z = \frac{(p_1 - p_2)}{\sqrt{\overline{p}(1 - \overline{p})\left(\frac{1}{n_1} + \frac{1}{n_2}\right)}} \quad \text{where } \overline{p} = \frac{n_1 p_1 + n_2 p_2}{n_1 + n_2}$$

and where n_1 and n_2 are the sample sizes, p_1 and p_2 are the sample proportions, and $\overline{p}$ is the pooled estimate of the population proportion as described above.

This approach assumes that $n_1 p_1$, $n_1(1 - p_1)$, $n_2 p_2$, and $n_2(1 - p_2)$ should all be ≥ 5 and each $n \geq 30$ so that the underlying binomial distribution (a proportion is equivalent to a binomial probability distribution with two outcomes) approaches the normal distribution; hence the ability to use the z-test.

For the independent means test, the two samples' means are tested using:

H_0: $\mu(\overline{x}_1 - \overline{x}_2) = 0$, there is no difference between the two datasets

H_a: $\mu(\overline{x}_1 - \overline{x}_2) \neq 0$, there is a difference between the two datasets

$$z = \frac{(\overline{x}_1 - \overline{x}_2) - (\mu_1 - \mu_2)}{\sqrt{\frac{s_1^2}{n_1} + \frac{s_2^2}{n_2}}}$$

Example: Suppose a medical experiment includes a total of 3,806 male heart patients that are divided into two equal groups of 1,903 each (Figure 5.11). In this case, $n_1 = n_2 = 1,903$, which satisfies the normal distribution requirements. A new heart drug was administered to the first group, and the number of mild coronary events was recorded for both groups. In the first group, 155 coronaries were recorded, while there were 187 events in the second group. We therefore compute the proportions where $p_1 = 155/1903 = 0.0815$ and p_2

$= 187/1903 = 0.0983$. In this example, we use a one-tail hypothesis where H_0 is $\mu(p_1 - p_2) \geq 0$ and H_a is $\mu(p_1 - p_2) < 0$ indicating that the new drug group 1 has a lower proportion of coronary events and, hence, the drug has a statistically significant effect. Figure 5.11 shows the manual computations in Excel, and the one-tail p-value is 0.0350. This means we reject the null hypothesis at the $\alpha = 0.05$ level, and we conclude that the drug does have a significant effect.

	A	B	C	D	E	F	G	H
1								
2		Proportion 1	0.081450					
3		Proportion 2	0.098266					
4		Count 1	1903					
5		Count 2	1903					
6								
7		Pooled P	0.089858		=(C4*C2+C5*C3)/(C4+C5)			
8		Z-Score	-1.8138		=(C2-C3)/SQRT(C7*(1-C7)*(1/C4+1/C5))			
9		P-Value	0.0349	1 Tail	=NORMSDIST(C8)			
10		P-Value	0.0697	2 Tail	=NORMSDIST(C8)*2			
11		Z Critical @ 0.10	-1.2816	Left 1 Tail	=NORMSINV(0.1)			
12		Z Critical @ 0.05	-1.6449	Left 1 Tail	=NORMSINV(0.05)			
13		Z Critical @ 0.01	-2.3263	Left 1 Tail	=NORMSINV(0.01)			

Figure 5.11: Z-Test for Proportions

Figure 5.12 illustrates the use of ROV BizStats using actual raw data where 1 represents a reduction and 0 represents no reduction. The proportions are automatically computed. The one-tail p-value shows 0.0349 and the same interpretation is applied as for the manual computations.

Z-TEST OF PROPORTIONS AND MEANS

Similarly, the z-test for means can be applied using the following:

$$z = \frac{(\bar{x}_1 - \bar{x}_2) - (\mu_1 - \mu_2)}{\sqrt{\left(\frac{s_1^2}{n_1} + \frac{s_2^2}{n_2}\right)}}$$

The hypotheses tested are typically:

H_0: $\mu_1 = \mu_2$, the samples' means are statistically similar

H_a: $\mu_1 \neq \mu_2$, the samples' means are statistically significantly different

This test is the alternative to the unequal variances t-test whenever both n_1 and $n_2 \geq 30$. The test can also be performed using ROV BizStats.

Figure 5.12: ROV BizStats' Z-Test for Proportions

The previously described t-tests, z-tests, and F-tests are applied to two variables at a time to determine if their means, proportions, or variances are statistically significantly different or if the small differences are attributable to random chance. When two or more sample means need to be tested at the same time, we resort to Analysis of Variance (ANOVA) tests.

The single ANOVA with multiple treatments tests one categorical independent variable (with multiple treatment levels, types, or categories) and one numerical dependent variable (randomly allocated into the multiple treatment categories) to determine if their population means are equal. Each data column will have a different treatment (e.g., a new method of manufacturing, a new training regimen, a new technology employed). This test assumes that the treatments are completely and randomly assigned to all the persons in the experiment and the underlying data is normally distributed with equal variance. Note that the nonparametric equivalent is the Kruskal–Wallis test, which is presented later in the chapter.

Example: Nine staff members in an organization were randomly divided into three teams each consisting of three individuals, and each team was provided a different type of training. There are three distinct training courses or treatments in this case. Upon completing the training course, each individual was assigned a task to complete, and the time it took to complete the task was recorded and shown in the data grid. Because the selection is random, we use the randomized single ANOVA with multiple treatments to test the following hypotheses:

H_0: $\mu_1 = \mu_2 = \ldots = \mu_t$ for treatments 1 to t

(there is no effect in the treatments)

H_a: Population means are not equal

(there is an effect in at least one of the treatments)

Figure 5.13 shows the results from Excel's Analysis Tool Pak, and Figure 5.14 shows the implementation and results from ROV BizStats.

	Method 1	Method 2	Method 3
Person 1	15	10	18
Person 2	20	15	19
Person 3	19	11	23

EXCEL ANALYSIS TOOL PAK
Anova: Single Factor

SUMMARY

Groups	Count	Sum	Average	Variance
Column 1	3	54	18	7
Column 2	3	36	12	7
Column 3	3	60	20	7

ANOVA

Source of Variation	SS	df	MS	F	P-value	F crit
Between Groups	104	2	52	7.4286	0.0238	5.1433
Within Groups	42	6	7			
Total	146	8				

Figure 5.13: Single ANOVA with Multiple Randomized Treatments

The specification tested is $x_{i,j} = \mu + \tau_j + \varepsilon_{ij}$ and the calculations proceed as follows:

The global average is $\tilde{x} = \dfrac{\displaystyle\sum_{j=1}^{t}\sum_{i=1}^{t} x_{ij}}{N}$

Sum of Squares of Treatment (SS Treatments) is $\displaystyle\sum_{j=1}^{t} n_j(\bar{x}_j - \tilde{x})^2$

Sum of Squares of Error (SS Error) is $\displaystyle\sum_{j=1}^{t}\sum_{i=1}^{n_j}(x_{ij} - \bar{x}_j)^2$

Sum of Squares of the Total (SS Total) is $\displaystyle\sum_{j=1}^{t}\sum_{i=1}^{n_j}(x_{ij} - \tilde{x})^2$

Mean Squares of Between Treatment (MS Treatment) is

(SS Treatment)/(Number of Treatments – 1)

Mean Squares of Errors or Mean Squares Within Treatments (MS Error) is computed as

(SS Error)/(Total Observations − Number of Treatments)

F Statistic is computed as MS Treatment / MS Error

The p-value of the F statistic has a degree of freedom set to (Number of Treatments − 1) in the numerator and (Total Observations − Number of Treatments) in the denominator.

Figure 5.15 shows the implementation of these calculations in Excel.

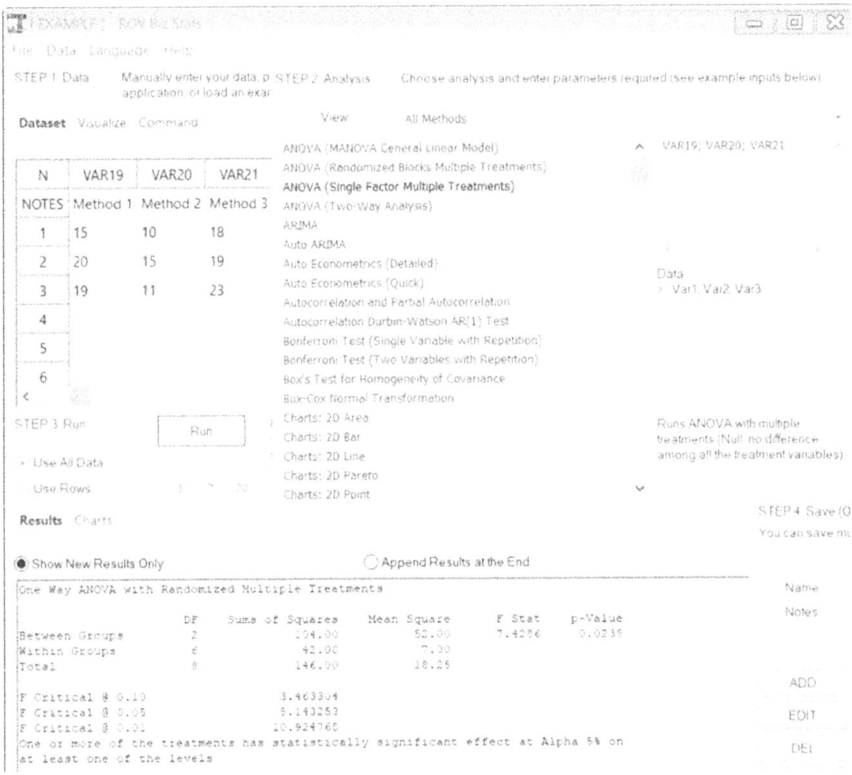

Figure 5.14: Single ANOVA with Multiple Randomized Treatments in ROV BizStats

	A	B	C	D	E	F	G	H	I	J
1		Method 1	Method 2	Method 3						
2	Person 1	15	10	18						
3	Person 2	20	15	19						
4	Person 3	19	11	23						
5										
6	Variable Average	18.0000	12.0000	20.0000						
7										
8	Global Average	16.6667	=AVERAGE(B2:D4)							
9	Sums of Squares	104.0000	=COUNT(B2:B4)*(B6-B8)^2+COUNT(C2:C4)*(C6-B8)^2+COUNT(D2:D4)*(D6-B8)^2							
10	Sums of Squares	42.0000	=(B2-B6)^2+(B3-B6)^2+(B4-B6)^2+(C2-C6)^2+(C3-C6)^2+(C4-C6)^2+(D2-D6)^2+(D3-D6)^2+(D4-D6)^2							
11	Sums of Squares	146.0000	=B9+B10							
12	Total Data Points	9	=COUNT(B2:D4)							
13	Number of Variables	3	=COUNTA(B1:D1)							
14	DF	2	=B13-1							
15	DF	6	=B12-B13							
16	DF	8	=B14+B15							
17	Mean Square	52.0000	=B9/B14							
18	Mean Square	7.0000	=B10/B15							
19	Mean Square	18.2500	=B11/B16							
20	Calculated F-Statistic	7.4286	=B17/B18							
21	P-Value	0.0238	=FDIST(B20,B14,B15)							
22										

Figure 5.15: Manual Computations of the Single ANOVA

Figure 5.16 revisits the single ANOVA results. The p-value was computed as under the 0.05 threshold, so we conclude that at least one of these treatments has a statistically significant effect. The issue with ANOVA is that we cannot determine which of the treatments is effective, just that at least one of them would be effective. To determine which specific treatment is effective, run pairwise t-tests of all possible combinations (AB, AC, BC) or use multivariate regression analysis.

One Way ANOVA with Randomized Multiple Treatments

	DF	SS	MS	F	P-Value
Between Groups	2	98.4000	49.2000	6.3778	0.0265
Within Groups	7	54.0000	7.7143		
Total	9	152.4000			
F Critical (Blocking) @ 0.10		3.2574			
F Critical (Blocking) @ 0.05		4.7374			
F Critical (Blocking) @ 0.01		9.5466			

One or more of the treatments has statistically significant effect at Alpha 5% on at least one of the levels

Figure 5.16: Single ANOVA Results

In the previous single ANOVA test, the assumption was that the treatments were completely and randomly assigned to all the persons in the experiment. This approach may result in overrepresentation and underrepresentation in some treatment groups simply by chance. If the properties or characteristics of the individuals participating in the experiment have a strong influence on the measurements and data obtained, the single ANOVA may end up measuring the differentials inside this experimental group instead of the effects of the treatments. To resolve this issue, ANOVA with Randomized Block can be used. Note that the nonparametric equivalent is Friedman's test.

The specification tested in this ANOVA is $x_{i,j} = \mu + \tau_j + \beta_i + \varepsilon_{ij}$

H_0: $\tau_j = 0$ for treatments j = 1 to t

(there is no effect in the treatments)

H_a: $\tau_j \neq 0$ for at least one treatment j = 1 to t

(one or more treatments has an effect)

where τ is the treatments and β is the blocking variable.

Example: Suppose that there are four auto headlamps under development. The manufacturer wishes to test the visibility of each lamp design by measuring how far someone can see using each of these headlamps. Now suppose 12 individuals were randomly selected to participate in this experiment, and suppose we categorize these participants as young (Y), middle-aged (M), and old (O). If we completely randomize the selection of these individuals, each of the methods may be over- or underrepresented in terms of age group, as seen in the first data grid in Figure 5.17. Now, further suppose that the participants' properties (e.g., age) have an influence on their vision (e.g., older participants cannot see as far as someone much younger). Consequently, completely randomizing the participants into these groups will yield biased results. The better approach is to *block* this intervening age variable. Figure 5.17's second data grid shows how to set up an ANOVA dataset with blocks. In this example, there are three blocks, and they are stratified into rows.

ANOVA One-Way Randomized Design

	Method 1	Method 2	Method 3	Method 4
Person 1	Y	M	O	Y
Person 2	Y	O	Y	M
Person 3	O	O	M	Y

ANOVA with Blocking Variable

	Method 1	Method 2	Method 3	Method 4
Block 1	Y	Y	Y	Y
Block 2	M	M	M	M
Block 3	O	O	O	O

Figure 5.17: Setting Up an ANOVA with Randomized Blocks

Calculations for the randomized block ANOVA are shown below:

The global average is $\tilde{x} = \dfrac{\sum\limits_{j=1}^{t}\sum\limits_{i=1}^{t} x_{ij}}{N}$

Sum of Squares of Treatment (SS Treatments) is $n\sum\limits_{j=1}^{t}(\bar{x}_j - \tilde{x})^2$

Sum of Squares of Error (SS Error) is

$$SS\ Total - SS\ Treatment - SS\ Block$$

Sum of Squares of Blocks (SS Block) is $t\sum\limits_{j=1}^{t}(\bar{x}_i - \tilde{x})^2$

Sum of Squares of the Total (SS Total) is $\sum\limits_{j=1}^{t}\sum\limits_{i=1}^{n_j}(x_{ij} - \tilde{x})^2$

Mean Squares of Between Treatment (MS Treatment) is

(SS Treatment)/(Number of Treatments – 1)

Mean Squares of Blocks (MS Block) is computed as

(SS Block)/(Total Observations – 1)

Mean Squares of Errors or Mean Squares Within Treatments (MS Error) is computed as

(SS Error)/((Total Observations – 1)(Number of Treatments – 1))

F Statistic is computed as

MS Treatment / MS Error

The p-value of the F statistic has a degree of freedom set to (Number of Treatments – 1) in the numerator and (Total Observations – 1)(Number of Treatments – 1) in the denominator.

Figure 5.18 illustrates a step-by-step approach to calculating this ANOVA model.

	A	B	C	D	E	F	G
1		Method 1	Method 2	Method 3	Method 4	Average	
2	Block 1	90	87	93	85	88.7500	
3	Block 2	86	79	87	83	83.7500	
4	Block 3	76	74	77	73	75.0000	
5	Average	84.0000	80.0000	85.6667	80.3333		
6							
7	Global Average	82.5000	=AVERAGE(B2:E4)				
8	Number of Rows (Blocks)	3	=COUNT(B2:B4)				
9	Number of Columns (Treatments)	4	=COUNT(B2:E2)				
10	SS Total	473.0000	=(B2-B7)^2+(B3-B7)^2+(B4-B7)^2+(C2-B7)^2+(C3-B7)^2+(C4-B7)^2+(D2-B7)^2+(D3-B7)^2+(D4-B7)^2+(E2-B7)^2+(E3-B7)^2+(E4-B7)^2				
11	SS Blocking (Rows)	387.5000	=B9*((F2-B7)^2+(F3-B7)^2+F4-B7)^2)				
12	SS Treatment (Columns)	69.6667	=B8*((B5-B7)^2+(C5-B7)^2+(D5-B7)^2+(E5-B7)^2)				
13	SS Errors	15.8333	=B10-B12-B11				
14	MS Block	193.7500	=B11/B17				
15	MS Treatment	23.2222	=B12/B18				
16	MS Error	2.6389	=B13/B19				
17	DF Block	2	=B8-1				
18	DF Treatment	3	=B9-1				
19	DF Error	6	=B17*B18				
20	F Statistic (Treatment)	8.8000	=B15/B16				
21	P-Value (Treatment)	0.0129	=FDIST(B20,B18,B19)				
22	F Statistic (Blocking)	73.4211	=B14/B16				
23	P-Value (Blocking)	0.0001	=FDIST(B22,B17,B19)				
24	F Critical (Treatment) @ 0.10	3.2888	=FINV(0.1,B18,B19)				
25	F Critical (Treatment) @ 0.05	4.7571	=FINV(0.05,B18,B19)				
26	F Critical (Treatment) @ 0.01	9.7795	=FINV(0.01,B18,B19)				
27	F Critical (Blocking) @ 0.10	3.4633	=FINV(0.1,B17,B19)				
28	F Critical (Blocking) @ 0.05	5.1433	=FINV(0.05,B17,B19)				
29	F Critical (Blocking) @ 0.01	10.9248	=FINV(0.01,B17,B19)				
30	The blocking variable has statistically significant effect at Alpha 5% on at least one of the levels						
31	The treatment variable has statistically significant effect at Alpha 1% on at least one of the levels						

Figure 5.18: Computing an ANOVA with Randomized Blocks

Figure 5.19 shows the results of the ANOVA with randomized blocks using ROV BizStats. The figure shows how the calculations can be implemented and the corresponding settings. The p-value for the treatment is 0.0129 and the p-value for the blocking variable (age, in this case) is 0.0001. This indicates that there is a statistically significant difference in at least one of the treatments and that the blocking variable (age) does have a statistically significant effect on the dataset.

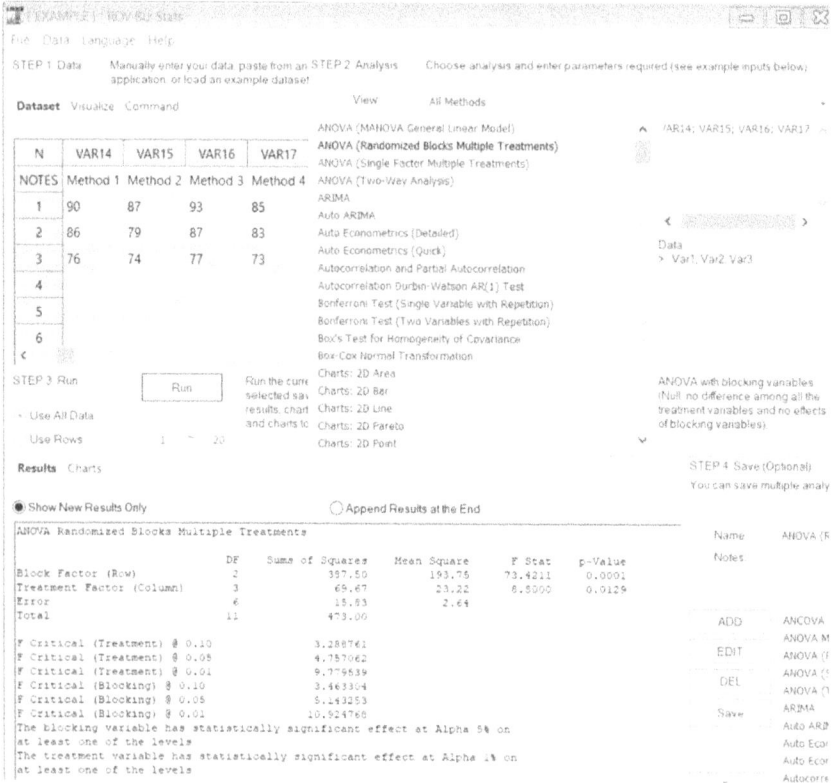

Figure 5.19: ANOVA with Randomized Blocks Results in ROV BizStats

The one-way ANOVA models presented above look at a single factor on the dependent variable. In this section, we introduce the two-way ANOVA, a method that simultaneously examines the effects of *two* factors (two categorical independent variables) on the *one* numerical dependent variable, as well as the interactions of different levels of the two factors. That is, random assignments are made such that two or more participants are subjected to each possible combination of the factor levels. The number of persons or participants within each of these combinations is termed the *number of replications (r)* and *r* has to be ≥ 2.

The specification in this ANOVA is $x_{i,j} = \mu + \alpha_i + \beta_j + (\alpha\beta)_{ij} + \varepsilon_{ijk}$

Testing the main effect, factor A:

H_0: $\alpha_i = 0$ for each level of factor A, for $i = 1$ to a (no level of factor A has an effect)

H_a: $\alpha_i \neq 0$ for at least one value of i, where $i = 1$ to a (at least one level has an effect)

Testing the main effect, factor B:

H_0: $\beta_j = 0$ for each level of factor B, for $j = 1$ to b (no level of factor B has an effect)

H_a: $\beta_j \neq 0$ for at least one value of j, where $j = 1$ to b (at least one level has an effect)

Testing the interaction effects, between levels of factors A and B:

H_0: $\alpha\beta_{ij} = 0$ for each combination of i and j (there are no interaction effects)

H_a: $\alpha\beta_{ij} \neq 0$ for at least one combination of i and j (at least one combination has an effect)

Example: Suppose an aircraft manufacturer is testing three different alloys (B1, B2, and B3) for its wing construction of a new plane, and each alloy type can be produced in four different thickness levels (A1 to A4). The number of twists and flexes is recorded until stress failure is detected. The data is then subjected to a two-way ANOVA as shown in Figure 5.20, which illustrates how the data is set up. The detailed calculations and results are shown in Figure 5.21, and Figure 5.22 shows how to set up the model in ROV BizStats.

	Factor B1	Factor B2	Factor B3
Factor A1	804	836	804
Factor A1	816	828	808
Factor A2	819	844	807
Factor A2	813	836	819
Factor A3	820	814	819
Factor A3	821	811	829
Factor A4	806	811	827
Factor A4	805	806	835

Figure 5.20: Two-Way ANOVA Settings and Results

The method's specifications are:

Sum of Squares for Factor A: $SSA = rb \sum_{i=1}^{a} (\bar{x}_i - \tilde{x})^2$

Sum of Squares for Factor B: $SSB = ra \sum_{j=1}^{b} (\bar{x}_j - \tilde{x})^2$

Sum of Squares Total: $SST = \sum_{i=1}^{a} \sum_{j=1}^{b} \sum_{k=1}^{r} (\bar{x}_{ijk} - \tilde{x})^2$

Sum of Squares of Error: $SSE = \sum_{i=1}^{a} \sum_{j=1}^{b} \sum_{k=1}^{r} (x_{ijk} - \bar{x}_{ij})^2$

The computed degrees of freedom (df) for factor A is $(a - 1)$, factor B is $(b - 1)$, Interaction AB is $(a - 1)(b - 1)$, Error is $ab(r - 1)$, and Total is $(abr - 1)$.

Mean Squares (MS) for factor A is $SSA/df(A)$, factor B is $SSB/df(B)$, factor AB is $SSAB/df(AB)$, Error is $SSE/df(E)$.

The calculated F Statistic for factor A is MS(A)/MS(E), factor B is MS(B)/MS(E), and AB interaction is MS(AB)/MS(E).

Figure 5.21 illustrates these calculations in more detail. In this figure, you can see that the row factor A is significant at the 0.10 level, while the column factor B and interaction AB are statistically significant at the 0.01 level. We can conclude that at least one level of A and B and at least one combination of A and B have a significant effect.

	Factor B1	Factor B2	Factor B3	Average
Factor A1	804	836	804	816.0000
Factor A1	816	828	808	
Factor A2	819	844	807	823.0000
Factor A2	813	836	819	
Factor A3	820	814	819	819.0000
Factor A3	821	811	829	
Factor A4	806	811	827	815.0000
Factor A4	805	806	835	
Average	813.0000	823.2500	818.5000	

Two Way ANOVA

Careful with column E. We average the number of rows based on user input of number of Replication/Rows there are

Replication/Rows (User Input)	2	This is a user input
Number of Rows	8	=COUNT(B2:B9)
Factors/Rows	4	=B14/B13
Factors/Columns	3	=COUNT(B2:D2)
Global Average	818.2500	=AVERAGE(B2:D9)
SS Total	3142.5000	see equation on the right
SS Factors Rows	232.5000	=B13*B16*((E3-B17)^2+(E5-B17)^2+(E7-B17)^2+(E9-B17)^2)
SS Factors Columns	421.0000	=B13*B15*((B11-B17)^2+(C11-B17)^2+(D11-B17)^2)
SS Interaction	2155.0000	=B18-B19-B20 watch out on this one... example has 2 Replication so we average two rows only, if replication 5 then average of all 5 rows and do the difference and square for all five items...
SS Errors	334.0000	see equation on the right
MS Factor Rows	77.5000	=B19/(B15-1)
MS Factor Columns	210.5000	=B20/(B16-1)
MS Interaction	359.1667	=B21/((B15-1)*(B16-1))
MS Errors	27.8333	=B22/(B15*B16*(B13-1))
F Statistic for Row Factors	2.7844	=B23/B26
F Statistic for Column Factors	7.5629	=B24/B26
F Statistic for Interaction	12.9042	=B25/B26
DF Row Factors	3	=B15-1
DF Column Factors	2	=B16-1
DF Interaction	6	=(B15-1)*(B16-1)
DF Both Factors	12	=B15*B16*(B13-1)
P-Value for Row Factors	0.0864	=FDIST(B27,B30,B33)
P-Value for Column Factors	0.0075	=FDIST(B28,B31,B33)
P-Value for Interaction	0.0001	=FDIST(B29,B32,B33)

B18=(B2-$B$17)^2+(B3-$B$17)^2+(B4-$B$17)^2+(B5-$B$17)^2+(B6-$B$17)^2+(B7-$B$17)^2+(B8-$B$17)^2+(B9-$B$17)^2+(C2-$B$17)^2+(C3-$B$17)^2+(C4-$B$17)^2+(C5-$B$17)^2+(C6-$B$17)^2+(C7-$B$17)^2+(C8-$B$17)^2+(C9-$B$17)^2+(D2-$B$17)^2+(D3-$B$17)^2+(D4-$B$17)^2+(D5-$B$17)^2+(D6-$B$17)^2+(D7-$B$17)^2+(D8-$B$17)^2+(D9-$B$17)^2

B22=(B2-AVERAGE(B2:B3))^2+(B3-AVERAGE(B2:B3))^2+(B4-AVERAGE(B4:B5))^2+(B5-AVERAGE(B4:B5))^2+(B6-AVERAGE(B6:B7))^2+(B7-AVERAGE(B6:B7))^2+(B8-AVERAGE(B8:B9))^2+(B9-AVERAGE(B8:B9))^2+(C2-AVERAGE(C2:C3))^2+(C3-AVERAGE(C2:C3))^2+(C4-AVERAGE(C4:C5))^2+(C5-AVERAGE(C4:C5))^2+(C6-AVERAGE(C6:C7))^2+(C7-AVERAGE(C6:C7))^2+(C8-AVERAGE(C8:C9))^2+(C9-AVERAGE(C8:C9))^2+(D2-AVERAGE(D2:D3))^2+(D3-AVERAGE(D2:D3))^2+(D4-AVERAGE(D4:D5))^2+(D5-AVERAGE(D4:D5))^2+(D6-AVERAGE(D6:D7))^2+(D7-AVERAGE(D6:D7))^2+(D8-AVERAGE(D8:D9))^2+(D9-AVERAGE(D8:D9))^2

Two Way ANOVA Results

	Df	SS	MS	F	p
Row Factor	3	232.5000	77.5000	2.7844	0.0864
Column Factor	2	421.0000	210.5000	7.5629	0.0075
Interaction	6	2155.0000	359.1667	12.9042	0.0001
Error	12	334.0000	27.8333		

Figure 5.21: Two-Way ANOVA Calculations

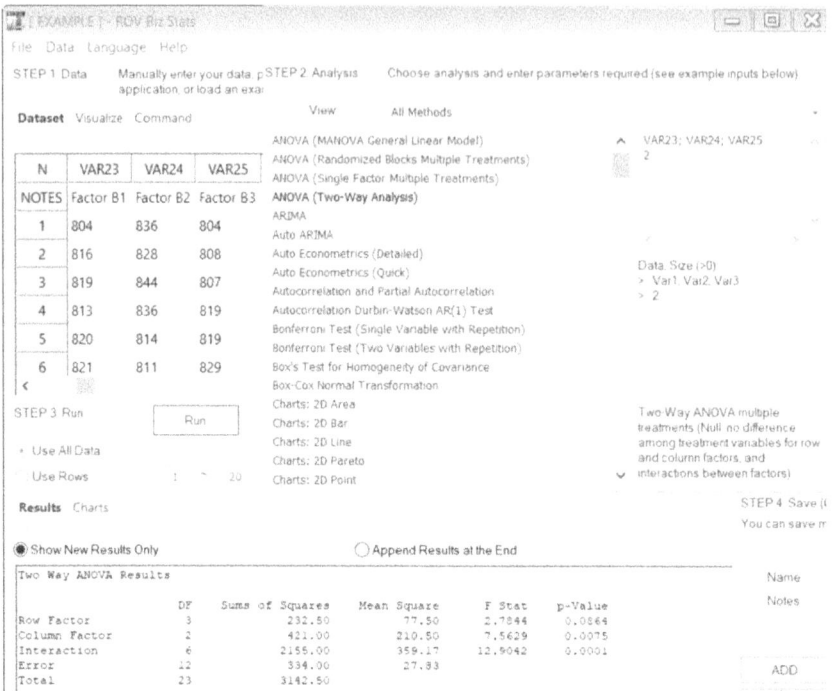

Figure 5.22: Two-Way ANOVA in ROV BizStats

ANCOVA, MANOVA, AND TWO-WAY MANOVA

The Multiple Analysis of Variance, or MANOVA, extends the ANOVA Single Factor Multiple Treatments model. The Two-Way MANOVA is an extension of the Two-Way ANOVA model. See Figure 5.23 for a comparison of these General Linear Models and Figure 5.24 for examples and the required data setup in BizStats.

As a reminder of the different ANOVA methods, the *ANOVA Single Factor Multiple Treatments* model variation is used to test for statistical differences of *one* continuous numerical dependent variable against *one* categorical independent variable (with multiple subcategories or treatment types). These treatments are collectively considered a single factor that is being tested. As an example, we collect and model math test scores of 90 students (the math test scores are continuous values and are collectively considered the single dependent variable) that have been randomly assigned into three different treatment groups (e.g., Russian Math, Singapore Math, U.S.

Math) to see if the three different teaching techniques generate statistically significant differences in math aptitude. In this example, the dependent variable is the math test scores (numerical values between 0% and 100%), and the independent variable is the different math teaching techniques (categorical nominal values of the three math teaching techniques).

The *ANOVA Single Factor Repeated Measures* is used when the researcher wishes to test the validity of the test instrument used. For example, a group of 30 students is subjected to three math tests at different times. Depending on the research question, these math tests are usually similar (e.g., identical difficulty levels, similar concepts with slightly different questions, identical questions asked slightly differently, similar questions but ordered differently, etc.). There is only *one* dependent variable (math test scores) and *one* independent variable (math tests, categorized into first test, second test, or third test).

The *ANOVA with Blocking Variables* is used to test *one* dependent variable against *one* independent variable, while controlling for, or *blocking*, an exogenous variable that may potentially impact the dependent variable. For example, the three different math teaching techniques (the independent variable) are tested on a group of students, but the type of school (private, public, home school) is controlled for.

A related approach is the *ANCOVA, or Analysis of Covariance*, where a single factor ANOVA model with repeated treatments (Group 1) removes the Group 2 covariate effects. The net effects after covariates have been accounted for will be to test the null hypothesis that the various treatments in Group 1 are identical to each other. The covariate effects are used as a benchmark, or base-case control values, of effects that are not of interest to the researcher. Examples of covariate effects may include different family wealth levels of the students or whether the schools are in urban or rural areas. The ANCOVA model requires that these two groups of variables have the same number of variables. Because some controversies surround the use of ANCOVA methods, it might be better to apply multiple regression instead.

Next, the *Two-Way ANOVA* provides an extension to include *one* dependent variable against *two* independent variables, or factors, and their interactions. For example, the same numerical math test scores (dependent variable) are collected but the students are divided into a 3 × 3 factorial design with two-factor treatments (independent variables). For example, Factor A is the different teaching techniques (Russian Math, Singapore Math, U.S. Math) and Factor B is the length of time the math techniques are taught (e.g., 1 month, 3 months, 6 months), to see if Factor A, Factor B, or the Interaction of Factors A & B, causes any perceivable statistical differences in math aptitude test scores.

The *Multiple Analysis of Variance, or MANOVA,* model extends the Single Factor ANOVA by allowing *multiple* dependent variables at once against *one* independent variable. For example, multiple continuous numerical variables are collected, such as math test scores, student satisfaction survey scores, and teacher ratings, and these dependent variables are compared against the single categorical independent variable (e.g., public, private, charter, and home school). MANOVA can be thought of as multiple simultaneous ANOVA runs. However, the MANOVA has a few key advantages over ANOVA. It protects against Type I Errors compared to running multiple and independently-run ANOVA models. Sometimes, MANOVA can potentially reveal statistical differences not discovered by running multiple independent ANOVA tests. However, MANOVA can be significantly more complicated than ANOVA, causing ambiguity in drawing concrete conclusions on which independent variable may or may not affect each of the dependent variables.

The *Two-Way MANOVA* allows for the testing of *multiple* dependent variables against *two* independent variables or factors. Extending the example above, we similarly collect multiple continuous numerical variables such as math test scores, student satisfaction survey scores, and teacher ratings, and these dependent variables are compared against two categorical independent variables. The first independent variable factor is the type of school (public, private, charter, and home school) and the second independent variable is the economic condition where the school district is located (wealthy, middle, poor). Figure 5.23 summarizes the main ANOVA and MANOVA methods.

Finally, in other multivariate situations, it would be more appropriate to apply multiple regression models using dummy variables in place of the categorical independent variables.

GENERAL LINEAR MODEL	Dependent Variable(s)	Independent Variable(s)	Notes
ANOVA Single Factor Multiple Treatments	One	One	One factor with multiple treatment types.
ANOVA Single Factor with Repeated Measures	One	One	Repeating similar tests for reliability.
ANOVA with Blocking Variables	One	One	Controls and tests for exogenous impacts.
Two-Way ANOVA	One	Two	Two factors with multiple treatment types each and testing for their interactions.
ANCOVA	One	One	Controls for baselines using covariates.
MANOVA	Multiple	One	Simultaneous ANOVA by testing multiple dependent variables at once.
Two-Way MANOVA	Multiple	Two	Two factors with multiple treatment types each and testing for their interactions on multiple dependent variables at once.

Figure 5.23: ANOVA and MANOVA Methods Comparison

ANOVA for Single Factor Multiple Treatments
1 Dependent Variable vs. 1 Independent Variable (One Factor Multiple Treatments)

Participants	Method 1 Treatment	Method 2 Treatment	Method 3 Treatment
Person 1	58	80	96
Person 2	68	82	92
Person 3	70	88	90
...	...	...	...
...	...	...	...
Person 30	72	86	88

* Method 1: Russian Math; Method 2: Singapore Math; Method 3: U.S. Math
* The Single Factor Tested: Different Teaching Techniques
* Dependent Variable = Math Scores (continuous numerical values in the table)
* Independent Variable = Teaching Techniques (column groups)

ANOVA for Single Factor Repeated Measures
1 Dependent Variable vs. 1 Independent Variable (Repeated Tests)

Participants	Test 1	Test 2	Test 3
Person 1	50	52	50
Person 2	88	90	92
Person 3	60	62	58
...	...	...	...
...	...	...	...
Person 30	78	80	80

* The same treatment is used but the participants are tested multiple times
* Dependent Variable = Math Scores (continuous numerical values in the table)
* The same students are subjected to multiple tests

ANOVA with Blocking Variable
1 Dependent Variable vs. 1 Independent Variable with Blocking Variable

Blocks	Method 1 Treatment	Method 2 Treatment	Method 3 Treatment
Private School	66	82	94
Public School	68	84	90
Home School	70	88	90

* Method 1: Russian Math; Method 2: Singapore Math; Method 3: U.S. Math
* The Single Factor Tested: Different Teaching Techniques
* Dependent Variable = Math Scores (continuous numerical values in the table)
* Independent Variable = Teaching Techniques (column groups)
* Blocking Variable = Type of school (variable to control)

TWO-WAY ANOVA
1 Dependent Variable vs. 2 Independent Variable (One Factor Multiple Treatments)

Factor B	Method 1 Factor A1	Method 2 Factor A2	Method 3 Factor A3
Factor B1: 1 Month	68	82	96
Factor B2: 3 Months	72	84	86
Factor B3: 6 Months	66	90	92

* The Two Factors Tested: Different Teaching Techniques vs. Length of Time Taught
* Factor A:: Method 1: Russian Math; Method 2: Singapore Math; Method 3: U.S. Math
* Factor B:: 1 Month, 3 Month, 6 Months
* Dependent Variable = Math Scores (continuous numerical values in the table)
* This example is a 3 x 3 Factorial Model

Figure 5.24: ANOVA and MANOVA Examples and Data Setup
(continues)

MANOVA
Multiple Dependent Variables vs. 1 Independent Variable

Independent Var Schools	Dependent Var 1 Math Scores	Dependent Var 2 Satisfaction	Dependent Var 3 Teacher Ratings
Public	76.7	29.5	7.5
Public	60.5	32.1	6.3
Public	96.1	40.7	4.2
Private	76.9	20.4	3.0
Private	66.9	23.9	1.1
Private	55.4	29.1	5.0
Charter	62.8	25.9	2.9
Charter	45.0	15.9	1.2
Charter	47.8	36.1	4.1
Home School	52.5	39.0	3.1
Home School	80.0	54.2	4.0
Home School	54.7	32.1	5.7

* Multiple Dependent Variables = The numerical values in the table include test scores, student satisfaction survey scores, and teacher ratings
* One Independent Variable = Type of school

TWO WAY MANOVA
Multiple Dependent Variables vs. 2 Independent Variables

Independent Var 1 Schools	Independent Var 2 Economic	Dependent Var 1 Math Scores	Dependent Var 2 Satisfaction	Dependent Var 3 Teacher Ratings
Public	Wealthy	29.50	29.50	7.50
Public	Wealthy	32.10	32.10	6.30
Public	Middle	40.70	40.70	4.20
Public	Middle	29.50	29.50	7.50
Public	Poor	32.10	32.10	6.30
Public	Poor	40.70	40.70	4.20
Private	Wealthy	20.40	20.40	3.00
Private	Wealthy	23.90	23.90	1.10
Private	Middle	29.10	29.10	5.00
Private	Middle	25.90	25.90	2.90
Private	Poor	15.90	15.90	1.20
Private	Poor	36.10	36.10	4.10
Home School	Wealthy	39.00	39.00	3.10
Home School	Wealthy	54.20	54.20	4.00
Home School	Middle	32.10	32.10	5.70
Home School	Middle	39.00	39.00	3.10
Home School	Poor	54.20	54.20	4.00
Home School	Poor	32.10	32.10	5.70

* Multiple Dependent Variables = The numerical values in the table include test scores, student satisfaction survey scores, and teacher ratings
* Two Independent Variable = Type of school vs. Economic status of the school district

Figure 5.24: ANOVA and MANOVA Examples and Data Setup
(continued)

Figures 5.25, 5.26, and 5.27 illustrate the results from MANOVA and Two-Way MANOVA models using BizStats. Similar to the ANOVA and Two-Way ANOVA models, the results indicate the various sums of squares, mean squares, degrees of freedom, F-statistics, and p-values for each of the independent variables or factors, as well as their interactions. These results are obtained by running between-subjects tests, similar to the ANOVA models. However, because MANOVA runs multiple dependent variables at once, to reduce the Type I Error impacts, the degrees of freedom and calculated F-statistics will need to be adjusted. The three adjustments for MANOVA are Pillai's Trace, Wilk's Lambda, and Hotelling's Trace. The computed F-statistics and p-values are interpreted exactly the same way as their ANOVA counterparts.

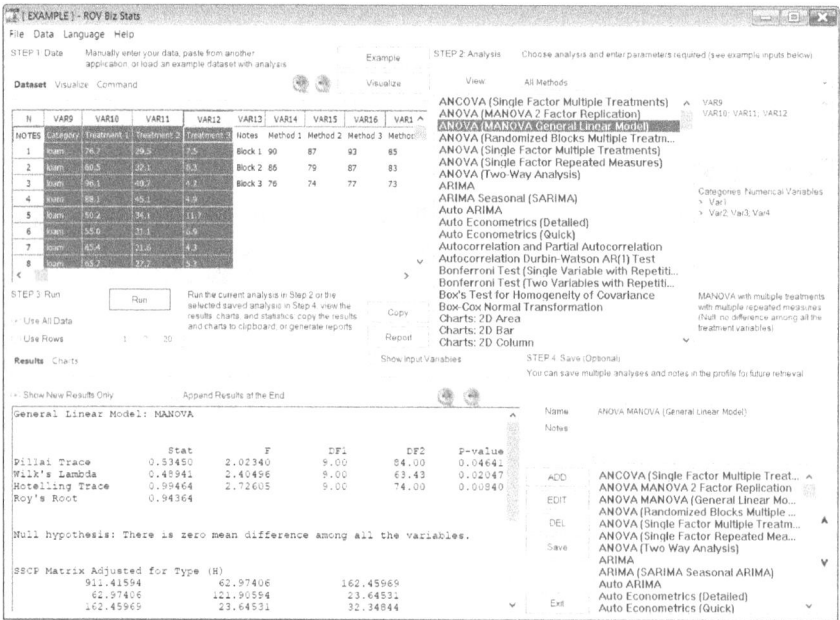

Figure 5.25: MANOVA Results in BizStats

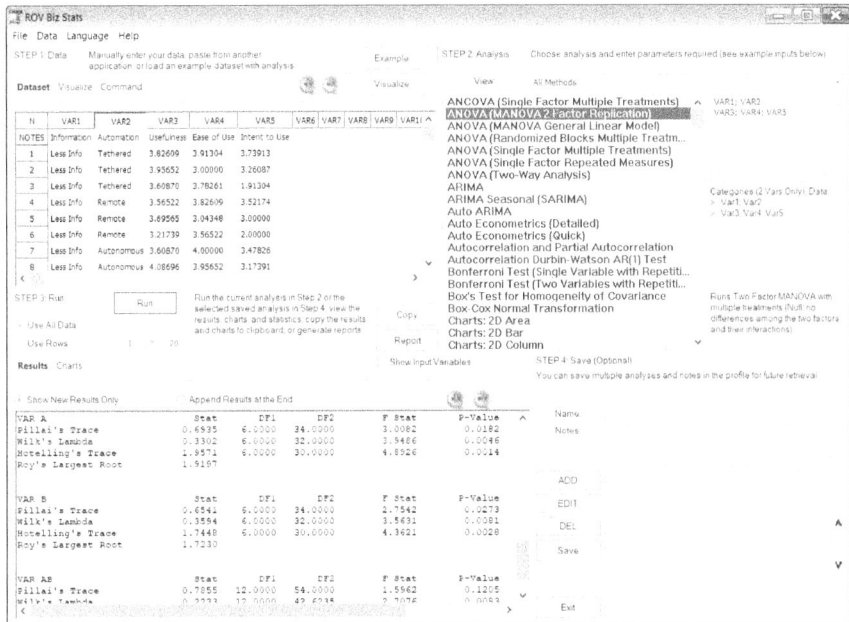

Figure 5.26: Two-Way MANOVA Results in BizStats

Between Subjects Effects Test

	Sum of Squares	DF	Mean Square	F Stat	P-Value
Variable A on Treatment 1	0.8313	2	0.4157	8.0235	0.0032
Variable A on Treatment 2	1.6406	2	0.8203	7.6865	0.0039
Variable A on Treatment 3	0.6323	2	0.3162	0.2977	0.7461
Variable B on Treatment 1	1.4715	2	0.7357	14.2013	0.0002
Variable B on Treatment 2	0.0267	2	0.0144	0.1346	0.8749
Variable B on Treatment 3	0.6737	2	0.3368	0.3172	0.7322
Interactions AB on Treatment 1	2.6117	4	0.6529	12.6030	0.0000
Interactions AB on Treatment 2	0.6232	4	0.1558	1.4599	0.2556
Interactions AB on Treatment 3	1.8303	4	0.4576	0.4308	0.7845
Errors on Treatment 1	0.9325	18	0.0518		
Errors on Treatment 2	1.9209	18	0.1067		
Errors on Treatment 3	19.1167	18	1.0620		

Multivariate Tests

VAR A	Stat	DF1	DF2	F Stat	P-Value
Pillai's Trace	0.6935	6.0000	34.0000	3.0082	0.0182
Wilk's Lambda	0.3302	6.0000	32.0000	3.9486	0.0046
Hotelling's Trace	1.9571	6.0000	30.0000	4.8926	0.0014
Roy's Largest Root	1.9197				

VAR B	Stat	DF1	DF2	F Stat	P-Value
Pillai's Trace	0.6541	6.0000	34.0000	2.7542	0.0273
Wilk's Lambda	0.3594	6.0000	32.0000	3.5631	0.0081
Hotelling's Trace	1.7448	6.0000	30.0000	4.3621	0.0028
Roy's Largest Root	1.7230				

VAR AB	Stat	DF1	DF2	F Stat	P-Value
Pillai's Trace	0.7855	12.0000	54.0000	1.5962	0.1205
Wilk's Lambda	0.2233	12.0000	42.6235	2.7076	0.0083
Hotelling's Trace	3.4382	12.0000	44.0000	4.2022	0.0002
Roy's Largest Root	3.4266				

Figure 5.27: Detailed Two-Way MANOVA Results in BizStats

CHI-SQUARE TESTS

The chi-square distribution is used to model three tests:

1. Goodness-of-Fit Test

    H_0: The sample is from the specified distribution.
    H_a: The sample is not from the specified distribution.

2. Test of Independence

    H_0: The variables are independent of each other.
    H_a: The variables are not independent of each other.

3. Comparing Proportions of Multiple Independent Samples

    H_0: $\pi_1 = \pi_2 = \ldots = \pi_k$ for the $j = 1$ to k populations.
    H_a: At least one of the π_j values differs from the others.

All three models are computed using ROV BizStats (see Figure 5.28).

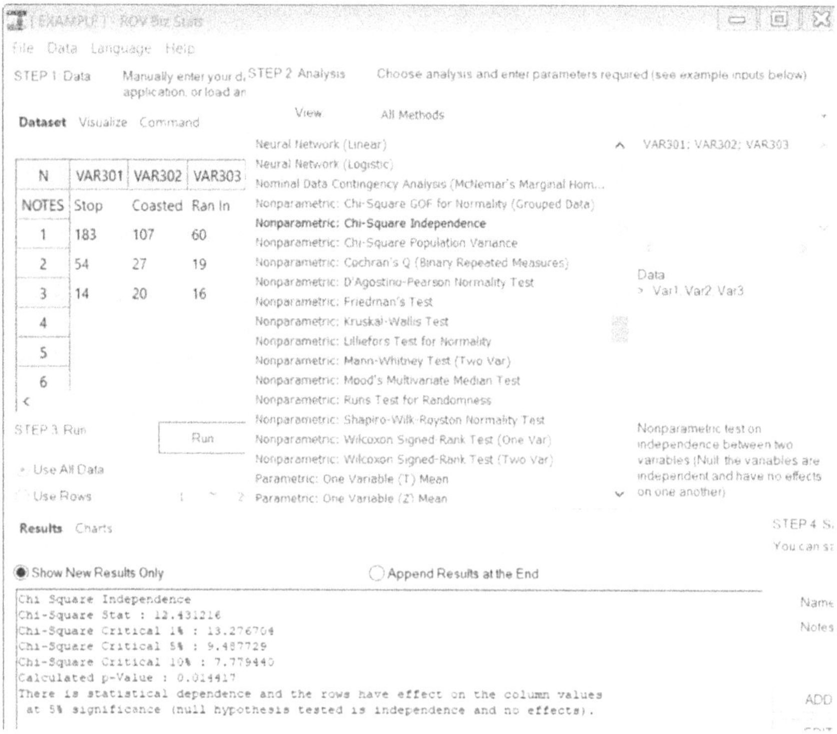

Figure 5.28: Chi-Square Tests in ROV BizStats

The correlation coefficient is a measure of the strength and direction of the relationship between two variables, and it can take on any values between −1.0 and +1.0. That is, the correlation coefficient can be decomposed into its sign (positive or negative relationship between two variables) and the magnitude or strength of the relationship (the higher the absolute value of the correlation coefficient, the stronger the relationship).

The correlation coefficient can be computed in several ways. The first approach is to manually compute the correlation r of two variables x and y using:

$$r_{x,y} = \frac{n \sum x_i y_i - \sum x_i \sum y_i}{\sqrt{n \sum x_i^2 - (\sum x_i)^2} \sqrt{n \sum y_i^2 - (\sum y_i)^2}}$$

The second approach is to use Excel's *CORREL* function. For instance, if the 10 data points for x and y are listed in cells A1:B10, then the Excel function to use is *CORREL (A1:A10, B1:B10)*.

The third approach is to run Risk Simulator's *Analytical Tools | Distributional Fitting | Multi-Variable,* and the resulting correlation matrix will be computed and displayed.

It is important to note that correlation does not imply causation. Two completely unrelated random variables might display some correlation, but this does not imply any causation between the two (e.g., sunspot activity and events in the stock market are correlated, but there is no causation between the two).

There are two general types of correlations: parametric and nonparametric correlations. Pearson's product-moment correlation coefficient is the most common correlation measure and is usually referred to simply as the correlation coefficient. However, Pearson's correlation is a parametric measure, which means that it requires both correlated variables to have an underlying normal distribution and that the relationship between the variables is linear. When these conditions are violated, which is often the case in Monte Carlo simulation, the nonparametric counterparts become more important. Spearman's rank correlation and Kendall's tau are the two nonparametric alternatives. The Spearman correlation is most commonly used and is most appropriate when applied in the context of Monte Carlo simulation—there is no dependence on normal distributions or linearity, meaning that correlations between different variables with different distributions can be applied. In order to compute the Spearman correlation, first rank all the x and y variable values and then apply the Pearson's correlation computation.

Figure 5.29 provides some visual examples of pairwise correlations between X and Y. Positive correlations (A and D) can be visualized as positive slopes, whereas negative correlations are negatively sloped (B). A flat line denotes zero correlation. The closer the values are to a linear line, the higher the absolute value of the correlation ($|C| > |B| > |A|$). The charts A–D indicate linear correlations whereas E and G show that nonlinear correlations are better fits than linear correlations F and H.

Correlation

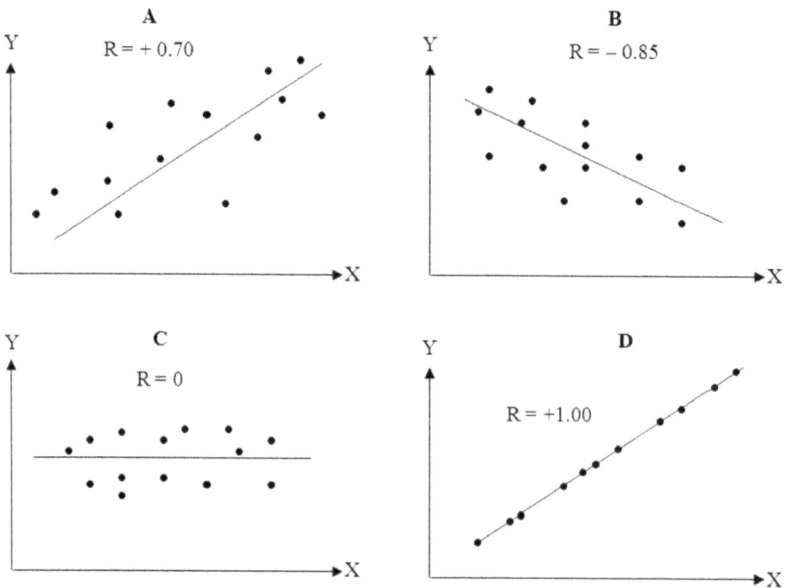

Figure 5.29: Linear and Nonlinear Correlations (*continues*)

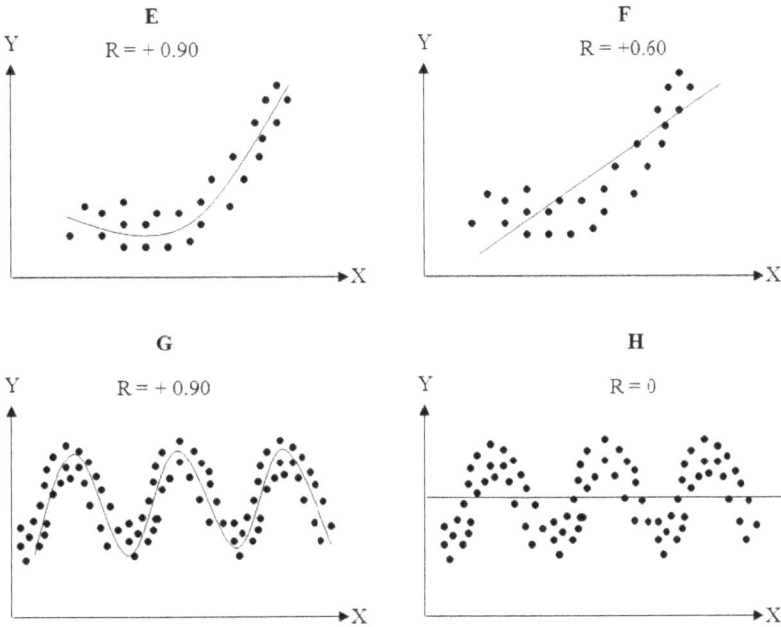

Figure 5.29: Linear and Nonlinear Correlations *(continued)*

In the case of Risk Simulator, the correlation used is the more robust nonparametric Spearman's rank correlation. However, to simplify the simulation process, and to be consistent with Excel's correlation function, the correlation inputs required are the Pearson's correlation coefficient. Risk Simulator will then apply its own algorithms to convert them into Spearman's rank correlation, thereby simplifying the process. Additionally, to simplify the user interface, we allow users to enter the more common Pearson's product-moment correlation (e.g., computed using Excel's *CORREL* function), while in the mathematical codes, we convert these simple correlations into Spearman's rank-based correlations for distributional simulations.

The following lists some key correlation effects and details that will be helpful in modeling:

- Correlation coefficients range from −1.00 to +1.00, with 0.00 as a possible value.

- The correlation coefficient has two parts: a sign and a value. The sign shows the directional relationship whereas the value shows the magnitude of the effect (the higher the value, the higher the magnitude, while zero values imply no relationship). Another way to think of a correlation's magnitude is the inverse of noise (the lower the value, the higher the noise).

- Correlation implies dependence and not causality. In other words, if two variables are correlated, it simply means both variables move together in the same or opposite direction (positive versus negative correlations) with some strength of co-movements. It does not, however, imply that one variable causes another. In addition, one cannot determine the exact impact or how much one variable *causes* another to move.

- If two variables are independent of one another, the correlation will be, by definition, zero. However, a zero correlation may not imply independence (because there might be some nonlinear relationships).

- Correlations can be visually approximated on an X-Y plot. If we generate an X-Y plot and the line is flat, the correlation is close to or equal to zero; if the slope is positive (data slopes upward), then the correlation is positive; if the slope is negative (data slopes downward), then the correlation is negative; the closer the scatter plot's data points are to a straight line, the higher the linear correlation value.

- The population correlation coefficient (ρ) can be defined as the standardized covariance:

  ○ $\rho_{x,y} = corr(X, Y) = \frac{cov(X,Y)}{\sigma_X \sigma_Y} = \frac{E[(X-\mu_X)(Y-\mu_Y)]}{\sigma_X \sigma_Y}$ where X and Y are the data from two variables' populations. The covariance measures the average or expectation (E) of the co-movements of all X values from its mean (μ_X) multiplied by the co-movements of all Y values from its population mean (μ_Y). The value of covariance is between negative and positive infinity, making its interpretation fairly difficult. However, by standardizing the covariance through dividing it by the population standard deviation (σ) of X and Y, we obtain the correlation coefficient, which is bounded between -1.00 and $+1.00$.

- However, in practice, we typically only have access to sample data, and the sample correlation coefficient (r) can be determined using the sample data from two variables x and y, their averages ($\bar{x}, \bar{y}$), their standard deviations (s_x, s_y), and the count (n) of x and y data pairs:

$$r_{x,y} = \frac{\sum_{i=1}^{n} x_i y_i - n\bar{x}\bar{y}}{(n-1)s_x s_y} = \frac{\sum_{i=1}^{n}(x_i - \bar{x})(y_i - \bar{y})}{(n-1)s_x s_y}$$

$$r_{x,y} = \frac{\sum_{i=1}^{n}(x_i - \bar{x})(y_i - \bar{y})}{\sqrt{\sum_{i=1}^{n}(x_i - \bar{x})^2 \sum_{i=1}^{n}(y_i - \bar{y})^2}}$$

$$r_{x,y} = \frac{n\sum_{i=1}^{n} x_i y_i - \sum_{i=1}^{n} x_i \sum_{i=1}^{n} y_i}{\sqrt{n\sum_{i=1}^{n} x_i^2 - \left(\sum_{i=1}^{n} x_i\right)^2} \sqrt{n\sum_{i=1}^{n} y_i^2 - \left(\sum_{i=1}^{n} y_i\right)^2}}$$

- Correlations are symmetrical. In other words, the $r_{A,B} = r_{B,A}$. Therefore, we sometimes call correlation coefficients *pairwise* correlations.

- If there are n variables, the number of total pairwise correlation is $C_x^n = \frac{n!}{x!(n-x)!}$. For example, if there are $n = 3$ variables, A, B, C, the number of pairwise ($x = 2$, or two items are chosen at a time) combinations total $C_2^3 = \frac{3!}{2!(3-2)!} = \frac{3!}{2!1!} = 3$ correlation pairs: $r_{A,B}$, $r_{A,C}$, and $r_{B,C}$.

- Correlations can be linear or nonlinear. Pearson's product moment correlation coefficient is used to model linear correlations, and Spearman's rank-based correlation is used to model nonlinear correlations.

- Linear correlations (also known as the Pearson's R) can be computed using Excel's *CORREL* function or using the equations described previously.

- Nonlinear correlations are computed by first ranking the nonlinear raw data, and then applying the linear Pearson's correlation. The result is a nonlinear rank correlation or Spearman's R. Use the correlation version (linear or nonlinear) that has a higher absolute value.

- Pearson's linear correlation is also a parametric correlation, with the implicit underlying assumption that the data is linear and close to being normally distributed. Spearman's rank correlation is nonparametric and has no dependence on the underlying data being normal.

- The square of the correlation coefficient (R) is called the coefficient of determination or R-squared. This is the same R-squared used in regression modeling, and it indicates the percentage variation in the dependent variable that is explained given the variation in the independent variable(s).

- R-squared is limited to being between 0.00 and 1.00 and is usually shown as a percentage. Specifically, because R has a domain between −1.00 and +1.00, squaring either a positive or negative R-value will always yield a positive R-squared value, and squaring any R-value between 0.00 and 1.00 will always yield an R-squared result between 0.00 and 1.00. This means that R-squared is localized to between 0% and 100% by construction.

- In a simple positively related model, negative correlations reduce total portfolio risk, whereas positive correlations increase total portfolio risk. Conversely, in a simple negatively related model, negative correlations increase total portfolio risk, whereas positive correlations decrease total portfolio risk.

    o Positive Model (+) with Positive Correlation (+) = Higher Risk (+).

    o Positive Model (+) with Negative Correlation (−) = Lower Risk (−).

    o Negative Model (−) with Positive Correlation (+) = Lower Risk (−).

    o Negative Model (−) with Negative Correlation (−) = Higher Risk (+).

- Portfolio Diversification typically implies the following condition: Positive Model (+) with a Negative Correlation (−) means a Lower Risk (−). For example, the portfolio level's (p) diversified risk is computed by taking $\sigma_P = \sqrt{\sum_{i=1}^{n} \omega_i^2 \sigma_i^2 + \sum_{i=1}^{n} \sum_{j=1}^{m} 2\omega_i \omega_j \rho_{i,j} \sigma_i \sigma_j}$ where $\omega_{i,j}$ are the respective weights or capital allocation across each project; $\rho_{i,j}$ are the respective cross-correlations between the assets, and $\sigma_{i,j}$ are the volatility risks. Hence, if the cross-correlations are negative, there are risk diversification effects, and the portfolio risk decreases.

- Examples of a simple positively related model are an investment portfolio (the total of the returns in a portfolio is the sum of each individual asset's returns, i.e., A + B + C = D, therefore, increase A or B or C, and the resulting D will increase as well, indicating a positive directional relationship) or the total of the revenues of a company, which is the sum of all the individual products' revenues. Negative correlations in such models mean that if one asset's returns decrease (losses), another asset's returns would increase (profits). The spread or distribution of the total net returns for the entire portfolio would decrease (lower risk). The negative correlation would, therefore, *diversify* the portfolio risk.

- Alternatively, an example of a simple negatively related model is revenue minus cost equals net income (i.e., A − B = C, which means that as B increases, C would decrease, indicating a negative relationship). Negatively correlated variables in such a model would increase the total spread of the net income distribution.

- In more complex or larger models where the relationship is difficult to determine (e.g., in a discounted cash flow model where we have revenues of one product being added to revenues of other products but minus costs to obtain the gross profits, and where depreciation is used as tax shields, then taxes are deducted, etc.), and both positive and negative correlations may exist between the various revenues (e.g., similar product lines versus competing product lines cannibalizing each other's revenues), the only way to determine the final effect is through simulations.

- Correlations typically affect only the second moment (risk) of the distribution, leaving the first moment (mean or expected returns) relatively stable. There is an unknown effect on the third and fourth moments (skew and kurtosis), and only after a simulation is run can the outcomes be empirically determined because the effects are wholly dependent on the distributions' type, skew, kurtosis, and shape. Therefore, in traditional single-point estimates where only the first moment is determined, correlations will not affect the results. When simulation models are used, the entire probability distribution of the results is obtained and, hence, correlations are critical.

- Correlations should be used in a simulation if there are historical data to compute its value. Even in situations without historical data but with clear theoretical justifications for correlations, one should still input them. Otherwise, the distributional spreads would not be accurate. For instance, a demand curve is theoretically negatively sloped (negatively correlated), where the higher the price, the lower the quantity demanded (due to income and substitution effects) and vice versa. Therefore, if no correlations are entered in the model, the simulation results may randomly generate high prices with high quantity demanded, creating extremely high revenues, as well as low prices and low quantity demanded, creating extremely low revenues. The simulated probability distribution of revenues would, hence, have wider spreads into the left and right tails. These wider spreads are not representative of the true nature of the distribution. Nonetheless, the mean or expected value of the distribution remains relatively stable. It is only the percentiles and confidence intervals that get biased in the model.

- Therefore, even without historical data, if we know that correlations do exist through experimentation, widely accepted theory, or even simply by logic and guesstimates, one should still input approximate correlations into the simulation model. This approach is acceptable because the first moment or expected values of the final results will remain unaffected (only the risks will be affected as discussed). Typically, the following approximate correlations can be applied even without historical data:

  o Use 0.00 if there are no correlations between variables.

  o Use ±0.25 for weak correlations (use the appropriate sign).

  o Use ±0.50 for medium correlations (use the appropriate sign).

  o Use ±0.75 for strong correlations (use the appropriate sign).

- It is theoretically very difficult, if not impossible, to have large sets of empirical data from real-life variables that are perfectly uncorrelated (i.e., a correlation of 0.0000000... and so forth). Therefore, given any random data, adding additional variables will typically increase the total absolute values of correlation coefficients in a portfolio (R-squared always increases, which is why the concept of Adjusted R-squared is introduced, which accounts for the marginal increase in total correlation compared against the number of variables; for now, think of Adjusted R-squared as the adjustment to R-squared by taking into account garbage correlations). Therefore, it is usually important to perform statistical tests on correlation coefficients to see if they are statistically significant or if their values can be considered random and insignificant. For example, we know that a correlation of 0.9 is probably significant, but what about 0.8, or 0.7, or 0.3, and so forth? That is, at what point can we statistically state that a correlation is insignificantly different from zero; would 0.10 qualify, or 0.05, or 0.03, and so forth?

- The t-test with $n - 2$ degrees of freedom hypothesis test can be computed by taking $t = r\sqrt{\frac{n-2}{1-r^2}}$. The null hypothesis is such that the population correlation $\rho = 0$.

- There are other measures of dependence such as Kendall's τ, Brownian correlation, Randomized Dependence Coefficient (RDC), entropy correlation, polychoric correlation, canonical correlation, and copula-based dependence measures. These are less applicable to most empirical data and are not as popular or applicable in most situations.

- Finally, here are some notes in applying and analyzing correlations in Risk Simulator:

    o Risk Simulator uses the Normal, T, and Quasi-Normal Copula methods to simulate correlated variable assumptions. The default is the Normal Copula, and it can be changed within the *Risk Simulator | Options* menu item. The T Copula is similar to the Normal Copula but allows for extreme values in the tails (higher kurtosis events), and the Quasi-Normal Copula simulates correlated values between the Normal and T Copulas.

    o After setting up at least two or more assumptions, you can set correlations between pairwise variables by selecting an existing assumption and using the *Risk Simulator | Set Input Assumption* dialog.

    o Alternatively, the *Risk Simulator | Analytical Tools | Edit Correlations* menu item can be used to enter multiple correlations using a correlation matrix.

    o If historical data from multiple variables exist, by performing a distributional fitting using *Risk Simulator | Analytical Tools | Distributional Fitting (Multi-Variable),* the report will automatically generate the best-fitting distributions with their pairwise correlations computed and entered as simulation assumptions. In addition, this tool allows you to identify and isolate correlations that are deemed statistically insignificant using a two-sample t-test.

NORMALITY TESTS AND DISTRIBUTIONAL FITTING

Several statistical tests exist for deciding if a sample set of data comes from a specific distribution. The most commonly used are the Kolmogorov–Smirnov test and the chi-square test. Each test has its advantages and disadvantages. The following sections detail the specifics of these tests as applied in distributional fitting in Monte Carlo simulation analysis. Other less powerful tests such as the Jacque–Bera and Wilkes–Shapiro are not used in Risk Simulator as these are parametric tests and their accuracy depends on the dataset being normal or near-normal. Therefore, the results of these tests are oftentimes suspect or yield inconsistent results.

Kolmogorov–Smirnov Test

The Kolmogorov–Smirnov (KS) test is a nonparametric test based on the empirical distribution function of a sample dataset. This nonparametric characteristic is the key to understanding the KS test, which simply means that the distribution of the KS test statistic does not depend on the underlying cumulative distribution function being tested. Nonparametric simply means no predefined distributional parameters are required. In other words, the KS test is applicable across a multitude of underlying distributions. Another advantage is that it is an exact test as compared to the chi-square test, which depends on adequate sample sizes for the approximations to be valid. Despite these advantages, the KS test has several important limitations. It only applies to continuous distributions, and it tends to be more sensitive near the center of the distribution than at the distribution's tails. Also, the distribution must be fully specified.

Given N ordered data points Y_1, Y_2, ... Y_N, the empirical distribution function is defined as $E_n = n_i / N$ where n_i is the number of points less than Y_i where Y_i are ordered from the smallest to the largest value. This is a step function that increases by $1/N$ at the value of each ordered data point.

The null hypothesis is such that the dataset follows a specified distribution, while the alternate hypothesis is that the dataset does not follow the specified distribution. The hypothesis is tested using the KS statistic defined as $KS = \max_{1 \le i \le N} \left| F(Y_i) - \frac{i}{N} \right|$, where F is the theoretical cumulative distribution of the continuous distribution being tested that must be fully specified (i.e., the location, scale, and shape parameters cannot be estimated from the data).

The hypothesis regarding the distributional form is rejected if the test statistic, KS, is greater than the critical value obtained from the table below. *Notice that 0.03 to 0.05 are the most common levels of critical values (at the 1%, 5%, and 10% significance levels). Thus, any calculated KS statistic less than these critical values implies that the null hypothesis is not rejected and that the distribution is a good fit.* There are several variations of these tables that use somewhat different scaling for the KS test statistic and critical regions. These alternative formulations should be equivalent, but it is necessary to ensure that the test statistic is calculated in a way that is consistent with how the critical values were tabulated. However, the rule of thumb is that a KS test statistic less than 0.03 or 0.05 indicates a good fit.

TWO-TAILED ALPHA LEVEL	KS CRITICAL
10%	0.03858
5%	0.04301
1%	0.05155

Chi-Square Test

The chi-square (CS) goodness-of-fit test is applied to binned data (i.e., data put into classes), and an attractive feature of the CS test is that it can be applied to any univariate distribution for which you can calculate the cumulative distribution function. However, the values of the CS test statistic are dependent on how the data is binned, and the test requires a sufficient sample size in order for the CS approximation to be valid. This test is sensitive to the choice of bins. The test can be applied to discrete distributions such as the binomial and the Poisson, while the KS test is restricted to continuous distributions.

The null hypothesis is such that the dataset follows a specified distribution, while the alternate hypothesis is that the dataset does not follow the specified distribution. The hypothesis is tested using the CS statistic defined as $\chi^2 = \sum_{i=1}^{k}(O_i - E_i)^2/E_i$, where O_i is the observed frequency for bin i and E_i is the expected frequency for bin i. The expected frequency is calculated by $E_i = N(F(Y_U) - F(Y_L))$, where F is the cumulative distribution function for the distribution being tested, Y_U is the upper limit for class i, Y_L is the lower limit for class i, and N is the sample size.

The test statistic follows a CS distribution with $(k - c)$ degrees of freedom where k is the number of non-empty cells and c is the number of estimated parameters (including location and scale parameters and shape parameters) for the distribution + 1. For example, for a three-parameter Weibull distribution, $c = 4$. Therefore, the hypothesis that the data are from a population with the specified distribution is rejected if $\chi^2 > \chi^2(\alpha, k - c)$ where $\chi^2(\alpha, k - c)$ is the CS percent point function with $k - c$ degrees of freedom and a significance level of α.

Again, as the null hypothesis is such that the data follow some specified distribution, when applied to distributional fitting in Risk Simulator, a low p-value (e.g., less than 0.10, 0.05, or 0.01) indicates a bad fit (the null hypothesis is rejected) while a high p-value indicates a statistically good fit.

Chi-Squared Goodness-of-Fit Test Sample Critical Values
Degrees of Freedom 23

ALPHA LEVEL	CUTOFF
10%	32.00690
5%	35.17246
1%	1.63840

Akaike Information Criterion, Anderson–Darling, Kuiper's Statistic, and Schwarz/Bayes Criterion

Following are methods of distributional fitting tests:

- Akaike Information Criterion (AIC). Rewards goodness-of-fit but also includes a penalty that is an increasing function of the number of estimated parameters (although it penalizes the number of parameters less strongly than other methods).

- Anderson–Darling (AD). When applied to testing if a normal distribution adequately describes a set of data, it is one of the most powerful statistical tools for detecting departures from normality and is powerful for testing normal tails. However, in non-normal distributions, this test lacks power compared to others.

- Kuiper's Statistic (K). Related to the KS test, making it as sensitive in the tails as at the median and also making it invariant under cyclic transformations of the independent variable, is invaluable when testing for cyclic variations over time. In comparison, the AD test provides equal sensitivity at the tails as at the median, but it does not provide for cyclic invariance.

- Schwarz/Bayes Information Criterion (SC/BIC). The SC/BIC test introduces a penalty term for the number of parameters in the model, with a larger penalty than AIC.

The null hypothesis being tested is such that the fitted distribution is the same distribution as the population from which the sample data to be fitted comes. Thus, if the computed p-value is lower than a critical alpha level (typically 0.10 or 0.05), then the distribution is the wrong distribution (reject the null hypothesis). Conversely, the higher the p-value, the better the distribution fits the data (do not reject the null hypothesis, which means the fitted distribution is the correct distribution, or null hypothesis of H_0: *Error = 0*, where the error is defined as the difference between the empirical data and the theoretical distribution). Roughly, you can think of p-value as a percentage explained; that is, for example, if the computed p-value of a fitted normal distribution is 0.9727, then setting a normal distribution with the fitted mean and standard deviation explains about 97.27% of the variation in the data, indicating an especially good fit. Both the results and the report show the test statistic, p-value, theoretical statistics (based on the selected distribution), empirical statistics (based on the raw data), the original data (to maintain a record of the data used), and the assumptions complete with the relevant distributional parameters (i.e., if you selected the option in Risk Simulator to automatically generate assumptions and if a simulation profile already exists). The results also rank all the selected distributions and how well they fit the data.

Figures 5.30 and 5.31 show Risk Simulator's Distributional Fitting method. The null hypothesis (H_0) being tested is such that the fitted distribution is the same distribution as the population from which the sample data to be fitted comes. Thus, if the computed p-value is lower than a critical alpha level (typically 0.10 or 0.05), then the distribution is the wrong distribution. Conversely, the *higher the p-value, the better the distribution fits the data*. Roughly, you can think of p-value as a *percentage explained,* that is, if the p-value is 0.9996 (Figure 5.31), then setting a normal distribution with a mean of 100.67 and a standard deviation of 10.40 explains about 99.96% of the variation in the data, indicating an especially good fit. The data was from a 1,000-trial simulation in Risk Simulator based on a normal distribution with a mean of 100 and a standard deviation of 10. Because only 1,000 trials were simulated, the resulting distribution is fairly close to the specified distributional parameters and, in this case, has about a 99.96% precision.

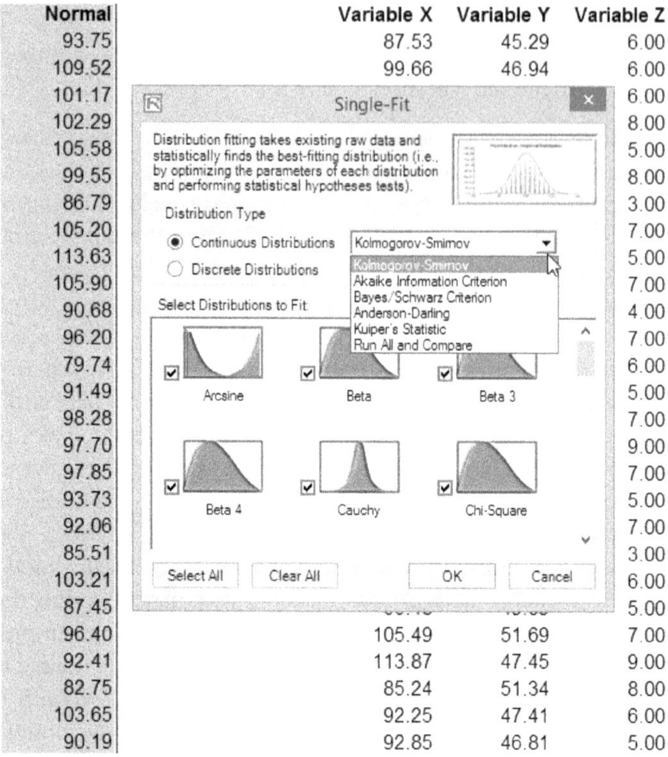

Normal	Variable X	Variable Y	Variable Z
93.75	87.53	45.29	6.00
109.52	99.66	46.94	6.00
101.17			6.00
102.29			8.00
105.58			5.00
99.55			8.00
86.79			3.00
105.20			7.00
113.63			5.00
105.90			7.00
90.68			4.00
96.20			7.00
79.74			6.00
91.49			5.00
98.28			7.00
97.70			9.00
97.85			7.00
93.73			5.00
92.06			7.00
85.51			3.00
103.21			6.00
87.45			5.00
96.40	105.49	51.69	7.00
92.41	113.87	47.45	9.00
82.75	85.24	51.34	8.00
103.65	92.25	47.41	6.00
90.19	92.85	46.81	5.00

Single-Fit

Distribution fitting takes existing raw data and statistically finds the best-fitting distribution (i.e., by optimizing the parameters of each distribution and performing statistical hypotheses tests).

Distribution Type

(●) Continuous Distributions   Kolmogorov-Smirnov ▼

(○) Discrete Distributions

Kolmogorov-Smirnov
Akaike Information Criterion
Bayes/Schwarz Criterion
Anderson-Darling
Kuiper's Statistic
Run All and Compare

Select Distributions to Fit:

☑ Arcsine   ☑ Beta   ☑ Beta 3

☑ Beta 4   ☑ Cauchy   ☑ Chi-Square

Select All   Clear All   OK   Cancel

Figure 5.30: Risk Simulator Distribution Fitting Setup

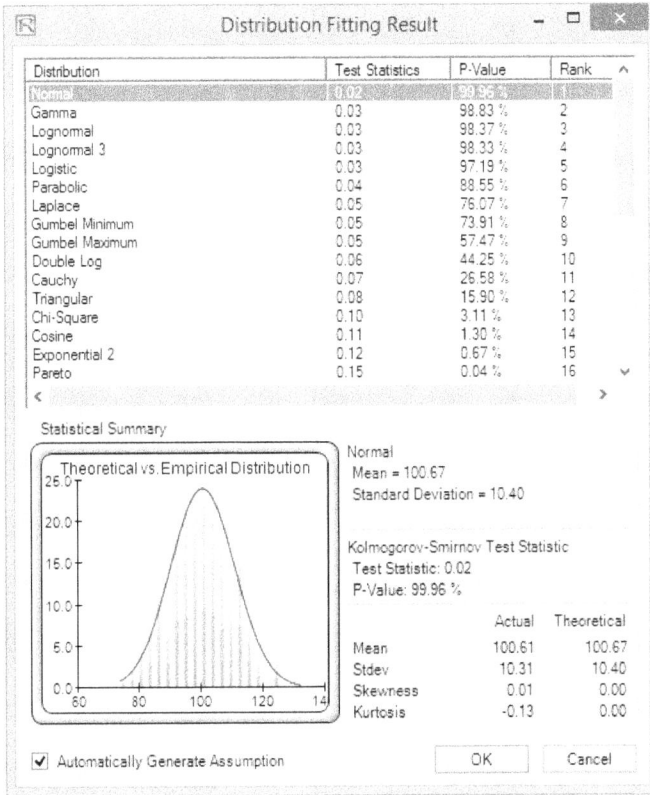

Figure 5.31: Risk Simulator Distribution Fitting Results

NONPARAMETRIC TESTS

There are some methods and tests that are considered nonparametric in nature. Compared to parametric tests (e.g., t-test, z-test, F-test, ANOVA), nonparametric tests have the following advantages and a single disadvantage:

- Fewer assumptions are required for the underlying data's population. Specifically, a nonparametric test does not require that the population be normally distributed. In fact, it does not require any specific distribution and, hence, is sometimes called distribution-free, or tests without specific population parameters (i.e., nonparametric).

- Smaller sample sizes can be used.

- Data with nominal and ordinal scales can be tested.

- Nonparametric methods have lower power and use the data less efficiently. Therefore, if assumptions have been met, it is better to use parametric tests whenever possible.

Some of the most common nonparametric tests are the Runs test for randomness, Wilcoxon test, Lilliefors test, Kruskal–Wallis test, and Friedman's test.

Runs Test for Randomness

The Runs test evaluates the randomness of a series of observations by analyzing the number of runs it contains. A run is a consecutive appearance of one or more observations that are similar. The null hypothesis tested is whether the data sequence is random, versus the alternate hypothesis that the data sequence is not random:

H_0: The sequence is random

H_a: The sequence is not random

For nominal data with two outcomes (e.g., heads and tails in a coin toss, arrival of male and female customers in a bank), the series of events are captured, and the number of runs is computed. For instance, in the series F M M M F F M, there would be a total of 4 runs, or in the series H H T T T T H H, there would be 3 runs. For ordinal, interval, and ratio data, the median is first calculated, and the runs are converted into + and – signs for above and below the median. Then, a z-statistic is computed based on the number of runs (T) observed, and the total number of observations in each of the types (n_1 and n_2):

$$z = \frac{T - \left(\dfrac{2n_1 n_2}{n_1 + n_2} + 1 \right)}{\sqrt{\dfrac{2n_1 n_2 (2n_1 n_2 - n_1 - n_2)}{(n_1 + n_2)^2 (n_1 + n_2 - 1)}}}$$

The standard normal p-value is then calculated, assuming, of course, that the sample sizes $n_1 \geq 10$ and $n_2 \geq 10$.

Figure 5.32 illustrates a series of 30 data points and the application of the Runs test. The computed z-statistic is –2.23 and the two-tailed p-value is 0.0257, which means we reject the null hypothesis. We conclude that the series is not sufficiently random at 5% significance, as the number of runs observed was only 10, whereas the expected number of runs to be considered statistically random is 16.

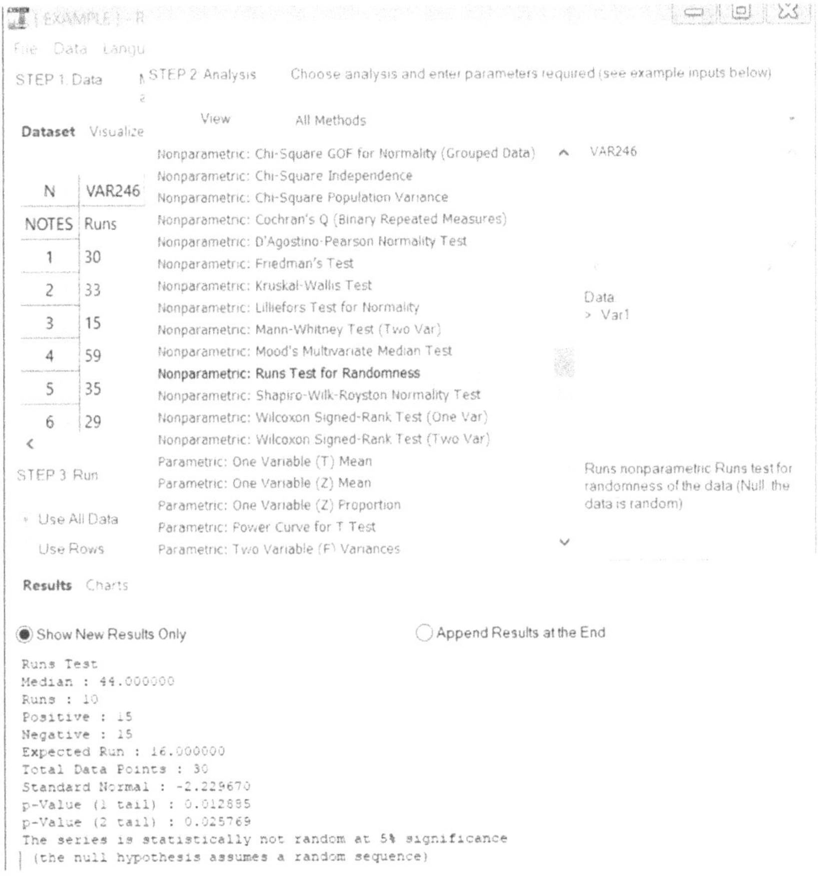

Figure 5.32: Nonparametric Runs Test for Randomness

Note that the Runs test is nonparametric, which means its statistical power is relatively low. For instance, the following shows some examples of random versus not random sequences.

Case A: 1, 1, 1, 1, 1, 2, 2, 2, 2, 2. This is clearly not random as the values are equal and then jump and stay equal. BizStats returns a two-tailed p-value of 0.0072 which allows us to reject the null hypothesis of randomness and conclude this series is not random.

Case B: 1, 3, 1, 3, 1, 3, 1, 3, 1, 3. This is clearly not random because there is a predictable sequence where it goes up and down and the series repeats. BizStats returns a two-tailed p-value of 0.0072 which allows us to reject the null hypothesis of randomness and conclude this series is not random.

Case C: 1, 1, 3, 3, 1, 1, 3, 3, 1, 1, 3, 3, 1, 1, 3, 3, 1, 1, 3, 3. This should be non-random but because of the lower testing power of the non-parametric Runs test, the two-tailed p-value computed is 0.6458, stating that this is a random series. Hence, be particularly careful with the Runs test. Other alternate methods should be employed as well, to check for randomness, including the statistical process Control C-Chart.

Case D: 1.25, 1.01, 3.99, 3.12, 1.01, 1.95, 3.02, 3.45, 1.11, 1.25, 3.33, 3.96, 1.55, 1.41, 3.15, 3.61, 1.18, 1.36, 3.05, 3.56. This is actually a similar sequence as Case C, but with additional decimals. At first glance, one might summarily decide that Case C is not random as it follows a discernible pattern, but Case D is random as there is no pattern. However, upon closer inspection, you will see that all we did was add decimals to the integers, but the same fluctuations around the median occur. In fact, BizStats computes the Run's test p-value to be exactly the same, at 0.6458, which leads us to conclude that this series is random.

Case E: 8.44, 15.01, 71.65, 32.68, 26.43, 7.00, 73.79, 49.05, 16.43, 39.05, 84.86, 92.15, 89.75, 49.10, 79.34, 37.82. This series looks somewhat random, and the computed p-value is 0.3006, so we cannot reject the null hypothesis and conclude that the series is random.

Wilcoxon Signed-Rank Test

As discussed, nonparametric techniques make no assumptions about the specific shape or distribution from which the sample is drawn. This lack of assumptions is different from the other hypotheses tests such as ANOVA or t-tests (parametric tests) where the sample is assumed to be drawn from a population that is normally or approximately normally distributed. If normality is assumed, the power of the test is higher due to this normality restriction. However, if flexibility on distributional requirements is needed, then nonparametric techniques are superior.

The nonparametric Wilcoxon Signed-Rank Test (WSRT) for a Single Variable looks at whether a sample dataset could have been randomly drawn from a particular population whose *median* is being hypothesized. The corresponding parametric test is the one-sample t-test, which should be used if the underlying population is assumed to be normal, providing a higher power on the test. In this single variable test, the following hypotheses are tested:

H_0: Population Median $= m$

H_a: Population Median $\neq m$

Of course, the null hypothesis can take the standard equality signs of $=$, $\geq$, or $\leq$, and m can be any hypothesized value to test. The alternate hypothesis will have the appropriate complementary sign of $\neq$, $<$, or $>$.

The WSRT uses a W-statistic, and its corresponding critical values are usually provided in a statistics table (these will be automatically calculated in a statistics software package such as ROV BizStats). The first step in calculating W is to take the difference $d_i = x_i - m$. All $d = 0$ values are ignored. Then, these $|d_i|$ values are ranked from smallest (rank of 1) to largest. All tied ranks are assigned their average values. For all ranks that have a positive value or where $x_i > m$, we sum all these positive ranks to obtain the W, that is, $W = \Sigma$ (R+). Figure 5.33 shows an example of the WSRT for a single variable. The calculated W statistic is 13, and the two-tailed critical limits at a 0.05 significance are 9 and 46. The W falls within these critical limits, which means we fail to reject the null hypothesis and conclude that the population median is statistically not different than the hypothesized median (in this example it is set as 40 in ROV BizStats, as seen in Figure 5.33).

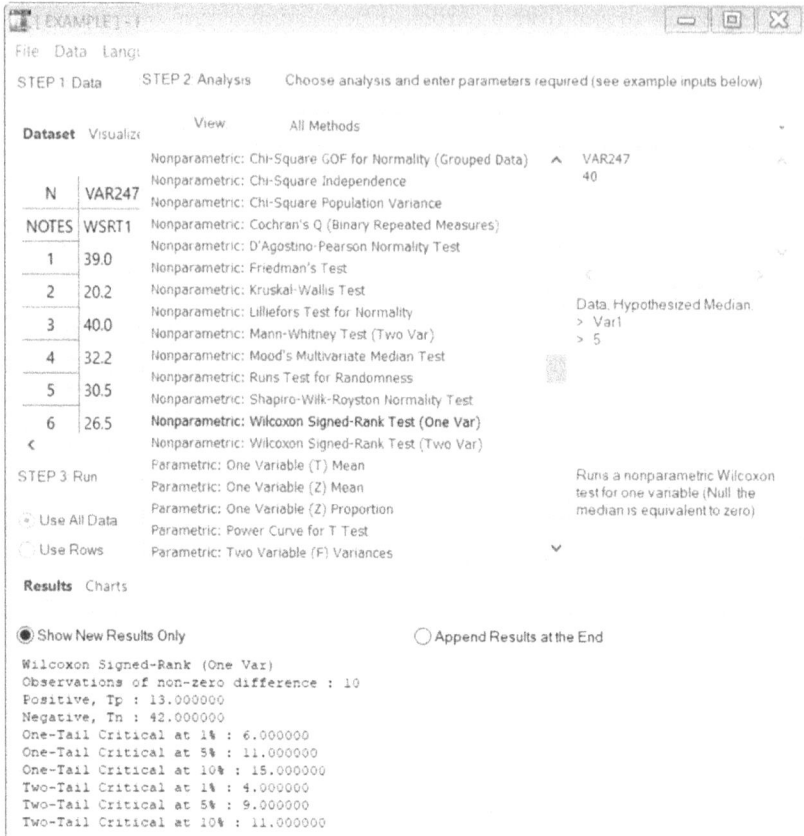

Figure 5.33: Wilcoxon Signed-Rank Test for One Variable

In contrast, the Nonparametric WSRT for Paired Variables looks at whether the *medians* of the differences between the two paired variables are equal. This test is specifically formulated for testing the same or similar samples before and after an event (e.g., measurements taken before a medical treatment are compared against those measurements taken after the treatment to see if there is a difference). The corresponding parametric test is the two-sample t-test with dependent means, which should be used if the underlying population is assumed to be normal, providing a higher power on the test. In this paired variable test, the following hypotheses are tested:

H_0: Population Median of Differences $m_d = 0$

H_a: Population Median of Differences $m_d \neq 0$

The approach is similar to the single-variable WSRT with the exception that the difference d is computed as $d_i = x_i - y_i$ where x and y are the two variables being tested. Figure 5.34 shows the WSRT for two variables. The calculated W is 44.5 (denoted W1) with a hypothesized difference of 0. Using a 0.10 significance level vs. the two-tailed p-value of 0.07, we reject the null hypothesis and conclude that the differences of x and y medians are statistically significant.

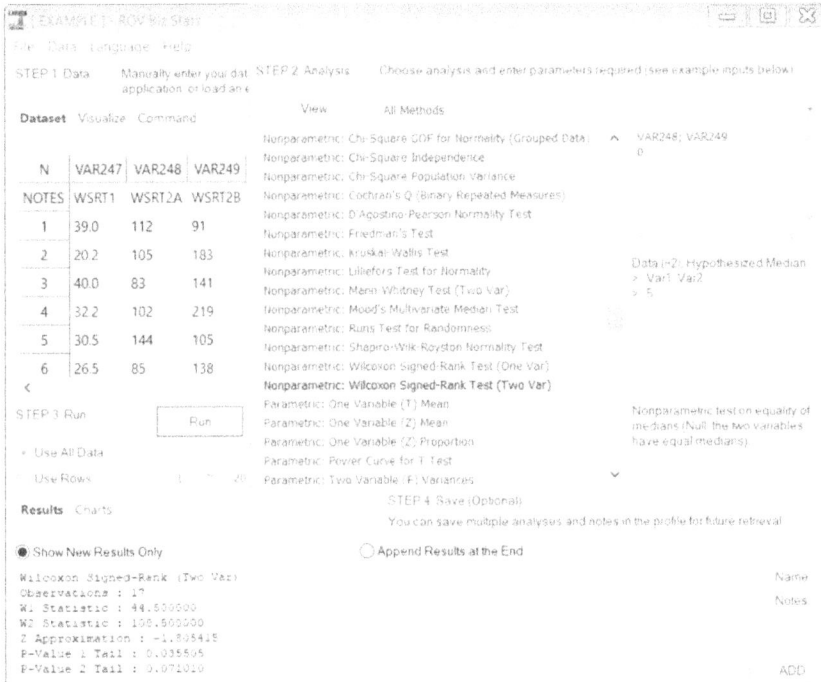

Figure 5.34: Wilcoxon Signed-Rank Test for Two Variables

Lilliefors Test

The Lilliefors test evaluates the null hypothesis of whether the data sample was drawn from a normally distributed population, versus an alternate hypothesis that the data sample is not normally distributed. This test relies on two cumulative frequencies: one derived from the sample dataset and one from a theoretical distribution based on the mean and standard deviation of the sample data. An alternative to this test is the chi-square test for normality. The chi-square test requires more data points to run compared to the Lilliefors test.

H_0: The sample is from a Normal Distribution

H_a: The sample is not from a Normal Distribution

In this test, the sample dataset is first arranged in order, from the smallest value to the largest value. Its observed (O) cumulative frequency is calculated, and a corresponding cumulative distribution function (CDF) of the normal distribution is computed based on the observed dataset's mean and standard deviation. The differences D between O and CDF are calculated, and the D statistic is computed as $D = max|O_i - CDF_i|$. Figure 5.35 illustrates a small sample set of five observations with the Lilliefors test administered. The computed D is 0.2782, which is less than the $\alpha = 5\%$ significance level threshold of 0.3370, which means we are unable to reject the null hypothesis and conclude that the small sample size is normally distributed.

Note that nonparametric methods have less power but are applicable in smaller sample sizes as illustrated in this example. However, if a larger dataset is available, it is always better to perform parametric distributional fittings such as those described previously (Kolmogorov–Smirnov, Akaike, Bayes Criterion, Kuiper, etc.).

Kruskal–Wallis Test

The Kruskal–Wallis test is the extension of the Wilcoxon Signed-Rank test by comparing more than two independent samples. The corresponding parametric test is the One-Way ANOVA, but unlike the ANOVA, the Kruskal–Wallis does not require that the dataset be randomly sampled from normally distributed populations with equal variances. The Kruskal–Wallis test is a two-tailed hypothesis test where the null hypothesis is such that the population medians of each treatment are statistically identical to the rest of the group; that is, there is no effect among the different treatment groups. Similar to the ANOVA method, the Kruskal–Wallis tests the following hypotheses:

H_0: $m_1 = m_2 = \ldots = m_K$ for $i = 1$ to k

(population medians are identical).

H_a: At least one of the medians m differs from the others.

The method starts off with k variables to be tested. For each variable, the data is ranked from smallest to largest, with the smallest value receiving the rank of 1, and all tied ranks are assigned their average values. Then, sum all the ranks for each variable, yielding a list of summed ranks $\Sigma(R_1)$, $\Sigma(R_2)$, ..., $\Sigma(R_K)$. Then, the H statistic is computed using:

$$H = \frac{12}{N(N+1)}\left[\frac{(\Sigma R_1)^2}{n_1} + \frac{(\Sigma R_2)^2}{n_2} + ... + \frac{(\Sigma R_K)^2}{n_K}\right] - 3(N+1)$$

The calculated H is compared to critical H values computed using a chi-square distribution with degrees of freedom $df = k - 1$. Figure 5.36 illustrates the Kruskal–Wallis test on three variables. The computed H statistic is over the 10% significance level, so we can reject the null hypothesis at this significance (but not at 5% or 1% significance) and conclude that at least one of the medians is statistically significantly different.

EXAMPLE 1 - ROW 8L ☐ ☐ ▣ ☒

File Data Language

STEP 1 Data   Manual STEP 2 Analysis   Choose analysis and enter parameters required (see example inputs below)
                 applica

Dataset Visualize Con   View   All Methods   ▾

		Nonparametric: Chi-Square GOF for Normality (Grouped Data)	∧	VAR240
N	VAR240	Nonparametric: Chi-Square Independence		
		Nonparametric: Chi-Square Population Variance		
NOTES	Small Normal	Nonparametric: Cochran's Q (Binary Repeated Measures)		
1	438	Nonparametric: D'Agostino-Pearson Normality Test		
		Nonparametric: Friedman's Test	<	
2	424	Nonparametric: Kruskal-Wallis Test		
3	213	**Nonparametric: Lilliefors Test for Normality**		Data
		Nonparametric: Mann-Whitney Test (Two Var)		> Var1
4	181	Nonparametric: Mood's Multivariate Median Test		
5	137	Nonparametric: Runs Test for Randomness		
		Nonparametric: Shapiro-Wilk-Royston Normality Test		
6		Nonparametric: Wilcoxon Signed-Rank Test (One Var)		
<		Nonparametric: Wilcoxon Signed-Rank Test (Two Var)		

STEP 3 Run   Parametric: One Variable (T) Mean   Runs nonparametric Lilliefors test
                  Parametric: One Variable (Z) Mean   for normality of your data (Null. the
 ◦ Use All Data   Parametric: One Variable (Z) Proportion   data is assumed to be normally
                  Parametric: Power Curve for T Test   distributed)
   Use Rows   Parametric: Two Variable (F) Variances   ∨

Results Charts   STEP 4 Save (Optional)
                                        You can save multiple analyses and notes in the profile for future retrieval
◉ Show New Results Only   ◯ Append Results at the End

```
Lilliefors Test

Average : 278.600000
Stdev : 141.800212
D Statistic : 0.278183
D Critical at 1% : 0.315000
D Critical at 5% : 0.337000
D Critical at 10% : 0.405000

The data is statistically normal at the 1%, 5% and 10% significance level
  (null hypothesis tested is that the data is normally distributed).
```

Data	Relative Frequency	Observed	Expected
137.000000	0.200000	0.200000	0.158997
181.000000	0.200000	0.400000	0.245634
213.000000	0.200000	0.600000	0.321817
424.000000	0.200000	0.800000	0.847410
438.000000	0.200000	1.000000	0.869518

Figure 5.35: Lilliefors Test for Normality

File   Data   Language   Help

STEP 1 Data   Manually enter your data, paste from   STEP 2 Analysis   Choose analysis and enter parameters required (see example inputs b
                  application, or load an example data

Dataset   Visualize   Command

N	VAR250	VAR251	VAR252
NOTES	Treatment 1	Treatment 2	Treatment 3
1	67	64	75
2	57	73	61
3	62	72	76
4	59	68	71
5	70	65	78
6	67		74

View   All Methods

Nonparametric: Chi-Square GOF for Normality (Grouped Data)   ∧   VAR250:VAR252
Nonparametric: Chi-Square Independence
Nonparametric: Chi-Square Population Variance
Nonparametric: Cochran's Q (Binary Repeated Measures)
Nonparametric: D'Agostino-Pearson Normality Test
Nonparametric: Friedman's Test
Nonparametric: Kruskal-Wallis Test   Data
Nonparametric: Lilliefors Test for Normality   > Var1 Var2 Var3
Nonparametric: Mann-Whitney Test (Two Var)
Nonparametric: Mood's Multivariate Median Test
Nonparametric: Runs Test for Randomness
Nonparametric: Shapiro-Wilk-Royston Normality Test
Nonparametric: Wilcoxon Signed-Rank Test (One Var)
Nonparametric: Wilcoxon Signed-Rank Test (Two Var)
Parametric: One Variable (T) Mean   Runs the nonparametric
Parametric: One Variable (Z) Mean   Kruskal-Wallis test, an e
Parametric: One Variable (Z) Proportion   of ANOVA with Multiple
Parametric: Power Curve for T Test   Treatments
Parametric: Two Variable (F) Variances

STEP 3 Run   Run   Run the
                                         selected
Use All Data   results
                                         and char
Use Rows

STEP 4 Save
You can save

Results   Charts

● Show New Results Only   ○ Append Results at the End

```
Kruskal-Wallis Test                                           Name
H Statistic : 7.489557
p-Value : 0.023661                                            Notes
H Critical at 1% : 9.210340
H Critical at 5% : 5.991465
H Critical at 10% : 4.605170
The population medians are statistically equal at 1% significance,   ADD
but are not statistically equal at 5% and 10% significance.
```

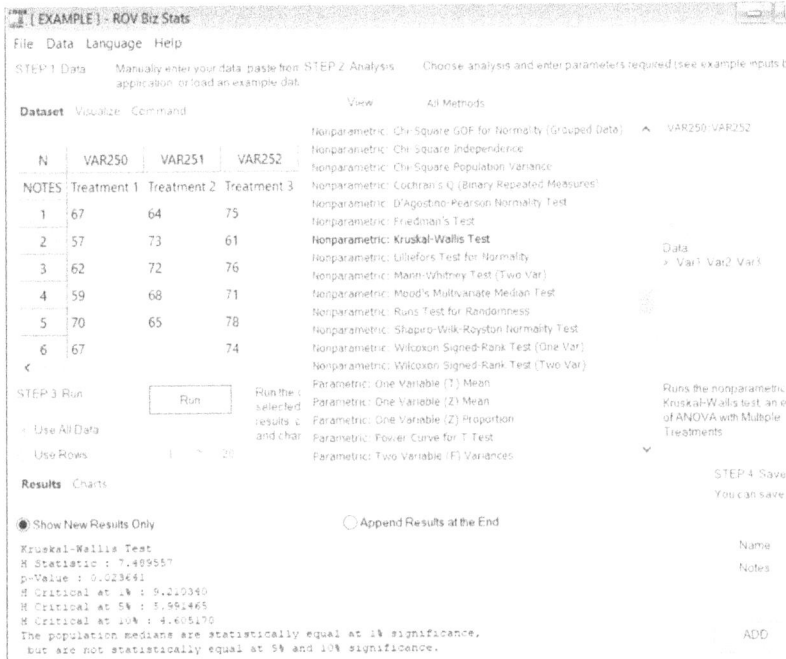

Figure 5.36: Kruskal–Wallis Test

Friedman's Test

The Friedman test is the extension of the Wilcoxon Signed-Rank test for paired samples. The corresponding parametric test is the Randomized Block Multiple Treatment ANOVA, but unlike the ANOVA, the Friedman test does not require that the dataset be randomly sampled from normally distributed populations with equal variances. The Friedman test uses a two-tailed hypothesis test where the null hypothesis is such that the population medians of each treatment are statistically identical to the rest of the group; that is, there is no effect among the different treatment groups. Similar to the ANOVA method, Friedman tests the following hypotheses:

H_0: $m_1 = m_2 = \ldots = m_K$ for $i = 1$ to k (identical population medians).

H_a: At least one of the medians m differs from the others.

$$F_r = \frac{12}{bt(t+1)} \sum_{j=1}^{t} R_j^2 - 3b(t+1)$$

Similar to the ANOVA with Blocking Variable, the data need to be set up in a $B \times T$ fashion, where the blocking variables (B) are listed in rows and the treatments (T) are in columns as different variables. Figure 5.37 illustrates an example with the correct data setup. As an example, assume that a company is testing a new stain remover liquid, and it has come up with four distinct formulations. These formulations are listed as the treatments, T, as different variables (columns). For each formulation or treatment, the stain remover was applied to various stain types (the blocking variable, B). In the example, there were six types of stains tested (e.g., chocolate, red wine, coffee, ink, paint, crayon) and these are listed in the rows. Each row represents one specific type of stain (e.g., row 1 may represent red wine). The numerical data in the grid is a value between 1 and 10, with a high number indicating that the stain was completely removed. The computed F_r statistic is 8.45, which is statistically significant at the 5% alpha level, so we can reject the null hypothesis and conclude that at least one of the formulations is different than the rest.

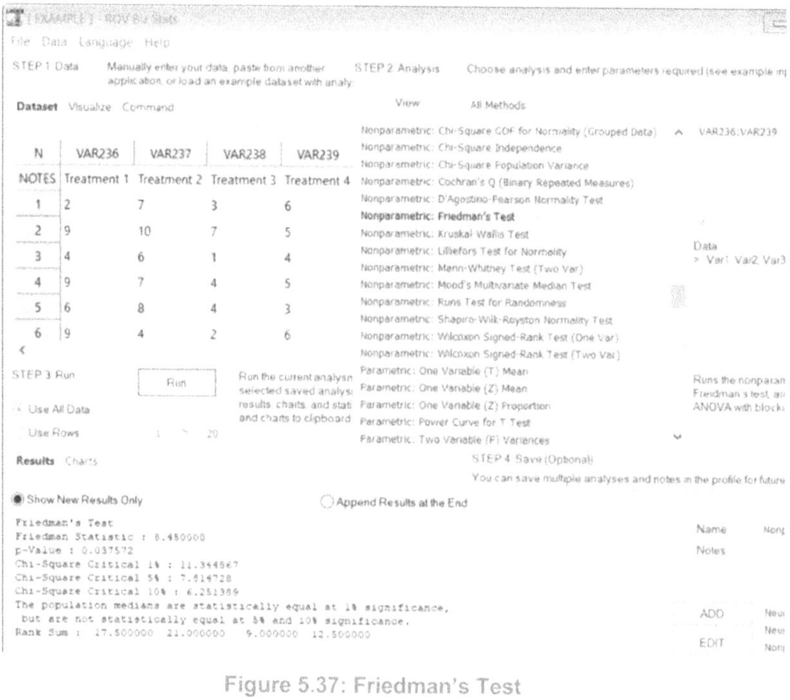

Figure 5.37: Friedman's Test

The concept of data reliability can be complicated and can take many forms. In general, reliability can be defined as how accurate the data is and the level of consistency of the collected data. In other words, the extent to which an experiment, test, or measuring procedure yields the same results on repeated trials is the measure of its reliability. For example, if one were to take a tape measure and find the length of a specific table, measuring the table repeatedly should yield the same result. If this is the case, then the data obtained are reliable.

Reliability can also be characterized as inter-rater (different people using the same measuring tape and measuring the same table multiple times) versus intra-rater (the same person measuring the same table several times, using the same measuring tape). There are statistical tests that can be run to identify the data's reliability and consistency.

Inter-Rater Reliability with Pairwise Cohen's Kappa

Cohen's Kappa test can be applied to test for the reliability of two raters. The null hypothesis tested is that both sets of judgments agree and are consistent. In the following table, we see four example cases. In each situation, there are two judges or raters.

In Case A, there are 50 patients, and the first rater (physician or healthcare worker) judges 15 of them as being psychotic, 24 borderline, and 11 neither. In comparison, the second rater or judge finds 16, 23, and 11 patients within these respective categories. The patients that fall within the same judgment categories are shown in the grid. Both judges agree that 10 are psychotic, 16 are borderline, and 8 are neither, with a total of 34 findings in agreement out of 50 cases (this can be read off the diagonal in the data grid). The results from BizStats indicate that Cohen's Kappa = 0.4959 or 49% agreement. In Case B, we see that the data grid is equally distributed with 200 patients in each block, and the computed Cohen's Kappa = 0.0000, indicating absolutely no consistency and reliability between these two raters spread evenly. Case C, as you would imagine, returns Cohen's Kappa = 1.0000. Finally, in Case D, where reliability is actually not just zero, but there is no value between the corresponding pairs, we obtain a Cohen's Kappa = –0.50902. Clearly, a high positive Cohen's Kappa measure is desirable for inter-rater reliability.

CASE A	Judge 2 Psychotic (16)	Judge 2 Borderline (23)	Judge 2 Neither (11)
Judge 1 Psychotic (15)	10	4	1
Judge 1 Borderline (24)	6	16	2
Judge 1 Neither (11)	0	3	8

CASE B	Judge 2 Psychotic (600)	Judge 2 Borderline (600)	Judge 2 Neither (600)
Judge 1 Psychotic (600)	200	200	200
Judge 1 Borderline (600)	200	200	200
Judge 1 Neither (600)	200	200	200

CASE C	Judge 2 Psychotic (100)	Judge 2 Borderline (100)	Judge 2 Neither (100)
Judge 1 Psychotic (100)	100	0	0
Judge 1 Borderline (100)	0	100	0
Judge 1 Neither (100)	0	0	100

CASE D	Judge 2 Psychotic (135)	Judge 2 Borderline (99)	Judge 2 Neither (114)
Judge 1 Psychotic (124)	0	55	69
Judge 1 Borderline (95)	50	0	45
Judge 1 Neither (129)	85	44	0

Internal Consistency and Reliability with Cronbach's Alpha for Binary Data

When there exist more than two raters or judges, we can use Cronbach's Alpha Analysis of Internal Consistency and Reliability. The null hypothesis for the Cronbach's Alpha is that there is zero alpha reliability, and, therefore, there is no internal consistency among the different raters. In Case E, there are 12 respondents to a survey comprising 11 different questions. Note that to run the Cronbach's Alpha test, the data obtained must be binary. If you look at the data carefully by *row*, we see that there are respondents such as Albert and Bob who tend to respond with the value 1 regardless of the question, whereas Kim and Larry might do the opposite, with a 0 response. One might even think that some respondents are too lazy to actually answer the questions and will simply fill in the blanks with similar responses throughout. In fact, the calculated Cronbach's Alpha p-value = 0.6659 in BizStats, which means we cannot reject the null hypothesis and conclude that in Case E, there is no internal consistency among the different respondents. The survey data is, therefore, not consistent, and not reliable.

Conversely, in Case F, we see that if you look down each *column*, there seems to be consistency among all the respondents. For instance, in Questions 6 and 7 (Q6 and Q7), almost all respondents agreed it would be a 0, as opposed to Q5, with all 1s in the column. Q2 and Q3 show that the respondents are equally spread between 0s and 1s. In this Case F, the computed Cronbach's Alpha p-value = 0.002723 in BizStats, indicating that the null can be rejected, and we conclude that there is, indeed, statistically significant alpha-level reliability among the respondents.

CASE E	Q1	Q2	Q3	Q4	Q5	Q6	Q7	Q8	Q9	Q10	Q11
Albert	1	1	1	1	1	1	1	1	1	1	1
Bob	1	1	1	1	1	1	1	1	0	1	0
Cathy	1	0	1	1	1	1	1	1	1	0	0
Derek	1	1	1	0	1	1	0	1	1	0	0
Eric	1	1	1	1	1	0	0	0	1	0	0
Florence	0	1	1	0	1	1	1	1	0	0	0
Gale	1	1	1	1	0	0	1	0	0	0	0
Henry	1	1	1	1	1	0	0	0	0	0	0
Indi	0	1	0	1	1	0	0	0	0	1	0
Jack	1	0	0	1	0	1	0	0	0	0	0
Kim	1	1	1	0	0	0	0	0	0	0	0
Larry	1	0	0	1	0	0	0	0	0	0	0

CASE F	Q1	Q2	Q3	Q4	Q5	Q6	Q7
Andy	1	1	0	1	1	0	1
Becky	0	1	0	1	1	0	0
Colin	1	1	0	0	1	0	0
Dave	0	1	0	0	1	0	0
Even	1	1	0	1	1	0	0
Flynn	0	1	0	1	1	0	0
George	1	0	1	0	1	0	0
Hope	0	0	1	0	1	0	0
Isaac	1	0	1	1	1	0	0
John	0	0	1	1	1	0	0
Kern	1	0	1	0	1	0	0
Lisa	0	0	1	0	1	0	0

Internal Consistency and Reliability with Guttman's Lambda

When the responses are not binary but categorical, we can use Guttman's Lambda test for inter-rater consistency and reliability. A quick scan of Case G in the following table indicates a familiar problem, where the vertical entries are almost identical in each column, but the columns themselves are not consistent across the different raters. For instance, Alex might always select a low score regardless of the question or issue posed, whereas Cory is an optimist and consistently provides a high score. The raters themselves might be consistent with themselves, but they are certainly not consistent with other raters. The computed Guttman's Lambda = 0.07563, with a corresponding Spearman–Brown Correlation Correction Factor = 0.07782 using BizStats (note that if multiple correlation correction factors are presented, we usually look at the more conservative measure). Low correlation corrections and low lambda scores mean there is low reliability and low consistency among the raters. Note that the data matrix is inverted in this test, as opposed to the Cronbach's test, where we show the questions as rows and respondents or judges/raters as columns. In comparison, for Case H, Guttman's Lambda = 0.99004 and the conservative Spearman–Brown Correlation Correction Factor = 0.9909. This indicates a very high consistency and reliability of the responses. For instance, Question

A received a very low score regardless of the rater, whereas Question C scored high consistently. Looking across the rows shows consistency and reliability in the data.

Case G	Alex	Ben	Cory	Dick	Emma	Flo	Ginny	Hale	Izzy	John
Question A	1	4	8	2	7	5	6	2	5	3
Question B	1	4	8	2	7	1	6	3	5	3
Question C	1	4	8	2	7	2	6	2	5	3
Question D	1	5	8	2	7	2	6	3	5	3
Question E	1	4	8	3	7	2	5	2	5	3
Question F	1	4	9	2	8	2	6	3	6	3
Question G	1	4	8	2	8	2	6	2	5	3
Question H	1	5	8	2	7	2	6	3	5	3
Question I	2	4	8	2	7	2	5	2	5	3
Question J	1	4	9	3	7	2	6	3	5	3
Question K	1	4	8	2	7	2	6	2	6	3
Question L	1	4	8	2	7	1	6	3	5	4
Question M	1	4	8	2	7	1	6	2	5	3
Question N	2	4	8	2	7	2	6	3	5	3
Question O	1	4	8	2	7	1	6	2	5	3

Case H	Arlo	Bex	Cal	Dale	Elsa	Fox	Guy	Ham	Illy	Jay
Question A	1	1	1	1	1	1	1	1	2	1
Question B	4	4	4	5	4	4	4	5	4	4
Question C	8	8	8	8	8	9	8	8	8	9
Question D	2	2	2	2	3	2	2	2	2	3
Question E	7	7	7	7	7	8	8	7	7	7
Question F	5	1	2	2	2	2	2	2	2	2
Question G	6	6	6	6	5	6	6	6	5	6
Question H	2	3	2	3	2	3	2	3	2	3
Question I	5	5	5	5	5	6	5	5	5	5
Question J	3	3	3	3	3	3	3	3	3	3

If we wish to test for both inter-rater and intra-rater reliability, we can use the Inter-Class Correlation (ICC) test. Cases I and J in the accompanying tables show some example data where we perform a double-blind test on eight wines (the wine bottles look identical, labels removed, and replaced with a generic label such as Wine 1, Wine 2, etc.). And suppose four sommeliers or expert wine judges were asked to grade the wines from a value of 1 (low quality) to 10 (high quality).

In Case I, we see that for each of the different wines, all four judges scored the wines consistently. For example, Wine 1 is by far the worst, whereas wines 7 and 8 are highly rated by all judges. This would indicate a high level of consistency and reliability in each row. The ICC test returns an Interclass Correlation = 0.9841, the row's p-value = 0.0000, and the column's p-value = 0.8538. This means there is a high level of consistency, as measured by the ICC, and we can reject the null hypothesis of having the same values in the rows and fail to reject regarding the columns. In other words, all the judges tend to be fairly consistent in their tastes (high ICC), possibly because they all have similar judging or sommelier training. In addition, the wines are different as compared to one another (p-value of 0.0000 for the rows), where we can say based on the scores, which we have now concluded are consistent and reliable, that the wines are certainly of varying quality. In contrast, when comparing the columns (i.e., comparing among the judges), we have consistency and statistically no difference in their ratings (high p-value of the columns at 0.8538), or, in other words, the judges have similar judgments.

Case J shows a very different situation. We see that Judge 1 is probably a snob, whereby no wine is considered good. Hence, Judge 1 is internally consistent with himself or has high intra-rater reliability. In contrast, Judge 4 simply loves wine and scores any and all wines highly. Judge 4 is also internally reliable to himself, but not to the other judges. The computed Interclass Correlation = 0.00149 (low inter-rater consistency and low reliability among the judges) with a row p-value of 0.3958 (we cannot reject the null hypothesis and state that the rows, when taken together, are statistically similar to each other, indicating, in this case, that there is high intra-rater reliability) and a column p-value of 0.0000 (we reject the null hypothesis and state that there is a statistically significant difference among the columns or judges, which means that there is no inter-rater consistency and no reliability in the wine scores).

Case I	Judge 1	Judge 2	Judge 3	Judge 4
Wine 1	1	1	1	1
Wine 2	2	3	3	2
Wine 3	3	3	3	3
Wine 4	6	6	6	6
Wine 5	6	5	5	6
Wine 6	2	2	2	2
Wine 7	8	9	9	9
Wine 8	9	9	9	8

Case J	Judge 1	Judge 2	Judge 3	Judge 4
Wine 1	1	3	5	8
Wine 2	2	3	5	9
Wine 3	3	3	6	9
Wine 4	1	2	6	7
Wine 5	1	2	5	9
Wine 6	1	2	5	9
Wine 7	2	3	4	9
Wine 8	3	1	5	8

Kendall's W Measure of Concordance Inter-rater Reliability Test (With or Without Ties)

Another test for the inter-rater reliability is Kendall's W measure, which can be run with ties or without ties. A tie means there are multiple data points with the same value, and, hence, we must split the difference between these ties. Regardless, the null hypothesis for these tests is that there is zero agreement ($W = 0$) among all the judges.

Case K in the table below returns a calculated Kendall's W = 1.1068, Kendall's R = 1.124646, and p-value = 0.0000. We reject the null hypothesis and conclude that there is agreement among the judges. For instance, we see that Issue 1 is critical for all judges, whereas Issues 3, 7, and 8 are rated lower. All ratings are consistent among all the judges.

In Case L, Kendall's W = 0.2261, Kendall's R = 0.0971, and p-value = 0.1352. This indicates that we cannot reject the null hypothesis and conclude that there is no statistical concordance among the different respondents answering the survey questions. Finally, in Case M, Kendall's W = 0.0028, Kendall's R = -0.1633, and p-value = 0.9999. This certainly indicates extremely low consistency and reliability among the respondents.

Case K	Issue 1	Issue 2	Issue 3	Issue 4	Issue 5	Issue 6	Issue 7	Issue 8
Judge 1	8	8	2	5	3	5	2	1
Judge 2	8	7	2	6	3	5	1	1
Judge 3	8	7	2	5	3	6	2	1
Judge 4	8	7	3	5	2	5	1	2
Judge 5	8	7	2	6	3	5	1	2
Judge 6	8	8	2	5	3	6	1	2
Judge 7	7	7	3	5	2	5	2	1

Case L	Q1	Q2	Q3	Q4	Q1	Q2	Q3	Q4
Person 1	7	8	5	4	1	7	2	1
Person 2	1	7	10	6	2	6	3	1
Person 3	3	1	7	10	3	5	10	1
Person 4	10	3	1	5	4	4	10	2
Person 5	3	2	1	1	5	3	1	4.5
Person 6	2	6	7.5	2.5	6	2	5	2.5
Person 7	6	10	4	8	7	1	6	1

Case M	Issue 1	Issue 2	Issue 3	Issue 4	Issue 5	Issue 6	Issue 7	Issue 8
Judge 1	5	5	5	5	5	5	5	5
Judge 2	8	8	8	8	7	8	7	8
Judge 3	1	1	1	2	2	1	1	1
Judge 4	5	5	5	5	5	5	5	5
Judge 5	6	7	6	7	6	7	6	7
Judge 6	9	9	9	9	9	9	9	9
Judge 7	2	1	2	2	3	2	2	1

Data Diversity with Shannon, Brillouin, and Simpson Diversity and Homogeneity Test

Another issue with regard to data reliability and consistency pertains to the randomized and stratified sampling that is performed. For instance, we may get a high level of data consistency and reliability but if the people sampled are from the same group or category, then the data may not be entirely reliable. As an example, suppose we wish to survey voter sentiment on a particular issue in a state. If all the voters selected were Democrats or predominantly Republicans, then the data might be skewed one way. Hence, to test for the diversity of a randomized and stratified sampling group, we can apply the Shannon, Brillouin, and Simpson model. In Case N in the accompanying table, suppose we have five categories of self-described voters (highly conservative, conservative, moderate, liberal, and highly liberal), and the data grid shows the number of people sampled within each category.

Case N	Scenario 1	Scenario 2	Scenario 3	Scenario 4
Category A	5	5	1	11
Category B	5	8	1	11
Category C	5	6	21	1
Category D	5	2	1	1
Category E	5	4	1	1

The following shows the results of the four samples. The higher the diversity index is to the maximum index, the higher the level of diversity. Clearly, we see that Scenario 1 has the highest homogeneity score and the diversity index is closest to the maximum index value. Scenario 2 has a 94.71% homogeneity score, while Scenarios 3 and 4 have the lowest diversity index relative to the maximum value.

Sample 1 Results	Shannon	Brillouin	Simpson
Diversity Index	1.6094	0.5918	0.2000
Max Index	1.6094	0.5918	
Homogeneity	1.0000	1.0000	

Sample 2 Results	Shannon	Brillouin	Simpson
Diversity Index	1.5243	0.5587	0.2320
Max Index	1.6094	0.5918	
Homogeneity	0.9471	0.9441	

Sample 3 Results	Shannon	Brillouin	Simpson
Diversity Index	0.6615	0.2193	0.7120
Max Index	1.6094	0.5918	
Homogeneity	0.4110	0.3706	

Sample 4 Results	Shannon	Brillouin	Simpson
Diversity Index	1.1087	0.3995	0.3920
Max Index	1.6094	0.5918	
Homogeneity	0.6889	0.6751	

Internal Validity

A related issue is that of model validity. When we discuss the validity of a model, we typically mean if the specified model does what it is intended to do. In other words, does the model actually model what we are looking to model? To answer the question, we look at the internal validity of a model and its external validity.

The internal validity of a model, such as multivariate regression, looks at whether the independent variables used are statistically significant; that is, are the internal constructs of the model valid? We typically use the p-value of regression to measure this internal validity. The null hypothesis tested is that each of the independent variables has zero effect on the dependent variable. Hence, low p-values, at or below the alpha significance level, imply that it is statistically significant and impacts the dependent variable. Hence, a model with only significant independent variables is deemed internally valid.

	Coeff	Std. Error	T-stat	P-value	Lower 5%	Upper 95%
Intercept	57.95550	108.79014	0.53273	0.59690	-161.29661	277.20762
VAR X1	-0.00354	0.00352	-1.00656	0.31965	-0.01064	0.00355
VAR X2	0.46437	0.25353	1.83159	0.01379	-0.04659	0.97533
VAR X3	25.23770	14.11723	1.78772	0.02071	-3.21371	53.68911
VAR X4	-0.00856	0.10156	-0.08433	0.93317	-0.21325	0.19612
VAR X5	16.55792	14.79957	1.11881	0.03929	-13.26866	46.38449

External Validity

A statistically significant and internally valid model may or may not have practical significance. This is where external validity comes in. While internal validity looks at the individual constructs of the model, external validity looks at the entire model and measures how much that model may explain the predicted variable. Typically, external validity is measured using a variety of error formulae. The typical measure is the R-square and adjusted R-square (the coefficient of determination and adjusted coefficient of determination). The R-square is simply the linear correlation (R) between the actual and predicted values, squared. While R has a domain between −1.00 and +1.00, its squared value will always lie between 0.00 and 1.00. Hence, the R-square is a percentage measure, which shows how much of the variation of the dependent variable can be explained simultaneously by all of the independent variables in the model. The higher the R-square, the higher the external validity of the model. However, in multivariate models, adding additional exogenous variables that may or may not be internally valid will usually increase the R-square value. This is where the adjusted R-square comes in. The adjusted R-square will adjust for the added independent variables and penalize the R-square for having too many independent variables that do not statistically significantly increase the R-square sufficiently. This means that with added extraneous variables, the adjusted R-square may actually decline, making it a more conservative and better estimate of a model's external validity.

In addition, along the lines of penalizing added variables, where holding everything else constant, if the predictive powers of two models are identical but one uses fewer predictor variables, then the more parsimonious model wins out. Based on the theory of parsimony and penalization of too many extraneous variables, other measures of external validity were created, such as the Akaike Information Criterion or the Bayes–Schwarz Criterion. These are relative measures of external model errors and are typically used to compare different model specifications to identify the lower error scores. The following are additional external validity error measures. Those denoted with an asterisk * are values that we would rather see an increase, versus the remaining error measures where the lower the error, the higher the external validity of the model.

*R-Squared
*Adjusted R-Squared
*Maximum Likelihood
Akaike Information Criterion (AIC)
Bayes and Schwarz Criterion (BSC)
Hannan–Quinn Criterion (HQC)
Mean Absolute Deviation (MAD)
Mean Absolute Percentage Error (MAPE)
Mean Squared Error (MSE)
Median Absolute Error (MdAE)
Median Absolute Percentage Error (MdAPE)
Root Mean Square Log Error (RMSLE)
Root Mean Square Percentage Error Loss (RMSPE)
Root Mean Squared Error (RMSE)
Root Median Square Percentage Error Loss (RMdSPE)
Sum of Squared Errors (SSE)
Symmetrical Mean Absolute Percentage Error (sMAPE)
Theil's U1 Accuracy (U1)
Theil's U2 Quality (U2)

Predictability and Accuracy: Akaike, Bayes, Hannan–Quinn, Diebold–Mariano, Pesaran–Timmermann

Another concept in data and modeling is that of predictability and accuracy. Multiple methods can be used to measure the accuracy of a predictive model. As previously mentioned, in a multivariate regression setting, we can use the R-square, Akaike Information Criterion, Bayes–Schwarz Criterion, and others. As an example, suppose we are comparing between two models' accuracy. One simple way is to look at the model predicted values and compare them against the historical actuals. The difference would constitute the model's prediction errors. The following shows two example sets of errors. We can see that model 2's errors are a lot smaller than model 1's errors. The computed results using BizStats' Forecast Accuracy model show that the second model has a lot lower errors and is, therefore, the preferred model with a higher level of accuracy.

Errors 1	Errors 2
221.4876	0.112161248
-120.1243	0.535868655
89.7211	0.663950485
88.6704	0.635762518
-162.1336	0.121139129
86.0007	0.432267702
-68.8718	0.200703196
84.3845	0.663499338
234.2450	0.004590278
79.2966	0.830036453
117.1991	0.568247701
....	....
....	....
-202.5301	0.697677820
-174.1671	0.234313273
-36.3149	0.530179776

Error Measures for Model 1
Maximum Log-Likelihood: -318.173405
Akaike Info Criterion (AIC): 12.926936
AIC Correction (AICC): 15.593603
Bayes and Schwarz Criterion (BSC): 13.118139
Hannan–Quinn Criterion (HQC): 12.999747
Mean Absolute Deviation (MAD): 114.467810
Mean Squared Errors (MSE): 19713.503554
Root Mean Squared Error (RMSE): 140.404785

Error Measures for Model 2
Maximum Log-Likelihood: -41.017947
Akaike Info Criterion (AIC): 1.840718
AIC Correction (AICC): 4.507385
Bayes and Schwarz Criterion (BSC): 2.031920
Hannan–Quinn Criterion (HQC): 1.913529
Mean Absolute Deviation (MAD): 0.475521
Mean Squared Errors (MSE): 0.302051
Root Mean Squared Error (RMSE): 0.549592

Even if the two models show a different level of forecast accuracy, the next question is whether the two forecasts are statistically significantly different from one another. The Diebold–Mariano Test of Forecast Differences and the Harvey, Leybourne, and Newbold Test allow us to determine if the errors are statistically significant. The null hypothesis tested is that there is no significant difference between the two forecasts.

Actual	Forecast 1	Forecast 2
1.2288	0.9028	0.8945
2.6684	2.4493	2.3214
3.4177	3.2076	2.5208
2.2392	2.4383	1.9081
2.1226	2.7751	0.9508
0.4638	0.5932	-0.6107

-0.5508	0.1085	-1.1155
1.1829	0.8785	1.1116
...	...	...
...	...	...
-0.5781	-0.0840	-0.4644
-0.7687	-0.0731	-0.9785

Diebold–Mariano Test of Forecast Differences
DM Stat: 1.00510
P-value: 0.31485

Harvey, Leybourne, and Newbold Test
HLN Stat: 1.12373
P-value: 0.27512

Finally, sometimes the exact forecast accuracy is not in question. Rather, it is the ability to predict directional change that is critical. The Pesaran–Timmerman tests for whether a model can adequately predict and track the directional changes over time. The null hypothesis tested is that the forecast does not track directional changes in the data.

Actual	Forecast
23	14
-2	3
56	45
51	23
...	...
...	...
-6	3
-7	-11
-39	-12
31	24
35	3

Pesaran–Timmermann Test
PT-Stat: 1.96834
P-value: 0.02451

One very powerful tool in Monte Carlo simulation is that of precision control. For instance, how many trials are considered sufficient to run in a complex model? Precision control takes the guesswork out of estimating the relevant number of trials by allowing the simulation to stop if the level of prespecified precision is reached.

The precision control functionality lets you set how precise you want your forecast to be. Generally speaking, as more trials are calculated, the confidence interval narrows, and the statistics become more accurate. The precision control feature in Risk Simulator uses the characteristic of confidence intervals to determine when a specified accuracy of a statistic has been reached. For each forecast, you can specify the specific confidence interval for the precision level (Figure 14.17). If the error precision is achieved within the number of trials you set, the simulation will run, as usual, otherwise, you will be informed that additional simulation trials are required to meet the more stringent required error precision.

Make sure that you do not confuse three very different terms: error, precision, and confidence. Although they sound similar, the concepts are significantly different from one another. A simple illustration is in order. Suppose you are a taco shell manufacturer and are interested in finding out how many broken taco shells there are on average in a box of 100 shells. One way to do this is to collect a sample of prepackaged boxes of 100 taco shells, open them, and count how many of them are actually broken. You manufacture 1 million boxes a year (this is your *population*), but you randomly open only 10 boxes (this is your *sample* size, also known as your number of *trials* in a simulation). The number of broken shells in each box is as follows: 24, 22, 4, 15, 33, 32, 4, 1, 45, and 2. The calculated average number of broken shells is 18.2. Based on these 10 samples or trials, the average is 18.2 units, while based on the sample, the 80% confidence interval is between 2 and 33 units (that is, 80% of the time, the number of broken shells is between 2 and 33 *based on this sample size or the number of trials run*). However, how sure are you that 18.2 is the correct average? Are 10 trials sufficient to establish this?

The confidence interval between 2 and 33 is too wide and too variable. Suppose you require a more accurate average value where the error is ±2 taco shells 90% of the time—this means that if you open *all* 1 million boxes manufactured in a year, 900,000 of these boxes will have broken taco shells on average at some mean unit ±2 tacos. How many more taco shell boxes would you then need to sample (or trials run) to obtain this level of precision? Here, the 2 tacos constitute the error level while the 90% is the level of precision. If sufficient numbers of trials are run, then the 90% confidence interval will be identical to the 90% precision level, where a more precise measure of the average is obtained such that 90% of the time, the error, and, hence, the confidence will be ±2 tacos. As an example, say the average is 20 units, then the 90% confidence interval will be between 18 and 22 units, where this interval is precise 90% of the time, where in opening all 1 million boxes, 900,000 of them will have between 18 and 22 broken tacos. The number of trials required to hit this precision is based on the sampling error equation of

$$\bar{x} \pm Z \frac{s}{\sqrt{n}}$$

where

$$Z \frac{s}{\sqrt{n}}$$

is the error of 2 tacos, $\bar{x}$ is the sample average, Z is the standard-normal Z-score obtained from the 90% precision level, s is the sample standard deviation, and n is the number of trials required to hit this level of error with the specified precision.

LINEAR AND NONLINEAR MULTIVARIATE REGRESSION

It is assumed that the user is sufficiently knowledgeable about the fundamentals of regression analysis. The general bivariate linear regression equation takes the form of $Y = \beta_0 + \beta_1 X + \varepsilon$, where β_0 is the intercept, β_1 is the slope, and ε is the error term. It is bivariate as there are only two variables, a Y or dependent variable, and an X or independent variable, where X is also known as the regressor (sometimes a bivariate regression is also known as a univariate regression as there is only a single independent variable X). The dependent variable is named as such as it *depends* on the independent variable; for example, sales revenue depends on the total marketing costs expended on a product's advertising and promotion, making the dependent variable sales and the independent variable marketing costs. An example of a bivariate regression is seen as simply inserting the best-fitting line through a set of data points in a two-dimensional plane, as seen on the left in Figure 5.38. In other cases, a multivariate regression can be performed, where there are multiple or k number of independent X variables or regressors, where the general regression equation will now take the form of $Y = \beta_0 + \beta_1 X_1 + \beta_2 X_2 + \beta_3 X_3 ... + \beta_k X_k + \varepsilon$. In this case, the best-fitting line will be within a $k + 1$ dimensional plane.

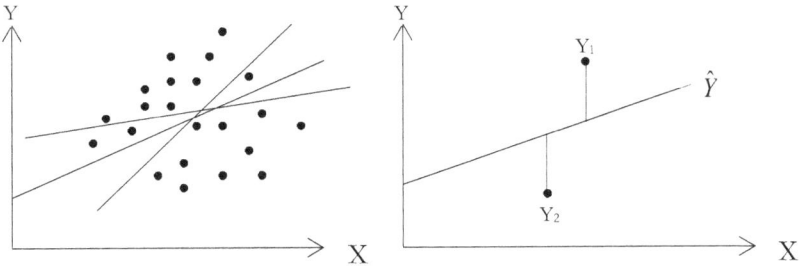

Figure 5.38: Bivariate Regression

However, fitting a line through a set of data points in a scatter plot as in Figure 5.38 may result in numerous possible lines. The best-fitting line is defined as the single unique line that minimizes the total vertical errors, that is, the sum of the absolute distances between the actual data points (Y_i) and the estimated line ($\hat{Y}$), as shown on the right in Figure 5.38. To find the best-fitting unique line that minimizes the errors, a more sophisticated approach is applied, using regression analysis. Regression analysis finds the unique best-fitting line by requiring that the total errors be minimized, or by calculating

$$Min \sum_{i=1}^{n} (Y_i - \hat{Y}_i)^2$$

where only one unique line minimizes this sum of squared errors. The errors (vertical distances between the actual data and the predicted line) are squared to avoid the negative errors from canceling out the positive errors. Solving this minimization problem with respect to the slope and intercept requires calculating first derivatives and setting them equal to zero:

$$\hat{\beta}_2 = \frac{\sum Y_i X_{2,i} \sum X_{3,i}^2 - \sum Y_i X_{3,i} \sum X_{2,i} X_{3,i}}{\sum X_{2,i}^2 \sum X_{3,i}^2 - \left(\sum X_{2,i} X_{3,i}\right)^2}$$

$$\hat{\beta}_3 = \frac{\sum Y_i X_{3,i} \sum X_{2,i}^2 - \sum Y_i X_{2,i} \sum X_{2,i} X_{3,i}}{\sum X_{2,i}^2 \sum X_{3,i}^2 - \left(\sum X_{2,i} X_{3,i}\right)^2}$$

which yields the bivariate regression's least squares equations:

$$\beta_1 = \frac{\sum_{i=1}^{n}(X_i - \bar{X})(Y_i - \bar{Y})}{\sum_{i=1}^{n}(X_i - \bar{X})^2} = \frac{\sum_{i=1}^{n} X_i Y_i - \frac{\sum_{i=1}^{n} X_i \sum_{i=1}^{n} Y_i}{n}}{\sum_{i=1}^{n} X_i^2 - \frac{\left(\sum_{i=1}^{n} X_i\right)^2}{n}}$$

$$\beta_0 = \bar{Y} - \beta_1 \bar{X}$$

For multivariate regression, the analogy is expanded to account for multiple independent variables, where $Y_i = \beta_1 + \beta_2 X_{2,i} + \beta_3 X_{3,i} + \varepsilon_i$ and the estimated slopes can be calculated by:

$$\hat{\beta}_2 = \frac{\sum Y_i X_{2,i} \sum X_{3,i}^2 - \sum Y_i X_{3,i} \sum X_{2,i} X_{3,i}}{\sum X_{2,i}^2 \sum X_{3,i}^2 - \left(\sum X_{2,i} X_{3,i}\right)^2}$$

$$\hat{\beta}_3 = \frac{\sum Y_i X_{3,i} \sum X_{2,i}^2 - \sum Y_i X_{2,i} \sum X_{2,i} X_{3,i}}{\sum X_{2,i}^2 \sum X_{3,i}^2 - \left(\sum X_{2,i} X_{3,i}\right)^2}$$

In running multivariate regressions, great care must be taken to set up and interpret the results. For instance, a good understanding of econometric modeling is required (e.g., identifying regression pitfalls such as structural breaks, multicollinearity, heteroskedasticity, autocorrelation, specification tests, nonlinearities, and so forth) before a proper model can be constructed.

Figure 5.39 shows how a multiple linear and nonlinear regression can be run in Risk Simulator. In Excel, type in or open your existing dataset (the illustration below uses *Risk Simulator | Example Models | 09 Multiple Regression* in the examples folder). Check to make sure that the data are arranged in columns and select the data including the variable headings and click on *Risk Simulator | Forecasting | Multiple Regression*. Select the dependent variable and check the relevant options (lags, stepwise regression, nonlinear regression, and so forth) and click *OK*. Figure 5.40 illustrates a sample multivariate regression result report generated. The report comes complete with all the regression results, analysis of variance results, fitted chart, and hypothesis test results.

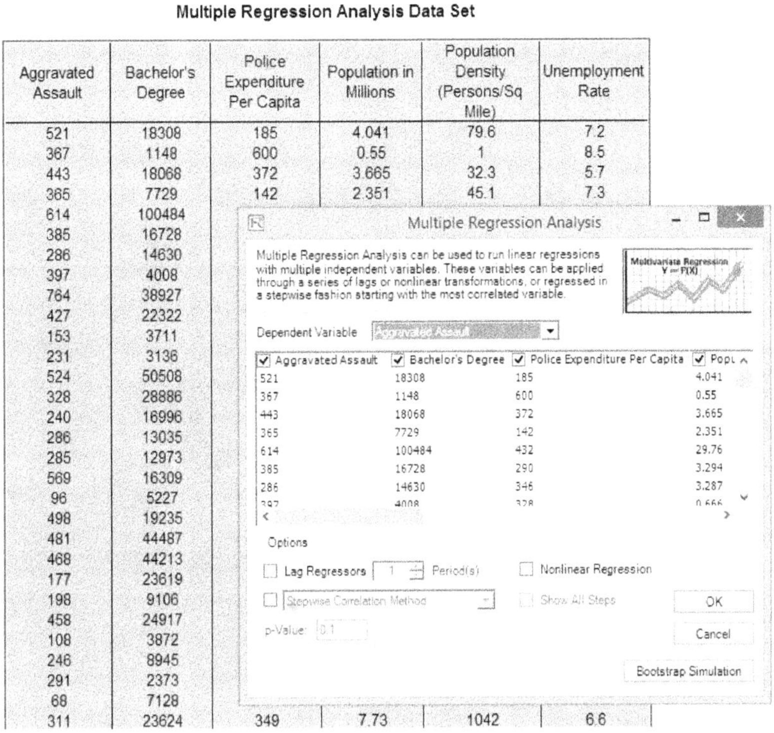

Multiple Regression Analysis Data Set

Aggravated Assault	Bachelor's Degree	Police Expenditure Per Capita	Population in Millions	Population Density (Persons/Sq Mile)	Unemployment Rate
521	18308	185	4.041	79.6	7.2
367	1148	600	0.55	1	8.5
443	18068	372	3.665	32.3	5.7
365	7729	142	2.351	45.1	7.3
614	100484				
385	16728				
286	14630				
397	4008				
764	38927				
427	22322				
153	3711				
231	3136				
524	50508				
328	28886				
240	16996				
286	13035				
285	12973				
569	16309				
96	5227				
498	19235				
481	44487				
468	44213				
177	23619				
198	9106				
458	24917				
108	3872				
246	8945				
291	2373				
68	7128				
311	23624	349	7.73	1042	6.6

Multiple Regression Analysis

Multiple Regression Analysis can be used to run linear regressions with multiple independent variables. These variables can be applied through a series of lags or nonlinear transformations, or regressed in a stepwise fashion starting with the most correlated variable.

Dependent Variable: Aggravated Assault

Aggravated Assault	Bachelor's Degree	Police Expenditure Per Capita	Popu
521	18308	185	4.041
367	1148	600	0.55
443	18068	372	3.665
365	7729	142	2.351
614	100484	432	29.76
385	16728	290	3.294
286	14630	346	3.287
397	4008	328	0.666

Options

Lag Regressors [1] Period(s)   Nonlinear Regression

Stepwise Correlation Method   Show All Steps   OK

p-Value [0.1]   Cancel

Bootstrap Simulation

Figure 5.39: Regression in Risk Simulator

143

Regression Analysis Report

Regression Statistics

R-Squared (Coefficient of Determination)	0.3272
Adjusted R-Squared	0.2508
Multiple R (Multiple Correlation Coefficient)	0.5720
Standard Error of the Estimates (SEy)	149.6720
Number of Observations	50

The R-Squared or Coefficient of Determination indicates that 0.33 of the variation in the dependent variable can be explained and accounted for by the independent variables in this regression analysis. However, in a multiple regression, the Adjusted R-Squared takes into account the existence of additional independent variables or regressors and adjusts this R-Squared value to a more accurate view of the regression's explanatory power. Hence, only 0.25 of the variation in the dependent variable can be explained by the regressors.

The Multiple Correlation Coefficient (Multiple R) measures the correlation between the actual dependent variable (Y) and the estimated or fitted (Y) based on the regression equation. This is also the square root of the Coefficient of Determination (R-Squared).

The Standard Error of the Estimates (SEy) describes the dispersion of data points above and below the regression line or plane. This value is used as part of the calculation to obtain the confidence interval of the estimates later.

Regression Results

	Intercept	Bachelor's Degree	Police Expenditure Per Capita	Population in Millions	Population Density (Persons/Sq Mile)	Unemployment Rate
Coefficients	57.9555	-0.0035	0.4644	25.2377	-0.0086	16.5579
Standard Error	108.7901	0.0035	0.2535	14.1172	0.1016	14.7996
t-Statistic	0.5327	-1.0066	1.8316	1.7877	-0.0843	1.1188
p-Value	0.5969	0.3197	0.0738	0.0807	0.9332	0.2693
Lower 5%	-161.2966	-0.0106	-0.0466	-3.2137	-0.2132	-13.2687
Upper 95%	277.2076	0.0036	0.9753	53.6891	0.1961	46.3845

Degrees of Freedom		Hypothesis Test	
Degrees of Freedom for Regression	5	Critical t-Statistic (99% confidence with df of 44)	2.6923
Degrees of Freedom for Residual	44	Critical t-Statistic (95% confidence with df of 44)	2.0154
Total Degrees of Freedom	49	Critical t-Statistic (90% confidence with df of 44)	1.6802

The Coefficients provide the estimated regression intercept and slopes. For instance, the coefficients are estimates of the true population b values in the following regression equation Y = b0 + b1X1 + b2X2 + ... + bnXn. The Standard Error measures how accurate the predicted Coefficients are, and the t-Statistics are the ratios of each predicted Coefficient to its Standard Error.

The t-Statistic is used in hypothesis testing, where we set the null hypothesis (Ho) such that the real mean of the Coefficient = 0, and the alternate hypothesis (Ha) such that the real mean of the Coefficient is not equal to 0. A t-test is is performed and the calculated t-Statistic is compared to the critical values at the relevant Degrees of Freedom for Residual. The t-test is very important as it calculates if each of the coefficients is statistically significant in the presence of the other regressors. This means that the t-test statistically verifies whether a regressor or independent variable should remain in the regression or it should be dropped.

The Coefficient is statistically significant if its calculated t-Statistic exceeds the Critical t-Statistic at the relevant degrees of freedom (df). The three main confidence levels used to test for significance are 90%, 95% and 99%. If a Coefficient's t-Statistic exceeds the Critical level, it is considered statistically significant. Alternatively, the p-Value calculates each t-Statistic's probability of occurrence, which means that the smaller the p-Value, the more significant the Coefficient. The usual significant levels for the p-Value are 0.01, 0.05, and 0.10, corresponding to the 99%, 95%, and 90% confidence levels.

The Coefficients with their p-Values highlighted in blue indicate that they are statistically significant at the 90% confidence or 0.10 alpha level, while those highlighted in red indicate that they are not statistically significant at any other alpha levels.

Analysis of Variance

	Sums of Squares	Mean of Squares	F-Statistic	p-Value	Hypothesis Test	
Regression	479388.49	95877.70	4.28	0.0029	Critical F-statistic (99% confidence with df of 5 and 44)	3.4651
Residual	985675.19	22401.71			Critical F-statistic (95% confidence with df of 5 and 44)	2.4270
Total	1465063.68				Critical F-statistic (90% confidence with df of 5 and 44)	1.9828

The Analysis of Variance (ANOVA) table provides an F-test of the regression model's overall statistical significance. Instead of looking at individual regressors as in the t-test, the F-test looks at all the estimated Coefficients' statistical properties. The F-Statistic is calculated as the ratio of the Regression's Mean of Squares to the Residual's Mean of Squares. The numerator measures how much of the regression is explained, while the denominator measures how much is unexplained. Hence, the larger the F-Statistic, the more significant the model. The corresponding p-Value is calculated to test the null hypothesis (Ho) where all the Coefficients are simultaneously equal to zero, versus the alternate hypothesis (Ha) that they are all simultaneously different from zero, indicating a significant overall regression model. If the p-Value is smaller than the 0.01, 0.05, or 0.10 alpha significance, then the regression is significant. The same approach can be applied to the F-Statistic by comparing the calculated F-Statistic with the critical F values at various significance levels.

Forecasting

Period	Actual (Y)	Forecast (F)	Error (E)
1	521.0000	299.5124	221.4876
2	367.0000	487.1243	(120.1243)
3	443.0000	353.2789	89.7211
4	365.0000	276.3296	88.6704
5	614.0000	776.1336	(162.1336)
6	385.0000	298.9993	86.0007
7	286.0000	354.8718	(68.8718)
8	397.0000	312.6155	84.3845
9	764.0000	529.7550	234.2450
10	427.0000	347.7034	79.2966
11	153.0000	266.2526	(113.2526)
12	231.0000	264.6375	(33.6375)
13	524.0000	406.8009	117.1991
14	328.0000	272.2226	55.7774
15	240.0000	231.7882	8.2118
16	286.0000	257.8862	28.1138
17	285.0000	314.9521	(29.9521)
18	569.0000	335.3140	233.6860
19	96.0000	282.0356	(186.0356)
20	498.0000	370.2062	127.7938
21	481.0000	340.8742	140.1258
22	468.0000	427.5118	40.4882
23	177.0000	274.5298	(97.5298)
24	198.0000	294.7795	(96.7795)
25	458.0000	295.2180	162.7820

RMSE: 140.4048

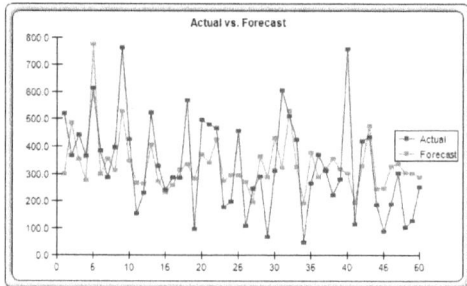

Actual vs. Forecast

Figure 5.40: Regression Results in Risk Simulator

Regression models can also take many functional forms or specifications. For instance, a linear regression will take the form of $Y = \beta_0 + \beta_1 X_1 + \beta_2 X_2 ... + \beta_n X_n + \varepsilon$ whereas a nonlinear regression can take the standard form of $Y = \beta_0 + \beta_1 ln(X_1) + \beta_2 ln(X_2)... + \beta_n ln(X_n) + \varepsilon$. However, there are other functional forms depending on the relationship of the variables. Typically, to test for functional form specifications, we revert to using a single independent variable at a time. The following are the most commonly used bivariate functional forms:

Linear	$Y = \beta_0 + \beta_1 X_1 + \varepsilon$
Linear Log	$Y = \beta_0 + \beta_1 ln(X_1) + \varepsilon$
Reciprocal	$Y = \beta_0 + \beta_1 (1/X_1) + \varepsilon$
Quadratic	$Y = \beta_0 + \beta_1 X_1 + \beta_2 X_1^2 + \varepsilon$
Log Linear	$ln(Y) = \beta_0 + \beta_1 X_1 + \varepsilon$
Log Reciprocal	$ln(Y) = \beta_0 + \beta_1 (1/X_1) + \varepsilon$
Log Quadratic	$ln(Y) = \beta_0 + \beta_1 X_1 + \beta_2 X_1^2 + \varepsilon$
Double Log	$ln(Y) = \beta_0 + \beta_1 ln(X_1) + \varepsilon$
Logistic	$Y/(1 - Y) = \beta_0 + \beta_1 X_1 + \varepsilon$

These functional forms are tested with one dependent variable and one independent variable. In the case of multivariate regressions, simply run the pairwise models and take the resulting functional forms and combine them into a more complex multivariate structure, with the understanding that when combining different functional forms, some previously statistically significant functions may drop out of the comprehensive model and integrate with other functions in the larger model. Figure 5.41 shows how these functional forms can be tested in BizStats, while Figure 5.42 shows their graphical representations (pay attention to the shape and the values on the axes).

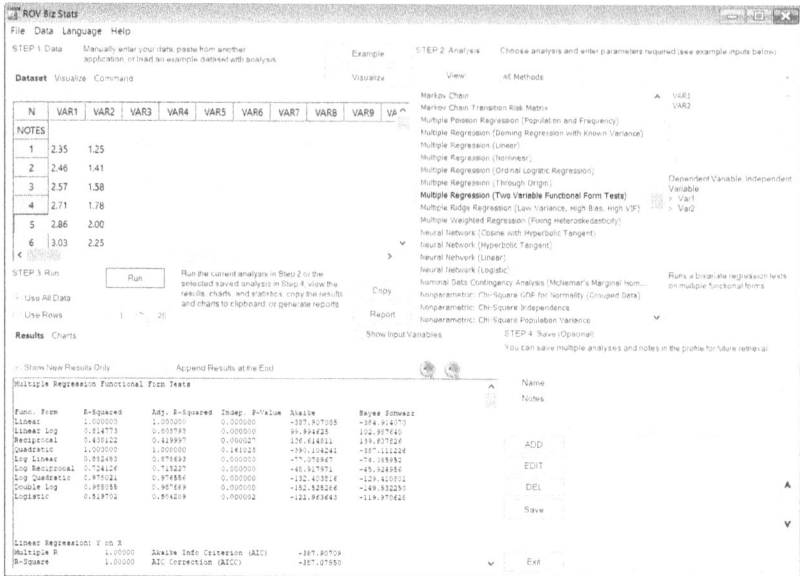

Figure 5.41: Bivariate Functional Forms

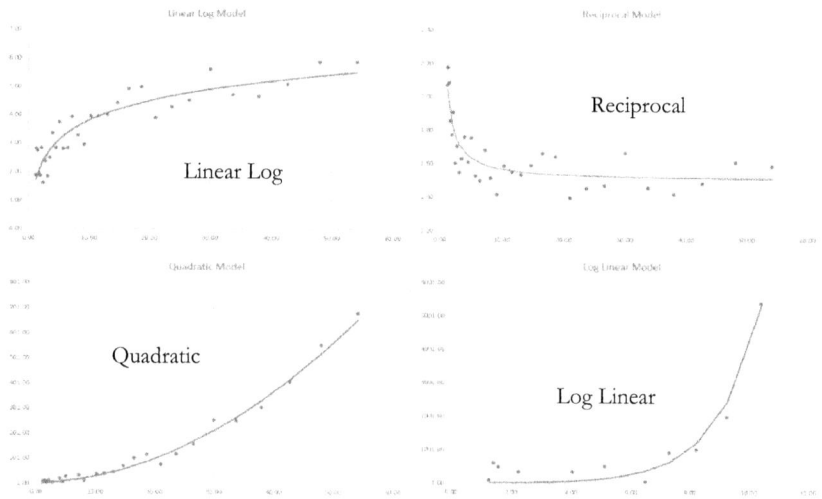

Figure 5.42: Graphical Representation of the Different Functional Forms (*continues*)

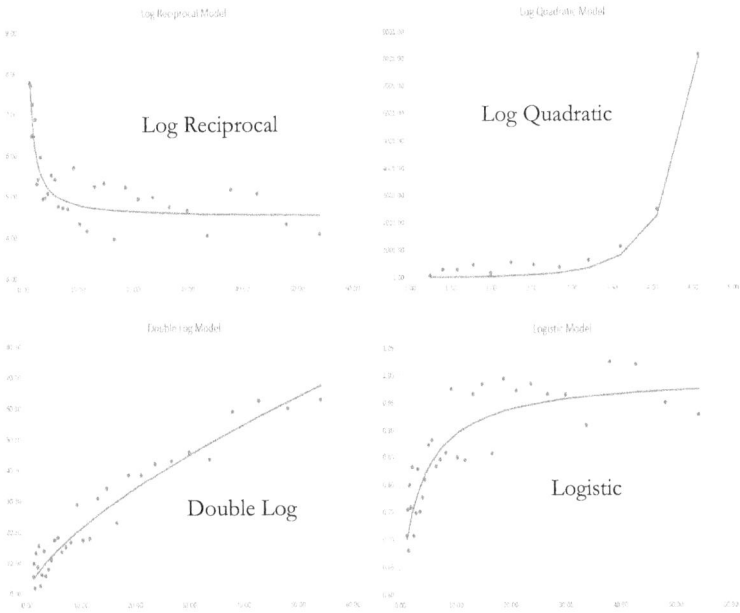

Figure 5.42: Graphical Representation of the Different Functional Forms (*continued*)

TESTS FOR MULTICOLLINEARITY AND HETEROSKEDASTICITY

Multicollinearity exists when there is a linear relationship between the independent variables. When this occurs, the regression equation cannot be estimated at all. In near collinearity situations, the estimated regression equation will be biased and provide inaccurate results. This situation is especially true when a stepwise regression approach is used, where the statistically significant independent variables will be thrown out of the regression mix earlier than expected, resulting in a regression equation that is neither efficient nor accurate. As an example, suppose the following multiple regression analysis exists, where $Y_i = \beta_1 + \beta_2 X_{2,i} + \beta_3 X_{3,i} + \varepsilon_i$. Then the estimated slopes can be calculated through

$$\hat{\beta}_2 = \frac{\sum Y_i X_{2,i} \sum X_{3,i}^2 - \sum Y_i X_{3,i} \sum X_{2,i} X_{3,i}}{\sum X_{2,i}^2 \sum X_{3,i}^2 - \left(\sum X_{2,i} X_{3,i}\right)^2}$$

$$\hat{\beta}_3 = \frac{\sum Y_i X_{3,i} \sum X_{2,i}^2 - \sum Y_i X_{2,i} \sum X_{2,i} X_{3,i}}{\sum X_{2,i}^2 \sum X_{3,i}^2 - \left(\sum X_{2,i} X_{3,i}\right)^2}$$

Now suppose that there is perfect multicollinearity, that is, there exists a perfect linear relationship between X_2 and X_3, such that $X_{3,i} = \lambda X_{2,i}$ for all positive values of λ. Substituting this linear relationship into the slope calculations for β_2, the result is indeterminate. In other words, we have

$$\hat{\beta}_2 = \frac{\sum Y_i X_{2,i} \sum \lambda^2 X_{2,i}^2 - \sum Y_i \lambda X_{2,i} \sum \lambda X_{2,i}^2}{\sum X_{2,i}^2 \sum \lambda^2 X_{2,i}^2 - \left(\sum \lambda X_{2,i}^2\right)^2} = \frac{0}{0}$$

The same calculation and results apply to β_3, which means that the multiple regression analysis breaks down and cannot be estimated given a perfect collinearity condition.

One quick test of the presence of multicollinearity in a multiple regression equation is that the R-squared value is relatively high while the t-statistics are relatively low. Another quick test is to create a correlation matrix between the independent variables. A high cross-correlation indicates a potential for multicollinearity. The rule of thumb is that a correlation with an absolute value greater than 0.75 is indicative of severe multicollinearity. Another test for multicollinearity is the use of the variance inflation factor (VIF), obtained by regressing each independent variable to all the other independent variables, obtaining the R-squared value, and calculating the VIF of that variable by estimating

$$VIF_i = \frac{1}{(1-R_i^2)}$$

A high VIF value indicates a high R-squared near unity. As a rule of thumb, a VIF value greater than 10 is usually indicative of destructive multicollinearity.

Another common violation is heteroskedasticity, that is, the variance of the errors increases over time. Figure 5.43 illustrates this case, where the width of the vertical data fluctuations increases or fans out over time. In this example, the data points have been changed to exaggerate the effect. However, in most time-series analyses, checking for heteroskedasticity is a much more difficult task. Figure 5.44 shows a comparative view of homoskedasticity (equal variance of the errors) versus heteroskedasticity.

If the variance of the dependent variable is not constant, then the error's variance will not be constant. The most common form of such heteroskedasticity in the dependent variable is that the variance of the dependent variable may increase as the mean of the dependent variable increases for data with positive independent and dependent variables.

Unless the heteroskedasticity of the dependent variable is pronounced, its effect will not be severe: the least-squares estimates will still be unbiased, and the estimates of the slope and intercept will either be normally distributed if the errors are normally distributed or at least normally distributed asymptotically (as the number of data points becomes large) if the errors are not normally distributed. The estimate for the variance of the slope and overall variance will be inaccurate, but the inaccuracy is not likely to be substantial if the independent-variable values are symmetric about their mean.

Heteroskedasticity of the dependent variable is usually detected informally by examining the X-Y scatter plot of the data before performing the regression. If both nonlinearity and unequal variances are present, employing a transformation of the dependent variable may have the effect of simultaneously improving the linearity and promoting equality of the variances. Otherwise, a weighted least-squares linear regression may be the preferred method of dealing with a nonconstant variance of the dependent variable.

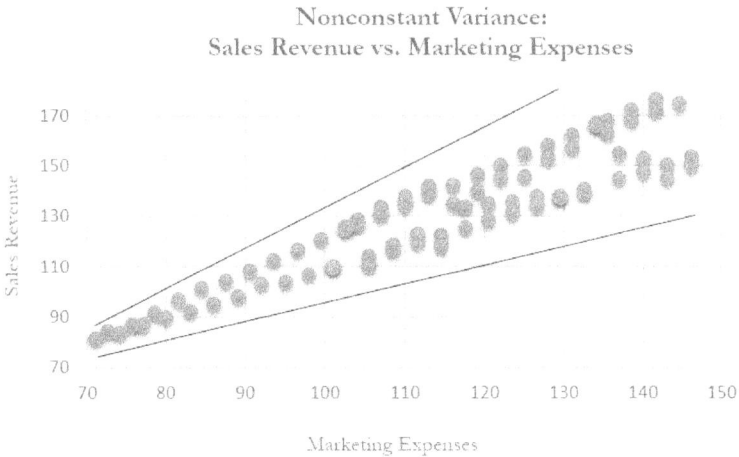

Figure 5.43: Scatter Plot Showing Heteroskedasticity with Nonconstant Variance

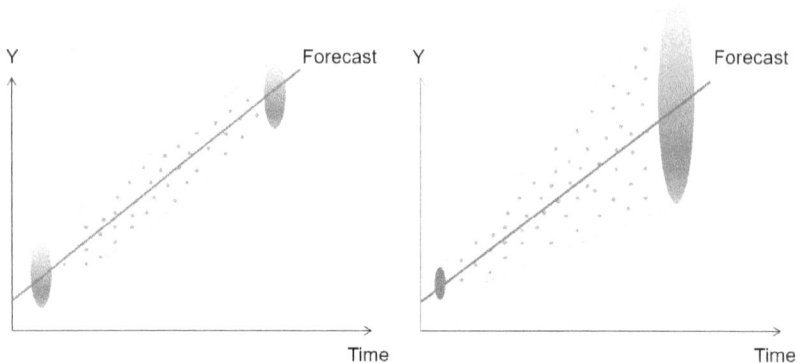

Figure 5.44: Homoskedasticity and Heteroskedasticity

Goodness-of-Fit

Goodness-of-fit statistics provide a glimpse into the accuracy and reliability of the estimated regression model. They usually take the form of a t-statistic, F-statistic, R-squared statistic, adjusted R-squared statistic, Durbin–Watson statistic, and their respective probabilities. (See the t-statistic, F-statistic, and critical Durbin–Watson tables at the end of this book for the corresponding critical values used later in this chapter). The following sections discuss some of the more common regression statistics and their interpretation.

The R-squared (R^2), or the coefficient of determination, is an error measurement that looks at the percent variation of the dependent variable that can be explained by the variation in the independent variable for regression analysis. The coefficient of determination can be calculated by:

$$R \ Squared = \frac{SS_{reg}}{SS_{total}} = 1 - \frac{SS_{error}}{SS_{total}} = 1 - \frac{\sum_{i=1}^{n}(y_i - \hat{y}_i)^2}{\sum_{i=1}^{n}(y_i - \bar{y})^2}$$

where the coefficient of determination is one less the ratio of the sums of squares of the errors (SSE) to the total sums of squares (TSS). In other words, the ratio of SSE to TSS is the unexplained portion of the analysis, thus, one less the ratio of SSE to TSS is the explained portion of the regression analysis.

Figure 5.45 provides a graphical explanation of the coefficient of determination. The estimated regression line is characterized by a series of predicted values ($\hat{Y}$); the average value of the dependent variable's data points is denoted $\bar{Y}$; and the individual data points are characterized by Y_i. Therefore, the total sum of squares, that is, the total variation in the data or the total variation about the average dependent value, is the total of the difference between the individual dependent values and its average (seen as the total squared distance of $Y_i - \bar{Y}$ in Figure 5.45). The explained sum of squares, the portion that is captured by the regression analysis, is the total of the differences between the regression's predicted value and the average dependent variable's dataset (seen as the total squared distance of $\hat{Y} - \bar{Y}$ in Figure 5.45). The difference between the total variation (TSS) and the explained variation (ESS) is the unexplained sums of squares, also known as the sums of squares of the errors (SSE).

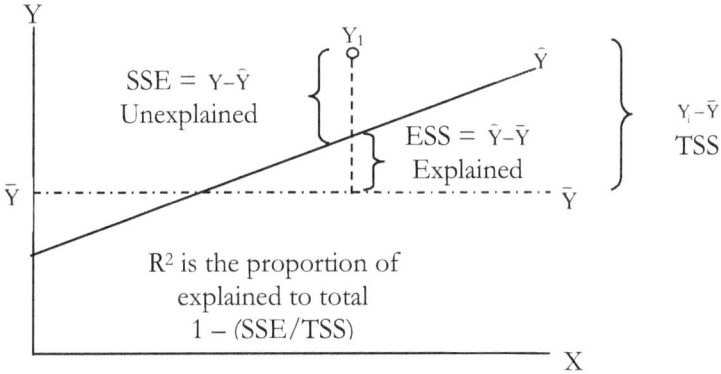

Figure 5.45: Explaining the Coefficient of Determination

Another related statistic, the adjusted coefficient of determination, or the adjusted R-squared ($\bar{R}^2$), corrects for the number of independent variables (k) in a multivariate regression through a degrees of freedom correction to provide a more conservative estimate:

$$\bar{R}^2 = 1 - \frac{\sum_{i=1}^{n}\left(Y_i - \frac{\hat{Y}_i)^2}{k-2}\right)}{\sum_{i=1}^{n}\left(Y_i - \frac{\bar{Y})^2}{k-1}\right)} = 1 - \frac{\frac{SSE}{k-2}}{\frac{TSS}{k-1}} = 1 - \left[\frac{(1-R^2)(n-1)}{n-k}\right]$$

The adjusted R-squared should be used instead of the regular R-squared in multivariate regressions because every time an independent variable is added into the regression analysis, the R-squared will increase; indicating that the percent variation explained has increased. This increase occurs even when nonsensical regressors are added. The adjusted R-squared takes the added regressors into account and penalizes the regression, providing a much better estimate of a regression model's goodness-of-fit. Next, the standard error of the regression $(SE_{y,x})$ and the standard errors of the intercept (SE_{b0}) and slope (SE_{b1}) are needed to compute the significant t-statistics for the regression coefficients:

$$SE_{y,x} = \sqrt{\frac{\Sigma(y_i - \hat{y})^2}{n - k}}$$

$$SE_{b1} = \frac{SE_{y,x}}{\sqrt{\Sigma x_i^2 - n(\bar{x})^2}} = \frac{SE_{y,x}}{\sqrt{\Sigma(x_i - \bar{x})^2}} = \sqrt{\frac{\frac{\Sigma(y_i - \hat{y}_i)^2}{n-k}}{\Sigma(x_i - \bar{x})^2}}$$

$$SE_{b0} = SE_{y,x}\sqrt{\frac{1}{n} + \frac{\bar{x}^2}{SS_x}} \qquad t = \frac{\hat{\beta}_i}{se_b}$$

Other goodness-of-fit statistics include the t-statistic and the F-statistic (Figure 5.46). The former is used to test if *each* of the estimated slope and intercept(s) is statistically significant, that is, if it is statistically significantly different from zero (therefore making sure that the intercept and slope estimates are statistically valid). The latter applies the same concepts but simultaneously for the entire regression equation including the intercept and slope(s). Using the previous example, the following illustrates how the t-statistic and F-statistic can be used in a regression analysis. (See the t-statistic and F-statistic tables at the end of the book for their corresponding critical values). It is assumed that the reader is somewhat familiar with hypothesis testing and tests of significance in basic statistics.

$$SS_{Reg} = \sum_{i=1}^{n}(\hat{y}_i - \bar{y})^2$$

$$SS_{Error} = \sum_{i=1}^{n}(y_i - \hat{y}_i)^2$$

$$SS_{Total} = \sum_{i=1}^{n}(y_i - \bar{y})^2$$

$$df_{Reg} = k - 1 \qquad\qquad df_{Error} = n - k - 1 \qquad\qquad df_{Tot} = n - 1$$

$$F_{k-1,n-k-1} = \frac{MS_{Treatment}}{MS_{Error}}$$

ANOVA

	df	SS	MS	F	Significance F
Regression	1	7.2014	7.2014	21.9747	0.0054
Residual	5	1.6386	0.3277		
Total	6	8.8400			

	Coefficients	Standard Error	t Stat	P-value
Intercept	4.3643	0.5826	7.4911	0.0007
X Variable 1	0.0845	0.0180	4.6877	0.0054

Figure 5.46: ANOVA and Goodness-of-Fit Table

Example: Given the information from the regression analysis output in Figure 5.46, interpret the following:

(a) Perform a hypothesis test on the slope and intercept to see if they are *each* significant at a two-tailed alpha (α) of 0.05.

The null hypothesis H_0 is such that the slope $\beta_1 = 0$ and the alternate hypothesis H_a is such that $\beta_1 \neq 0$. The t-statistic calculated is 4.6877, which exceeds the t-critical (2.9687 obtained from the t-statistic table at the end of this book) for a two-tailed alpha of 0.05 and degrees of freedom $n - k = 7 - 1 = 6$.[36] Therefore, the null hypothesis is rejected, and one can state that the slope is statistically significantly different from 0, indicating that the regression's estimate of the slope is statistically significant. This hypothesis test can also be performed by looking at the t-statistic's corresponding p-value (0.0054), which is less than the alpha of 0.05, which means the null hypothesis is rejected. The hypothesis test is then applied to the intercept, where the null hypothesis H_0 is such that the intercept $\beta_0 = 0$ and the alternate hypothesis H_a is such that $\beta_0 \neq 0$. The t-statistic calculated is 7.4911, which exceeds the critical *t* value of 2.9687 for $n - k$ (7 − 1 = 6) degrees of freedom, so, the null hypothesis is rejected indicating that the intercept is statistically significantly different from 0, meaning that the regression's estimate of the intercept if statistically significant. The calculated p-value (0.0007) is also less than the alpha level, which means the null hypothesis is also rejected.

(b) Perform a hypothesis test to see if both the slope and intercept are significant as a whole. In other words, if the estimated model is statistically significant at an alpha (α) of 0.05.

The simultaneous null hypothesis H_0 is such that $\beta_0 = \beta_1 = 0$ and the alternate hypothesis H_a is $\beta_0 \neq \beta_1 \neq 0$. The calculated F-value is 21.9747, which exceeds the critical F-value (5.99 obtained from the table at the end of this book) for k (1) degrees of freedom in the numerator and $n - k$ (7 - 1 = 6) degrees of freedom for the denominator, so the null hypothesis is rejected indicating that both the slope and intercept are simultaneously significantly different from 0 and that the model as a whole is statistically significant. This result is confirmed by the p-value of 0.0054 (significance of F), which is less than the alpha value, thereby rejecting the null hypothesis and confirming that the regression as a whole is statistically significant.

(c) Using Risk Simulator's regression output in Figure 5.47, interpret the R^2 value. How is it related to the correlation coefficient?

The calculated R^2 is 0.8146, meaning that 81.46% of the variation in the dependent variable can be explained by the variation in the independent variable. The R^2 is simply the square of the correlation coefficient, that is, the correlation coefficient between the independent and dependent variable is 0.9026.

Regression Statistics		
R-Squared (Coefficient of Determination)		0.8146
Adjusted R-Squared		0.7776
Multiple R (Multiple Correlation Coefficient)		0.9026
Standard Error of the Estimates (SEy)		0.5725
Regression Results		
	Intercept	Ad Size
Coefficients	4.3643	0.0845
Standard Error	0.5826	0.0180
t-Statistic	7.4911	4.6877
p-Value	0.0007	0.0054
Lower 5%	2.8667	0.0382
Upper 95%	5.8619	0.1309

Figure 5.47: Additional Regression Output from Risk Simulator

A manual computation example is now in order. To truly understand and peel back the mystique of regression analysis, it is important to see how the math works. Figure 5.48 illustrates an example dataset and its corresponding bivariate regression results in BizStats. Using the BizStats results, we can see how the manual calculations proceed in Figure 5.49. Finally, Figure 5.50 shows how the intercept and slope coefficients can be computed using matrix math. The use of matrix math falls outside the purview of this book, but, briefly, the coefficients can be computed using: $B = (X'X)^{-1}X'Y$. For regressions with an intercept coefficient, the X matrix requires a column of identities (the value of 1 is repeated for every row) prior to the x values (see columns AD and AE in Figure 5.50). This approach can be implemented in Excel using the following formula:

$$MMULT(MINVERSE(MMULT(TRANSPOSE(xmatrix),$$
$$xmatrix)),$$
$$MMULT(TRANSPOSE(xmatrix), ymatrix))$$

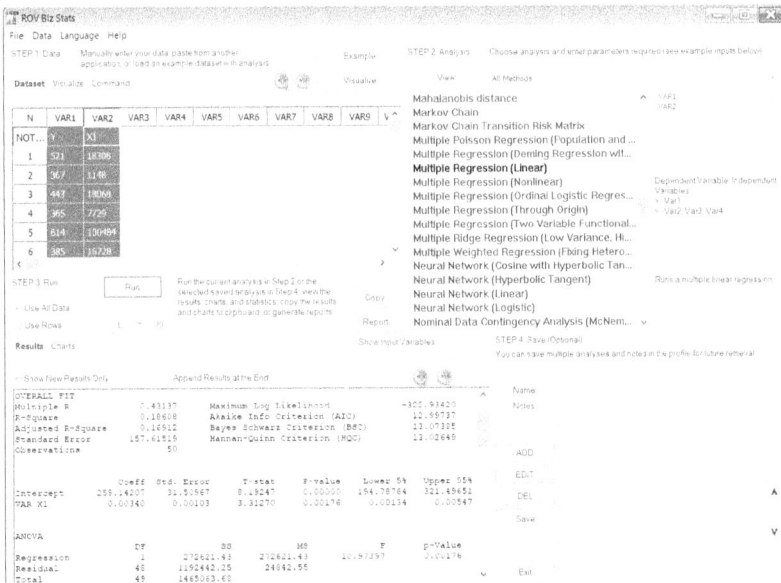

Figure 5.48: Bivariate Regression in BizStats

Manual Computations of Simple Regression, Coefficients, Standard Errors, Akaike, Bayes, Schwarz, Hannan Quinn, Adjusted R-Squared, Adjusted R-Squared, for Regression, T-Stat, etc.

N (Rows)	50	<< COUNTA(F6:F55)
K (Variables)	2	<< COUNTA(F5:G5)
Multiple R	0.43137	<< CORREL(F6:F55,N6:N55)
R-Squared	0.18608	<< J8*J8
Adj R-Squared	0.16912	<< 1-((1-J9)*(J5-1))/(J5-J6))
S.E. Estimates	157.61519	<< SQRT(P3/(J5-J6))
Max Likelihood	-322.93420	<< -J5/2*LN(2*PI())-J5/2*LN(P3/J5)-J5/2
Akaike Criterion	12.99737	<< 2*J13/J5+2*J6/J5
Bayes and Schwarz	13.07385	<< -2*J13/J5+J6*LN(J5)/J5
Hannan-Quinn	13.02649	<< -2*J13/J5+2*J6*LN(LN(J5))/J5
Slope B1	0.00340	<< R3/Q3
SE Slope	0.00103	<< J11/SQRT(Q3)
T-Stat B1	3.31270	<< J18/J19
P-value	0.00176	<< TDIST(J20,$J$5-$J$6,2)
CI Lower B1	0.00134	<< J18-TINV(0.05,$J$5-$J$6)*J19
CI Upper B1	0.00547	<< J18+TINV(0.05,$J$5-$J$6)*J19
Intercept	258.14207	<< AVERAGE($E$6:$E$55)-J18*AVERAGE(G6:G55)
SE Intercept Bo	31.50967	<< J11*(SQRT(1/J5+(AVERAGE(G6:G55)*AVERAGE(G6:G55))/Q3))
T-Stat Bo	8.19247	<< J25/J26
P-value	0.00000	<< TDIST(J27,$J$5-$J$6,2)
CI Upper Bo	194.78764	<< J25-TINV(0.05,$J$5-$J$6)*J26
CI Upper Bo	321.49651	<< J25+TINV(0.05,$J$5-$J$6)*J26
DF Regression	1	<< J6-1
DF Residual	48	<< J5-J6
DF Total	49	<< J5-1
SS Regression	272621.43	<< P3
SS Residual	1192442.25	<< S3
SS Total	1465063.68	<< J35/J32
MS Regression	272621.43	<< J36/J33
MS Residual	24842.55	<< J38/J39
F Statistic	10.97397	<< FDIST(J40,J32,J33)
P-value	0.00176	<< J35/J37
Eta-Square	0.18608	
MATRIX:	258.14207	<< =MMULT(MINVERSE(MMULT(TRANSPOSE(AD94:AE143),AD94:AE143)),MMULT(TRANSPOSE(AD94:AE143),W94:W143))
	0.00340	AD94:AE143)),MMULT(TRANSPOSE(AD94:AE143),W94:W143))

Y	X1	Y Pred	Error	SS Error: 1192442.249 SUM(O6:O55) Error^2	23513989216.42 SUM(P6:P55) (X - X Avg)^2	80065082.16 SUM(Q6:Q55) (X - X Avg)(Y - Y Avg)	SS Total: 1465063.68 SUM(R6:R55) (Y - Y Avg)^2	SS Regression: 272621.43 SUM(S6:S55) (Y Pred - Y Avg)^2
521	18308	320.48	200.52	40207.96	11286509.01	-635221.82	35751.25	130.86
367	1148	262.05	104.95	11014.29	4210151521.81	-719825.46	1230.61	4881.68
443	18068	319.66	123.34	15211.87	12956688.21	-399836.90	12338.77	150.22
365	7729	284.46	80.54	6486.80	194282897.33	-461086.90	1094.29	2252.52
614	100484	600.29	13.71	187.97	6212034366.93	22232547.04	79569.43	72022.39
385	16728	315.10	69.90	4885.89	24399055.41	-262190.78	2817.49	282.88
286	14630	307.96	-21.96	482.12	49526969.25	323163.84	2108.65	574.22
397	4008	271.79	125.21	15677.72	311859353.01	-1149282.86	4235.41	3615.70
764	38927	390.69	373.31	139361.53	297888959.49	7457467.48	18669.13	3453.73
427	22322	334.15	92.85	8621.41	428317.89	62226.00	9040.21	4.97
153	3711	270.78	-117.78	13871.66	3244373287.77	3212784.14	32012.37	3738.34
231	3136	268.82	-37.82	1430.36	343417974.77	1870203.02	10184.85	3981.59
524	50508	430.12	93.88	8813.13	817727133.01	5539675.56	36894.73	9643.57
328	28886	356.50	-28.50	812.18	52106164.77	-28296.36	15.37	604.12
240	16996	316.01	-76.01	5778.04	21823285.97	429407.96	8449.29	253.02
286	13035	302.53	-16.53	273.12	74520746.85	396406.24	2108.65	863.99
285	12973	302.32	-17.32	299.81	75595025.81	407947.82	2201.49	876.45
569	16309	313.67	255.33	65191.27	28713950.93	-1270402.66	56206.93	332.91
96	5227	275.94	-179.94	32378.40	270291355.49	3878652.20	55658.25	3133.76
498	19235	323.64	174.36	30402.38	5917250.85	-403996.24	27582.57	68.60
481	44487	409.62	71.38	5095.07	520727754.69	3401925.10	22224.85	6037.32
468	44213	408.69	59.31	3518.00	508297766.61	3067986.20	18517.77	5893.21
177	23619	338.56	-161.56	26103.16	3808196.13	-302320.18	24000.21	44.15
198	9106	289.15	-91.15	8307.95	157739287.17	1682241.44	17934.57	1829.45
458	24917	342.98	115.02	13228.59	10558990.29	409691.92	15896.17	122.42
108	3872	271.33	-163.33	26675.46	316681243.89	3984777.32	50140.17	3671.61
246	8945	288.60	-42.60	1814.74	161863024.05	1093120.64	7382.25	1876.64
291	2373	266.22	24.78	613.94	372279273.81	789532.58	1674.45	4316.21
68	7128	282.41	-214.41	45972.89	211398223.41	3837275.40	69653.77	2450.95
311	23824	338.58	-27.58	760.75	3827735.73	-40929.14	437.65	44.38
606	5242	275.99	330.01	108905.89	269798364.29	4501912.00	75119.85	3128.04
512	92629	573.54	-61.54	3787.62	5035528805.33	12778739.72	32428.81	58381.97
426	28795	356.19	69.81	4873.58	50800686.05	670551.44	8851.05	588.98
47	4487	273.42	-226.42	51266.15	295170954.69	4895079.46	81179.41	3422.22
265	48799	424.30	-159.30	25377.31	736116121.73	-1815637.30	4478.29	8534.54
370	14067	306.04	63.96	4090.86	57768208.29	-289428.56	1450.09	669.77
312	12693	301.36	10.64	113.17	80542368.21	178772.84	396.81	933.81
222	62184	469.88	-247.88	61443.73	16415833090.93	4453569.28	12082.41	19032.54
280	9153	289.31	-9.31	86.64	1556613711.41	649754.92	2695.69	1815.78
759	14250	306.66	452.34	204608.50	3167882.98	-3167882.98	182397.73	637.90
114	3680	270.67	-156.67	24546.26	3235515952.5	3919844.72	47489.13	3751.26
419	18063	319.65	99.35	9871.11	12992708.61	-313883.34	7582.93	150.64

Figure 5.49: Bivariate Regression Manual Computations

	W	X	Y	Z	AA	AB	AC	AD	AE
84	**MATRIX APPROACH:**								
85	258.14207	<< =MMULT(MINVERSE(MMULT(TRANSPOSE(AD94:AE143),							
86	0.00340	AD94:AE143)),MMULT(TRANSPOSE(AD94:AE143),W94:W143))							
87									
88									
89	*Using Excel:*		0.43137	<< =CORREL(W94:W143,X94:X143)					
90	**Correlation R**		0.43137	<< =SUM(AA94:AA143)/SQRT(SUM(AB94:AB143)*SUM(AC94:AC143))					
91	**R-Squared**		0.18608	<< =Y90*Y90					
92									

	Y	Y Pred	Y-Mu	Y Pred - Mu	Product	Sq Y-Mu	Sq Y Pred - Mu	UNIT	X
93	Y	Y Pred	Y-Mu	Y Pred - Mu	Product	Sq Y-Mu	Sq Y Pred - Mu	UNIT	X
94	521	320.481	189.0800	-11.4392	-2162.93	35751.2	130.8559005	1	18308
95	367	262.051	35.0800	-69.8690	-2451	1230.61	4881.675636	1	1148
96	443	319.664	111.0800	-12.2564	-1361.44	12338.8	150.2199752	1	18068
97	365	284.459	33.0800	-47.4607	-1570	1094.29	2252.517892	1	7729
98	614	600.290	282.0800	268.3699	75701.8	79569.1	72022.38978	1	100484
99	385	315.101	53.0800	-16.8191	-892.759	2817.49	282.8828972	1	16728
100	286	307.957	-45.9200	-23.9628	1100.37	2108.65	574.2161864	1	14630
101	397	271.789	65.0800	-60.1307	-3913.31	4235.41	3615.700518	1	4008
102	764	390.688	432.0800	58.7684	25392.7	186693	3453.727633	1	38927
103	427	334.148	95.0800	2.2284	211.88	9040.21	4.965922002	1	22322
104	153	270.778	-178.9200	-61.1420	10939.5	32012.4	3738.341677	1	3711
105	231	268.820	-100.9200	-63.0999	6368.04	10184.8	3981.5915	1	3136
106	524	430.122	192.0800	98.2017	18862.6	36894.7	9643.57459	1	50508
107	328	356.499	-3.9200	24.5788	-96.3491	15.3664	604.1194055	1	28886
108	240	316.013	-91.9200	-15.9066	1462.13	8449.29	253.0194	1	16996
109	286	302.526	-45.9200	-29.3938	1349.76	2108.65	863.9942987	1	13035
110	285	302.315	-46.9200	-29.6049	1389.06	2201.49	876.4494999	1	12973
111	569	313.674	237.0800	-18.2458	-4325.72	56206.9	332.9098398	1	16309
112	96	275.940	-235.9200	-55.9800	13206.8	55658.2	3133.760731	1	5227
113	498	323.637	166.0800	-8.2828	-1375.61	27582.6	68.6046667	1	19235
114	481	409.620	149.0800	77.7002	11583.5	22224.8	6037.322896	1	44487
115	468	408.687	136.0800	76.7672	10446.5	18517.8	5893.209488	1	44213
116	177	338.565	-154.9200	6.6447	-1029.4	24000.2	44.15226477	1	23619
117	198	289.148	-133.9200	-42.7720	5728.03	17934.6	1829.445386	1	9106
118	458	342.984	126.0800	11.0644	1395	15896.2	122.4210411	1	24917
119	108	271.326	-223.9200	-60.5938	13568.2	50140.2	3671.60557	1	3872
120	246	288.600	-85.9200	-43.3202	3722.07	7382.25	1876.641551	1	8945
121	291	266.222	-40.9200	-65.6979	2688.36	1674.45	4316.209696	1	2373
122	68	282.413	-263.9200	-49.5071	13065.9	69653.8	2450.953157	1	7128
123	311	338.582	-20.9200	6.6617	-139.364	437.646	44.37880709	1	23624
124	606	275.991	274.0800	-55.9289	-15329	75119.8	3128.044986	1	5242
125	512	573.544	180.0800	241.6236	43511.6	32428.8	58381.9723	1	92629
126	426	356.189	94.0800	24.2690	2283.23	8851.05	588.983672	1	28795
127	47	273.420	-284.9200	-58.4997	16667.7	81179.4	3422.215058	1	4487
128	265	424.303	-66.9200	92.3826	-6182.24	4478.29	8534.53782	1	48799
129	370	306.040	38.0800	-25.8798	-985.504	1450.09	669.7651958	1	14067
130	312	301.362	-19.9200	-30.5583	608.721	396.806	933.8090381	1	12693
131	222	469.878	-109.9200	137.9585	-15164.4	12082.4	19032.53619	1	62184
132	280	289.308	-51.9200	-42.6120	2212.41	2695.69	1815.780967	1	9153
133	759	306.663	427.0800	-25.2567	-10786.6	182397	637.9012775	1	14250
134	114	270.672	-217.9200	-61.2475	13347.1	47489.1	3751.260494	1	3680
135	419	319.647	87.0800	-12.2735	-1068.77	7582.93	150.6375961	1	18063
136	435	479.848	103.0800	147.9283	15248.4	10625.5	21882.77953	1	65112
137	186	296.755	-145.9200	-35.1653	5131.31	21292.6	1236.594895	1	11340
138	87	273.645	-244.9200	-58.2750	14272.7	59985.8	3395.972302	1	4553
139	188	356.751	-143.9200	24.8308	-3573.65	20713	616.5691474	1	28960
140	303	323.521	-28.9200	-8.3986	242.886	836.366	70.53586613	1	19201
141	102	283.792	-229.9200	-48.1281	11065.6	52863.2	2316.311889	1	7533
142	127	347.840	-204.9200	15.9199	-3262.31	41992.2	253.4442073	1	26343
143	251	263.730	-80.9200	-68.1903	5517.96	6548.05	4649.920445	1	1641

Figure 5.50: Regression Using Matrix Math

Apart from the standard multivariate regression and bivariate regressions (and their corresponding functional forms), there are other regression variations and regression-related methods. The following provides a summary of the related models you can run in BizStats.

- **Cointegration Test or Engle–Granger Cointegration Test.** The Engle–Granger test is used to identify if there exists any cointegration of two nonstationary time-series variables. First of all, the two variables need to be nonstationary, otherwise a simple linear and nonlinear correlation would typically suffice in identifying if there is a co-movement relationship between them. If two time-series variables are nonstationary to order one, $I(1)$, and if a linear combination of these two series is stationary at $I(0)$, then these two variables are, by definition, cointegrated. Many macroeconomic data are $I(1)$, and conventional forecasting and modeling methods do not apply due to the nonstandard properties of unit root $I(1)$ processes. This cointegration test can be applied to identify the presence of cointegration, and if confirmed to exist, a subsequent Error Correction Model can then be used to forecast the time-series variables.

- **Cox Regression.** Cox's proportional hazards model for survival time is used to test the effect of several variables at the time a specified event takes to happen. For example, in medical research, we can use the Cox model to investigate the association between the survival time of patients using one or more predictor variables.

- **Discriminate Analysis (Linear and Nonlinear).** Discriminant Analysis is related to ANOVA and multivariate regression analysis, where it attempts to model one dependent variable as a linear or nonlinear combination of other independent variables. A Discriminant Analysis has continuous independent variables and a categorical dependent variable. Think of the discriminant analysis as a statistical analysis using a linear or nonlinear discriminant function to assign data to one of two or more categories or groups.

- **Endogeneity Test with Two-Stage Least Squares (Durbin–Wu–Hausman).** This tests if a regressor is endogenous using the two-stage least squares (2SLS) method and applying the Durbin–Wu–Hausman test. A Structural Model and a (2SLS) Reduced Model are both computed in a 2SLS paradigm, and a Hausman test is administered to test if one of the variables is endogenous.

- **Endogenous Model (Instrumental Variables with Two-Stage Least Squares).** If the regressor is endogenous, we can apply a two-stage least squares (2SLS) with instrumental variables (IV) on a bivariate model to estimate the model.

- **Error Correction Model (Engle–Granger).** This is also known as an Error Correction Model where we assume that the variables exhibit cointegration. That is, if two time-series variables are nonstationary in the first order, I(1), and when both variables are found to be cointegrated (the I(0) relationship is stationary), we can run an error correction model for estimating short-term and long-term effects of a time series on another. The error correction comes from previous periods' deviation from a long-run equilibrium, where the error influences its short-run dynamics.

- **Granger Causality.** This test is applied to see if one variable Granger causes another variable and vice versa, using restricted autoregressive lags and unrestricted distributive lag models. Predictive causality in finance and economics is tested by measuring the ability to predict the future values of a time series using prior values of another time series. A simpler definition might be that a time-series variable X Granger causes another time-series variable Y if predictions of the value of Y are based solely on its own prior values and on the prior values of X, and these are comparatively better than predictions of Y based solely on its own past values. The causality loop is modeled using these data leads and lags.

- **Multiple Poisson Regression (Population and Frequency).** The Poisson Regression is like the Logit Regression in that the dependent variables can only take on non-negative values, but also that the underlying distribution of the data is a Poisson distribution, drawn from known population sizes.

- **Multiple Regression (Deming Regression with Known Variance).** In regular multivariate regressions, the dependent variable Y is modeled and predicted by independent variables X_i with some error ε. However, in a Deming regression, we further assume that the data collected for Y and X have additional uncertainties and errors, or variances, that are used to provide a more relaxed fit in a Deming model.

- **Multiple Regression (Ordinal Logistic Regression).** This model runs a multivariate ordinal logistic regression with two dependent variables and multiple independent variables. Ordinal logistic regression models the relationship between one or more predictors and an ordinal response variable. The ordinal or categorical variable needs to have three or more levels with a natural ordering, such as those in a survey, with coded responses for strongly disagree, disagree, neutral, agree, and strongly agree.

- **Multiple Regression (Through Origin).** This model runs a multiple linear regression but without an intercept. This method is used when an intercept may not conceptually or theoretically apply to the data being modeled. Examples include a factory cannot produce outputs if the equipment is not running, or the gravitational force of a large object does not exist when there is zero mass.

- **Multiple Ridge Regression (Low Variance, High Bias, High VIF).** A Ridge Regression model's results come with a higher bias than an Ordinary Least Squares standard multiple regression but with less variance. It is more suitable in situations with high Variance Inflation Factors and multicollinearity or when there is a high number of variables compared to data points. Clearly, in the case of high VIF with multicollinearity, some of the highly colinear variables will need to be dropped, but for whatever reason these colinear variables need to be included, a ridge-based regression is a better alternative.

- **Multiple Weighted Regression for Heteroskedasticity.** The Multivariate Regression on Weighted Variables is used to correct for heteroskedasticity in all the variables. The weights used to adjust these variables are the user input standard deviations. Clearly, this method is only applicable for time-series variables, due to the heteroskedastic assumption.

- **Stepwise Regression.** When there are multiple independent variables vying to be in a multivariate regression model, it can be cumbersome to identify and specify the correct combinations of variables in the model. A stepwise regression can be run to systematically identify which variables are statistically significant and should be inserted into the final model. Several simple algorithms exist for running stepwise regressions:

  - **Stepwise Regression (Backward).** In the backward method, we run a regression with Y on all X variables and, reviewing each variable's p-value, systematically eliminate the variable with the largest p-value. Then run a regression again, repeating each time until all p-values are statistically significant.

  - **Stepwise Regression (Correlation).** In the correlation method, the dependent variable Y is correlated to all the independent variables X and starting with the X variable with the highest absolute correlation value, a regression is run. Then subsequent X variables are added until the p-values indicate that the new X variable is no longer statistically significant. This approach is quick and simple but does not account for interactions among variables, and an X variable, when added, will statistically overshadow other variables.

  - **Stepwise Regression (Forward).** In the forward method, we first correlate Y with all X variables, run a regression for Y on the highest absolute value correlation of X, and obtain the fitting errors. Then, correlate these errors with the remaining X variables and choose the highest absolute value correlation among this remaining set and run another regression. Repeat the process until the p-value for the latest X variable coefficient is no longer statistically significant and then stop the process.

- **Stepwise Regression (Forward and Backward).** In the forward and backward method, apply the forward method to obtain three X variables, and then apply the backward approach to see if one of them needs to be eliminated because it is statistically insignificant. Repeat the forward method and then the backward method until all remaining X variables are considered.

BEYOND MULTIPLE REGRESSION: STRUCTURAL EQUATION MODELING (SEM) WITH PARTIAL LEAST SQUARES (PLS) ON PATH ESTIMATION

Another extension to multiple regression analysis is the Structural Equation Model (SEM), which uses the Partial Least Squares (PLS) method. SEM is typically used to solve path-dependent structures such as the one illustrated in Figure 5.51. Suppose that there are five variables in your research, where the final dependent variable is technology acceptance (VAR5). We are trying to determine what drives and predicts the level of technology acceptance in different organizations. If we collected data on the corporate culture of the various organizations (VAR1) using a Likert scale in terms of openness to new technology, we can run a simple bivariate regression. However, we also understand from organizational behavior theory and decision theory that other intervening variables can also contribute to an organization's acceptance of new technology, such as what types of decisions are relegated to technology, that is, the decision criticality (VAR2) and whether new artificial intelligence (AI) technology is used or more traditional technology is used (VAR3). For example, letting a smart AI computer system make frequent orders of paper clips is a lot less critical than allowing AI full and complete access to the nation's nuclear arsenal. Mistakes made on the former have little consequence compared to the latter. However, we also know from technology acceptance theory that there are other latent and hidden effects that drive technology trust (VAR4). If a technology is not trusted, then the technology is probably not going to be accepted for use in the organization. Technology trust might include whether the AI technology has transparent algorithms or comes as a black box.

In such a research paradigm, one might be inclined to simply run the first four independent variables on the fifth dependent variable. That would be a major mistake and the results will be erroneous at best, because VAR2, VAR3, and VAR4 are endogenous. That is, based on various theories, we know that the type of organization drives the types of decision criticality (a local office-supplies store versus the U.S. Department of Defense, VAR1 drives VAR2), the type of advanced AI technology employed (paperclip reordering system has rudimentary code versus national cybersecurity defense against state-sponsored actors that requires much more sophisticated AI technology, VAR1 drives VAR3), and so forth. In addition, the level of decision criticality drives whether AI is needed (VAR2 drives VAR3). Whether AI is applied will drive trust in the new technology (VAR3 drives VAR4) and then acceptance. Figure 5.51 shows the tangled web known as a path model. Simple multiple regression analysis cannot be used. Instead, partial least squares or sequential regression models will need to be applied. The SEM approach is used to handle such complex path models.

In typical path models, the pathways move in a single direction, where one or multiple paths can originate from a box and one or many paths can recombine into a box, and the pathways all end at the main dependent model (in this example, that would be VAR5). The direct effects on VAR5 are pathways C, F, I, and J, from the four independent variables. However, these variables also have indirect effects (e.g., VAR3 has indirect impacts on VAR5 through path HJ; VAR2 has indirect effects on VAR5 through paths EJ, GI, and GHJ; and VAR1 has indirect impacts on VAR5 through paths AEJ, AF, AGI, AGHJ, BJ, DHJ, and DI). Notice that VAR4 does not have any indirect effects on VAR5, only a single direct impact path. The summation of the direct and indirect effects equals the total effects.

Due to the existence of endogenous variables (the tangled web where an independent variable can also be a dependent variable), the regular regression coefficients would not mean much as these would change depending on the combinations of variables modeled. Therefore, in path models, we use the Standardized Beta coefficients instead. Instead of a unitary impact of the independent variable on the dependent variable, these standardized beta estimates look at the movement of one standard deviation of the independent variable on the number of beta standard deviations of the dependent variable. These are the numerical values in Figure 5.51. You can also add in p-values (typically typeset in a smaller font in parenthesis) to show if a certain path is statistically significant or not. The variables denoted as D are the disturbances or errors in the model and are typically computed as $D = \sqrt{1 - R^2}$. Figure 5.52 shows the BizStats procedure for running an SEM PLS model and the model results. Pay close attention to how the SEM inputs are entered in BizStats in Figure 5.52. Look for the bold letters beside the results to identify where they are along the SEM path model. As mentioned, the total effect is the sum of the direct and indirect effects. For example, the indirect effects (see the bottom section of Figure 5.52) are:

```
VAR1 on VAR5: 0.94828 = (0.48406 × -0.56521 × 0.43355) +
                        (0.48406 × 0.2447) + (0.48406 ×
                        0.00253 × 0.45264) + (0.48406 ×
                        0.00253 × 0.98713 × 0.43355) +
                        (0.15673 × 0.43355) + (0.99864 ×
                        0.98713 × 0.43355) + (0.99864 ×
                        0.45264)

VAR2 on VAR5: -0.24282 = (-0.56521 × 0.43355) + (0.00253
                        × 0.45264) + (0.00253 × 0.98713
                        × 0.43355)

VAR3 on VAR5: 0.42798 = (0.98713 × 0.43355)

VAR4 on VAR5: no indirect effects; only direct effects
```

The results indicate that the use of AI technology and trust in said technology has the highest direct impact on whether the technology is accepted and widely used in the organization. However, the organizational structure and culture also have the largest total impact, where the bulk of the impact comes from indirect sources.

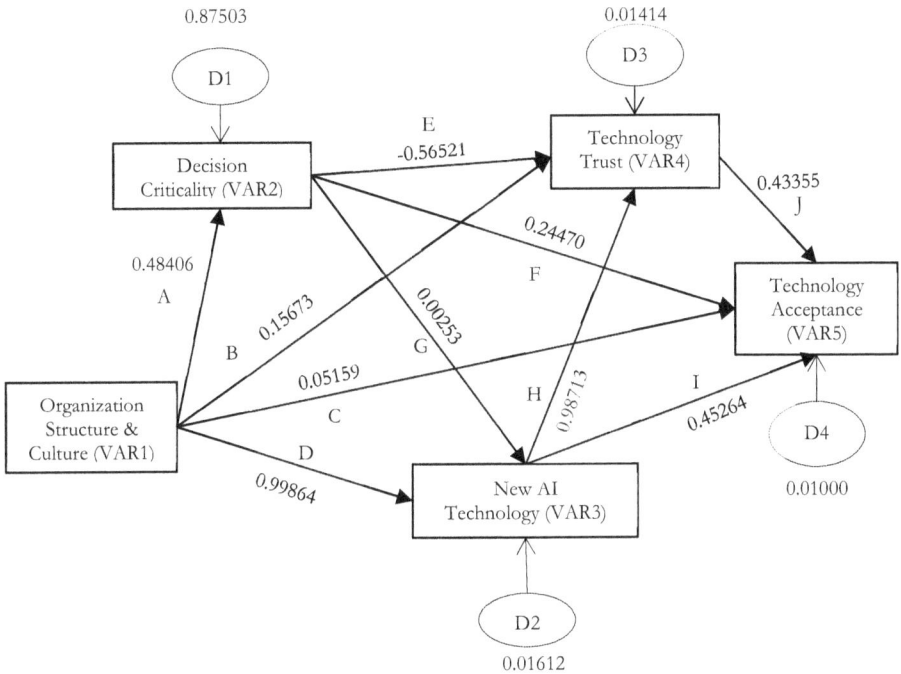

Figure 5.51: Structural Equation Model and Partial Least Squares

```
Model Inputs:
VAR1;VAR2; VAR3; VAR4; VAR5
VAR1;VAR2; VAR3; VAR4
VAR1;VAR2; VAR3
VAR1;VAR2
```

Structural Equations Model with Partial Least Squares
Direct Effects Path

Dep. Var:	VAR5	Tech Acceptance		
R-Square	0.99990	Disturbance	0.01000	

Var Name	Ind. Var	Coeff	P-Value	Std. Beta	
Intercept		0.34030	0.34366		
Culture Org.	VAR1	0.51562	0.21713	0.05159	**C**
Criticality	VAR2	7.74992	0.00000	0.24470	**F**
New AI Tech	VAR3	1.68941	0.00000	0.45264	**I**
Tech Trust	VAR4	15.49786	0.00000	0.43355	**J**

Partial Direct Effects Path

Dep. Var:	VAR4	Tech Trust		
R-Square	0.99980	Disturbance	0.01414	

Var Name	Ind. Var	Coeff	P-Value	Std. Beta	
Intercept		0.11916	0.00000		
Culture Org.	VAR1	0.04382	0.17074	0.15673	**B**
Criticality	VAR2	-0.50070	0.00000	-0.5652	**E**
New AI Tech	VAR3	0.10307	0.00000	0.98713	**H**

Partial Direct Effects Path

Dep. Var:	VAR3	New AI Tech		
R-Square	0.99974	Disturbance	0.01612	

Var Name	Ind. Var	Coeff	P-Value	Std. Beta	
Intercept		0.89306	0.00036		
Culture Org.	VAR1	2.67416	0.00000	0.99864	**D**
Criticality	VAR2	0.02146	0.35062	0.00253	**G**

Partial Direct Effects Path

Dep. Var:	VAR2	Criticality		
R-Square	0.23432	Disturbance	0.87503	

Var Name	Ind. Var	Coeff	P-Value	Std. Beta	
Intercept		-0.03350	0.98190		
Culture Org.	VAR1	0.15276	0.00037	0.48406	**A**

Total Effects
Dep. Var VAR5   Tech Acceptance

Var Name	Ind. Var	Coeff	P-Value	Std. Beta
Culture Org.	VAR1	9.99326	0.00000	0.99987
Criticality	VAR2	0.05966	0.47689	0.00188
New AI Tech	VAR3	3.28678	0.00000	0.88061
Tech Trust	VAR4	15.49786	0.00000	0.43355

Summary Standardized Path Effects
Dep. Var VAR5   Tech Acceptance

Var Name		Direct		Indirect	Total
Culture Org.	VAR1	0.05159	**C**	**0.94828**	0.99987
Criticality	VAR2	0.24470	**F**	**-0.2428**	0.00188
New AI Tech	VAR3	0.45264	**I**	**0.42798**	0.88061
Tech Trust	VAR4	0.43355	**J**	**0.00000**	0.43355

Figure 5.52: SEM PLS Results

Endogeneity occurs when a dependent variable in a model is also the independent variable in another model. The simplest example would be the structural equation model with partial least squares as shown previously. The SEM model is best used when there are complex combinations of pathways. Sometimes there are only two equations in the system, and, hence, these can be solved using a simultaneous equations model approach. Recall from basic algebra when you have two equations and two unknowns, you can solve them using simultaneous equations. The same applies here when we have a system of two equations.

Suppose we have two equations:

$$M_t = a_0 + a_1 Y_t + u_{1t}$$

$$Y_t = b_0 + b_1 M_t + b_2 I_t + u_{2t}$$

M_t is money supply at time t, Y_t is income at time t, and I_t is the investment at time t. We see that M depends on Y in the first equation, but Y depends on M and I in the second equation. In this example, M and Y are endogenous or jointly determined, meaning that they cannot be modeled by themselves, and must be modeled together or simultaneously. However, I is an exogenous variable, which can be determined outside of this system of equations. In this example, the number of endogenous variables (k) is 2 and the number of exogenous variables (r) is 1. If $r = k - 1$, then it is considered to be exactly identified. The system of equations is overidentified or underidentified if r exceeds or is smaller than $k - 1$. The system can only be modeled when the system is exactly identified or overidentified. Figure 5.53 illustrates the two-stage least squares model. The calculated model returns the following: $M_t = 85.853 + 0.132Y_t$.

As another example, when we have an overidentification system, where the second equation above has an additional exogenous variable G, such that:

$$Y_t = b_0 + b_1 M_t + b_2 I_t + b_3 G_t + u_{2t}$$

The result is shown in Figure 5.54, where the computed model is: $M_t = 84.398 + 0.133Y_t$. The two-stage least squares approach involves regressing each of the endogenous variables on all the exogenous variables to obtain the predicted values of these endogenous variables to estimate the structural equations model.

Sometimes, with random data, it is hard to determine if a certain variable is endogenous. The Durbin–Wu–Hausman test can be used to determine endogeneity. For example, Figure 5.55 illustrates the test, where the null hypothesis is that there is no endogeneity. With a low p-value of 0.003, we reject this null hypothesis and conclude that there is, indeed, endogeneity among the variables.

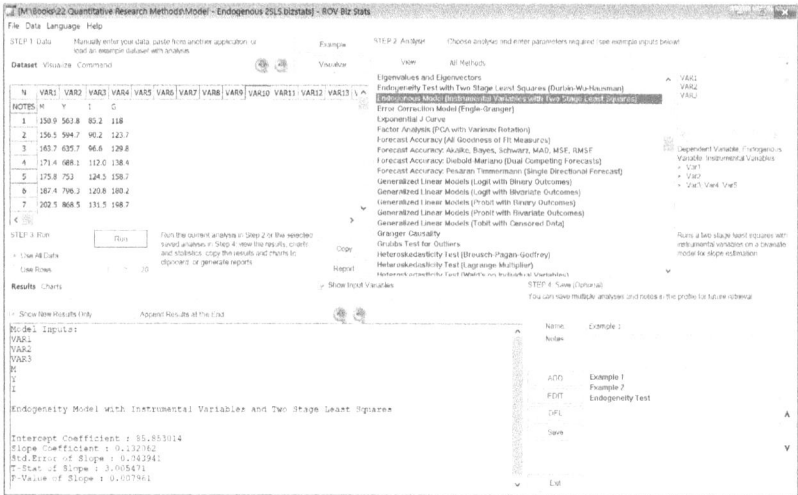

```
Model Inputs:
VAR1
VAR2
VAR3
```

Endogeneity Model Results with Instrumental Variables and Two Stage Least Squares

```
Intercept Coefficient: 85.853014
Slope Coefficient: 0.132062
Std. Error of Slope: 0.043941
T-Stat of Slope: 3.005471
P-Value of Slope: 0.007961
```

Figure 5.53: Two-Stage Least Squares I

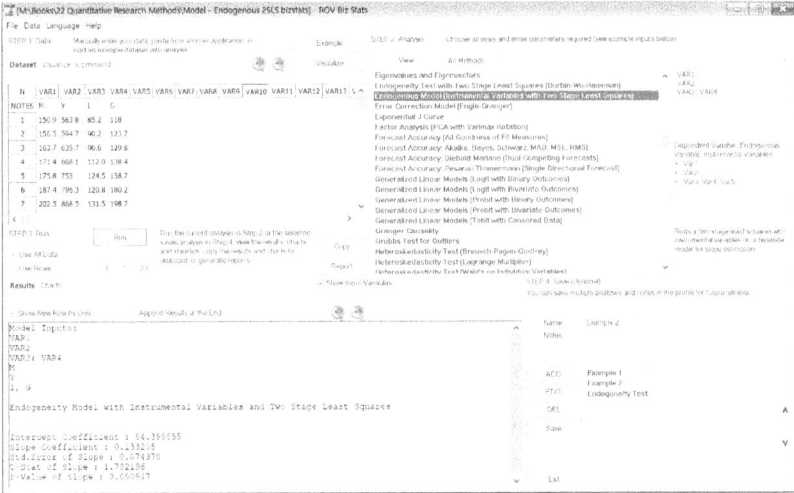

Model Inputs:
VAR1
VAR2
VAR3; VAR4

**Endogeneity Model Results with Instrumental Variables
and Two Stage Least Squares**
Intercept Coefficient: 84.398855
Slope Coefficient: 0.133285
Std. Error of Slope: 0.074370
T-Stat of Slope: 1.792196
P-Value of Slope: 0.090917

Figure 5.54: Two-Stage Least Squares II

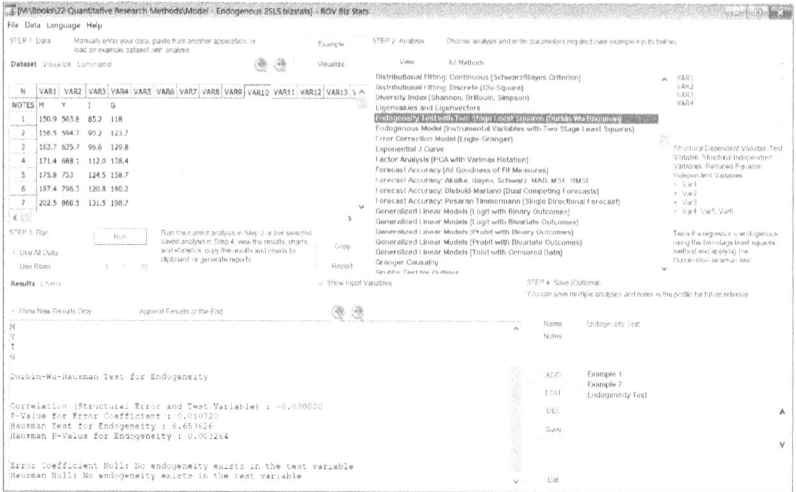

Model Inputs:
VAR1
VAR2
VAR3
VAR4

Durbin-Wu-Hausman Test for Endogeneity
Correlation (Structural Error and Test Variable): -0.000000
P-Value for Error Coefficient: 0.010720
Hausman Test for Endogeneity: 8.653626
Hausman P-Value for Endogeneity: 0.003264

Error Coefficient Null: No endogeneity exists in the test variable
Hausman Null: No endogeneity exists in the test variable

Figure 5.55: Testing for Endogeneity

The Granger causality tests if one variable "Granger causes" another variable and vice versa, using restricted autoregressive lags and unrestricted distributive lag models. Typically, predictive causality in finance and economics is tested by measuring the ability to predict the future values of a time series using prior values of another time series. A simpler definition might be that a time-series variable A can Granger cause another time-series variable B if predictions of the value of B based solely on its own prior values and on the prior values of A are comparatively better than predictions of B based solely on its own past values. For example, Figure 5.56 illustrates two time-series variables, A and B. The two null hypotheses tested are that there is no Granger causality of A on B and also between B and A. We see that the p-values for both directions are greater than alpha of 0.05, so we cannot reject the null hypothesis and conclude that neither A Granger causes B nor B Granger causes A when both are lagged for 3 periods (this is the value 3 in the input box).

The Granger causality model can only be run pairwise and assumes that the time-series variable is stationary or not stochastic. If a time series is suspected to have nonstationary effects, we can run the Augmented Dickey–Fuller test (see Figure 5.57), where the null hypothesis is that the series is nonstationary, has a unit root, or I(1) process, and is potentially stochastic. The example BizStats results indicate that the variable is stationary (the null hypothesis is rejected with a p-value of 0.0442). However, if a time-series variable is nonstationary and stochastic, you can still attempt to forecast this series in several ways:

- Compute the difference to potentially make the series stationary. For example, stock prices are nonstationary and stochastic, whereas its difference, i.e., the calculated stock returns, tend to be stationary and more predictable than the raw stock prices.

- Run a stochastic process model, for example, a geometric Brownian motion random walk process, mean-reversion process, jump-diffusion process, or other mixed processes. These are typically used to forecast stock prices for the purposes of modeling and valuing stock options, real options, and employee stock options. Both Risk Simulator and BizStats (Figure 5.58) support these methods.

- If there is another nonstationary variable, you can test if these two series are cointegrated. For example, you can use the Engle–Granger Error Correction Model assuming the variables exhibit cointegration. If two time-series variables are nonstationary in the first order, $I(1)$, as tested using the Augmented Dickey–Fuller test, and when both variables are cointegrated, the error correction model can be used for estimating short-term and long-term effects of one time-series on the another. The error correction comes from previous periods' deviation from a long-run equilibrium, where the error influences its short-run dynamics (Figure 5.59).

- Apply a data filter to smooth out the disturbances such as the Hodrick–Prescott filter (Figure 5.60). This filter allows you to remove the cyclical effects of raw time-series data. The filter helps generate a smoothed curve of a time-series variable that is sensitive to longer-term fluctuations rather than short-term impacts. The key is to choose the correct smoothing parameter, which can sometimes require trial and error.

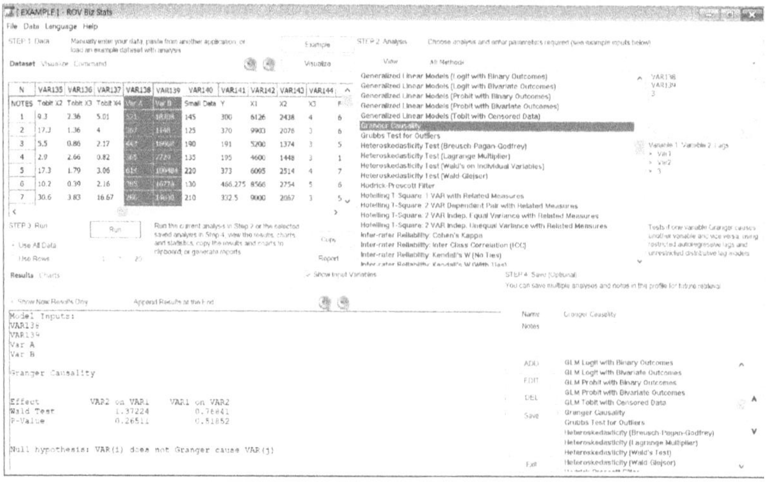

Figure 5.56: Granger Causality (*continues*)

```
Model Inputs:
VAR138
VAR139
3
```

Granger Causality

```
Effect                VAR2 on VAR1:    VAR1 on VAR2:
Wald Test             1.37224          0.76841
P-Value               0.26511          0.51852
```

```
Null hypothesis: VAR(i) does not Granger cause VAR(j)
```

Figure 5.56: Granger Causality (*continued*)

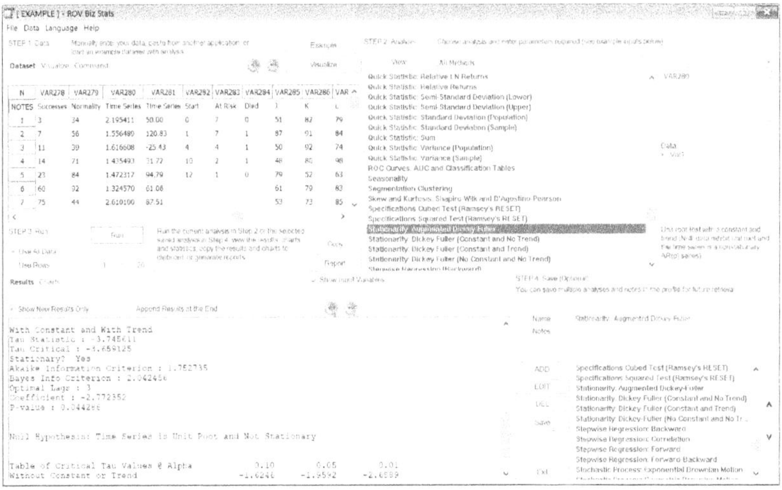

```
Model Inputs:
VAR280
```

Augmented Dickey-Fuller Stationarity Test for AR(p)

```
              With Constant and With Trend
              Tau Statistic: -3.745611
              Tau Critical: -3.659125
              Stationary? Yes
              Akaike Information Criterion: 1.752735
              Bayes Info Criterion: 2.042456
              Optimal Lags: 3
              Coefficient: -2.772352
              P-value: 0.044286
```

```
Null Hypothesis: Time Series is Unit Root and Not Stationary
```

Figure 5.57: Augmented Dickey–Fuller Test for Stationarity

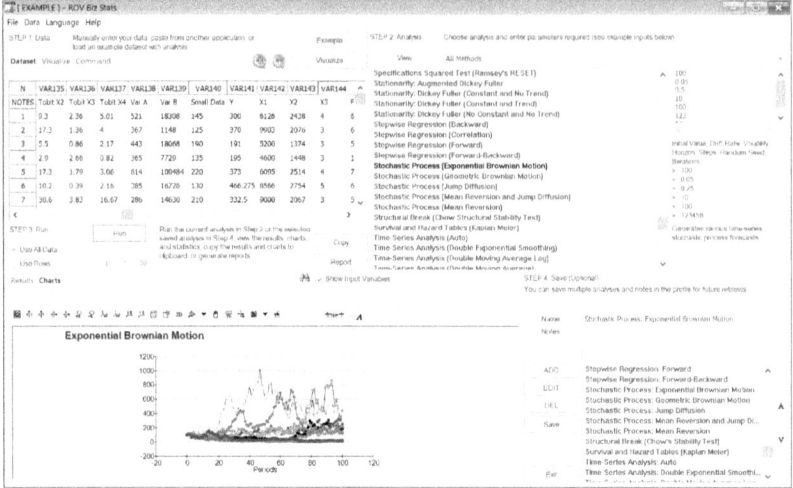

Figure 5.58: Stochastic Processes

Model Inputs:
100, 0.05, 0.5, 10, 100, 123, 10 (entered as input rows)

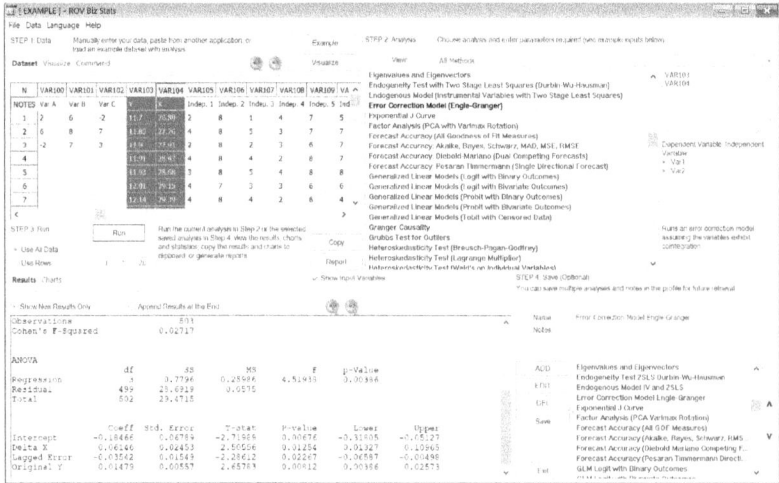

Figure 5.59: Error Correction Model

Model Inputs:
VAR103
VAR104

Error Correction Model

Multiple R	0.16264
R-Square	0.02645
Adjusted R-Square	0.02060

	Coeff	Std. Error	T-stat	P-value
Standard Error		0.23979		
Observations		503		
Cohen's F-Squared		0.02717		

	Coeff	Std. Error	T-stat	P-value
Intercept	-0.18466	0.06789	-2.71989	0.00676
Delta X	0.06146	0.02453	2.50556	0.01254
Lagged Error	-0.03542	0.01549	-2.28612	0.02267
Original Y	0.01479	0.00557	2.65783	0.00812

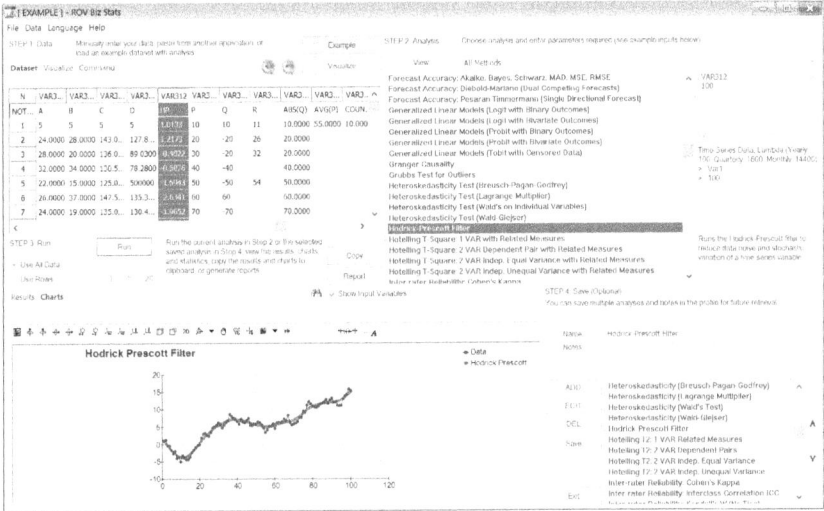

Model Inputs: VAR312, 100 on Hodrick-Prescott Filter

Figure 5.60: Hodrick–Prescott Filtering

BEYOND MULTIPLE REGRESSION: POISSON REGRESSION, DEMING REGRESSION, ORDINAL LOGISTIC REGRESSION, RIDGE REGRESSION, AND WEIGHTED REGRESSION

Finally, there are also other types of unique multiple regression methods that are available in BizStats. Each of these multiple regression variations has a specific purpose and requires different data setups, and the results are slightly different than a standard multiple regression. Nonetheless, the interpretations of the results are similar to a standard regression model. The following lists five types of advanced regression methods, an example of the data requirements (the full dataset is available inside BizStats), how to set up the model's data inputs, and the results.

Multiple Poisson Regression (Population and Frequency)

The Poisson regression is like the Logit regression in that the dependent variable can only take on non-negative values, but also that the underlying distribution of the data is a Poisson distribution, drawn from known population sizes. Recall that the Poisson distribution is a discrete distribution used to model the probability that an event occurs within the context of time and area. Typically, this generalized linear model approach runs a log-linear regression model, where the dependent variable is the event count (see VAR1 in the sample dataset below), and an additional variable for the population size (VAR2) and categorical independent variables (VAR3 to VAR5) are needed.

In Poisson regression, the logarithm of the expected value is a linear combination of the independent variables, that is, $\log[E(Y \mid \mathbf{x})] = \alpha + \beta'\mathbf{x}$. In the sample results below, we can say that the coefficient for X_1 is 0.76457, which is the expected log count of each unit increase in X_1. Alternatively, $e^{0.76457} = 2.148$, which means that there is a 114.8% (a 2.148-fold) increase in Y for every unit increase in X_1. Similarly, X_2 has an expected log count of 0.38873, or $e^{0.38873} = 1.475$, which means that there is a 47.5% (a 1.475-fold) increase in Y for every unit increase in X_2. In addition, the interpretation of the p-values, R-square, and Akaike Information Criterion (AIC) are the same as a regular multiple regression. The new goodness-of-fit and error measures, such as Pearson's Phi and Cohen's F-Squared, test the null hypothesis that the current model is a good fit (null hypothesis states that the error is zero), which means we want these error measures to be small. These measures are typically used to compare against running other Poisson regression models, where a model with lower Pearson's Phi, F-squared, and AIC indicates a better fit. R-square is an *absolute* measure in the sense that it has a fixed domain between 0 and 1 and can be readily interpreted (the percent variation in the dependent variable that can be explained by the variation in the independent variable). However, these other goodness-of-fit error measures like Phi, F-squared, and AIC are *relative* measures, where there is little interpretation by themselves, and are only used when comparing across multiple models.

Poisson Regression Example Dataset

VAR1 Cancer (Y)	VAR2 Population	VAR3 X1	VAR4 X2	VAR5 X3
45	24786	1	0	0
77	32125	1	0	0.5
95	34706	1	0	1
...	...	...	...	...
...	...	...	...	...
62	41707	0	0	1
57	26319	0	0	1.5
71	22978	0	0	2

Model Inputs:
VAR1
VAR2
VAR3; VAR4; VAR5

Multiple Poisson Regression

R-Square	0.96413
AIC	19.62304
Pearson Phi	1.07152
Sqrt Phi	1.03514
Cohen's F-Squared	26.87470

	Coeff	Std. Error	Wald Test	P-value
Intercept	-7.30714	0.08931	6693.69972	0.00000
X1	**0.76457**	0.07958	92.29805	0.00000
X2	**0.38873**	0.09882	15.47465	0.16178
X3	0.76612	0.05376	203.06012	0.00000

With Phi Correction   1.035141

	Coeff	Std. Error	Wald Test	P-value
Intercept	-7.30714	0.09245	6693.69972	0.00000
X1	0.76457	0.08238	92.29805	0.00000
X2	0.38873	0.10229	15.47465	0.16178
X3	0.76612	0.05565	203.06012	0.00000

Multiple Regression (Deming Regression with Known Variance)

In regular multivariate regressions, the dependent variable Y is modeled and predicted by independent variables X_i with some error ε. However, in a Deming regression, we further assume that the data collected for the X variables have additional uncertainties and errors, or variances, that is used to provide a more relaxed fit in a Deming model. This implies that the predicted Y values will have a higher level of variance and uncertainty. The estimated variances are used to determine the lambda, where $\lambda = s_x^2/s_y^2$, and this parameter is minimized to determine the value of the slope and intercept coefficients. The optimized coefficients will be unbiased estimators of the true population parameters, and the error residuals are assumed to be normally distributed. The following illustrates a sample dataset needed when using BizStats to compute a Deming regression, as well as the required input parameters. This bivariate model requires the dependent and independent variables, followed by the known variance for both variables.

```
          Deming Regression
          Example Dataset

            VAR1      VAR2
            Dep       Indep
            5.4       5.1
            5.6       5.6
            6.3       6.8
            ...       ...
            ...       ...
            6.8       6.7
            4.6       5.2
            4.1       4.5
```

Model Inputs:
VAR1
VAR2
0.02
0.09

Deming Regression

	Coefficient	S.E.	DF	T-Stat	P-value
Intercept	-0.30704	1.29693	9	-0.23674	0.81816
Slope	1.04233	0.21194	9	4.91812	0.00083
Lambda	4.500000				

An Ordinal Logistic regression runs a multivariate ordinal logistic regression with two predictor variables and multiple frequencies of ordered variables, for instance, the two categorical variables of Gender (0/1) and Age (1–5), with five variables filled with the numbers or frequencies of people who responded Strongly Agree, Agree, Neutral, Disagree, or Strongly Disagree, which are presumably ordered. Note that this is an ordinal dataset where the Age variables are ordered, and it is multinomial because we are forecasting the four variables VAR3–VAR6 values.

Note that this is an extension of the binary logistic model, but in this example, there are multiple probabilities or frequency forecasts (VAR3–VAR6). Alternatively, you can collapse these four variables into a single variable and run the Logit regression multiple times. For instance, combine these four variables into a single variable that is binary (e.g., Strongly Agree = 1 and All Others = 0) to run a Logit model. Then, repeat the process with Agree = 1 and All Others = 0, and repeat the process. Remember to run only $k - 1$ models, where k is the number of frequency or count variables, and the last variable's predicted probability should be the complement of the remaining variables such that the total probability equals 100%. Hence, in the results below, although there are four variables VAR3–VAR6, the results only return VAR4–VAR6.

The following illustrates some sample datasets used in BizStats, the required input parameter format, and the results. Typically, the computed coefficients are interpreted in a log-logistic function and can seem complicated at times. Nonetheless, it is much simpler to look at the predicted probabilities (relative frequencies) and forecasted values (frequencies) given all the possible combinations of the two predictor variables of gender and age. Unfortunately, this approach can only accommodate two predictor variables. If more predictors are needed, use the Logit model as described above.

```
Ordinal Logistic Regression Example Dataset
VAR1    VAR2    VAR3      VAR4    VAR5      VAR6
Gender  Age     Strongly  Agree Disagree  Strongly
                Agree                      Disagree
0       0       3         9       18        24
0       1       6         13      16        28
0       5       9         13      17        20
...     ...     ...       ...     ...       ...
...     ...     ...       ...     ...       ...
1       4       8         14      20        18
1       2       10        15      16        12
1       3       5         14      12        8
```

Model Inputs:
VAR1; VAR2
VAR3; VAR4; VAR5; VAR6

Multiple Ordinal Logistic Regression

	VAR4	VAR5	VAR6
Intercept	0.70462	1.30649	1.91678
VAR1	0.03091	-0.29433	-0.51153
VAR2	-0.06285	-0.15006	-0.39874

Maximum Log-Likelihood	-88.16470
Initial Log-Likelihood	-58.71436
Chi-Square Statistic	-58.90066
Degrees of Freedom	6

Predicted Probabilities

VAR1	VAR2	VAR3	VAR4	VAR5	VAR6	Total
0.00	0.00	7.40%	14.97%	27.33%	50.31%	100.00%
0.00	1.00	9.40%	17.85%	29.87%	42.88%	100.00%
0.00	2.00	11.65%	20.79%	31.87%	35.69%	100.00%
0.00	3.00	14.11%	23.65%	33.23%	29.01%	100.00%
1.00	0.00	10.09%	21.05%	27.75%	41.12%	100.00%
1.00	1.00	12.40%	24.30%	29.37%	33.93%	100.00%
1.00	2.00	14.89%	27.41%	30.35%	27.35%	100.00%
1.00	3.00	17.50%	30.24%	30.70%	21.57%	100.00%

Forecasted Values

VAR1	VAR2	VAR3	VAR4	VAR5	VAR6	Total
0.00	0.00	4.00	8.08	14.76	27.17	54.00
0.00	1.00	5.92	11.25	18.82	27.02	63.00
0.00	2.00	6.87	12.27	18.81	21.05	59.00
0.00	3.00	6.21	10.40	14.62	12.76	44.00
1.00	0.00	4.84	10.10	13.32	19.74	48.00
1.00	1.00	7.44	14.58	17.62	20.36	60.00
1.00	2.00	7.89	14.52	16.09	14.49	53.00
1.00	3.00	6.82	11.79	11.97	8.41	39.00

A Ridge regression comes with a higher bias than an Ordinary Least Squares (OLS) multiple regression but has less variance. It is more suitable in situations with high Variance Inflation Factors (VIF) and multicollinearity or when there is a high number of variables compared to data points. In a standard multiple regression model, we minimize the fitted sum of squared errors where $SSE = \sum_{i=1}^{n}(y_i - \hat{y}_i)^2$, but in a high VIF dataset with near perfect collinearity, the matrix is not invertible and cannot be solved. In this situation, the sum of squares is penalized with an added term where $SSE = \sum_{i=1}^{n}(y_i - \hat{y}_i)^2 + \lambda \sum_{j=0}^{k} b_i^2$ and λ is considered the adjustment parameter. When $\lambda = 0$, the results revert to an OLS approach. A small λ generates estimates with less bias but with a higher variance, versus a large λ that generates higher bias with less variance. The idea is to select a value that balances bias and variance, which might require trial and error. Finally, ridge-based regressions are suitable only when there is high VIF or significant multicollinearity. As discussed, multicollinearity can be solved by simply removing the offending independent variable(s) and running a standard regression. A sample dataset and results from BizStats are shown below.

```
          Ridge Regression Example Dataset
    VAR1      VAR2      VAR3      VAR4      VAR5
     Y         X1        X2        X3        X4
     3         3         6         2         8
    15         7         7        11        14
    19        11        11        23        33
    ...       ...       ...       ...       ...

    ...       ...       ...       ...       ...
    23        23        17        16        10
    31        28        22        22        15
    39        31        16        28        24


  Model Inputs:
  VAR1
  VAR2; VAR3; VAR4; VAR5

  Multiple Ridge Regression


OVERALL FIT
Multiple R      0.96818     Maximum Log-Likelihood          -0.09243
R-Square        0.93737     Akaike Info Criterion (AIC)      0.56583
Adj R-Square    0.91947     Bayes Schwarz Criterion (BSC)    0.81315
Std Error       0.27578     Hannan-Quinn Criterion (HQC)     0.59993
Observations         18     Cohen's F-Squared               14.96580


ANOVA
                 DF         SS         MS          F       p-Value
Regression        4    15.93522    3.98381    52.38029    0.00000
Residual         14     1.06478    0.07606
Total            18    17.00000
```

```
            Coeff     Std. Error    T-stat      P-value    Lower 5%    Upper 95%
VAR X1      0.42021    0.26106      1.60965     0.12978   -0.13970     0.98012
VAR X2     -0.12370    0.25386     -0.48727     0.63361   -0.66817     0.42077
VAR X3      0.79884    0.26794      2.98141     0.00991    0.22416     1.37351
VAR X4     -0.26279    0.11732     -2.23987     0.04184   -0.51443    -0.01116
```

*Ridge Regression has a higher bias than OLS regression but with less variance. It is more suitable in situations with high VIF and multicollinearity or a high number of variables compared to data points.

```
Lambda    0.00000    0.00170    0.01700    0.17000    1.70000   17.00000   170.00000
VAR X1    0.41543    0.41602    0.42020    0.42021    0.36398    0.25379     0.07428
VAR X2   -0.37140   -0.36783   -0.33685   -0.12370    0.23040    0.23845     0.07251
VAR X3    1.11241    1.10725    1.06388    0.79884    0.39040    0.22834     0.07024
VAR X4   -0.38094   -0.37902   -0.36284   -0.26279   -0.09478    0.01508     0.02177
```

Multiple Weighted Regression (Fixing Heteroskedasticity)

A Multiple Weighted regression runs a Multivariate Regression on Weighted Variables (also known as weighted least squares, or WLS) to correct for heteroskedasticity in all the variables. The weights used to adjust these variables are the user input standard deviations. As mentioned, the standard OLS approach minimizes the sum of squares of the errors $SSE = \sum_{i=1}^{n}(y_i - \hat{y}_i)^2$, but in a weighted least squares approach, we add an additional weight variable w_i such that we have $SSE = \sum_{i=1}^{n} w_i(y_i - \hat{y}_i)^2$. Similarly, in matrix notation, the standard regression's $B = (X'X)^{-1}(X'Y)$ becomes $B = (X'WX)^{-1}(X'WY)$. These weights are used as an additional input variable to the model in situations where the errors are heteroskedastic.

The following provides an example dataset and results from Biz-Stats using a weighted regression model. Notice that a new input variable called standard deviation is required.

Finally, the regression results will show $1/Stdev$ as a representation of the weighted intercept and $X/Stdev$ as a representation of the weighted X variable. These variables can be used exactly as in a standard regression model to determine the predicted dependent variable's values. In fact, the results from a WLS should be relatively close to those in an OLS model.

```
   Weighted Regression
    Example Dataset
VAR1          VAR2                VAR3
  Y            X                  Stdev
266.7        2.60269             60.5
342.5        3.62434             68.3
418.1        4.31749             81.4
  ...          ...               98.8
608.3        5.92693             110.6
798.3        6.62007             145.6
950.6        8.00637             173.1
1216.5       8.92266             238.3
```

Model Inputs:
VAR221
VAR222
VAR223

Multiple Weighted Regression

OVERALL FIT

Multiple R	0.99552	Maximum Log-Likelihood	-5.59816
R-Square	0.99107	Akaike Info Criterion (AIC)	2.14954
Adj R-Square	0.98809	Bayes Schwarz Criterion (BSC)	2.17933
Std Error	0.56252	Hannan-Quinn Criterion (HQC)	1.94861
Observations	8	Cohen's F-Squared	110.93199

ANOVA

	DF	SS	MS	F	p-Value
Regression	2	210.61	105.31	332.79596	0.00000
Residual	6	1.90	0.32		
Total	8	212.51			

	Coeff	Std. Error	T-stat	P-value
X1/Stdev	126.84523	11.82915	10.72311	0.00004
1/Stdev	-100.84543	53.29659	-1.89216	0.10733

ARTIFICIAL INTELLIGENCE & MACHINE LEARNING

Artificial Intelligence (AI) is a broad catch-all term for a group of inorganic computer science technologies that are used to simulate intelligence. The science of AI was established in the 1950s to determine whether inorganic robots could execute human-level intelligence capabilities. Significant interest in AI resurfaced about the same time as Big Data computer capacity became more widely available to researchers and businesses, allowing them to apply the science to a variety of practical applications. Manufacturing robots, smart assistants, proactive healthcare management, illness mapping, automated financial investing, virtual travel-booking agents, social media monitoring, conversational marketing bots, natural language processing tools, and inventory supply chain management are all examples of commercially feasible AI applications.

The timeline of AI and Data Science development reveals a long journey, where mathematical statistics evolved into applied statistics, data science, artificial intelligence, and machine learning (ML). For instance, in 1962, John Tukey's work as a mathematical statistician can be considered one of the early seminal works in data analytics. In 1977, the International Association for Statistical Computing (IASC) was founded to link traditional statistical methodology, modern computer technology, and the knowledge of domain experts to convert data into information and knowledge. Database marketing started a trend in 1994, and by 1996, the term "Data Science" appeared for the first time at the International Federation of Classification Societies in Japan. The inaugural topic was entitled,

"Data Science, Classification, and Related Methods." In 1997, Jeff Wu gave an inaugural lecture titled simply "Statistics = Data Science?" In 2001, William Cleveland published "Data Science: An Action Plan for Expanding the Technical Areas of the Field of Statistics." He put forward the notion that data science was an independent discipline and named various areas in which he believed data scientists should be educated: multidisciplinary investigations, models, and methods for data analysis; computing with data; pedagogy; tool evaluation; and theory. By 2008, the term "data scientist" was often attributed to Jeff Hammerbacher and D. J. Patil, then of Facebook and LinkedIn, respectively, and in 2010, the term "data science" had fully infiltrated the vernacular. Between 2011 and 2012, "data scientist" job listings increased by 15,000%. Around 2016, data science started to be entrenched in Machine Learning and Deep Learning. This implies that AI/ML techniques are based solidly on the foundations of traditional mathematical statistics, but with smart algorithmic steps wrapped around these methods.

The term AI typically conjures up the nebulous concept of machine learning, which, in reality, is a subset of AI where a computer system is programmed to identify and categorize external real-world stimuli. AI can be loosely defined as the ability of machines to perform tasks that normally require human intelligence—for example, recognizing patterns, learning from experience, drawing conclusions, making predictions, or taking action—whether digitally or as the smart software behind autonomous physical systems. AI processes that are most appropriate for data science, quantitative research analytics, prediction, and forecast modeling include applications of Machine Learning (ML), Natural Language Processing (NLP), and Robotic Process Automation (RPA).

Whereas AI, in general, involves the use of algorithms exhibiting "smart" behavior, the use of AI algorithms in Machine Learning (ML)— that detect patterns and use them for prediction and decision making—can be broadly divided into supervised and unsupervised methods. *Supervised* learning means that the correct answers are provided by humans to train the algorithm, whereas *unsupervised* learning does not include the correct results. Supervised algorithms are taught patterns using past data and then detect them automatically in new data. For example, a multiple regression model requires historical data of the dependent variable Y and one or more independent variables X_i and because the results (dependent variable) are provided, this is considered a supervised ML algorithm. In contrast, unsupervised algorithms are programmed to detect new and interesting patterns in completely new data. Without supervision, the algorithm is not expected to surface specific correct answers; instead, it looks for logical patterns within raw data. For example, a factor analysis where there are multiple independent variables X_i but the a priori groupings of these variables are not known would be considered an unsupervised method. Reinforcement Learning is where the algorithm helps to make decisions on how to act in certain situations, and the behavior is rewarded or penalized depending on the consequences. Deep Learning is another class of ML inspired by the human brain where artificial neural networks progressively improve their ability to perform a task.

NLP is a set of algorithms for interpreting, transforming, and generating human language in a way that people can understand. It is used in devices that appear to be able to understand and act on written or spoken words, such as translation apps or personal assistants like Apple Siri, Amazon's Alexa, or Google Home. Speech soundwaves are converted into computer code that the algorithms understand. The code then translates that meaning into a human-readable, precise response that can be applied to normal human cognition. This is performed using semantic parsing, which maps a passage's language to categorize each word and, using ML, creates associations to represent not just the definition of a term, but the meaning within a specific context.

Finally, while RPA, the algorithms that mimic human actions to reduce simple but repetitive back-office tasks benefits from AI application, RPA is not a simulation of human intelligence, but, rather, it only mimics capabilities. Strictly speaking, it is not AI; it is an existing process that has been augmented by AI. RPA can be loosely defined as the use of technology to set up computer software or robots to capture and interpret current applications for processing transactions, altering data, triggering reactions, and communicating with other digital systems. When used correctly, robotic automation offers numerous benefits because it is not constrained by human limitations such as weariness, morale, discipline, or survival requirements. Robots, unlike their human creators, have no ambitions. Due to the applications of NLP and RPA that are beyond the realm of decision analytics, data analytics, and quantitative research methods, we will only focus on ML applications in BizStats going forward.

Figure 6.1 provides a visualization of AI/ML methods. In the figure, AI/ML is divided into supervised learning and unsupervised learning. K-Nearest Neighbor can be considered the in-between method of semi-supervised in the sense that both training and testing sets are required, whereas strictly speaking, both supervised and unsupervised methods do not require a testing set. However, in practice, testing sets are typically used in order to apply the training set's fitted parameters to the testing data points for forecasting or classification.

The following sections describe the AI/ML algorithms that are available in BizStats. Each method is first discussed, then an example is shown on how BizStats is applied, followed by results interpretation. Note that AI/ML methods rely heavily on standard statistics and analytical methods, and where appropriate, cross-referencing to other standard methods will be discussed.

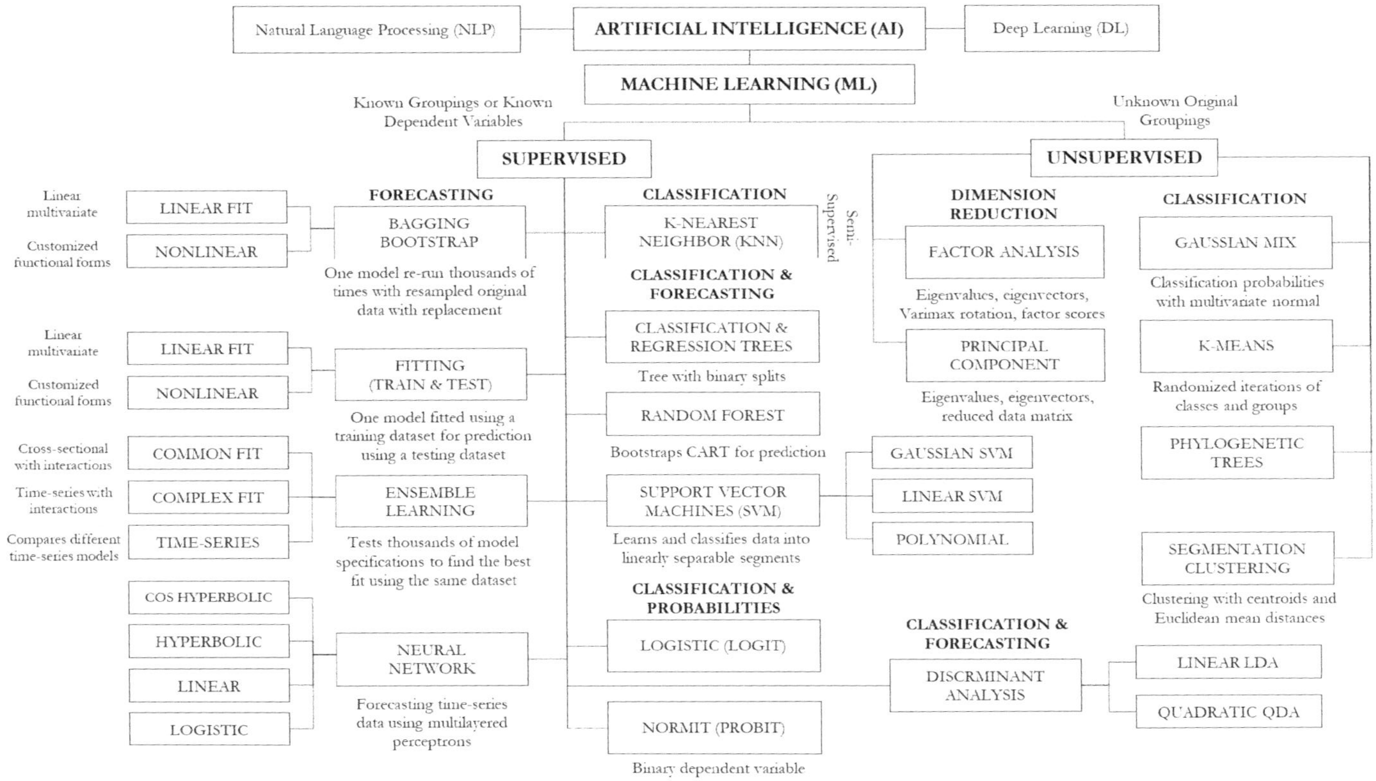

Figure 6.1: Artificial Intelligence Machine Learning Methods

Related AI/ML Methods: Bagging Nonlinear Fit Bootstrap

Ensemble Common & Complex Fit

Related Traditional Methods: Bootstrap Simulation, Bootstrap Regression

This method applies a Bootstrap Aggregation (Bagging) Linear Fit Model of hundreds of models via resampled data to generate the best consensus forecasts. The idea is that in a random selection of data, taking the average forecast of an ensemble of models provides a more accurate prediction than a single sample. In a typical multivariate linear regression, the relationship structure and characteristics of a dependent variable and how it depends on other independent exogenous variables can be modeled. The model can be used to understand the relationship among these variables as well as for the purposes of forecasting and predictive modeling. The accuracy and goodness of fit for this model can also be determined. Similar to a linear multivariate regression model, we first train the algorithm using the training dependent and training independent variables, which will identify the optimized parameters to use on the testing dataset. Then, the dataset is resampled, and the algorithm is again run. This process is repeated or bootstrapped hundreds of times, and the output forecasts will be a consensus of all these bootstrapped models.

In an ensemble forecast, we would apply different models to the same dataset, whereas in a bagging or bootstrap aggregation approach, we use the same model but applied multiple times to a random selection of the existing dataset. The latter's algorithm is trivial. Suppose we have a dependent response variable Y and k number of predictor independent variables $\mathbf{X} = X_1, X_2, \ldots, X_k$, each with N rows of data. Then, we would initialize B, the number of bootstrap models to be fitted, as well as n, the number of data rows to use in the bootstrap, where $n < N$. Starting with $B = 1$, we take a bootstrap resampling of n data rows and fit the model; specifically, we sample with replacement, to fit $\mathbf{X}_B$ to Y_B and obtain a forecast fit $\hat{f}_B(\mathbf{X})$. Repeat the process applying a resampling with replacement and generating the aggregate consensus forecast. Recall that this bootstrap approach assumes that the model is correctly specified, and we are simply re-running the same model specification on resampled data. In contrast, the Ensemble Learning methods such as the

AI/ML Ensemble Common Fit and the Ensemble Complex Fit will take the same dataset and apply hundreds or even thousands of models to test for the best-fitting model specification.

Bootstrapping works well in situations where the dataset consists of N *i.i.d.* data points. This means that the sequential order of the data points is not important in fitting the underlying process. For example, if we sufficiently resample rows of data (one row may consist of multiple columns of independent variables) with replacement, the fitted parameters will be distributed around the true population parameters. There might be situations where bootstrap regression is problematic, especially when the data points are not *i.i.d.* such as when the data points are clumpy or sensitive to extreme values.

Figure 6.2 illustrates the AI Machine Learning Bagging Linear Fit Bootstrap supervised model in BizStats. To get started, the standard practice is to divide your data into training and testing sets. The training set (one dependent with one or more independent variables) is used to train the algorithm and obtain the best-fitting parameters. Note that Risk Simulator also provides a variation of this bootstrap regression by resampling the residual errors as well as randomizing the data and generating probabilistic Monte Carlo simulation assumptions as a result.

The algorithm also allows you to optionally enter known testing set dependent values. Sometimes these are known and sometimes they are unknown and are to be forecasted. If the values are unknown, simply leave the input empty or enter a 0 in the input if you wish to enter the next input, which is the forecast results save location in the data grid.

Simply enter the variables you need to classify and enter the number of clusters desired. For instance, the required model inputs look like the following:

```
Model Inputs:
VAR373          Training Y (1 variable)
VAR374:VAR375   Training X (≥ 1 variables)
VAR380:VAR381   Testing X (matches Training X's number of variables)
1000            Number of Bootstraps (1-1000)
45              Number of data points (< number of data rows)
0               Testing Y (optional, 1 variable)
VAR442          Forecast save location (optional, 1 variable)
```

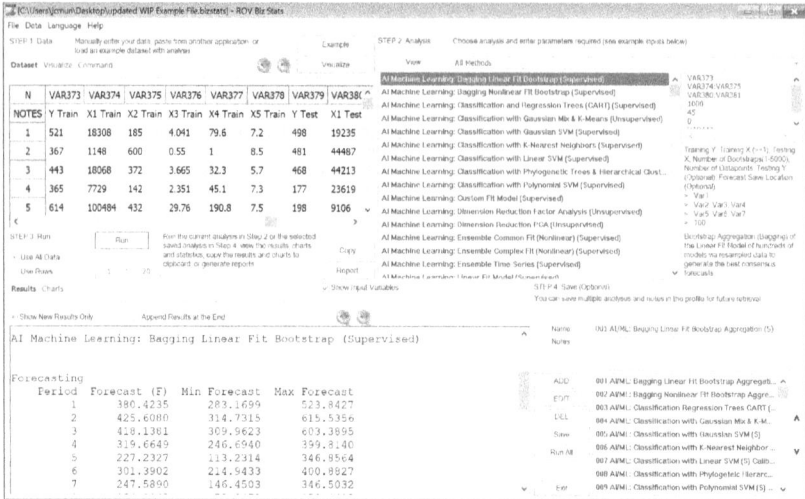

Figure 6.2: AI/ML Linear Fit Bootstrap Aggregation or Bagging

Some sample results are shown next. Because there could be hundreds to thousands of bootstrap models, there is no reason to display all the coefficients. The only critical results we care about are the averages of forecast predictions. The interpretations of these forecast values are the same as in multiple linear regression, except that these forecasts are based on the average of hundreds to thousands of bootstrapped regressions to generate a consensus prediction. If you need the fitted coefficients and goodness of fit for the linear fit model, use the AI/ML Linear Fit Model (Supervised) to generate the results of a single model.

```
AI Machine Learning: Bagging Linear Fit Bootstrap (Supervised)

      Forecasting
      Period  Forecast (F)  Min Forecast  Max Forecast
         1      380.4235      283.1699      523.8427
         2      425.6080      314.7315      615.5356
         3      418.1381      309.9623      603.3895
         .           .             .             .
        30      349.5307      277.0782      440.0635
```

Related AI/ML Methods: Bagging Linear Fit Bootstrap, Ensemble Common & Complex Fit

Related Traditional Methods: Nonparametric Bootstrap Simulation, Bootstrap Regression

This method computes a Bagging or Bootstrap Aggregation on your custom nonlinear fit model hundreds of times via resampled data to generate the best consensus forecasts. This approach is similar to the Bagging Linear Fit Bootstrap model described previously. The main difference is that the regression model is a customized nonlinear model that the user can enter. Again, do note the differences between bootstrap aggregation versus ensemble learning methods as described in the previous method.

As usual, the standard practice is to divide your data into training and testing sets. The training set (one dependent with one or more independent variables) is used to train the algorithm and obtain the best-fitting parameters. In this model, you can create your custom equations (Figure 6.3). Note that only one variable is allowed as the Training *Y* Dependent Variable, whereas multiple variables are allowed in the Training *X* Independent Variables section, separated by a semicolon (;), and that basic mathematical functions can be used (e.g., *LN, LOG, LAG*, +, -, /, *, *TIME, RESIDUAL, DIFF*). For instance, the training set's dependent variable is *VAR373* and the independent variables are *VAR374*; *(VAR375)^2*; *LN(VAR376)*, and so forth. You need to use the same functional form for the testing set's independent variables as well (but with the same or different variables), otherwise, the model will not run properly. For example, the complementary testing independent variables set might be *VAR380*; *(VAR381)^2*; *LN(VAR382)*. Notice that the same functional form is used but applied to different variables. Applying it to the same variables would be the same as running a customized econometric model instead.

The algorithm also allows you to optionally enter known testing set dependent values. Sometimes these are known and sometimes they are unknown and are to be forecasted. If the values are unknown, simply leave the input empty or enter a 0 in the input if you wish to enter the next input, which is the forecast results save location in the data grid. Simply enter the variables you need to classify and enter the number of clusters desired. For instance, the required model inputs look like the following:

```
Model Inputs:
VAR373                          Training Y (1 variable)
VAR374; (VAR375)^2; LN(VAR376)  Training X (customized)
VAR380; (VAR381)^2; LN(VAR382)  Testing X (match Training X)
1000                            Bootstraps (1-1000)
45                              Data points (< rows)
VARX                            Testing Y (optional, 1 var)
VARX                            Save location (optional)
```

Similar to the Bagging Linear model, the nonlinear fit model aggregation method is only interested in the average forecast prediction based on the testing variables.

AI Machine Learning: Bagging Nonlinear Fit Bootstrap (Supervised)

Period	Forecast (F)	Min Forecast	Max Forecast
1	460.6380	330.5135	624.2640
2	375.6430	196.8459	447.4713
3	432.1997	299.2141	521.3108
4	349.8022	268.4462	436.7163
.	.	.	.
30	378.2814	294.0299	466.1581

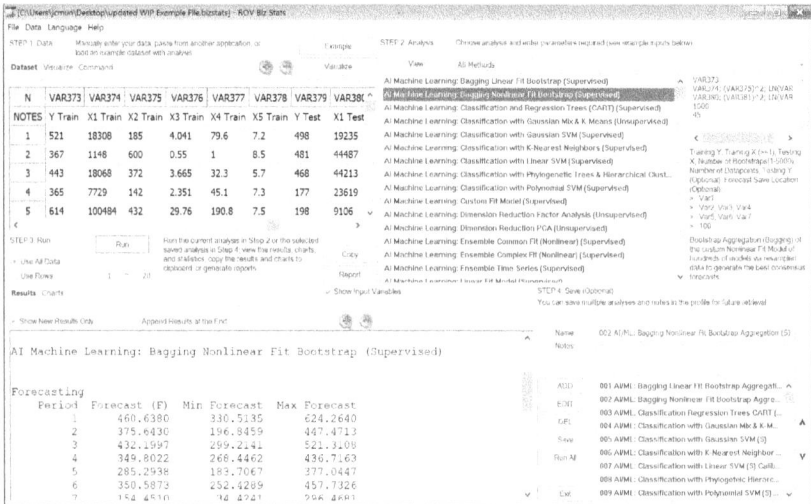

Figure 6.3: AI/ML Nonlinear Fit Bootstrap Aggregation or Bagging

Related AI/ML Methods: Multivariate Discriminant Analysis, Random Forest

Related Traditional Methods: Linear Discriminant Analysis

The Classification and Regression Trees (CART) model generates branches and subgroups of the categorical dependent Y variable using characteristic X variables. CART is typically used for data mining and constitutes a supervised machine learning approach. This is a classification approach when the dependent variable is categorical, and the tree is used to determine the class or group within which a target testing variable is most likely to fall. The data is split into branches along a tree, and each branch split will be determined using Gini coefficients and information loss coefficients based on the questions asked along the way. Specifically, $Gini = 1 - \sum_{i=1}^{c} p_i^2$. If this Gini index is 0, it means the data are perfectly classified. Therefore, using a recursive algorithm, we can apply the splits that have the lowest Gini index. The final structure looks like a tree with its many branches. Additional splitting and stopping rules are applied along the way, and the terminal branches will provide predictions of the target testing variable.

Figure 6.4 provides a visual illustration and the results of a CART model. Simply enter the variables you need to classify and enter the number of clusters desired. The CART model then generates if-then-else rules that are simple to understand and implement as a forecasting tool. The tree can identify patterns that are oftentimes obscured in the complex interactions of the data.

The CART algorithm runs the optimal splits according to the Gini coefficient and then retests the regression tree against the actual Training Y variable to identify its accuracy. If a different set of Testing X variables is entered, it will also project and classify the relevant groupings (Figure 6.5). The sample data shows the information on 10 individuals, where each individual's preferred transportation mode is the dependent variable (a categorical variable 1, 2, 3 for bus, train, or car). The independent predictors are the individuals' gender (1, 2 for male or female), whether the person owns a car (1, 0 for yes or no), the cost of transportation (1, 2, 3 for cheap, medium, or expensive), and the individual's income level category (1, 2, 3 for low, medium, or high). Back in Figure 6.4, we see the tree visually, with all the relevant splits and Gini coefficients. The tree is then used to back-fit the original data. For the example data (Figure 6.5), the first individual who ended up taking the Bus (Transportation Mode = 1) has the following dependent variable values: Gender = 1, Car Ownership = 0, Transportation Cost = 1, and Income Level = 1. We start from the top of the tree in Figure 6.4 and see that for cost = 1, we take the first right branch, then going down the next level, we take the right branch where travel cost = 1. Then, we take the left branch where gender = 1. The path is bolded for easier identification. This happens to be the terminal branch, which means the model predicts that the transport mode is 1, corresponding to the original data. All rows of data are fed through this tree according to their own pathways.

The required model inputs look like the following:

```
Model Inputs:
VAR433          Training Y (1 variable)
VAR434:VAR437   Training X (≥ 1 variables)
VAR438:VAR441   Testing X (optional, match # of var)
VAR442          Forecast save location (optional, 1 var)
```

The complete results from the algorithm are shown next. The CART method will return the various unique numerical categories in the Training Y set, and, in this example, we have three categories: 1, 2, and 3. It will show the fit of the training dataset, where here we see the actuals versus CART predicted results, with a perfect 100% accuracy match in each category. The actual categories based on the training set are shown, together with the model's predicted categorization. This fitted model and its comparison to actuals allow one to see the accuracy of the model. Then, using this fitted model, if the optional Testing X variables are provided, the algorithm takes this testing dataset and computes the predicted categories.

Node 1   Count   %
Class 1   4   40%
Class 2   3   30%
Class 3   3   30%

Gini = 0.66   Travel Cost = 3   Travel Cost < 3

Terminal 1 Count   %
Class 1   0   0%
Class 2   0   0%
Class 3   3   100%

Node 2   Count   %
Class 1   4   57%
Class 2   3   43%
Class 3   0   0%

Gini = 0.34   Travel Cost = 2   Travel Cost = 1

Terminal 2 Count   %
Class 1   0   0%
Class 2   2   100%
Class 3   0   0%

Node 3   Count   %
Class 1   4   80%
Class 2   1   20%
Class 3   0   0%

Gini = 0.23   Gender = 1   Gender = 2

Terminal 3 Count   %
Class 1   3   100%
Class 2   0   0%
Class 3   0   0%

Terminal 4 Count   %
Class 1   1   50%
Class 2   1   50%
Class 3   0   0%

Gini = 0.20   Car Owner = 1   Car Owner = 0

Terminal 3 Count   %
Class 1   0   0%
Class 2   1   100%
Class 3   0   0%

Terminal 4 Count   %
Class 1   1   100%
Class 2   0   0%
Class 3   0   0%

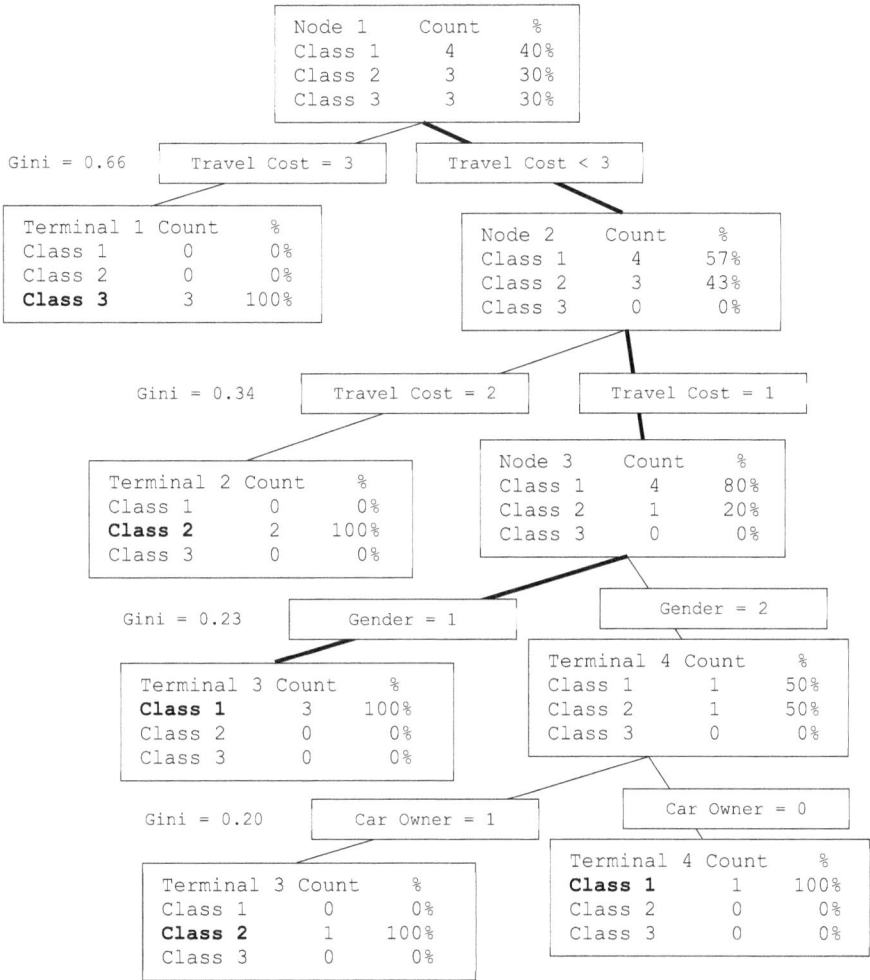

Figure 6.4: Classification and Regression Tree (CART)

AI Machine Learning: Classification Regression Tree (Supervised)

Category	Actual	Predicted	Accuracy
1	4	4	100.00%
2	3	3	100.00%
3	3	3	100.00%

Training Dataset

Actual	Forecast
1.00	1.00
1.00	1.00
2.00	2.00
1.00	1.00
1.00	1.00
2.00	2.00
2.00	2.00
3.00	3.00
3.00	3.00
3.00	3.00

Testing Dataset Forecast
1.00
1.00
2.00
1.00
1.00
. .
3.00

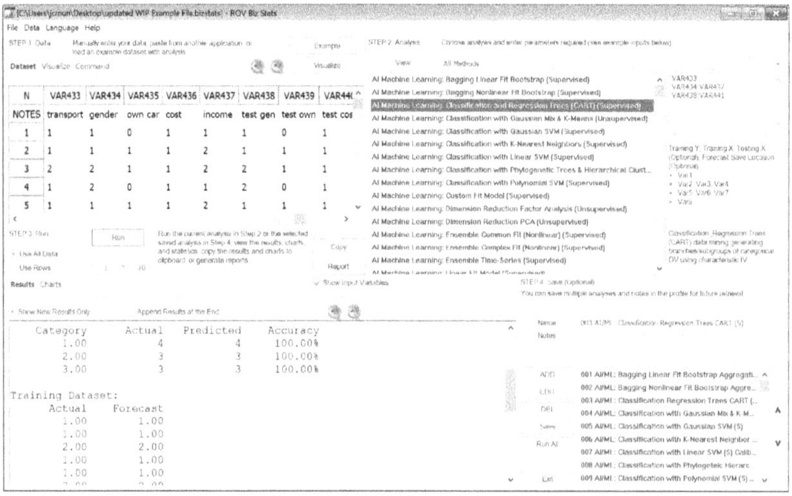

Figure 6.5: AI/ML Classification and Regression Tree CART

Related AI/ML Methods: Multivariate Discriminant Analysis (Quadratic), Segmentation Clustering

Related Traditional Methods: Quadratic Discriminant Analysis

The AI Machine Learning Gaussian Mix with K-Means Segmentation model assumes multiple overlaying normal distributions. This is an unsupervised machine learning method that is applicable when we do not know where the clusters come from initially. Typically, the dataset has n rows of data with m columns of multidimensional-space characteristics, and where we typically have $1 \leq m \leq 4$. The results show the probabilities of a certain value belonging to a particular cluster. When there is a single cluster, we would typically perform a distributional fitting routine such as a Kolmogorov–Smirnov model, but when there are multiple such k normal distribution clusters (with μ_k, COV_k mean and covariance), the total probability density is a linear function of the densities across all these clusters, where $p(x) = \sum_{k=1}^{k} \pi_k G(x|\mu_k, COV_k)$ and π_k is the mix-coefficient for the k-th distribution. An expectations maximization algorithm is used to estimate the maximum likelihood function of the fit, while the Bayes Information Criterion is used to automatically select the best covariance parameters.

A Gaussian Mix is related to the K-Means approach and is fairly simple and uses some Naïve Bayes and likelihood estimations. Sometimes the results are not as reliable as, say, a supervised Support Vector Machine (SVM) method. This is because of the Gaussian Mix's unsupervised algorithm, which may not converge. Run the same model several times to see if the model converges (i.e., the results will be the same each time when you click Run). If the results are not identical, try increasing the number of iterations and test again. If the results obtained are not as expected, reduce the number of variables, and increase the number of rows and try again with a higher iteration. The best model is the one with the maximum log-likelihood value (be careful here as log-likelihood is typically a negative value, which means a model with −100 is better than a model with a −300 log-likelihood measure). Alternatively, try the unsupervised AI/ML Segmentation Clustering methodology, which is typically more reliable. Whenever possible and if the data allow for it, the recommendation is to use the supervised SVM methods or the unsupervised AI/ML Segmentation Clustering method.

Figure 6.6 illustrates a dataset of 50 states and their reported 10-year averages of criminal activities, including the number of murders, aggravated assaults, and breaking and entering events, as well as the population (in millions). Suppose we want to, without any supervision, categorize the states into 5 clusters. Simply enter the variables you need to classify and enter the number of clusters desired. For instance, the required model inputs look like the following:

```
Model Inputs:
VAR416:VAR419    The variables to classify
5                The number of clusters to group the data into
1000             Max iterations (Optional=100, 1-5000)
VARX             Location to save the forecasted categories
```

The results will show both the K-Means Clustering as well as the Gaussian Mix models. As mentioned, if the same model is re-run several times and the results remain the same, the model has converged; otherwise, add more iterations and try again. If the model converges, use the results from that run. If convergence is not achieved, either apply a different method completely or re-run the same model several times and select the one with the maximum log-likelihood value. Also, when the cluster means of K-Means and Gaussian Mix are close to each other, the results are relatively reliable. These means usually do not equal each other as they run different algorithms.

Figure 6.6: AI/ML Classification with Gaussian Mix

As shown in Figure 6.6, the K-Means and Gaussian Mix cluster means are provided for the requested 5 clusters (shown as rows in the results) for each of the 4 independent variables (shown as columns). Then, the K-Means counts of the number of states in each category are provided, as are the K-Means assignments of these states into the various categories. The Gaussian Mix results also provide the probabilities that a certain state falls within a specific category. For instance, we see from the results that there are 10 rows grouped into Cluster 1, 10 into Cluster 2, and so forth. The Gaussian Mix probabilities show that there is a 99.81% chance the first row's data fall into Cluster 1, the second row's data has a 100% chance of being in Cluster 1, the third row's data has a 99.68% chance of being in Cluster 4, and so forth You can also run the analysis using AI/ML Cluster Segmentation but be aware that similar rows will be clustered together although the numbering of the clusters may differ due to the different algorithms used. For example, Cluster 1 may be called Cluster 5, and so on.

```
AI Machine Learning: Classification with Gaussian Mix & K-Means
(Unsupervised)

Log-Likelihood:      -532.6046
K-Means Average          X1          X2          X3          X4
Cluster 1            12.3800     246.6000     67.2000     27.7800
Cluster 2             2.9500      62.7000     53.9000     11.5100
Cluster 3             7.5077     170.3846     71.4615     22.6154
Cluster 4            11.8000     300.8571     68.7143     28.8571
Cluster 5             5.5900     112.4000     65.6000     17.2700
Gaussian Mix Average
                         X1          X2          X3          X4
Cluster 1            12.1347     248.1784     67.3133     27.5988
Cluster 2             2.9546      62.8118     53.9251     11.5229
Cluster 3             7.8164     171.4283     71.0373     22.6710
Cluster 4            11.8121     298.4321     68.9918     29.1794
Cluster 5             5.6117     112.3859     65.5904     17.2776


K-Means Count

          Cluster 1   Cluster 2   Cluster 3   Cluster 4   Cluster 5
             10          10          13           7          10

K-Means Assignments for Each Row

              1
              1
              4
              3
              4
              3
              .
              2
              2
              3
```

Gaussian Mix Probabilities for Each Row

Cluster 1	Cluster 2	Cluster 3	Cluster 4	Cluster 5
0.9981	0.0000	0.0019	0.0000	0.0000
1.0000	0.0000	0.0000	0.0000	0.0000
0.0032	0.0000	0.0000	**0.9968**	0.0000
0.0000	0.0000	1.0000	0.0000	0.0000
0.0235	0.0000	0.0000	0.9765	0.0000
0.0013	0.0000	0.9850	0.0136	0.0000
. . .	. . .	. . .	. . .	. . .
0.0000	1.0000	0.0000	0.0000	0.0000
0.0000	0.0000	1.0000	0.0000	0.0000

AI MACHINE LEARNING: CLASSIFICATION WITH K-NEAREST NEIGHBORS (SUPERVISED)

Related AI/ML Methods: Segmentation Clustering

Related Traditional Methods: Segmentation Clustering

The K-Nearest Neighbor (KNN) algorithm is used to classify and segregate the data into groups. Another name for this method is the k-dimensional tree structure, useful for partitioning data points into a few small dimensions. Simply enter the variables you need to classify and enter the number of clusters desired. For instance, the required model inputs look like the following:

```
Model Inputs:
VAR105:VAR107   Training X (≥ 1 variable)
VAR108:VAR110   Testing X (match Training X's number of var)
```

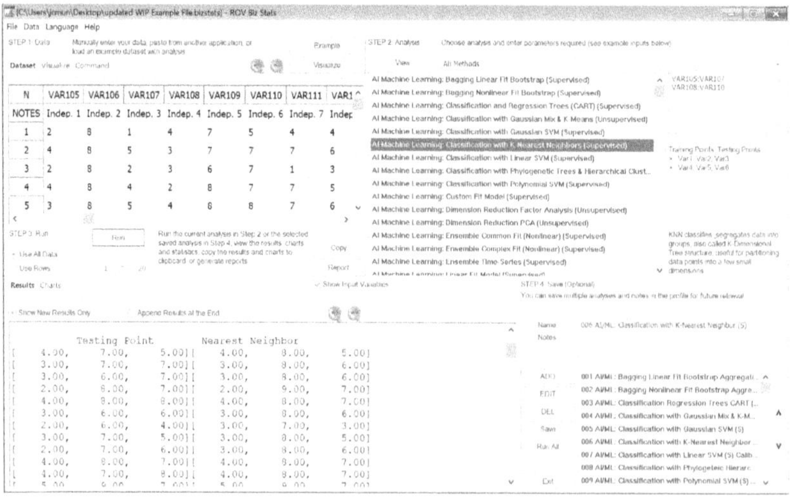

Figure 6.7: AI/ML K-Nearest Neighbor

As illustrated in Figure 6.7, the KNN results will show the testing points and identify the nearest neighbors. For example, in the first row of the testing data, we have the values 4, 7, 5 and this numerical sequence, as compared to all the other data, is most closely related to 4, 8, 5 (this can be either in the testing set or the training set).

```
AI Machine Learning: Classification with K-Nearest Neighbors
(Supervised)

        Testing Points              Nearest Neighbor
     [4.00,   7.00,   5.00]      [4.00,   8.00,   5.00]
     [3.00,   7.00,   7.00]      [3.00,   8.00,   6.00]
     [3.00,   6.00,   7.00]      [3.00,   8.00,   6.00]
     [2.00,   8.00,   7.00]      [2.00,   9.00,   7.00]
     [4.00,   8.00,   8.00]      [4.00,   8.00,   7.00]
     [3.00,   6.00,   6.00]      [3.00,   8.00,   6.00]
      . . .   . . .   . . .       . . .   . . .   . . .
     [5.00,   8.00,   3.00]      [5.00,   8.00,   3.00]
     [4.00,   7.00,   4.00]      [4.00,   8.00,   4.00]
     [5.00,   5.00,   6.00]      [5.00,   8.00,   5.00]
```

AI MACHINE LEARNING: CLASSIFICATION WITH PHYLOGENETIC TREES & HIERARCHICAL CLUSTERING (UNSUPERVISED)

Related AI/ML Methods: Segmentation Clustering, K-Nearest Neighbor

Related Traditional Methods: Segmentation Clustering

In this method, the algorithm runs phylogenetic trees for data classification by applying a hierarchical clustering algorithm. Phylogenetic trees are typically used in biomedical and genetic research, such as looking at DNA sequences. This method is unsupervised, and the algorithm is applied to figure out how to cluster a set of data that is unordered without being provided with any training data having the correct responses. The result is a hierarchical cluster with multiple fully nested sets where the smallest sets are the individual elements of the set, and the largest set is the entire dataset.

To apply a phylogenetic tree using hierarchical clustering, the dataset is typically a set of sequences or distance matrices. Simply enter the variables you need to classify and enter the number of clusters desired. The input variable is a sample genetic DNA sequence, and the results show a hierarchical 5-level phylogenetic tree (Figure 6.8). The 5-level tree (vertical lines indicate branching events, and there are 5 vertical lines starting from the first branch to the longest path). The required model inputs look like the following:

```
Model Inputs:
VAR462      Genetic Chain
0           Chain Name (Optional)
1           Distance Type (Optional, 1-5)
```

DNA Sequence	Names	DNA Sequence	Names
CGGTTGGGAGCT	A	AGGCGGTGCGGG	I
AGGTCGTGAGGT	B	GGGCGGGGCGGG	J
TGGGTGCGAGTT	C	GGGCGCTGCGGG	K
ACGTTTGGGTGA	D	GGACGGAGGCTG	L
AAGGTTGGGGAA	E	GGGTGGGAGCTG	M
GTCTTTCGGGTG	F	AGGAGGCTGATG	N
CACTTGCGGGGG	G	TGGCGGATGATG	O
GCGCGGTGCAGC	H	TGGGTGCGAGTT	P

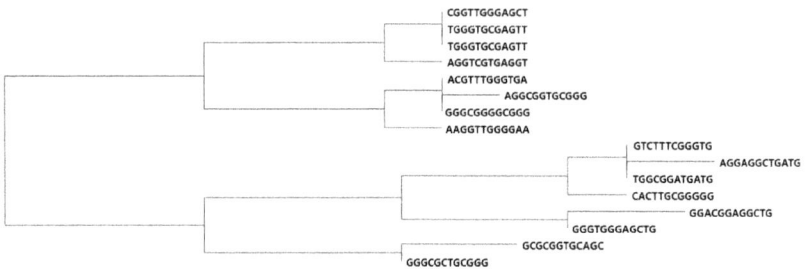

Figure 6.8: AI/ML Phylogenetic Trees

Related AI/ML Methods: Multivariate Discriminant Analysis, Segmentation Clustering

Related Traditional Methods: Linear Discriminant Analysis, Segmentation Clustering

Support Vector Machines (SVM) is a class of supervised machine learning algorithms used for classification. The term "machine" in SVM might be a misnomer in that it is only a vestige of the term "machine learning." SVM methods are simpler to implement and run than complex neural network algorithms. In supervised learning, we typically start with a set of training data. The algorithm is trained using this dataset (i.e., the parameters are optimized and identified), and then the same model parameters are applied to the testing set, or to a new dataset never before seen by the algorithm. The training dataset comprises m data points, placed as rows in the data grid (Figure 6.9), where there is an outcome or dependent variable y_i, followed by one or more independent predictors x_i for $i = 1, ..., m$. Each of the dependent (also known as predictor or feature) variables has n dimensions (number of columns). In contrast, there is only a single y_i variable, with a binary outcome (e.g., 1 and 0, or 1 and 2, indicating if an item is in or out of a group). Note that the training set can also be used as the testing set, and the results will typically yield a high level of segregation accuracy. However, in practice, we typically use a smaller subset of the testing dataset as the training dataset and unleash the optimized algorithm on the remaining testing set. One of the few limiting caveats of SVM methods is a requirement that there exists some n-dimensional hyperplane that separates the data.

The hyperplane is defined by an equation $f(\mathbf{x}) = \mathbf{w} \cdot \mathbf{x} + b = 0$, which completely separates the training dataset into two groups. The parameters $\mathbf{w}$ (the normal vector to the hyperplane) and b (an offset parameter such as a virtual intercept) can be scaled as needed, to adjust the forecast back into the original two groups. Applying some analytical geometry, we see that the parameters are best fitted by applying an internal optimization routine to minimize $\frac{1}{2}\mathbf{w} \cdot \mathbf{w}$, which reduces to a Lagrangian problem where we maximize the likelihood of $\mathcal{L}(\alpha, \beta) = \frac{1}{2} f(\mathbf{w}) + \sum_j \alpha_j g_j(\mathbf{w}) + \sum_k \beta_k h_k(\mathbf{w})$, where all parameters are positive.

Finally, SVM algorithms are best used in conjunction with a kernel density estimator, and the three most commonly used are the Gaussian, Linear, and Polynomial kernels. Try each of these approaches and see which fits the data the best by reviewing the accuracy of the results.

o **Gaussian SVM.** Applies a normal kernel estimator $exp\left[-\frac{1}{2}|\mathbf{x_i} - \mathbf{x_j}|^2/\sigma^2\right]$.

o **Linear SVM.** Applies a standard linear kernel estimator $\mathbf{x_i} \cdot \mathbf{x_j}$.

o **Polynomial SVM.** Applies a polynomial (e.g., quadratic nonlinear programming) kernel density estimator such as $|a\mathbf{x_i} \cdot \mathbf{x_j} + b|^c$.

Figure 6.9 illustrates the SVM supervised model. The same procedure applies to all three SVM subclasses. To get started, we use an example dataset where the weights and sizes of 40 fruits were measured. These fruits were either apples or oranges. Recall that SVMs are best used for separations into two groups. The data grid shows VAR408 with the alphanumeric category of the dependent or classified variable (apples or oranges). However, the SVM algorithms require numerical inputs, hence, the dependent groupings have been coded to a numerical value of 1 and 2 in VAR407 (bivariate numerical categories). VAR405 and VAR406 are the predictors or features set (the weights and sizes of the fruits) that we will use as the training set to calibrate and fit the model. These are the first two sets of inputs in the model. Note that we have VAR407 entered in the first row as the training dependent variable and in the second row, VAR405; VAR406 as the training independent variables (predictor feature set). To get started, we use the default Sigma, Lambda, and Omega values of 2, 1000, and 0.5. Depending on the SVM subclass, only some or all three of these will be used. Start with the defaults and change as required. The main variable that impacts the results is the Omega, which is a value between 0 and 1. If you set the Calibrate Option to 1, it will test various Omega values and shows the accuracy levels of each. Select the Omega value with the highest accuracy and rerun the model.

You can access the dataset and input parameters in BizStats by
loading the default example. The following illustrates the required
input parameters and some examples:

```
Model Inputs:
VAR407              Training dependent variable (1)
VAR405; VAR406      Training independent variables (≥ 1)
2.00                Sigma
1000                Lambda
0.50                Omega (this is tested for accuracy)
1                   Calibrate (1 = calibrate Omega, 0 = do not)
VAR409; VAR410      Testing independent variables
VAR411              Paste the forecast results (optional)
VAR412              Paste the grouped results (optional)
```

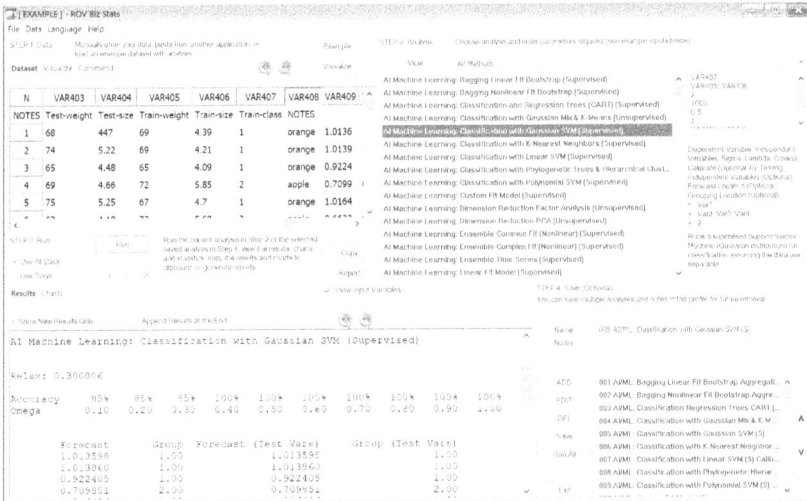

Figure 6.9: AI/ML Classification with Support Vector Machines (SVM)

The results provide a series of forecast values and forecast
groups for the training set as well as for the testing dataset, showing
the numerical segmentation results and the final resulting groups.
Note that the example results indicate a relatively high goodness of
fit to the training dataset at 95% fit. This fit applies to the training
dataset and assuming the same data structure holds, the testing dataset should also have a fit that is close to this result. Typically, only
the testing dataset's forecast values and grouping membership are
important to the user; hence, you can optionally enter the location in
the data grid to save the results, for example, VAR411 and VAR412.
If these inputs are left empty, the results will not be saved in the data
grid, and they will only be available in the results area.

```
AI Machine Learning: Classification with Gaussian SVM (Supervised)

Accuracy    85%    85%    85%    100%   100%   100%   100%   100%
Omega       0.10   0.20   0.30   0.40   0.50   0.60   0.70   0.80

Forecast           Group        Forecast (Test Vars)   Group (Test Vars)
1.013598           1.00                 1.013598                1.00
1.013860           1.00                 1.013860                1.00
0.922405           1.00                 0.922405                1.00
0.709851           2.00                 0.709851                2.00
1.016426           1.00                 1.016426                1.00
 . . .              . .                   . . .                  . .
0.670190           2.00                 0.670190                2.00
```

AI MACHINE LEARNING: CUSTOM FIT MODEL (SUPERVISED)

Related AI/ML Methods: Linear Fit Model

Related Traditional Methods: Basic Econometric Model, Multiple Regression

The AI Machine Learning Custom Fit model is applicable in forecasting time-series and cross-sectional data for modeling relationships among variables. It allows you to create custom-fit multiple regression models. Econometrics refers to a branch of business analytics, modeling, and forecasting techniques for modeling the behavior of or forecasting certain business, financial, economic, physical science, and other variables. Running the Custom Fit model is like regular econometric regression analysis except that the dependent and independent variables can be modified before a regression is run. For more detailed explanations of regression models, see the sections on Linear and Nonlinear Multivariate Regression and Regression Analysis, as well as the associated sections on pitfalls of regression modeling.

As usual, the standard practice is to divide your data into training and testing sets. The training set (one dependent with one or more independent variables) is used to train the algorithm and obtain the best-fitting parameters. In this model, you can create your custom equations (Figure 6.10). Note that only one variable is allowed as the Training Y Dependent Variable, whereas multiple variables are allowed in the Training X Independent Variables section, separated by a semicolon (;), and that basic mathematical functions can be used (e.g., LN, LOG, LAG, +, -, /, *, TIME, RESIDUAL, DIFF). For instance, you can use your training set's dependent variable as VAR373 and independent variables VAR374; (VAR375)^2; LN(VAR376), and so forth. You need to use the same functional form for the testing set's independent variables as well (but with the same or different variables), otherwise, the model will not run properly. For example, a complementary set of testing independent variables would be VAR380; (VAR381)^2; LN(VAR382). Notice that the same functional form is used but applied to different variables. Applying it to the same variables would be the same as running a customized econometric model instead.

The algorithm also allows you to optionally enter known testing set dependent values. Sometimes these are known and sometimes they are unknown and are to be forecasted. If the values are unknown, simply leave the input empty or enter a 0 in the input if you wish to enter the next input, which is the forecast results save location in the data grid. Figure 6.10 shows these last two inputs treated as optional and left empty.

```
Model Inputs:
VAR373                          Training set dependent variable
VAR374; (VAR375)^2; LN(VAR376)  Training set custom ind. var.
VAR380; (VAR381)^2; LN(VAR382)  Test set ind. var.
{VARx or 0 or empty}            Test set dep. var. (optional)
{VARxx or empty}                Forecast location (optional)
```

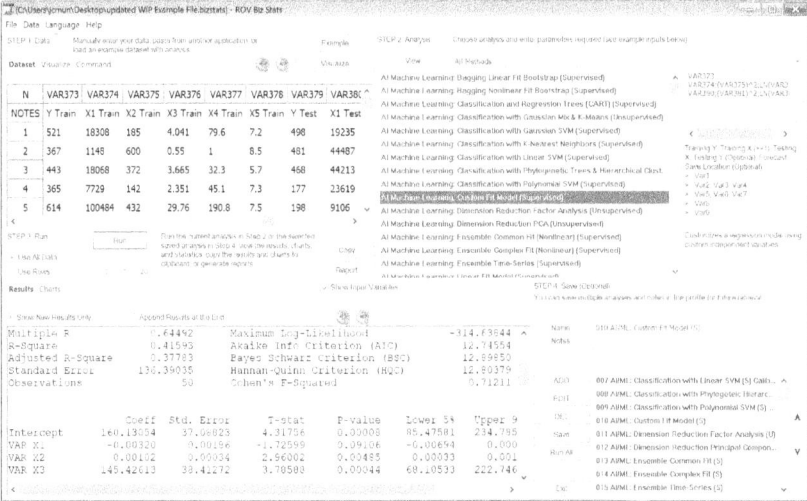

Figure 6.10: AI/ML Custom Fit Model (Supervised)

The results interpretation would be similar to that for the basic econometric analysis. The goodness-of-fit results and fitted parameter estimations pertain to the training dataset, whereas the forecast values are based on the testing dataset when applied to these fitted parameters. Sometimes, you may wish to hold some data back from the training dataset and apply it to the testing dataset to test the accuracy of the model and its ability to forecast, as well as to view the forecast errors. In other words, the optional testing set's dependent variable can be used and because these known values are applied, forecast errors can also be generated as a result. For example, the VARx value above can be set to VAR379.

```
AI Machine Learning: Custom Fit Model (Supervised)

Multiple R             0.64492    Maximum Log-Likelihood         -314.63844
R-Square               0.41593    Akaike Info Criterion (AIC)     12.74554
Adjusted R-Square      0.37783    Bayes Schwarz Criterion (BSC)   12.89850
Standard Error       136.39035    Hannan-Quinn Criterion (HQC)    12.80379
Observations               50     Cohen's F-Squared                0.71211

                     Coeff   Std. Error    T-stat     P-value
Intercept         160.13054    37.08823    4.31756    0.00008
VAR X1             -0.00320     0.00186   -1.72599    0.09106
VAR X2              0.00102     0.00034    2.96002    0.00485
VAR X3            145.42613    38.41272    3.78588    0.00044


ANOVA
                   DF          SS          MS          F       p-Value
Regression          3    609356.63   203118.88    10.91900   0.00002
Residual           46    855707.05    18602.33
Total              49   1465063.68

Forecasting
          Period       Forecast (F)
            1            456.4715
            2            379.5395
            3            436.1389

            .             . .
           25            252.1756
           26             96.8285
           27            401.1761
           28            398.0723
           29            235.0797
           30            379.7052
```

Related AI/ML Methods: Dimension Reduction Factor Analysis

Related Traditional Methods: Principal Component Analysis, Factor Analysis

Principal component analysis, or PCA, makes multivariate data easier to model and summarize. To understand PCA, suppose we start with N variables that are unlikely to be independent of one another, such that changing the value of one variable will change another variable. PCA modeling will replace the original N variables with a new set of M variables that are less than N but are uncorrelated to one another, while at the same time, each of these M variables is a linear combination of the original N variables so that most of the variation can be accounted for using fewer explanatory variables.

PCA is a way of identifying patterns in data and recasting the data in such a way as to highlight their similarities and differences. Patterns of data are very difficult to find in high dimensions when multiple variables exist, and higher dimensional graphs are very difficult to represent and interpret. Once the patterns in the data are found, they can be compressed, and the number of dimensions is now reduced. This reduction of data dimensions does not mean much reduction in loss of information. Instead, similar levels of information can now be obtained by a fewer number of variables.

PCA is a statistical method that is used to reduce data dimensionality using covariance analysis among independent variables by applying an orthogonal transformation to convert a set of correlated variables data into a new set of values of linearly uncorrelated variables named principal components. The number of computed principal components will be less than or equal to the number of original variables. This statistical transformation is set up such that the first principal component has the largest possible variance accounting for as much of the variability in the data as possible, and each subsequent component has the highest variance possible under the constraint that it is orthogonal to or uncorrelated with the preceding components. Thus, PCA reveals the internal structure of the data in a way that best explains the variance in the data. Such a dimensional reduction approach is useful to process high-dimensional datasets while still retaining as much of the variance in the dataset as possible. PCA essentially rotates the set of points around their mean to align with the principal components. Therefore, PCA creates variables that are linear combinations of the original variables. The new variables have the property that the variables are all orthogonal. Factor analysis is similar to PCA, in that factor analysis also involves linear combinations of variables using correlations, whereas PCA uses covariance to determine eigenvectors and eigenvalues relevant to the data using a covariance matrix. Eigenvectors can be thought of as preferential directions of a dataset or main patterns in the data. Eigenvalues can be thought of as quantitative assessments of how much a component represents the data. The higher the eigenvalues of a component, the more representative it is of the data.

As an example, PCA is useful when running multiple regression or basic econometrics when the number of independent variables is large or when there is significant multicollinearity in the independent variables. It can be run on the independent variables to reduce the number of variables and to eliminate any linear correlations among the independent variables. The extracted revised data obtained after running PCA can be used to rerun the linear multiple regression or linear basic econometric analysis. The resulting model will usually have slightly lower R-squared values but potentially higher statistical significance (lower p-value). Users can decide to use as many principal components as required based on the cumulative variance.

Suppose there are k variables, X_k, there are exactly k principal components, $Z_i \in i = 1 \ldots k$, and $Z_i = w_{i,1}X_1 + w_{i,2}X_2 + \ldots + w_{i,k}X_k$, where $w_{i,k}$ are the weights or component loadings. The first principal component Z_1 is a linear combination that best explains the total variation, while the second principal component Z_2 is orthogonal or uncorrelated to the first and explains as much as it can of the remaining variation in the data, and so forth, all the way until the final Z_k component.

Related to another method called Factor Analysis, PCA makes multivariate data easier to model and summarize. Figure 6.11 illustrates an example where we start with 5 independent variables that are unlikely to be independent of one another, such that changing the value of one variable will change another variable. Recall that this multicollinearity effect can cause biases in a multiple regression model. Both principal component and factor analysis can help identify and eventually replace the original independent variables with a new set of fewer variables that are less than the original but are un-correlated to one another, while, at the same time, each of these new variables is a linear combination of the original variables. This means most of the variation can be accounted for by using fewer explanatory variables. Similarly, factor analysis is used to analyze interrelationships within large numbers of variables and simplifies said factors into a smaller number of common factors. The method condenses information contained in the original set of variables into a smaller set of implicit factor variables with minimal loss of information. The analysis is related to the principal component analysis by using the correlation matrix and applying principal component analysis coupled with a varimax matrix rotation to simplify the factors.

The data input requirement is simply the list of variables you want to analyze (separated by semicolons for individual variables or separated by a colon for a contiguous set of variables, such as VAR29:VAR33 for all 5 variables).

```
Model Inputs:
VAR29; VAR30; VAR31; VAR32; VAR33    List of variables
```

As shown in Figure 6.11, we started with 5 independent variables, which means the factor analysis or principal component analysis results will return a 5×5 matrix of eigenvectors and 5 eigenvalues. Typically, we are only interested in components with eigenvalues >1. Hence, in the results, we are only interested in the first three or four factors or components (some researchers would plot these eigenvalues and call it a scree plot, which can be useful for identifying where the kinks are in the eigenvalues).

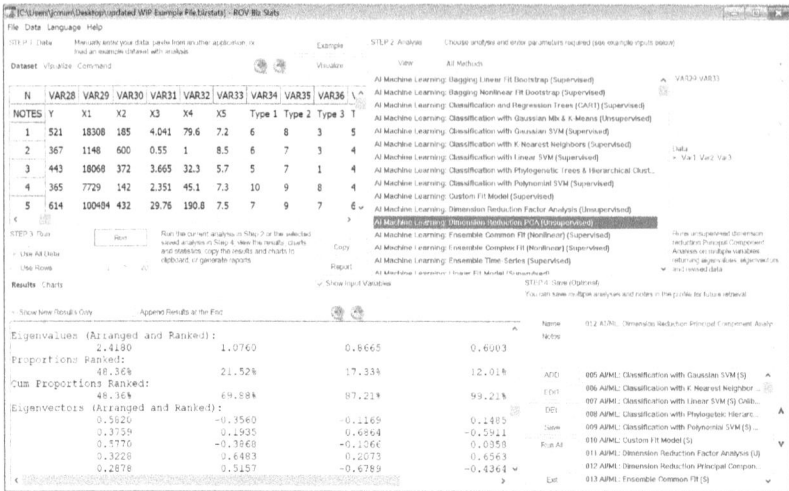

Figure 6.11: AI/ML Dimension Reduction PCA (Unsupervised)

Notice that the first and second factors (the first two result columns) return a cumulative proportion of 69.88%. This means that using these two factors will explain approximately 70% of the variation in all the independent factors themselves. Next, we look at the absolute values of the eigenvalue matrix. It seems that variables 1 and 3 can be combined into a new variable in factor 1, with variables 4 and 5 as the second factor. This can be done separately and outside of principal component analysis. Notice that the results are not as elegant with only 5 variables. The idea of PCA and Factor Analysis is that the more variables you have, the better the algorithm will perform in terms of reducing the number of data variables or the data dimensionality size.

```
Eigenvalues (Arranged and Ranked):
2.4180          1.0760          0.8665          0.6003          0.0393

Proportions Ranked:
48.36%         21.52%          17.33%         12.01%           0.79%

Cum Proportions Ranked:
48.36%         69.88%          87.21%         99.21%         100.00%

Eigenvectors (Arranged and Ranked):
0.5820         -0.3560         -0.1169          0.1485          0.7063
0.3759          0.1935          0.6864         -0.5911          0.0257
0.5770         -0.3868         -0.1066          0.0858         -0.7062
0.3228          0.6483          0.2073          0.6563         -0.0429
0.2878          0.5157         -0.6789         -0.4364          0.0021

Revised Data:
-0.0652          0.0004         -0.1386         -0.0046          0.0010
  . .              . .             . .             . .             . .
-0.0141         -0.0306          0.1469         -0.1321          0.0151
```

Figure 6.12 shows the results of multiple linear regressions to illustrate how orthogonality works in PCA. For instance, the first multiple regression is run using the original dataset (VAR28 against VAR29:VAR33). The second regression is run based on the revised PCA data (VAR28 against the converted data). Notice that the goodness-of-fit measures such as R-square, Adjusted R-square, Multiple R, and Standard Error of the Estimates are identical. The estimated coefficients will differ because different data were used in each situation. Some of the variables are not significant in the models because this is only meant as an illustration of the PCA method and not about calibrating a good regression model. In fact, using the reduced model, the Adjusted R-square of only using two variables is 23% as opposed to 25% using all 5 independent variables in the original dataset. This showcases the power of PCA, where fewer variables are used while retaining a high level of variability explained.

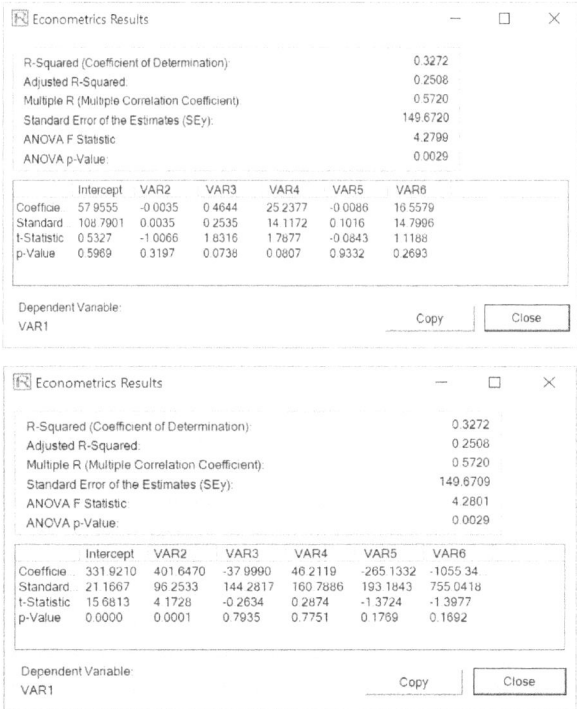

Econometrics Results						— □ ✕
R-Squared (Coefficient of Determination):						0.3272
Adjusted R-Squared:						0.2508
Multiple R (Multiple Correlation Coefficient):						0.5720
Standard Error of the Estimates (SEy):						149.6720
ANOVA F Statistic						4.2799
ANOVA p-Value:						0.0029

	Intercept	VAR2	VAR3	VAR4	VAR5	VAR6
Coefficie	57.9555	-0.0035	0.4644	25.2377	-0.0086	16.5579
Standard	108.7901	0.0035	0.2535	14.1172	0.1016	14.7996
t-Statistic	0.5327	-1.0066	1.8316	1.7877	-0.0843	1.1188
p-Value	0.5969	0.3197	0.0738	0.0807	0.9332	0.2693

Dependent Variable:
VAR1   Copy   Close

Econometrics Results						— □ ✕
R-Squared (Coefficient of Determination):						0.3272
Adjusted R-Squared:						0.2508
Multiple R (Multiple Correlation Coefficient):						0.5720
Standard Error of the Estimates (SEy):						149.6709
ANOVA F Statistic						4.2801
ANOVA p-Value:						0.0029

	Intercept	VAR2	VAR3	VAR4	VAR5	VAR6
Coefficie	331.9210	401.6470	-37.9990	46.2119	-265.1332	-1055.34
Standard	21.1667	96.2533	144.2817	160.7886	193.1843	755.0418
t-Statistic	15.6813	4.1728	-0.2634	0.2874	-1.3724	-1.3977
p-Value	0.0000	0.0001	0.7935	0.7751	0.1769	0.1692

Dependent Variable:
VAR1   Copy   Close

Figure 6.12: PCA Regression Comparability (continues)

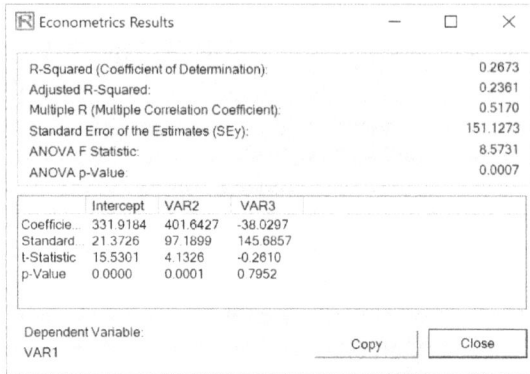

Figure 6.12: PCA Regression Comparability (*continued*)

AI MACHINE LEARNING: DIMENSION REDUCTION FACTOR ANALYSIS (UNSUPERVISED)

Related AI/ML Methods: Dimension Reduction PCA

Related Traditional Methods: Factor Analysis, Principal Component Analysis

This method runs Factor Analysis to analyze interrelationships within large numbers of variables and simplifies said factors into a smaller number of common factors. The method condenses information contained in the original set of variables into a smaller set of implicit factor variables with minimal loss of information. The analysis is related to Principal Component Analysis (PCA) by using the correlation matrix and applying PCA coupled with a Varimax matrix rotation to simplify the factors. The same results interpretation is used for Factor Analysis as for PCA. For instance, Figure 6.13 illustrates an example where we start with 9 independent variables that are unlikely to be independent of one another, such that changing the value of one variable will change another variable. Factor analysis helps identify and eventually replace the original independent variables with a new set of smaller variables that are less than the original but are uncorrelated to one another, while, at the same time, each of these new variables is a linear combination of the original variables. This means most of the variation can be accounted for by using fewer explanatory variables. Factor analysis is therefore used to analyze interrelationships within large numbers of variables and simplifies said factors into a smaller number of common factors. The method condenses information contained in the original set of variables into a smaller set of implicit factor variables with minimal loss of information.

The data input requirement is simply the list of variables you want to analyze (separated by semicolons for individual variables or separated by a colon for a contiguous set of variables, such as VAR105:VAR113 for all 9 variables).

```
Model Inputs:
VAR105:VAR113    The list of variables to analyze
```

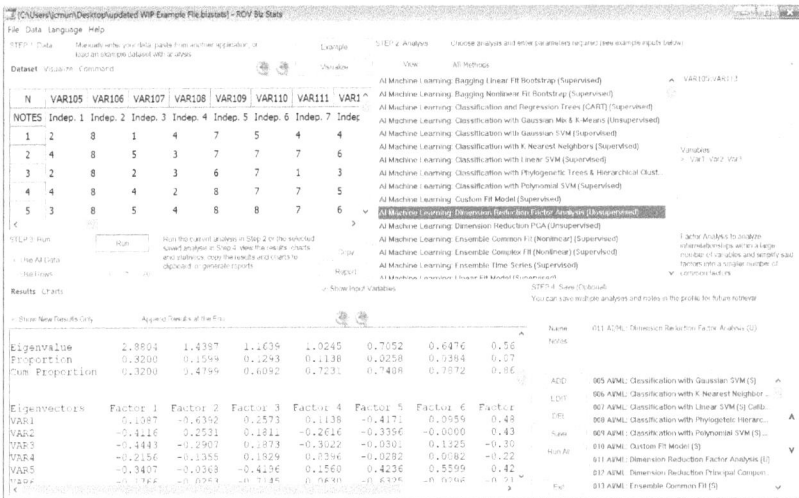

Figure 6.13: AI/ML Dimension Reduction Factor Analysis

As shown in Figure 6.13, we started with 9 independent variables, which means the factor analysis results will return a 9×9 matrix of eigenvectors and 9 eigenvalues. Typically, we are only interested in components with eigenvalues >1. Hence, in the results, we are only interested in the first four factors or components. Notice that the first four factors (the first four result columns) return a cumulative proportion of 72.31%. This means that using these four factors will explain 72.31% of the variation in all the independent factors themselves. Next, we look at the absolute values of the eigenvalue matrix. It seems that variables 2, 3, 7, 8 can be combined into a new variable in factor 1, with variables 1 and 9 as the second factor, and so forth.

```
Factor Analysis (Eigenvalues and Eigenvectors)

Eigenvalue   2.8804   1.4387   1.1639   1.0245   0.7052   0.6476   0.5624 …
Proportion   0.3200   0.1599   0.1293   0.1138   0.0258   0.0384   0.0784 …
Cumulative   0.3200   0.4799   0.6092   0.7231   0.7488   0.7872   0.8656 …

Eigenvectors  Fact1     Fact2    Fact3    Fact4    Fact5    Fact6    Fact7 …
VAR1          0.1087  -0.6392   0.2573   0.1138  -0.4171   0.0959   0.4808 …
VAR2         -0.4116   0.2531   0.1811  -0.2616  -0.3396  -0.0000   0.4365 …
VAR3         -0.4443  -0.2907   0.1873  -0.3022  -0.0301   0.1325  -0.3009 …
VAR4         -0.2156  -0.1355   0.1829   0.8396  -0.0282   0.0082  -0.2214 …
VAR5         -0.3407  -0.0368  -0.4196   0.1560   0.4236   0.5599   0.4245 …
VAR6         -0.1766  -0.0253  -0.7145   0.0630  -0.6325  -0.0296  -0.2161 …
VAR7         -0.4815  -0.1996   0.1803  -0.1644   0.0891   0.0992  -0.3614 …
VAR8         -0.4053  -0.0294  -0.1076   0.1162   0.2150  -0.7828   0.2818 …
VAR9         -0.1776   0.6179   0.3190   0.2312  -0.2744   0.1903   0.0417 …
```

AI MACHINE LEARNING: ENSEMBLE COMMON FIT (NONLINEAR) (SUPERVISED)

Related AI/ML Methods: Ensemble Complex Fit,

Bagging Nonlinear Fit Bootstrap

Related Traditional Methods: Detailed Autoeconometrics

Custom Econometrics

This algorithm computes thousands of possible nonlinear and interaction models (suitable for cross-sectional data for pattern recognition); it calibrates the best model with the training dataset and forecasts outcomes using the testing dataset. In other words, it performs an ensemble learning approach (Figure 6.14).

Simply enter the variables you need to classify and enter the number of clusters desired. For instance, the required model inputs look like the following:

```
Model Inputs:
VAR373          Training Y (1 variable)
VAR374:VAR378   Training X (≥ 1 variables)
VAR380:VAR384   Testing X (optional, match Training X)
VAR379          Forecast Save Location (optional, 1 variable)
0.10            P-value Threshold (optional, default at 0.1)
0               Time Series Lags (optional, default at 0)
```

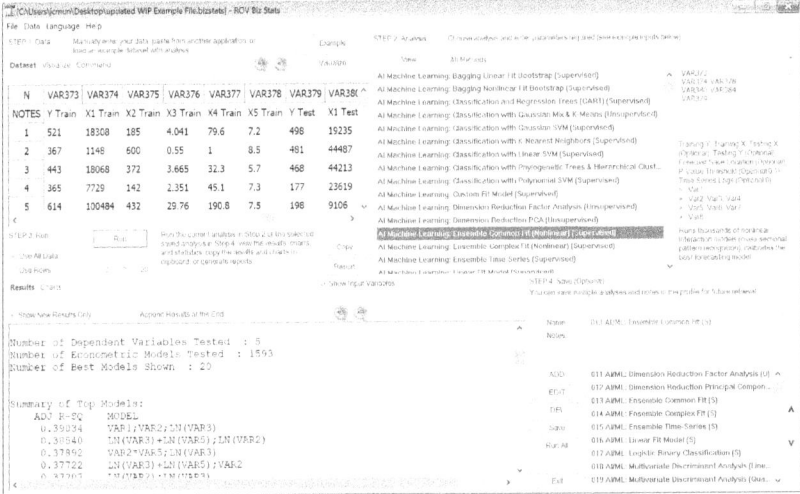

Figure 6.14: AI/ML Ensemble Learning Common Fit

The sample results illustrate the ensemble algorithm where over 1,593 combinations of linear, nonlinear, interacting, and mixed models were tested, and the 10 best models are shown. The models are selected based on the independent variables' p-values ≤ 0.10 and ranked by Adjusted R-squares. A stricter p-value can be entered if required.

```
AI Machine Learning: Ensemble Common Fit (Nonlinear) (Supervised)

Number of Dependent Variables Tested: 5
Number of Econometric Models Tested:  1593
Number of Best Models Shown:          20

Summary of Top Models:
    ADJ R-SQ    MODEL
     0.39034    VAR1;VAR2;LN(VAR3)
     0.38540    LN(VAR3)+LN(VAR5);LN(VAR2)
     0.37892    VAR2*VAR5;LN(VAR3)
     0.37722    LN(VAR3)+LN(VAR5);VAR2
     0.37207    LN(VAR2);LN(VAR3)
     0.36811    LN(VAR1)+LN(VAR3)+LN(VAR5);LN(VAR2)
     0.36811    LN(VAR1)+LN(VAR5)+LN(VAR3);LN(VAR2)
     0.36572    VAR2;LN(VAR3)
     0.36135    LN(VAR1)+LN(VAR3);VAR2*VAR5
     0.36135    VAR2*VAR5;LN(VAR1)+LN(VAR3)
     0.36059    LN(VAR2)+LN(VAR5)+LN(VAR3);LN(VAR1)
     0.36059    LN(VAR2)+LN(VAR3)+LN(VAR5);LN(VAR1)
     0.35811    LN(VAR1)+LN(VAR3)+LN(VAR5);VAR2
     0.35811    LN(VAR1)+LN(VAR5)+LN(VAR3);VAR2
     0.35724    LN(VAR1)+LN(VAR3);LN(VAR2)
     0.35229    LN(VAR3)+LN(VAR5);LN(VAR1)
     0.35220    LN(VAR2)+LN(VAR3);LN(VAR1)
     0.34890    LN(VAR1)+LN(VAR3);VAR2
     0.34489    LN(VAR2)+LN(VAR5);LN(VAR3)
     0.33791    LN(VAR3)+LN(VAR5)+LN(VAR4);LN(VAR2)
```

```
Top Model Result: VAR1;VAR2;LN(VAR3)

Regression Results
Multiple R        0.65396    Maximum Log-Likelihood      -314.13076
R-Square          0.42767    Akaike Info Criterion (AIC)   12.80523
Adj. R-Square     0.39034    Bayes Schwarz Criterion (BSC) 13.03467
Standard Error 135.01252     Hannan-Quinn Criterion (HQC)  12.89260
Observations         50      Cohen's F-Squared              0.74723

                     Coeff    Std. Error    T-stat    P-value
Intercept         59.91680     60.90323     0.98380   0.33036
VAR1              -0.00308      0.00181    -1.70238   0.09543
VAR2               0.70340      0.22372     3.14406   0.00292
LN(VAR3)         138.21002     37.29707     3.70565   0.00056

ANOVA         DF       SS           MS          F       p-Value
Regression     3   626558.21    208852.74   11.45756   0.00001
Residual      46   838505.47     18228.38
Total         49  1465063.68
```

AI MACHINE LEARNING: ENSEMBLE COMPLEX FIT (NONLINEAR) (SUPERVISED)

Related AI/ML Methods: Ensemble Common Fit, Bagging Nonlinear Fit Bootstrap

Related Traditional Methods: Quick Autoeconometrics, Custom Econometrics

Using an ensemble learning approach, this model computes thousands of possible nonlinear and interaction models (suitable for time-series data for pattern recognition); it calibrates the best model with the training dataset and forecasts outcomes using the testing dataset (Figure 6.15).

Simply enter the variables you need to classify and enter the number of clusters desired. For instance, the required model inputs look like the following:

```
Model Inputs:
VAR373          Training Y (1 variable)
VAR374:VAR378 Training X (≥ 1 variables)
VAR380:VAR384 Testing X (optional)
VAR379          Forecast Save Location (optional, 1 variable)
0.10            P-value Threshold (optional, default=0.1)
0               Time Series Lags (optional, default=0)
0               Autoregressive AR(p) (optional, default=0)
```

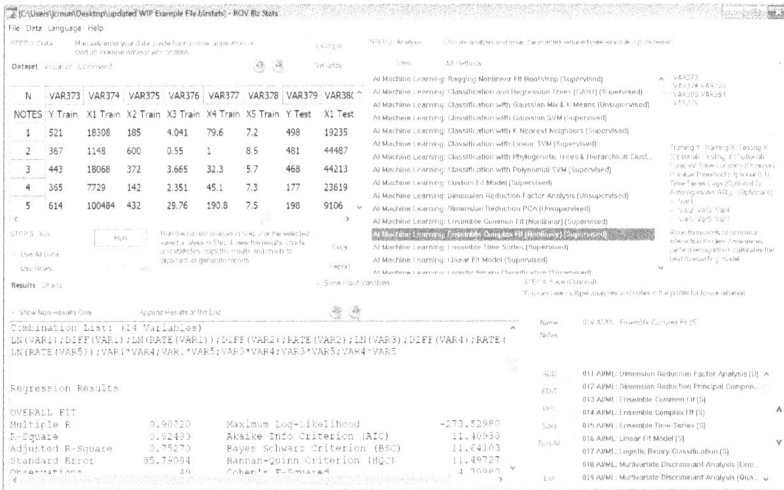

Figure 6.15: AI/ML Ensemble Learning Complex Fit

The results illustrate the complex ensemble model where thousands of combinations of linear, nonlinear, interacting, time-series (lags, rate, and differences), and mixed models were tested, and the best model is shown. The models are selected based on the independent variables' p-values ≤ 0.10 and ranked by Adjusted R-squares. A stricter p-value can be entered if required.

```
AI Machine Learning: Ensemble Complex Fit (Nonlinear) (Supervised)

Detailed Combination list Results:

Combination List: (14 Variables)
LN(VAR1);DIFF(VAR1);LN(RATE(VAR1));DIFF(VAR2);RATE(VAR2);LN(VAR3);DI
FF(VAR4);RATE(VAR5);LN(RATE(VAR5));VAR1*VAR4;VAR1*VAR5;VAR3*VAR4;VAR
3*VAR5;VAR4*VAR5

Regression Results
OVERALL FIT
Multiple R          0.90820     Maximum Log-Likelihood     -273.52980
R-Square            0.82483     Akaike Info Criterion (AIC)  11.40938
Adj. R-Square       0.75270     Bayes Schwarz Criterion (BSC) 11.64103
Standard Error     85.79084     Hannan-Quinn Criterion (HQC) 11.49727
Observations             49     Cohen's F-Squared             4.70880

                     Coeff   Std. Error      T-stat    P-value
Intercept        3664.81960   805.12137     4.55188    0.00006
LN(VAR1)         -321.07588    83.62231    -3.83960    0.00051
DIFF(VAR1)          -0.00469     0.00144    -3.26953    0.00247
LN(RATE(VAR1))    138.86285    31.87150     4.35696    0.00012
DIFF(VAR2)           0.83499     0.36471     2.28944    0.02839
RATE(VAR2)       -137.48661    77.44510    -1.77528    0.08480
LN(VAR3)          286.43034    66.04043     4.33720    0.00012
DIFF(VAR4)          -0.35191     0.05970    -5.89427    0.00000
RATE(VAR5)       -497.73236   156.06627    -3.18924    0.00306
LN(RATE(VAR5))    431.68094   163.34071     2.64283    0.01234
```

```
VAR1*VAR4        0.00004    0.00001    3.46983    0.00143
VAR1*VAR5       -0.00193    0.00077   -2.49557    0.01759
VAR3*VAR4       -0.15513    0.04131   -3.75557    0.00065
VAR3*VAR5        8.92027    2.57281    3.46713    0.00145
VAR4*VAR5        0.03743    0.01553    2.40975    0.02152

ANOVA           DF          SS           MS          F         p-Value
Regression      14     1178340.49    84167.18    11.43565    0.00000
Residual        34      250242.33     7360.07
Total           48     1428582.82
```

AI MACHINE LEARNING: ENSEMBLE TIME-SERIES (SUPERVISED)

Related AI/ML Methods: Ensemble Complex Fit

Related Traditional Methods: Detailed Autoeconometrics, ARIMA, Time-Series Forecasting

This algorithm computes and calibrates an ensemble of different time-series forecast models, selects the best combination, and generates forecasts for the single historical time-series variable. An ensemble of time-series forecast methods such as Holt–Winters, deseasonalized forecasts, ARIMA, and others are applied, the best model combinations are used, and the consensus forecasts are provided (Figure 6.16). A visual representation of the back-fitting and forecast fit is also provided in the results (Figure 6.17). An alternative is to run each of these models manually in BizStats. Enter the variables you need to classify and enter the number of clusters desired. For instance, the required model inputs look like the following:

```
Model Inputs:
VAR64      Historical time series (1 variable)
4          Seasonality (e.g., 1, 4, 12, 250, 365)
8          Forecast periods (positive integer)
VARX       Forecast save location (optional, 1 variable)
```

Another related process is the Combinatorial Fuzzy Logic method available in BizStats. The term fuzzy logic is derived from fuzzy set theory to deal with reasoning that is approximate rather than accurate—as opposed to crisp logic, where binary sets have binary logic, fuzzy logic variables may have a truth value that ranges between 0 and 1 and is not constrained to the two truth values of classic propositional logic. This fuzzy weighting schema is used together with a combinatorial method to yield time-series forecast results.

Figure 6.16: AI/ML Ensemble Learning Time-Series Forecast

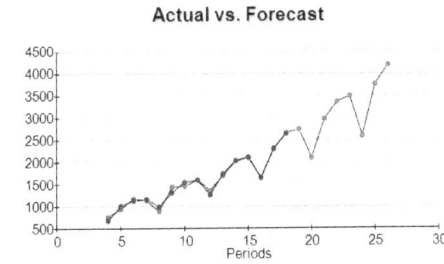

Actual vs. Forecast

Figure 6.17: AI/ML Ensemble Learning Time-Series Forecast

BEST RMSE: 249.495091

Auto ARIMA(Autoregressive Integrated Moving Average)

P,D,Q	Adj R-Sq	AIC	SC	DW Stat	Iter.	Rank
3,2,0	0.975310	10.9575	11.1463	3.00222	0	1
3,3,0	0.974249	12.8944	13.0770	3.08095	0	2
3,0,0	0.810734	13.2187	13.4148	3.13092	0	3
1,0,0	0.757283	13.5117	13.6111	2.35762	0	4
0,0,2	0.755534	14.3154	14.4648	1.11343	36	5
3,1,0	0.738737	13.1115	13.3046	0.66057	0	6
2,0,0	0.732178	14.3405	14.4889	2.14685	0	7
2,1,2	0.706057	12.4512	12.6962	2.00422	33	8
0,3,2	0.647397	14.3629	14.5100	1.88313	15	9
0,0,1	0.457153	15.0703	15.1699	1.07554	51	10
2,3,0	0.383042	14.9030	15.0446	2.48489	0	11
1,3,0	0.382042	15.8116	15.9082	2.28473	0	12
2,1,0	0.329073	13.1377	13.2847	2.93179	0	13
2,2,0	0.271308	14.9692	15.1141	2.85595	0	14
0,1,1	0.237051	13.2015	13.3010	1.68375	88	15
1,2,0	0.164739	14.1176	14.2157	2.31989	0	16
1,1,0	-0.005812	14.2302	14.3291	2.12907	0	17

```
ARIMA (P, D, Q): 3, 2, 0

Regression Statistics
 R-Squared (Coefficient of Determination)      0.9806010
 Adjusted R-Squared                            0.9753100
 Multiple R (Multiple Correlation Coefficient) 0.9902530
 Standard Error of the Estimates (SEy)         478.74859
 Number of Observations                        15
 Akaike Information Criterion (AIC)            10.957458
 Schwarz Criterion (SC)                        11.146272
 Log-Likelihood                               -78.180937
 Durbin-Watson (DW) Statistic                  3.0022200
 Number of Iterations                          1

Regression Results
                   Intercept         AR(1)         AR(2)         AR(3)
 Coefficients     27.051029     -1.097853     -1.155977     -1.254295
 Standard Error   19.571112      0.052945      0.069607      0.067098
 t-Statistic       1.382192    -20.735646    -16.607232    -18.693438
 p-Value           0.194334      0.000000      0.000000      0.000000
```

AI MACHINE LEARNING: LINEAR FIT MODEL (SUPERVISED)

Related AI/ML Methods: Custom Fit Model

Related Traditional Methods: Basic Econometric Model, Multiple Regression

Multivariate linear regression is used to model the relationship structure and characteristics of a certain dependent variable as it depends on other independent exogenous variables. Using the modeled relationship, we can forecast the future values of the dependent variable. The accuracy and goodness of fit for this model can also be determined. Linear and nonlinear models can be fitted in the multiple regression analysis. Similar to the custom fit model, running the Linear Fit model is like regular regression analysis except that we first train the algorithm using the training dependent and training independent variables, which will identify the optimized parameters to use on the testing dataset. Figure 6.18 illustrates the AI Machine Learning Linear Fit supervised model. For more detailed explanations of regression models, see Linear and Nonlinear Multivariate Regression in Chapter 9 and Regression Analysis in Chapter 12, as well as the associated sections on the pitfalls of regression modeling.

Similar to the custom fit model explained previously, we divide the dataset into a training set and a testing set. In Figure 6.18, the example used VAR373 as the training dependent variable and VAR374; VAR375 as the training independent variables, making this a form of supervised learning. Using these training data, the model is calibrated, and the parameters estimated. Then, the testing independent variables are entered, such as VAR380; VAR381. Please note that there can only be a single dependent variable versus one or more independent variables. Also, the number of independent variables in the testing set and training set must match.

The algorithm also allows you to optionally enter known testing set dependent values. Sometimes these are known and sometimes they are unknown and are to be forecasted. If the values are unknown, simply leave the input empty or enter a 0 in the input if you wish to enter the next input, which is the forecast results save location in the data grid. Figure 6.18 shows these last two inputs are treated as optional and left empty.

```
Model Inputs:
VAR373                    Training set dependent variable
VAR374; VAR375           Training set independent variable(s)
VAR380; VAR381           Testing set matching dep. var.
{VARx or 0 or empty}     Testing set dep. Var. (optional or 0)
{VARxx or empty}         Forecast save location (optional)
```

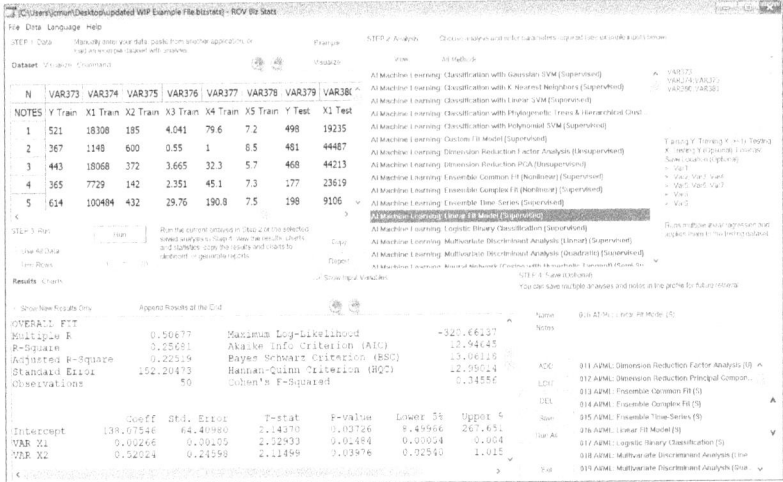

Figure 6.18: AI/ML Linear Fit Model (Supervised)

The results interpretation would be similar to the multiple linear regression. The goodness-of-fit results and fitted parameter estimations pertain to the training dataset, whereas the forecast values are based on the testing dataset when applied to these fitted parameters. Sometimes, you may wish to hold some data back from the training dataset and apply it to the testing dataset to test the accuracy of the model and its ability to forecast, as well as to view the forecast errors.

In other words, the optional testing set's dependent variable can be used and because these known values are applied, forecast errors can also be generated as a result. For example, the VARx value above can be set to VAR379.

```
AI Machine Learning: Linear Fit Model (Supervised)

Training Fit Results

Multiple R          0.50677    Maximum Log-Likelihood      -320.66137
R-Square            0.25681    Akaike Info Criterion (AIC)   12.94645
Adj. R-Square       0.22519    Bayes Schwarz Criterion (BSC) 13.06118
Standard Error    152.20473    Hannan-Quinn Criterion (HQC)  12.99014
Observations             50    Cohen's F-Squared              0.34556


                 Coeff    Std. Error    T-stat    P-value    Std. Beta
Intercept     138.07546    64.40980    2.14370    0.03726
VAR X1          0.00266     0.00105    2.52933    0.01484     0.33735
VAR X2          0.52024     0.24598    2.11499    0.03976     0.28209


ANOVA          DF           SS           MS          F       p-Value
Regression      2       376248.51    188124.26   8.12061    0.00093
Residual       47      1088815.17     23166.28
Total          49      1465063.68


           Forecasting
             Period       Forecast (F)
                1           375.5419
                2           420.4133
                3           413.4408
                4           319.5842
                .            . . .
               30           347.6475
```

AI MACHINE LEARNING: MULTIVARIATE DISCRIMINANT ANALYSIS (LINEAR) (SUPERVISED)

Related AI/ML Methods: Regression Trees CART, Gaussian Mix, Support Vector Machines

Related Traditional Methods: Linear Discriminant, Logistic Regression (Logit)

A Linear Discriminant Analysis (LDA) approach classifies a categorical dependent Training Y variable using one or more characteristic Training X variables (Figure 6.19). This supervised method applies maximum linear discriminant ratios (i.e., the ratio of between-class variance to within-class variance), which allows a clear separation or groupings of the Testing X variable. In other words, the separations are obtained through the maximization of $ss_{between}/ss_{within}$ or the sum of squares ratio of a linear combination $w_x x + w_y y + w_z z$. The optimized coefficient results help identify how each of the independent variables contributes towards the categorization. The group assignment will be based on the maximum estimated impact scores. To run the model, enter the variables you need to classify and enter the number of clusters desired. For instance, the required model inputs look like the following:

```
Model Inputs:
VAR444            Training Y (1 variable)
VAR445:VAR447     Training X (≥ 1 variables)
VAR448:VAR450     Testing X (optional, match Training X)
VAR451            Forecast save location (optional)
```

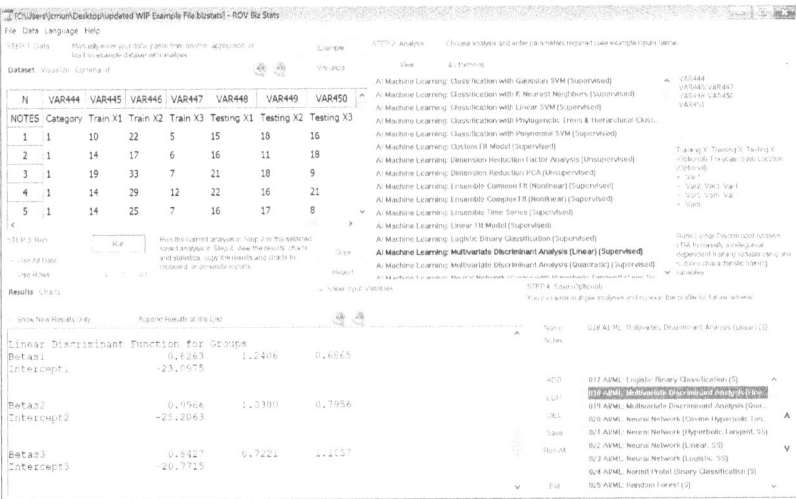

Figure 6.19: AI/ML Linear Discriminant Analysis

The results are self-explanatory in that the group counts are provided, as well as the model's classification ("Put Into Group") compared to the actual group ("True Group") or the training dataset's dependent variable. For instance, we see in the original data of 244 rows (N = 244 or 85 + 93 + 66), that 34.84% were in category 1, 38.11% in category 2, and 27.05% in category 3. Out of the 85 originally in category 1 from the training dataset, the model selected 68 of these into group 1, 13 into group 2, and 4 into group 3, which means there is an 80% accuracy (68/85). In total, there were 185 correctly grouped values out of 244, providing a 75.82% accuracy. The groups' means are also shown, as are the estimated coefficients for the three groups. Recall that LDA uses a linear discriminant model to maximize the sums of squares ratio, and we can use these coefficients in the same manner. For example, suppose the first row for the testing dataset (Figure 6.19) has the following: 15, 18, 16. We can then apply the three groups' coefficients and select the one with the highest discriminant value.

$$-23.0975 + 0.6263 \times 15 + 1.2406 \times 18 + 0.6865 \times 16 = 19.6118$$

$$-25.2063 + 0.9966 \times 15 + 1.0380 \times 18 + 0.7956 \times 16 = 21.1563$$

$$-20.7715 + 0.8427 \times 15 + 0.7221 \times 18 + 1.1057 \times 16 = 22.5580$$

Therefore, this first line item belongs to group 3. All other rows of testing data are computed in a similar fashion and categorized appropriately.

```
AI Machine Learning: Multivariate Discriminant Analysis (Linear)
(Supervised)
```

Group	1	2	3
Count	85	93	66
Prior	0.3484	0.3811	0.2705

Classification Results		True Group	
Put Into Group	1	2	3
1	68	16	3
2	13	67	13
3	4	10	50
Total N	85	93	66
N Correct	68	67	50
Proportion	0.8000	0.7204	0.7576

N: **244**
N Correct: **185**
Proportion Correct: **0.758197**

VAR	1	2	3
Global Mean Vector	15.6393	20.6762	10.5902

Means of Features in Groups			
1	12.5176	24.2235	9.0235
2	18.5376	21.1398	10.1398
3	15.5758	15.4545	13.2424

Linear Discriminant Function for Groups			
Betas1	0.6263	1.2406	0.6865
Intercept1	-23.0975		
Betas2	0.9966	1.0380	0.7956
Intercept2	-25.2063		
Betas3	0.8427	0.7221	1.1057
Intercept3	-20.7715		

```
        Forecast Group
             3
             3
             2
             3
             2
             1
             1
```

Related AI/ML Methods: Regression Trees CART, Gaussian Mix, Support Vector Machines

Related Traditional Methods: Quadratic Discriminant Analysis, Cluster Segmentation

This approach classifies the categorical dependent Y variable using characteristic X variables via Quadratic Discriminant Analysis (QDA) as shown in Figure 6.20. This method is similar to LDA, but the covariance matrix is used in the group assignment as well as the estimated coefficients because LDA assumes homoskedasticity in the prediction errors whereas QDA allows for some heteroskedasticity. This allows for second-order and second-moment approximations to calibrate the relevant group assignments. To get started, enter the variables you need to classify and enter the number of clusters desired. For instance, the required model inputs look like the following:

```
Model Inputs:
VAR444              Training Y (1 variable)
VAR445:VAR447       Training X (≥ 1 variables)
VAR448:VAR450       Testing X (optional, match Training X)
VAR452              Forecast location (optional)
```

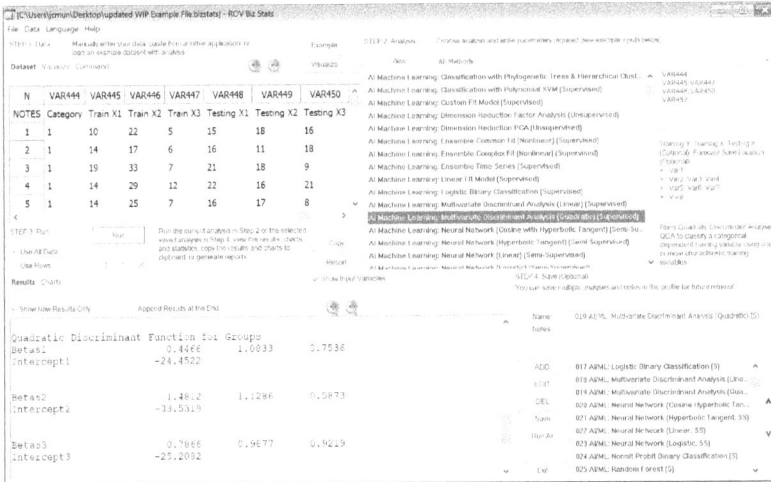

Figure 6.20: AI/ML Quadratic Discriminant Analysis

Notice that the forecasted classification groups for the QDA model below are identical to the LDA model shown previously. While the LDA model's category is easily predicted using a multiple regression equation and selecting the category with the highest likelihood result, QDA requires the inclusion of the inverse covariance matrix. This means you will have to rely on the results presented and not readily be able to compute the likelihood results directly.

```
Quadratic Discriminant Analysis (QDA)

Group                           1         2         3
Count                          85        93        66
Prior                      0.3484    0.3811    0.2705

Classification Results
                        True Group
Put Into Group                  1         2         3
1                              68        16         3
2                              14        68        14
3                               3         9        49
Total N                        85        93        66
N Correct                      68        68        49
Proportion                 0.8000    0.7312    0.7424

N : 244
N Correct : 185
Proportion Correct : 0.758197

VAR                             1         2         3
Global Mean Vector        15.6393   20.6762   10.5902

Means of Features in Groups

1                         12.5176   24.2235    9.0235
2                         18.5376   21.1398   10.1398
3                         15.5758   15.4545   13.2424

Quadratic Discriminant Function for Groups

Betas1                     0.4466    1.0833    0.7536
Intercept1               -24.4522

Betas2                     1.4812    1.1286    0.5873
Intercept2               -33.5319

Betas3                     0.7866    0.9877    0.9219
Intercept3               -25.2082

            Forecast Group
                  3
                  3
                  2
                  3
                  2
                  1
                  1
```

Related AI/ML Methods: Custom Fit Model, Ensemble Complex Fit

Related Traditional Methods: ARIMA, Time-Series Forecasting

Commonly used to refer to a network or circuit of biological neurons, modern usage of the term *neural network* often refers to artificial neural networks that consist of artificial neurons, or nodes, recreated in a software environment. Such networks attempt to mimic the neurons in the human brain in ways of thinking and identifying patterns and, in our situation, identifying patterns for the purposes of forecasting time-series data.

Note that the number of hidden layers in the network is an input parameter and will need to be calibrated with your data. Typically, the more complicated the data pattern, the higher the number of hidden layers you would need and the longer it would take to compute. It is recommended that you start at 3 layers. The testing period is simply the number of data points used in the final calibration of the Neural Network model, and we recommend using at least the same number of periods you wish to forecast as the testing period.

- Linear. Applies a linear function, where $f(x) = x$.

- Nonlinear Logistic. Applies a nonlinear logistic function, where $f(x) = (1 + e^{-x})^{-1}$.

- Nonlinear Cosine with Hyperbolic Tangent. Applies a nonlinear cosine with hyperbolic tangent function, where $f(x) = \cos\left[(e^x - e^{-x})(e^x + e^{-x})^{-1}\right]$.

- Nonlinear Hyperbolic Tangent. Applies a nonlinear hyperbolic tangent function, where $f(x) = (e^x - e^{-x})(e^x + e^{-x})^{-1}$.

The neural mapping (Figure 6.21) assumes that y_4 is the dependent variable, whereas y_1, y_2, y_3 and constant terms are the independent variables. The neural network has an input layer, a hidden layer, and an output layer. There are 3 inputs in the input layer, a neuron for the biases, 4 neurons in the hidden layer, and 1 neuron in the output layer.

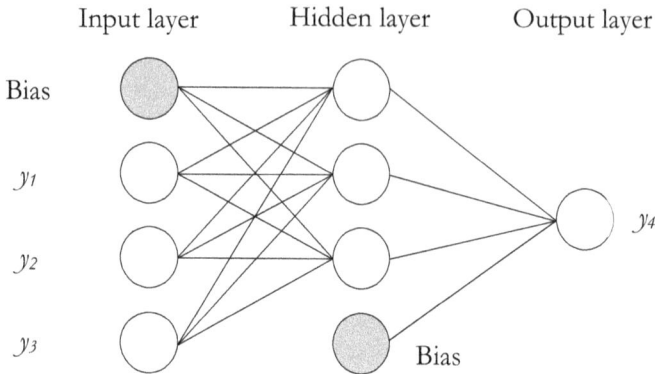

Figure 6.21: Multiple-layered Perceptron Neural Network

Figure 6.22 illustrates the neural network algorithms in BizStats. The historical time-series data is entered as the first variable, VAR227. Then, 3 perceptron layers are requested, and 20 data points are used as the testing set. The dataset has 420 data points and entering 20 indicates that we use the first 400 of these data to perform training and calibration on the model, leaving the last 20 data points for testing the model. On completion of the testing, the model is then used to forecast the next future 2 data points. The number of forecast periods has to be ≥ 1. Finally, the model is run through internal multiphasic optimization routines. Setting this to 1 (for "yes") makes it slightly longer to run but provides a more accurate calibration of the results. A chart is also provided (Figure 6.23) in the results to visually examine how good the forecast fit is.

```
Model Inputs:

VAR227     Historical time-series data to fit
3          Number of perceptron layers
20         Testing data points to withhold
2          Number of periods to forecast
1          Apply multiphased optimization (1=Yes, 0=No)
```

Figure 6.22: AI/ML Neural Network (Supervised)

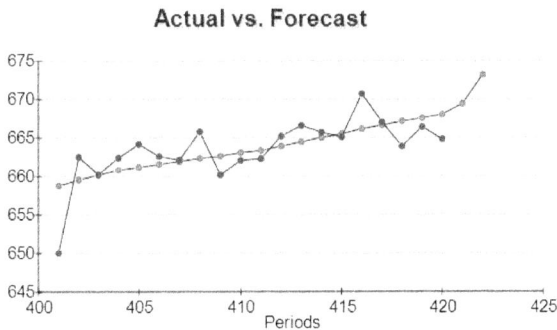

Actual vs. Forecast

Figure 6.23: AI/ML Neural Network (Supervised)

Neural Network (Cosine with Hyperbolic Tangent)
Sum of Squared Errors (Training): 0.740693
RMSE (Training): 0.043194
Sum of Squared Errors (Modified): 167.402055
RMSE (Modified): 2.893113

Forecasting

Period	Actual (Y)	Forecast (F)	Error (E)
401	650.0200	665.1658	-15.1458
402	662.4900	660.0630	2.4270
403	660.2300	658.6152	1.6148
404	662.3800	659.7383	2.6417
.	. . .	. . .	. . .
420	664.8100	667.3111	-2.5011
421		668.0264	
422		668.9191	

AI MACHINE LEARNING: LOGISTIC
BINARY CLASSIFICATION (SUPERVISED)

Related AI/ML Methods: Normit Probit Binary Classification, Multivariate Discriminant Analysis

Related Traditional Methods: Generalized Linear Models, Logit, Probit, Tobit

Limited dependent variables techniques are used to forecast the probability of something occurring given some independent variables (e.g., predicting if a credit line will default given the obligor's characteristics such as age, salary, credit card debt levels; or the probability a patient will have lung cancer based on age and number of cigarettes smoked annually, and so forth). The dependent variable is limited (i.e., binary 1 and 0 for default/cancer, or limited to integer values 1, 2, 3, etc.). Traditional regression analysis will not work as the predicted probability is usually less than 0 or greater than 1, and many of the required regression assumptions are violated (e.g., independence and normality of the errors). We also have a vector of independent variable regressors, X, which are assumed to influence the outcome, Y. A typical ordinary least squares regression approach is invalid because the regression errors are heteroskedastic and non-normal, and the resulting estimated probability estimates will return nonsensical values of above 1 or below 0. This analysis handles these problems using an iterative optimization routine to maximize a log-likelihood function when the dependent variables are limited.

The AI Machine Learning Logistic Binary Classification (Figure 6.24) regression is used for predicting the probability of occurrence of an event by fitting data to a logistic curve. It is a Generalized Linear Model used for binomial regression, and, like many forms of regression analysis, it makes use of several predictor variables that may be either numerical or categorical. Maximum Likelihood Estimation (MLE) is applied in a binary multivariate logistic analysis to determine the expected probability of success of belonging to a certain group.

```
Model Inputs:
VAR421              Training set dependent var (binary 0/1)
VAR422:VAR425       Training set independent variables
VAR427:VAR430       Testing set (optional)
VAR432              Forecast probability save (optional)
```

The estimated coefficients for the Logistic model are the logarithmic odds ratios and cannot be interpreted directly as probabilities. A quick computation is first required. Specifically, the Logit model is defined as Estimated Y or $(\hat{Y})$ using $\hat{Y} = ln[P_i/(1 - P_i)]$ or, conversely, $P_i = e^{\hat{Y}}/(1 + e^{\hat{Y}})$, and the coefficients β_i are the log odds ratios. So, taking the antilog or e^{β_i} we obtain the odds ratio of $P_i/(1 - P_i)$. This means that with an increase in a unit of β_i, the log odds ratio increases by this amount. Finally, the rate of change in the probability is $dP/dX = \beta_i P_i (1 - P_i)$. The standard error measures how accurate the predicted coefficients are, and the t-statistics are the ratios of each predicted coefficient to its standard error and are used in the typical regression hypothesis test of the significance of each estimated parameter. To estimate the probability of success of belonging to a certain group (e.g., predicting if a smoker will develop chest complications given the amount smoked per year), simply compute the estimated $\hat{Y}$ value using the MLE coefficients. For example, if the model is $\hat{Y} = 1.1 + 0.005 \ (Cigarettes)$, then for someone smoking 100 packs per year, $\hat{Y} = 1.1 + 0.005(100) = 1.6$. Next, compute the inverse antilog of the odds ratio by doing: $e^{\hat{Y}}/[1 + e^{\hat{Y}}] = e^{1.6}/(1 + e^{1.6}) = 0.8320$. So, such a person has an 83.20% chance of developing some chest complications in his or her lifetime.

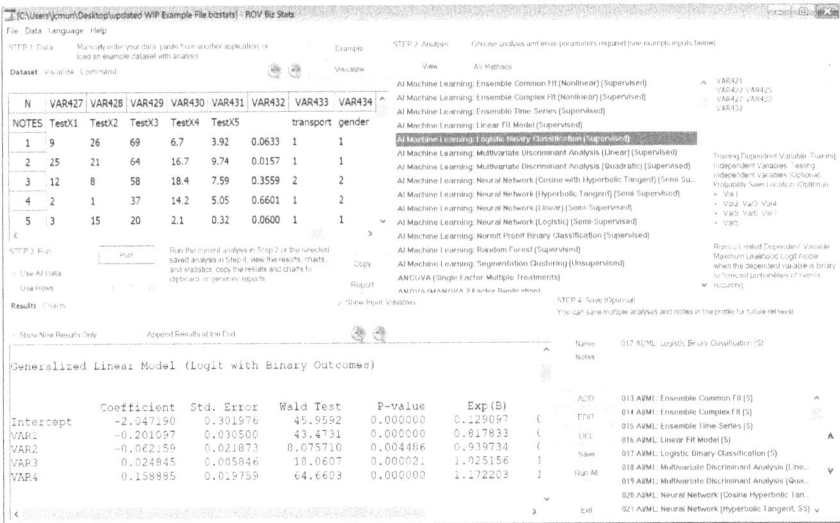

Figure 6.24: AI/ML Logistic Binary Classification (Supervised)

The results interpretation is similar to that of a standard multiple regression, with the exception of computing the probability. For example, in Figure 6.24, the first row of the testing variable's data points are 9, 26, 69, 6.7, which means that the $\hat{Y} = -2.047190 - 0.201097(9) - 0.062159(26) + 0.024845(69) + 0.158885(6.7) = -2.6944$. Next, we can compute the inverse antilog of the odds ratio by doing: $e^{\hat{Y}}/[1 + e^{\hat{Y}}] = e^{-2.6944}/(1 + e^{-2.6944}) = 6.33\%$. The remaining rows are similarly computed.

In addition, the results also return a confusion matrix, which lists the true responses based on the training set's dependent variable and the predicted responses. The matrix shows the various positivity and recall rates as well as the specificity, prevalence of false positives, and false negatives. True Positive (TP) is where the actual is 1 and the predicted is 1, and we see that 67.37% of the dataset was predicted correctly as a true positive. The same interpretation applies to False Negatives (FN), False Positives (FP), and True Negatives (TN).

In addition, Positive Sensitivity Recall is TP/(TP+FN) and it measures the ability to predict positive outcomes. Negative Specificity is TN/(TN+FP) and it measures the ability to predict negative outcomes. Event Prevalence is the amount of Actual Y=1 and it measures the positive outcomes in the original data. False Positives is FP/(FP+TP) or Type I error. False Negatives is FN/(FN+TN) or Type II error. Positive Precision is TP/(TP+FP) and it measures the accuracy of a predicted positive outcome. Negative Precision is TN/(TN+FN) and it measures the accuracy of a predicted negative outcome. The Accuracy of the overall prediction is the % of TP and TN.

Finally, the results show the Receiver Operating Characteristic (ROC) curve (Figure 6.25). It plots the Positive Sensitivity Rate against the Negative Specificity, where the area under the curve (AUC) is another measure of the accuracy of the classification model. The ROC plots the model's performance at all classification thresholds. AUC ranges from 0%–100%, where 100% indicates a perfect fit. The ROC is available by clicking on the Charts subtab in BizStats while the AUC result is shown as one of the accuracy measures in the Confusion Matrix section.

Generalized Linear Model (Logit with Binary Outcomes)

	Coefficient	Std. Error	Wald Test	P-value	Exp(B)
Intercept	**-2.047190**	0.301976	45.9592	0.000000	0.129097
VAR1	**-0.201097**	0.030500	43.4731	0.000000	0.817833
VAR2	**-0.062159**	0.021873	8.07571	0.004486	0.939734
VAR3	**0.024845**	0.005846	18.0607	0.000021	1.025156
VAR4	**0.158885**	0.019759	64.6603	0.000000	1.172203

Log-Likelihood	-214.8162
Restricted Log-Likelihood	-285.4773
McFadden R-squared	0.247519
Cox and Snell R-squared	0.246212
Nagelkerke R-squared	0.361656
Raw Akaike Info. Criterion	439.6324
Raw Bayes Criterion	460.7054
Chi-Square	141.3222
Degrees of Freedom	4
P-value	0.000000

Confusion Matrix

	Predicted Response	
True Response	y = 1	y = 0
y = 1	**True Positive TP**	**False Negative FN**
y = 0	**False Positive FP**	**True Negative TN**

	Predicted Response	
True Response	**y = 1**	y = 0
y = 1	**64**	65
y = 0	31	340

	Predicted Response	
True Response	**y = 1**	y = 0
y = 1	**67.37%**	16.05%
y = 0	32.63%	83.95%

Positive Sensitivity Recall	49.61%
Negative Specificity	91.64%
Event Prevalence	25.80%
False Positives	32.63%
False Negatives	16.05%
Positive Precision	67.37%
Negative Precision	83.95%
Accuracy	80.80%
ROC Curve's AUC Measure	72.61%

Forecast Y	Probability
-2.6944	**6.33%**
-4.1365	1.57%
-0.5931	35.59%
0.6639	66.01%
-2.7523	6.00%
-0.6550	34.19%
-1.2852	21.67%
-0.9458	27.97%
-2.3878	8.41%
1.5601	82.64%

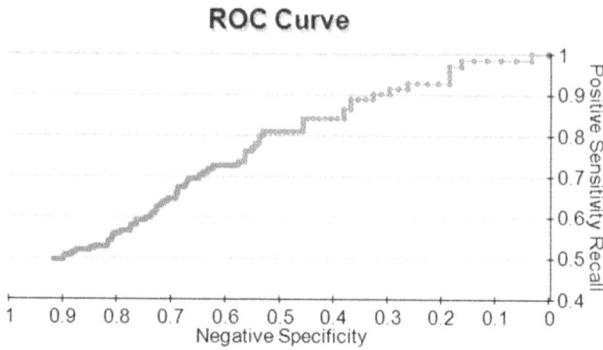

ROC Curve

Figure 6.25: ROC & AUC

AI MACHINE LEARNING: NORMIT PROBIT
BINARY CLASSIFICATION (SUPERVISED)

Related AI/ML Methods: Logistic Binary, Multivariate Discriminant Analysis

Related Traditional Methods: Generalized Linear Models, Logit, Probit, Tobit

The AI Machine Learning Normit Probit model (Figure 6.26) is a popular alternative specification for the Logistic binary response model. It employs a Normit-Probit function estimated using maximum likelihood estimation and is also sometimes called a Probit regression. The Probit and logistic regression models tend to produce very similar predictions. The choice of using a Probit or Logit is entirely up to convenience, and the main distinction is that the logistic distribution has a higher kurtosis (fatter tails) to account for extreme values. For example, suppose that house ownership is the decision to be modeled, and this response variable is binary (home purchase or no home purchase) and depends on a series of independent variables X_i such as income, age, and so forth, such that $I_i = \beta_0 + \beta_1 X_1 + \cdots + \beta_n X_n$, where the larger the value of I_i, the higher the probability of homeownership. For each family, a critical threshold I^* exists, where, if exceeded, the house is purchased, otherwise, no home is purchased, and the outcome probability (P) is assumed to be normally distributed, such that $P_i = CDF(I)$ using a standard-normal cumulative distribution function (CDF). Therefore, use the estimated coefficients exactly like that of a regression model and, using the estimated $\hat{Y}$, apply a standard-normal distribution to compute the probability.

```
Model Inputs:
VAR421              Training set dependent var. (binary 0/1)
VAR422:VAR425       Training set independent var.
VAR427:VAR430       Testing set (optional)
VAR432              Forecast probability location (optional)
```

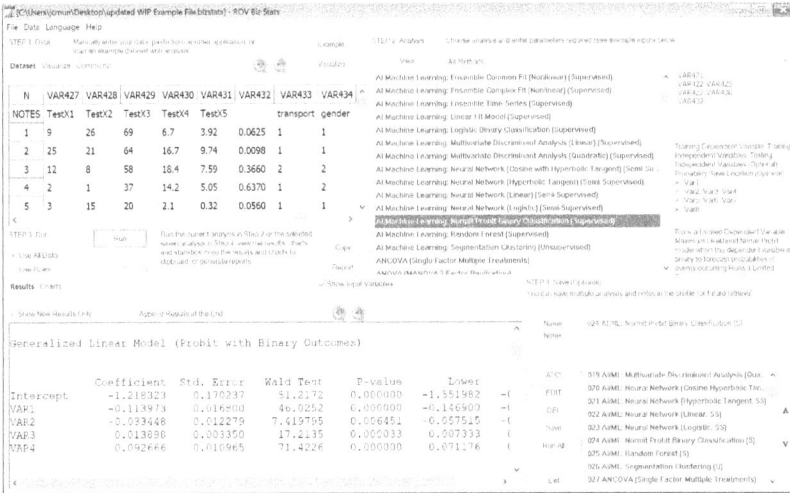

Figure 6.26: AI/ML Normit Probit Binary Classification (Supervised)

The results interpretation is similar to that of a standard multiple regression and the AI/ML Logistic Binary Classification model, with the exception of computing the probability, which, in the case of a Normit Probit model, requires a standard normal distribution. For example, in Figure 6.26, the first row of the testing variable's data points are 9, 26, 69, 6.7, which means that the $\hat{Y} = -1.218323 - 0.113973(9) - 0.033448(26) + 0.013898(69) + 0.092666(6.7) = -1.5339$ (rounded). Next, we can compute the normal cumulative distribution function $\Phi(-1.5339) = 6.25\%$. The resulting forecasted probability for Normit is typically fairly close to the Logit result seen previously. The remaining rows are similarly computed. Finally, the ROC, AUC, and Confusion Matrix results such as positivity, specificity, false positives, false negatives, and so forth, are also computed and their interpretations are identical to the AI/ML Logistic Binary Classification model.

```
       Generalized Linear Model (Probit with Binary Outcomes)

              Coefficient   Std. Error   Wald Test     P-value
Intercept       -1.218323     0.170237     51.2172    0.000000
VAR1            -0.113973     0.016800     46.0252    0.000000
VAR2            -0.033448     0.012279      7.419795  0.006451
VAR3             0.013898     0.003350     17.2135    0.000033
VAR4             0.092666     0.010965     71.4226    0.000000

Log-Likelihood                            -214.3784
Restricted Log-Likelihood                 -285.4773
McFadden R-squared                           0.249053
Cox and Snell R-squared                      0.247531
Nagelkerke R-squared                         0.363593
Raw Akaike Info. Criterion                 438.7567
Raw Bayes Criterion                        459.8298
Chi-Square                                 142.1979
Degrees of Freedom                                 4
P-value                                      0.000000
```

Confusion Matrix

```
                        Predicted Response
   True Response          y = 1                 y = 0
      y = 1         True Positive TP      False Negative FN
      y = 0         False Positive FP     True Negative TN

                        Predicted Response
   True Response          y = 1                 y = 0
      y = 1               70                     59
      y = 0               39                    332

                        Predicted Response
   True Response          y = 1                 y = 0
      y = 1             64.22%                 15.09%
      y = 0             35.78%                 84.91%


Positive Sensitivity Recall       54.26%
Negative Specificity              89.49%
Event Prevalence                  25.80%
False Positives                   35.78%
False Negatives                   15.09%
Positive Precision                64.22%
Negative Precision                84.91%
Accuracy                          80.40%
ROC Curve's AUC Measure           72.40%


   Forecast Y Probability
      -1.5339        6.25%
      -2.3330        0.98%
      -0.3424       36.60%
       0.3504       63.70%
      -1.5894        5.60%
      -0.3880       34.90%
      -0.7630       22.27%
      -0.5542       28.97%
      -1.4084        7.95%
       0.8985       81.55%
```

AI MACHINE LEARNING: RANDOM FOREST (SUPERVISED)

Related AI/ML Methods: Regression Trees CART

Related Traditional Methods: Bootstrap Simulation, Bootstrap Regression

In this approach, bootstraps of regression trees are run multiple times with different combinations of data points and variables to develop a consensus forecast of group assignments. Using a single set of Training Y and Training X variables, the data and variables are bootstrapped and resampled. Each resampling will be run in the CART or classification and regression tree model, and the consensus categorization results will be generated (Figure 6.27). The benefit of random forests is that it provides a consensus forecast (wisdom of the crowd) through a resampling with replacement of both the variables and the data points. However, the individual CART model and tree process will no longer be available. To get started with this approach, enter the variables you need to classify and enter the number of clusters desired. The required model inputs look like this:

```
Model Inputs:
VAR433              Training Y (1 variable)
VAR434:VAR437       Training X (≥ 1 variables)
3                   Min variables (< the total X variables)
9                   Min data points (< the total number of rows)
300                 Max Bootstrap trials (2-1000)
VAR438:VAR441       Testing X (optional)
VARX                Forecast save location (optional)
```

Figure 6.27: AI/ML Random Forest

Suppose we apply the entire dataset and bootstrapped it (i.e., minimum variables is 4 and the minimum data points to use is 10, which means the entire dataset is utilized), the results will be identical to the AI/ML Classification and Regression Tree CART model. Recall that the CART results had 100% for all three categories. In this random forest model, if we only apply a minimum of 3 variables with 9 data rows, we see the results shown next. Hundreds of CART models are bootstrapped, and the averages of the results are obtained. The testing dataset's categorization shows that the highest probability events are in categories 1, 1, 2, 1, 1, 2, 2, 3, 3, 3, which also corresponds to the single CART model results.

```
AI Machine Learning: Random Forest (Supervised)

Category      Average Accuracy
   1.00            76.17%
   2.00           100.00%
   3.00            94.89%
```

```
Training Dataset
    Actual       Category 1        Category 2        Category 3
     1.00         100.00%            0.00%             0.00%
     1.00          75.00%           25.00%             0.00%
     2.00           0.00%          100.00%             0.00%
     1.00         100.00%            0.00%             0.00%
     1.00          75.00%           25.00%             0.00%
     2.00           0.00%          100.00%             0.00%
     2.00           0.00%          100.00%             0.00%
     3.00           0.00%            0.00%           100.00%
     3.00           0.00%            0.00%           100.00%
     3.00           0.00%            0.00%           100.00%
```

```
Testing Dataset
             Category 1        Category 2        Category 3
              100.00%            0.00%             0.00%
               75.00%           25.00%             0.00%
               19.17%           80.83%             0.00%
              100.00%            0.00%             0.00%
               75.00%           25.00%             0.00%
                0.00%          100.00%             0.00%
                0.00%          100.00%             0.00%
                0.00%            0.00%           100.00%
                0.00%            0.00%           100.00%
                0.00%            0.00%           100.00%
```

AI MACHINE LEARNING: SEGMENTATION CLUSTERING (UNSUPERVISED)

Related AI/ML Methods: Multivariate Discriminant Analysis (LDA & QDA)

Related Traditional Methods: Quadratic Discriminant Analysis (LDA & QDA)

Taking the original dataset, we run some internal algorithms (a combination of k-means hierarchical clustering and other methods-of-moments to find the best-fitting groups or natural statistical clusters) to statistically divide or segment the original dataset into multiple groups. Segment this dataset into as many groups as you wish. This technique is valuable in a variety of settings including marketing (market segmentation of customers into various customer relationship management groups etc.), physical sciences, engineering, and others.

Figure 6.28 illustrates the AI Machine Learning Segmentation Clustering algorithm at work. VAR415 shows the various states, whereas VAR416:VAR419 provides the characteristics in terms of each state's number of murders, number of assaults, the state population in millions, and number of breaking-and-entering events. Using these numerical values (VAR416:VAR419), the states can be segmented into various groups.

```
Model Inputs:
VAR416:VAR419    Variables to cluster
0                Optional (0=Show Up To X, 1=Show Cluster X)
5                Cluster X
```

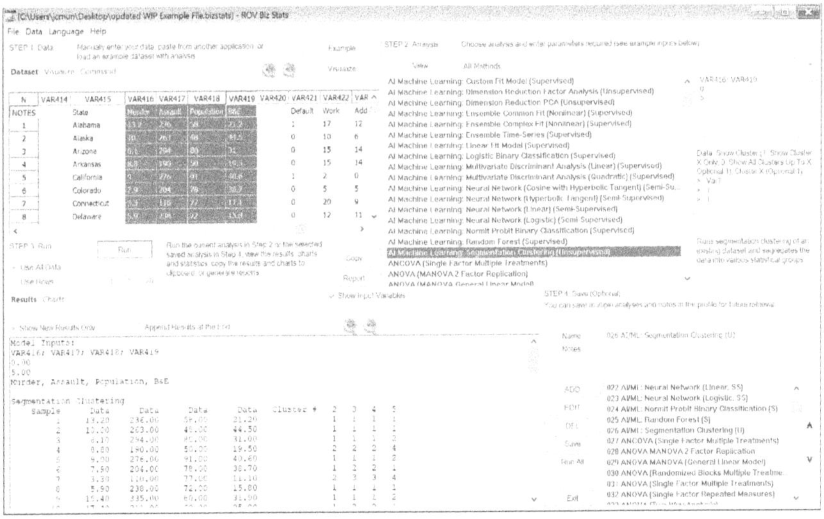

Figure 6.28: AI/ML Segmentation Clustering (Unsupervised)

The results from cluster analysis shown next generate clusters of multiple groups partitioned based on data similarity for exploratory data analysis and data mining (e.g., machine learning, pattern recognition, image analysis, bioinformatics, etc.). The objects in the same cluster are more similar to each other than to those in other clusters.

In addition, cluster analysis can be used to discover data structures without providing an explanation or interpretation of the relationship among variables. The results will show the cluster membership number as well as the centroid's mean values and counts of members within each cluster subgroup. For example, if we need to segregate the data into 3 segments, we see that one segment has Alaska, Alabama, Arizona, and so forth, while the second segment includes states like Arkansas and so forth (i.e., the 3 Cluster result shows 1, 1, 1, 2, 1, and so forth, indicating that the first three sample rows are categorized into Cluster 1, followed by Cluster 2, and then Cluster 1, etc.). These segments group similar characteristics together as cohorts, where states within these cohorts have the highest amounts of statistical similarities.

```
Segmentation Clustering                                    Clusters
N      Data      Data      Data      Data        C2  C3  C4  C5
1     13.20    236.00     58.00     21.20         1   1   1   1
2     10.00    263.00     48.00     44.50         1   1   1   1
3      8.10    294.00     80.00     31.00         1   1   1   2
4      8.80    190.00     50.00     19.50         2   2   2   4
5      9.00    276.00     91.00     40.60         1   1   1   2
.     . . .     . . .     . . .     . . .         .   .   .   .
48     5.70     81.00     39.00      9.30         2   3   4   5
49     2.60     53.00     66.00     10.80         2   3   4   3
50     6.80    161.00     60.00     15.60         2   2   2   4

Cluster Centroids [1]
No. of Clusters           2         3         4         5
              1       11.95     11.81     11.81     12.03
              2        5.24      8.21      8.54     11.80
              3                  4.27      5.45      3.73
              4                            2.95      6.43
              5                                      2.70
Cluster Centroids [2]
No. of Clusters           2         3         4         5
              1      261.95    272.56    272.56    239.25
              2      114.87    173.29    175.46    300.86
              3                 87.55    115.36     68.25
              4                           62.70    141.60
              5                                     65.14
Cluster Centroids [3]
No. of Clusters           2         3         4         5
              1       69.00     68.31     68.31     69.17
              2       63.42     70.64     70.46     68.71
              3                 59.75     66.27     69.25
              4                           53.90     68.25
              5                                     46.29
Cluster Counts
No. of Clusters           2         3         4         5
              1          19        16        16        12
              2          31        14        13         7
              3                    20        11         4
              4                              10        20
              5                                         7
```

BIZSTATS ANALYTICS

The following is a quick reference guide to all the analytics and methods in ROV's BizStats software. It begins with an alphabetical presentation of each model that includes a description of what the method or model does, a short tip that is also visible in the BizStats software, the required data inputs, and examples of data inputs. Note that additional examples of data types and how data variables should be arranged are provided in the data type sections at the end of this chapter. In those sections, the methods and models are also arranged by categories (e.g., multivariate methods versus single variable methods, or stochastic models versus reliability and consistency methods).

- **Artificial Intelligence Machine Learning (AI/ML): Bagging Linear Fit Bootstrap (Supervised).** This method applies a Bootstrap Aggregation (Bagging) Linear Fit Model of hundreds of models via resampled data to generate the best consensus forecasts. The idea is that in a random selection of data, taking the average forecast of an ensemble of models provides a more accurate prediction than a single sample. In a typical multivariate linear regression, the relationship structure and characteristics of a dependent variable and how it depends on other independent exogenous variables can be modeled. The model can be used to understand the relationship among these variables as well as for the purposes of forecasting and predictive modeling. The accuracy and goodness of fit for this model can also be determined. Similar to a linear multivariate regression model, we first train the algorithm using the training dependent and training independent variables, which will identify the optimized parameters to use on the testing dataset. Then, the dataset is resampled, and the algorithm is again run. This process is repeated or bootstrapped hundreds of times, and the output forecasts will be a consensus of all these bootstrapped models.

- o Short Tip: Bootstrap Aggregation (Bagging) of the Linear Fit Model of hundreds of models via resampled data to generate the best consensus forecasts.

- o Model Input: Data Type C. Multiple variables.

  - Training Y, Training X, Testing X, Number of Bootstraps (1–1000), Number of Data Points (< Number of Rows), Testing Y (Optional), Forecast Save Location (Optional):

    - >VAR1
    - >VAR2:VAR5
    - 1000
    - 45
    - >VAR6:VAR9
    - >VAR10

- **Artificial Intelligence Machine Learning (AI/ML): Bagging Nonlinear Fit Bootstrap (Supervised).** This method computes a Bagging or Bootstrap Aggregation on a custom nonlinear fit model hundreds of times via resampled data to generate the best consensus forecasts. This approach is similar to the Bagging Linear Fit Bootstrap model described previously. The main difference is that the regression model is a customized nonlinear model that the user can enter. Again, do note the differences between bootstrap aggregation versus ensemble learning methods as described in the previous method.

  - o Short Tip: Bootstrap Aggregation (Bagging) of the custom Nonlinear Fit Model of hundreds of models via resampled data to generate the best consensus forecasts.

  - o Model Input: Data Type C. Multiple variables.

    - Training Y, Training X, Testing X, Number of Bootstraps (1–1000), Number of Data Points (< Number of Rows), Testing Y (Optional), Forecast Save Location (Optional):

      - >VAR1
      - >VAR2:VAR5
      - 1000
      - 45
      - >VAR6:VAR9
      - >VAR10

- **Artificial Intelligence Machine Learning (AI/ML): Classification and Regression Trees (CART) (Supervised).** The Classification and Regression Trees (CART) model generates branches and subgroups of the categorical dependent Y variable using characteristic X variables. CART is typically used for data mining and constitutes a supervised machine learning approach. This is a classification approach when the dependent variable is categorical, and the tree is used to determine the class or group within which a target testing variable is most likely to fall. The data is split into branches along a tree, and each branch split will be determined using Gini coefficients and information loss coefficients based on the questions asked along the way.

  o Short Tip: Classification & Regression Trees (CART) data mining generating branches/subgroups of the categorical dependent variable using characteristic independent variables.

  o Model Input: Data Type C. Multiple variables.

    ▪ Training Y, Training X, Testing X (Optional), Forecast Save Location (Optional):

      - >VAR1
      - >VAR2:VAR5
      - >VAR6:VAR9
      - >VAR10

- **Artificial Intelligence Machine Learning (AI/ML): Classification with Gaussian Mix & K-Means Segmentation (Unsupervised).** Runs a Gaussian Mix Cluster Model assuming multiple overlaying normal distributions. This is an unsupervised machine learning method that is applicable when the origins of the clusters are unknown. The results show the probabilities of a certain value belonging to a particular cluster.

  o Short Tip: Runs an unsupervised Gaussian Mix model with K-Mean Cluster classification when the origins of the clusters are unknown.

  o Model Input: Data Type C. Multiple variables.

    ▪ Variables to Classify, Number of Clusters, Max Iterations, Forecast Save Location (Optional):

      - >VAR1:VAR4
      - >5
      - >1000
      - >VAR5

- Artificial Intelligence Machine Learning (AI/ML): Classification with K-Nearest Neighbor (Supervised). The K-Nearest Neighbor algorithm, also known as the K-Dimensional Tree structure, is used to classify and segregate the data into a few small dimensions. Simply enter the variables you need to classify and enter the number of clusters desired.

  o Short Tip: KNN classifies and segregates data into groups, also called K-Dimensional Tree structure, useful for partitioning data points into a few small dimensions.

  o Model Input: Data Type C. Multiple variables.

    ▪ Training X, Testing X:

      • >VAR1:VAR4
      • >VAR5:VAR9

- Artificial Intelligence Machine Learning (AI/ML): Classification with Phylogenetic Trees & Hierarchical Clustering (Unsupervised). This method is unsupervised, and the algorithm is applied to figure out how to cluster a set of data that is unordered without being provided with any training data having the correct responses. The result is a hierarchical cluster with multiple fully nested sets where the smallest sets are the individual elements of the set, and the largest set is the entire dataset. To apply a phylogenetic tree using hierarchical clustering, the dataset is typically a set of sequences or distance matrices.

  o Short Tip: Phylogenetic Trees with Hierarchical Clustering for unsupervised classification of unordered data.

  o Model Input: Data Type C. Multiple variables.

    ▪ Training Y, Training X:

      • >VAR1
      • >VAR2

- Artificial Intelligence Machine Learning (AI/ML): Classification with Support Vector Machines (Supervised). Support Vector Machines (SVM) is a class of supervised machine learning algorithms used for classification. SVM methods are simpler to implement and run than complex neural network algorithms. In supervised learning, we typically start with a set of *training* data. The algorithm is trained using this dataset (i.e., the parameters are optimized and identified), and then the same model parameters are applied to the *testing* set or to a new dataset never before seen by the algorithm.

- o Gaussian SVM. Applies a normal kernel estimator $exp\left[-|\mathbf{x}_i - \mathbf{x}_j|^2/2\sigma^2\right]$.

- o Linear SVM. Applies a standard linear kernel estimator $\mathbf{x}_i \cdot \mathbf{x}_j$.

- o Polynomial SVM. Applies a polynomial (e.g., quadratic or nonlinear programming) kernel density estimator $|a\mathbf{x}_i \cdot \mathbf{x}_j + b|^c$.

- o Short Tip: Runs a supervised machine learning algorithm using support vector machines for the classification of data.

- o Model Input: Data Type C. One dependent variable and multiple independent variables are required.

  - ▪ Training Dependent Variable, Training Independent Variables, Sigma, Lambda, Omega, Calibration (Optional: 0), Testing Independent Variables (Optional but Highly Recommended), Forecast Location (Optional), Groupings (Optional):

    - >VAR1
    - >VAR2; VAR3
    - >2
    - >1000
    - >0.5
    - >VAR4; VAR5
    - >VAR6
    - >VAR7

- Artificial Intelligence Machine Learning (AI/ML): Custom Fit Model (Supervised). Applicable for forecasting time-series and cross-sectional data and for modeling relationships among variables. It allows you to create customized multiple regression models. Econometrics refers to a branch of business analytics, modeling, and forecasting techniques for modeling the behavior of or forecasting certain business, financial, economic, physical science, and other variables. Running the AI Machine Learning Custom Fit models is like regular econometric regression analysis except that the dependent and independent variables can be modified before a regression is run.

- Short Tip: Customizes a regression model using custom independent variables.

- Model Input: Data Type C. One dependent variable and multiple independent variables are required.

  - Training Dependent Variable, Training Independent Variables, Testing Independent Variable, Testing Dependent Variables (Optional), Save Forecast Location (Optional):

    - >VAR1
    - >VAR2; LN(VAR3); (VAR4)^2; LAG(VAR5,1); (VAR6*VAR7)
    - >VAR9; LN(VAR10); (VAR11)^2; LAG(VAR12,1); (VAR13*VAR14)

- **Artificial Intelligence Machine Learning (AI/ML): Dimension Reduction Factor Analysis (Unsupervised).** Runs Factor Analysis to analyze interrelationships within large numbers of variables and simplifies said factors into a smaller number of common factors. The method condenses information contained in the original set of variables into a smaller set of implicit factor variables with minimal loss of information. The analysis is related to Principal Component Analysis (PCA) by using the correlation matrix and applying PCA coupled with a Varimax matrix rotation to simplify the factors.

  - Short Tip: Factor Analysis to analyze interrelationships within a large number of variables and simplify said factors into a smaller number of common factors.

  - Model Input: Data Type C. Requires at least three or more variables, each with an equal number of rows.

    - Variables:

      - >VAR1; VAR2; VAR3; …

- **Artificial Intelligence Machine Learning (AI/ML): Dimension Reduction Principal Component Analysis (Unsupervised).** Principal component analysis, or PCA, makes multivariate data easier to model and summarize. To understand PCA, suppose we start with N variables that are unlikely to be independent of one another, such that changing the value of one variable will change another variable. PCA modeling will replace the original N variables with a new set of M variables that are less than N but are uncorrelated to one another, while at the same time, each of these M variables is a linear combination of the original N variables so that most of the variation can be accounted for using fewer explanatory variables.

- o Short Tip: Runs unsupervised dimension reduction Principal Component Analysis on multiple variables, returning eigenvalues, eigenvectors, and revised data.

- o Model Input: Data Type C. Three or more input variables are required. Different variables are arranged in columns, and all variables must have at least 5 data points each, with the same number of total data points or rows per variable.

  - Variables:

    - >VAR1; VAR2; VAR3; …

- **Artificial Intelligence Machine Learning (AI/ML): Ensemble Common Fit (Supervised).** This algorithm computes thousands of possible nonlinear and interaction models (suitable for cross-sectional data for pattern recognition); it calibrates the best model with the training dataset and forecasts outcomes using the testing dataset. In other words, it performs an ensemble learning approach.

  - o Short Tip: Runs thousands of nonlinear interaction models (cross-sectional pattern recognition); calibrates the best forecasting model.

  - o Model Input: Data Type C. Multiple variables.

    - Training Y, Training X, Testing X (Optional), Forecast Save Location (Optional), P-value Threshold (Optional, Default = 0.10), Time-Series Lags (Optional, Default = 0):

      - >VAR1
      - >VAR2:VAR5
      - >VAR6:VAR9
      - >VAR10
      - >0.10
      - >0

- **Artificial Intelligence Machine Learning (AI/ML): Ensemble Complex Fit (Supervised).** Using an ensemble learning approach, this model computes thousands of possible nonlinear and interaction models (suitable for time-series data for pattern recognition); it calibrates the best model with the training dataset and forecasts outcomes using the testing dataset.

  - Short Tip: Runs thousands of nonlinear interaction models (time-series pattern recognition); calibrates the best forecasting model.

  - Model Input: Data Type C. Multiple variables.
    - Training Y, Training X, Testing X (Optional), Forecast Save Location (Optional), P-value Threshold (Optional, Default = 0.10), Time-Series Lags (Optional, Default = 0), Autoregressive Lags (Optional, Default = 0):

      - >VAR1
      - >VAR2:VAR5
      - >VAR6:VAR9
      - >VAR10
      - >0.10
      - >0
      - >0

- **Artificial Intelligence Machine Learning (AI/ML): Ensemble Time-Series Fit (Supervised).** This algorithm computes and calibrates an ensemble of different time-series forecast models, selects the best combination, and generates forecasts for the single historical time-series variable. An ensemble of time-series forecast methods such as Holt–Winters, deseasonalized forecasts, ARIMA, and others are applied, the best model combinations are used, and the consensus forecasts are provided.

  - Short Tip: Computes an ensemble of different time-series models, selects the best combination, and generates forecasts.

  - Model Input: Data Type C. Multiple variables.
    - Historical Time-series Data, Seasonality, Forecast Periods, Forecast Save Location (Optional):

      - >VAR1
      - 4
      - 8
      - >VAR2

- **Artificial Intelligence Machine Learning (AI/ML): Linear Fit Model (Supervised).** Multivariate linear regression is used to model the relationship structure and characteristics of a certain dependent variable as it depends on other independent exogenous variables in the training dataset. Using the modeled relationship, we can forecast the future values of the dependent variable using the testing set's independent variables. The accuracy and goodness of fit for this model can also be determined. Linear and nonlinear models can be fitted in the multiple regression analysis.

  - o Short Tip: Runs multiple linear regressions and applies them to the testing dataset.

  - o Model Input: Data Type C. Two sets of variables are required: One Dependent Variable and One or Multiple Independent Variables, with at least 5 rows of data in each variable and the same number of total data points or rows per variable.

    - ▪ Training Dependent Variable, Training Independent Variables (one or more), Testing Independent Variables (same as training), Testing Dependent (Optional), Save Forecasts (Optional):

      - • >VAR1
      - • >VAR2; VAR3; …
      - • >VAR4; VAR5;…

- **Artificial Intelligence Machine Learning (AI/ML): Multivariate Discriminant Analysis (Linear) (Supervised).** A Linear Discriminant Analysis (LDA) approach classifies a categorical dependent Training Y variable using one or more characteristic Training X variables. This supervised method applies maximum linear discriminant ratios (i.e., the ratio of between-class variance to within-class variance), which allows a clear separation or groupings of the Testing X variable. In other words, the separations are obtained through the maximization of the sum of squares ratio of a linear combination. The optimized coefficient results help identify how each of the independent variables contributes towards the categorization. The group assignment will be based on the maximum estimated impact scores.

  - o Short Tip: Runs Linear Discriminant Analysis LDA to classify a categorical dependent training variable using one or more characteristic training variables.

- Model Input: Data Type C. Multiple variables.

  - Training Y, Training X, Testing X (Optional), Forecast Save Location (Optional):

    - >VAR1
    - >VAR2:VAR5
    - >VAR6:VAR9
    - >VAR10

- **Artificial Intelligence Machine Learning (AI/ML): Multivariate Discriminant Analysis (Quadratic) (Supervised).** The approach classifies the categorical dependent Y variable using characteristic X variables via Quadratic Discriminant Analysis (QDA). This method is similar to LDA, but the covariance matrix is used in the group assignment as well as the estimated coefficients. This is because LDA assumes homoskedasticity in the prediction errors whereas QDA allows for some heteroskedasticity. This allows for second-order and second-moment approximations to calibrate the relevant group assignments.

  - Short Tip: Runs Quadratic Discriminant Analysis QDA to classify a categorical dependent training variable using one or more characteristic training variables.

  - Model Input: Data Type C. Multiple variables.

    - Training Y, Training X, Testing X (Optional), Forecast Save Location (Optional):

      - >VAR1
      - >VAR2:VAR5
      - >VAR6:VAR9
      - >VAR10

- **Artificial Intelligence Machine Learning (AI/ML): Neural Network.** Commonly used to refer to a network or circuit of biological neurons, modern usage of the term *neural network* often refers to artificial neural networks that consist of artificial neurons, or nodes, recreated in a software environment. Such networks attempt to mimic the neurons in the human brain in ways of thinking and identifying patterns and, in our situation, identifying patterns for the purposes of forecasting time-series data.

  - **Linear.** Applies a linear function.

  - **Nonlinear Logistic.** Applies a nonlinear logistic function.

- o **Nonlinear Cosine with Hyperbolic Tangent.** Applies a nonlinear cosine with hyperbolic tangent function.

- o **Nonlinear Hyperbolic Tangent.** Applies a nonlinear hyperbolic tangent function.

- o Short Tip: Runs a time-series neural network forecast through pattern recognition algorithms (linear, logistic, cosine, hyperbolic).

- o Model Input: Data Type A. Data Variable, Layers, Testing Set, Forecast Periods, and Apply Multiphased Optimization (Optional, default set to 0 or no optimization).

  - Data Variable, Layers, Testing Set, Forecast Periods:

    - >VAR1
    - >3
    - >20
    - >5
    - >1

- **Artificial Intelligence Machine Learning (AI/ML): Logistic Binary Classification (Supervised).** Limited dependent variables techniques are used to forecast the probability of something occurring given some independent variables (e.g., predicting if a credit line will default given the obligor's characteristics such as age, salary, credit card debt levels; or the probability a patient will have lung cancer based on age and number of cigarettes smoked monthly, and so forth). The dependent variable is limited (i.e., binary 1 and 0 for default/cancer, or limited to integer values 1, 2, 3, etc.). Traditional regression analysis will not work as the predicted probability is usually less than 0 or greater than 1, and many of the required regression assumptions are violated (e.g., independence and normality of the errors). We also have a vector of independent variable regressors, X, which are assumed to influence the outcome, Y. A typical ordinary least squares regression approach is invalid because the regression errors are heteroskedastic and non-normal, and the resulting estimated probability estimates will return nonsensical values of above 1 or below 0. This analysis handles these problems using an iterative optimization routine to maximize a log-likelihood function when the dependent variables are limited.

- Short Tip: Runs a Limited Dependent Variable Maximum Likelihood Logit model when the dependent variable is binary to forecast probabilities of events occurring.

- Model Input: Data Type C. One binary dependent variable is required with 0 and 1 values and multiple continuous or categorical independent variables.

  - Dependent Variable, Independent Variables:

    - >VAR1
    - >VAR2; VAR3; …

- **Artificial Intelligence Machine Learning (AI/ML): Normit Probit Binary Classification (Supervised).** A Probit model (sometimes also known as a Normit model) is a popular alternative specification for a binary response model. It employs a Probit function estimated using maximum likelihood estimation and is called Probit regression. The Probit and logistic regression models tend to produce very similar predictions where the parameter estimates in a logistic regression tend to be 1.6 to 1.8 times higher than they are in a corresponding Probit model. The choice of using a Probit or Logit is entirely up to convenience, and the main distinction is that the logistic distribution has a higher kurtosis (fatter tails) to account for extreme values. For example, suppose that house ownership is the decision to be modeled, and this response variable is binary (home purchase or no home purchase) and depends on a series of independent variables X_i such as income, age, and so forth, such that $I_i = \beta_0 + \beta_1 X_1 + ... + \beta_n X_n$, where the larger the value of I_i, the higher the probability of homeownership. For each family, a critical I^* threshold exists, where, if exceeded, the house is purchased, otherwise, no home is purchased, and the outcome probability (P) is assumed to be normally distributed, such that $P_i = CDF(I)$ using a standard-normal cumulative distribution function (CDF). Therefore, use the estimated coefficients exactly like that of a regression model and, using the estimated Y, apply a standard-normal distribution to compute the probability.

  - Short Tip: Runs a Limited Dependent Variable Maximum Likelihood Normit Probit model when the dependent variable is binary to forecast probabilities of events occurring.

  - Model Input: Data Type C. One binary dependent variable is required with 0 and 1 values and multiple continuous or categorical independent variables.

- Dependent Variable, Independent Variables:
  - >VAR1
  - >VAR2; VAR3; …

- **Artificial Intelligence Machine Learning (AI/ML): Random Forest (Supervised).** In this approach, bootstraps of regression trees are run multiple times with different combinations of data points and variables to develop a consensus forecast of group assignments. Using a single set of Training Y and Training X variables, the data and variables are bootstrapped and resampled. Each resampling will be run in the CART or regression tree model, and the consensus categorization results will be generated. The benefit of the random forest is that it provides a consensus forecast (wisdom of the crowd) through a resampling with replacement of both the variables and the data points. However, the individual CART model and tree process will no longer be available.

  - Short Tip: Bootstraps CART regression trees multiple times with different resampled data points and variables for consensus group assignment forecasts.

  - Model Input: Data Type C. Multiple variables.
    - Training Y, Training X, Testing X, Min Variables to Use, Min Data Points to Use, Forecast Save Location (Optional):
      - >VAR1
      - >VAR2:VAR5
      - >VAR6:VAR9
      - 3
      - 30
      - >VAR10

- **Artificial Intelligence Machine Learning (AI/ML): Segmentation Clustering (Unsupervised).** Taking the original dataset, we run some internal algorithms (a combination of k-means hierarchical clustering and other methods-of-moments in order to find the best-fitting groups or natural statistical clusters) to statistically divide or segment the original dataset into multiple groups.

  - Short Tip: Runs segmentation clustering of an existing dataset and segregates the data into various statistical groups.

  - Model Input: Data Type B. One or multiple input variables are required with at least 3 data points or rows of data. You can optionally request that a specific cluster be shown instead of the entire matrix (recommended if you have a lot of data).

- Variables:
  - >VAR1; VAR2; VAR3;…
  - 1
  - 3

- **ANCOVA (Single Factor Multiple Treatments).** Performs ANCOVA or Analysis of Covariance with multiple repeated treatments (Group 1) that removes the Group 2 covariate effects. The net effects after covariates have been accounted for will be tested against the null hypothesis that the various treatments in Group 1 are identical to each other after accounting for the effects of covariates in Group 2.
  - Short Tip: Analysis of Covariance with multiple repeated treatments (Group 1) that removes the Group 2 covariate effects (H_0: the various treatments are identical).
  - Model Input: Data Type D. Two groups of variables are required. Both groups are required to have the same number of variables. Group 1 has the main variables to test where each variable is a type of treatment like ANOVA. Group 2 has the covariates whose effects the analysis will integrate into the model.
    - Group 1 Main Variables, Group 2 Covariate Variables:
      - >VAR1; VAR2; VAR3; VAR4; …
      - >VAR5; VAR6; VAR7; VAR8; …

- **ANOVA (MANOVA General Linear Model).** Runs the Multiple ANOVA (MANOVA) with *multiple* numerical dependent variables against *one* alphanumeric categorical independent variable. Extends the ANOVA single factor multiple treatments to include multiple simultaneous de-pendent variables. The null hypothesis tested is that there is zero mean difference among all the variables. The computed statistics include the standard F statistics as well as Pillai's Trace, Wilk's Lambda, and Hotelling's Trace, which modifies the degrees of freedom and sums of squares to adjust for the simultaneous tests of multiple dependent variables.
  - Short Tip: MANOVA with multiple numerical dependent variables and one alpha-numeric categorical independent variable (H0: no difference among all the variables).
  - Model Input: Data Type C. Three or more input variables are required. Different variables are arranged in columns and all variables must have at least 6 data points

each, with the same number of total data points or rows per variable. Must also have one variable for Categories, which can be alpha-numeric.

- Categories, Variables:
  - >VAR10
  - >VAR1; VAR2; VAR3; …

- **ANOVA (MANOVA Two-Factor Replication General Linear Model).** Runs the Multiple ANOVA (MANOVA) with *multiple* numerical dependent variables against *two* alphanumeric categorical independent variables. Extends the Two-Way ANOVA to include multiple simultaneous dependent variables. The null hypothesis tested is that there is zero mean difference among all the variables. The computed statistics include the standard F statistics as well as Pillai's Trace, Wilk's Lambda, and Hotelling's Trace, which modifies the degrees of freedom and sums of squares to adjust for the simultaneous tests of multiple dependent variables.

  - Short Tip: MANOVA with multiple numerical dependent variables and two alphanumeric categorical independent variables (H_0: no difference among all the dependent variables compared against the independent variables and their interactions).
  - Model Input: Data Type C. Four or more input variables are required. Different variables are arranged in columns and all variables must have at least 6 data points each, with the same number of total data points or rows per variable. Must also have two variables for Categories, which can be alphanumeric.
    - Categories, Variables:
      - >VAR10; VAR11
      - >VAR1; VAR2; VAR3; …

- **ANOVA (Randomized Blocks Multiple Treatments).** The sampling distribution is assumed to be approximately normal and there exists a block variable for which ANOVA will control (i.e., block the effects of this variable by controlling it in the experiment). This analysis can test for the effects of the *one* dependent variable divided into *different treatment groups* as well as the effectiveness of the different levels of the *one* control or block variable. If the calculated p-value for the treatment or block is less than or equal to the significance level used in the test, then reject the null hypothesis and conclude that there is a significant difference among the different treatments or blocks.

- o Short Tip: ANOVA with blocking variables (H_0: no difference among all the treatment variables and no effects of blocking variables).
- o Model Input: Data Type C. Three or more input variables are required. Different treatment variables are arranged in columns and blocking variables are arranged in rows, and all variables must have at least 3 data points each, with the same number of total data points or rows per variable.
  - ▪ Variables: >VAR1; VAR2; VAR3; …

- **ANOVA (Single Factor Multiple Treatments).** An extension of the two-variable t-test, looking at *one* numerical dependent variable against *one* categorical independent variable that is separated into *multiple treatment groups*, and when the sampling distribution is assumed to be approximately normal. A two-tailed hypothesis tests the null hypothesis such that the population means of each treatment is statistically identical to the rest of the group, indicating that there is no effect among the different treatment groups.
  - o Short Tip: Runs ANOVA with multiple treatments (H_0: no difference among all the treatment variables).
  - o Model Input: Data Type C. Three or more input variables are required. Different treatment variables are arranged in columns and all variables must have at least 3 data points each, with the same number of total data points or rows per variable.
    - ▪ Variables: >VAR1; VAR2; VAR3; …

- **ANOVA (Single Factor Repeated Measures).** A modification of the ANOVA single-factor model looking at *one* numerical dependent variable that is *tested repeatedly*. These repeated measures are separated into multiple columns or test groups. A two-tailed hypothesis tests the null hypothesis such that the population means of each treatment is statistically identical to the rest of the group, indicating that there is no effect among the different repeated measurements groups.
  - o Short Tip: Runs ANOVA with repeated measures (H_0: no difference among all the repeated tests).
  - o Model Input: Data Type C. Three or more input variables are required. Different repeated test values are arranged in columns and all variables must have at least 3 data points each, with the same number of total data points or rows per variable.
    - ▪ Variables: >VAR1; VAR2; VAR3; …

- ANOVA (Two-Way Analysis). An extension of the Single Factor and Randomized Block ANOVAs by simultaneously examining the effects of *one* numerical dependent variable against *two* categorical independent variables (two factors along with the effects of interactions between the different levels of these two factors). Unlike the randomized block design, this model examines the interactions between different levels of the factors or independent variables. In a two-factor experiment, interaction exists when the effect of a level for one factor depends on which level of the other factor is present. There are three null hypotheses.
  o Short Tip: Runs Two-Way ANOVA with multiple treatments with one numerical dependent variable and two categorical independent variables (H_0: no difference among all the treatment variables for each row factor, column factor, and interactions between factors).
  o Model Input: Data Type C. Three or more input variables are required. Different column factor variables are arranged in columns and second replicated row factors are arranged as rows where all variables must have at least 4 data points each, with the same number of total data points or rows per variable. The total number of rows must be divisible by the number of row replications. For example, row factors can be arranged as A1, A1, A2, A2, A3, A3, A4, A4 for 8 rows with 4 factors, implying a replication of 2.
    ▪ Variables, Replication:
      - >VAR1; VAR2; VAR3; ...
      - >2
- ARIMA. Autoregressive Integrated Moving Average is used for forecasting time-series data using its own historical data by itself or with exogenous or independent variables. The first segment is the autoregressive (AR) term corresponding to the number of lagged values of the residual in the unconditional forecast model. The model captures the historical variation of actual data to a forecasting model and uses this variation or residual to create a better predicting model. The second segment is the integration order (I) term corresponding to the number of differencing the time series to be forecasted goes through to make the data stationary. This element accounts for any nonlinear growth rates existing in the data. The third segment is the moving average (MA) term, which is essentially the moving average of lagged forecast errors. By incorporating this lagged forecast errors term, the model learns from its forecast errors or mistakes and corrects for them through a moving average calculation. The ARIMA model follows the Box–Jenkins methodology with each term representing steps taken in the model construction until only random noise remains.

- Short Tip: Runs the Autoregressive Integrated Moving Average (ARIMA) (p,d,q) model using historical time series and optionally with other exogenous variables.
- Model Input: Data Types A and C. One input variable is required, although additional exogenous variables can be added as needed.
  - Historical Time-Series Variable, AR(p), I(d), MA(q), Iterations (Optional, default set at 100), Forecast Periods (Optional, default set at 5), Backcasting (Optional, default set at 0), Use Exogenous Variables (Optional, default set at 0):
    - >VAR1
    - >1
    - >0
    - >1

- **Auto ARIMA.** Runs some common combinations of ARIMA models (low-order PDQ) and returns the best models.
  - Short Tip: Runs the multiple ARIMA (p,d,q) models with low order p, d, q values, ranks and returns the best models.
  - Model Input: Data Types A and C. One input variable is required, although additional exogenous variables can be added as needed. ARIMA models typically require large amounts of data (e.g., 30–50 data points).
    - Historical Time-Series Variable, Iterations (Optional, default set at 100), Forecast Periods (Optional, default set at 5), Backcasting (Optional, default set at 0), Use Exogenous Variables (Optional, default set at 0):
      - >VAR1

- **Auto Econometrics (Detailed and Quick).** Runs some common combinations of Basic Econometrics and returns the best models using different algorithms.
  - Short Tip: Runs Auto Econometrics by testing multiple combinations of models that provide the best fit for your data, including linear, nonlinear, logarithmic, and interaction models.
  - Model Input: Data Type C. One dependent variable and one or multiple independent variables are required.
    - Dependent Variable, Independent Variables:
      - >VAR1
      - >VAR2; VAR3; …

- **Autocorrelation and Partial Autocorrelation.** One very simple approach to test for autocorrelation is to graph the time series of a regression equation's residuals. If these residuals exhibit some cyclicality, then autocorrelation exists. Another more robust approach to detect autocorrelation is the use of the Durbin–Watson statistic, which estimates the potential for first-order autocorrelation. The Durbin–Watson test employed also identifies model misspecification, that is, if a time-series variable is correlated to itself one period prior. Many time-series data tend to be autocorrelated to their historical occurrences. Autocorrelation is applicable only to time-series data. This relationship can exist for multiple reasons, including the variables' spatial relationships (similar time and space), prolonged economic shocks and events, psychological inertia, smoothing, seasonal adjustments of the data, and so forth.
  - o Short Tip: Runs Autocorrelation and Partial Autocorrelation on your time-series data up to 20 time-lag periods depending on data availability.
  - o Model Input: Data Type A. One input variable is required with at least 5 data points or rows of data.
    - Variable:
      - >VAR1
- **Autocorrelation Durbin–Watson AR(1) Test.** Runs the Durbin–Watson test for autocorrelation of one lag or AR(1) process.
  - o Short Tip: Runs the Durbin–Watson test for autocorrelation of one lag or AR(1) process.
  - o Model Input: Data Type C. One dependent variable and one or multiple independent variables are required.
    - Dependent Variable, Independent Variables:
      - >VAR1
      - >VAR2; VAR3; …
- **Bonferroni Test (Single Variable with Repetition).** The Bonferroni test is an adjustment made to p-values when multiple dependent or independent statistical t-tests are being performed simultaneously on a single dataset. Simultaneous confidence intervals are computed and compared against multiple individual tests. This single variable with repetition corrections test is applied on one group of multiple variables at once.
  - o Short Tip: Corrects for p-values on multiple independent tests and runs simultaneous confidence intervals (H_0: the individual expected means are equal to the goals).
  - o Model Input: Data Type C. Two or more input variables are required. Different variables are arranged in columns and all variables must have the same number of data

points or rows. The total number of goals needs to match the number of variables. Alpha is 0.05 by default and can optionally be changed by the user.

- Variables, Goals Tested, Alpha Level (Optional, default is 0.05):
  - \>VAR1; VAR2; VAR3; …
  - \>7; 8; 5; …
  - \>0.05

- **Bonferroni Test (Two Variables with Repetition).** The Bonferroni test is an adjustment made to p-values when multiple dependent or independent statistical t-tests are being performed simultaneously on a single dataset. Simultaneous confidence intervals are computed and compared against multiple individual tests. This two-variable with repetition corrections test is applied on two groups of multiple variables each. The null hypothesis tested is that the individual expected differences are all equal to zero.
  - Short Tip: Corrects for p-values on multiple independent tests and runs simultaneous confidence intervals (H_0: the individual expected differences are equal to zero).
  - Model Input: Data Type D. Two groups of variables are required. In each group, two or more input variables are required with the same number of data points or rows.
    - Group 1's Variables, Group 2's Variables, Alpha Level (Optional, default is 0.05):
      - \>VAR1; VAR2; VAR3; …
      - \>VAR4; VAR5; VAR6; …
      - \>0.05

- **Box–Cox Normal Transformation.** Takes your existing dataset and transforms it into normally distributed data. The original dataset is tested using the Shapiro–Wilk test for normality (H_0: data is assumed to be normal), then transformed using the Box–Cox method either using your custom Lambda parameter or internally optimized Lambda. The transformed data is tested again for normality using Shapiro–Wilk.
  - Short Tip: Transforms your existing data into normally distributed data that is tested using Shapiro–Wilk (H_0: data is assumed to be normal) and visualized in a QQ Chart.
  - Model Input: Data Type A. One input variable is required with at least 5 rows of data. Optionally, enter a nonzero Lambda value (positive or negative values only, but no zeros are allowed).
    - Variable, Lambda (Optional, default computed internally but can be overridden with any nonzero value):

- >VAR1
- >0.2

- **Box's Test for Homogeneity of Covariance.** Runs the Box Test of Covariance Homogeneity of two groups of variables' covariance matrices. The null hypothesis tested is that there is zero difference between the two covariance matrices.
  - Short Tip: Tests if two covariance matrices are homogeneous (H_0: no difference between the two covariance matrices).
  - Model Input: Data Type D. Two groups of variables are required. In each group, two or more input variables are required with at least 5 data points each and the same total number of data points or rows.
    - Group 1's Variables, Group 2's Variables:
      - >VAR1; VAR2; VAR3; …
      - >VAR4; VAR5; VAR6; …

- **Charts.** Generates various 2D and 3D charts (area, bar, line, point, and scatter) as well as QQ charts, Box-Whisker charts, and Pareto charts. Most of these charts take Data Types A and C (this just means either one or multiple series will be charted), with the exception of Pareto charts, which require only Data Type C.
  - **2D and 3D Area, Bar, Line, Point, Scatter.**
    - Short Tip: Generates the selected 2D or 3D chart with one, two, three, or multiple variables.

    - Model Input: Data Types A and C. One or more input variables are required with at least 3 rows of data. Optionally, add other variables to chart.
      - Variables: >VAR1; VAR2; VAR3; …
  - **Box-Whisker Chart.** Box plots or box-and-whisker plots graphically depict numerical data using their descriptive statistics: the smallest observation (Minimum), First Quartile or 25th Percentile (Q1), Median or Second Quartile or 50th Percentile (Q2), Third Quartile (Q3), and largest observation (Maximum). A box plot may also indicate which observations, if any, might be considered outliers.
    - Short Tip: Generates a Box-Whisker chart with one, two, three, or multiple variables.
    - Model Input: Data Types A and C. At least one input variable is required with at least 3 rows of data. Optionally, add other variables to chart.
      - Variables: >VAR1; VAR2; VAR3; …

- o **2D and 3D Pareto Chart.** A Pareto chart contains both a bar chart and a line graph. Individual values are represented in descending order by the bars and the cumulative total is represented by the ascending line. Also known as the "80-20" chart, whereby you see that by focusing on the top few variables, we are already accounting for more than 80% of the cumulative effects of the total.
    - Short Tip: Generates a 2D and 3D Pareto chart with two, three, or multiple variables. Each variable has one data point only.
    - Model Input: Data Type C. At least two or more input variables are required with exactly 1 row of data for each variable. Optionally, add other variables to chart.
        - Variables:
            - o >VAR1; VAR2; VAR3; …
- o **Q-Q Normal Chart.** This Quantile-Quantile chart is a normal probability plot, which is a graphical method for comparing a probability distribution with the normal distribution by plotting their quantiles against each other.
    - Short Tip: Generates QQ Normal chart where the CDF distribution is mapped against the user's raw data to see its fit.
    - Model Input: Data Type A. Only one input variable is required.
        - Variable:
            - o >VAR1
- **Coefficient of Variation Homogeneity Test.** Returns the coefficient of variation (CV) calculations for each of the input variables (standard deviation divided by the mean), as a unitless and relative measure of risk and uncertainty. Then, a pooled Chi-Square test is applied to test the null hypothesis that these CV values are homogeneous and statistically similar, and a Shapiro–Wilk test is also applied to test the normality of the variables' dataset.
    - o Short Tip: Tests if the coefficient of variations from different variables are similar (H_0: all CVs are equal or homogeneous).
    - o Model Input: Data Type C. Two or more input variables are required. Different variables are arranged in columns and all variables must have at least 3 data points each. A different number of total data points or rows per variable is allowed.
        - Variables: >VAR1; VAR2; VAR3; …

- **Cointegration Test (Engle–Granger).** Runs the Engle–Granger test for any cointegration of two nonstationary time-series variables. If there are two time-series variables that are nonstationary to order one, I(1), and if a linear combination of these two series is stationary at I(0), then these two variables are, by definition, cointegrated. Many macroeconomic data are I(1), and conventional forecasting and modeling methods do not apply due to the nonstandard properties of unit root processes. The Cointegration test can be applied to identify the presence of cointegration, and if confirmed to exist, a subsequent Error Correction Model can then be used to forecast the time-series variables.
  - Short Tip: Runs the Engle–Granger test for any cointegration of two nonstationary time-series variables.
  - Model Input: Data Type B. Exactly two input variables are required. Variables are arranged in columns and both variables must have at least 3 data points each, with the same number of total data points or rows per variable.
    - Variables:
      - >VAR1; VAR2
- **Combinatorial Fuzzy Logic.** Applies fuzzy logic algorithms for forecasting time-series data by combining forecast methods to create an optimized model. Fuzzy logic is a probabilistic logic dealing with the reasoning that is approximate rather than fixed and exact, where fuzzy logic variables may have a truth value that ranges in degree between 0 and 1.
  - Short Tip: Computes time-series forecasts using fuzzy logic combining and optimizing multiple forecast methods into one unified forecast.
  - Model Input: Data Type A. Only one input variable is required.
    - Variable
      - >VAR1
- **Control Charts: C, NP, P, R, U, X, XMR.** Sometimes specification limits of a process are not set; instead, statistical control limits are computed based on the actual data collected (e.g., the number of defects in a manufacturing line). The upper control limit (UCL) and lower control limit (LCL) are computed, as are the central line (CL) and other sigma levels. The resulting chart is called a control chart, and if the process is out of control, the actual defect line will be outside of the UCL and LCL lines for a certain number of times.
  - **C Chart.** The variable is an attribute (e.g., defective or nondefective), the data collected are in the total number of defects (actual count in units), and there are multiple measurements in a sample experiment; when multiple

experiments are run and the average number of defects of the collected data is of interest; and a constant number of samples is collected in each experiment.

- Short Tip: Control C Chart depicting and measuring upper and lower control levels on the number of defects.
- Model Input: Data Type A. Only one input variable is required.
  - Defective Units
    - >VAR1

- NP Chart. The variable is an attribute (e.g., defective or nondefective), the data collected are in proportions of defects (or the number of defects in a specific sample), and there are multiple measurements in a sample experiment; when multiple experiments are run and the average proportion of defects of the collected data is of interest; and a constant number of samples is collected in each experiment.
  - Short Tip: Control NP Chart depicting and measuring upper and lower control levels on the proportions of defects.
  - Model Input: Data Type A. Only one input variable is required, and a second manual numerical input of the sample size.
    - Defective Units, Sample Size:
      - >VAR1
      - 20

- P Chart. The variable is an attribute (e.g., defective or nondefective), the data collected are in proportions of defects (or the number of defects in a specific sample), and there are multiple measurements in a sample experiment; when multiple experiments are run and the average proportion of defects of the collected data is of interest; and with a different number of samples in each experiment.
  - Short Tip: Control P Chart depicting and measuring upper and lower control levels using defective units compared to sample size.
  - Model Input: Data Type B. Only one input variable is required, and a second manual numerical input of the sample size.
    - Defective Units, Sample Size:
      - >VAR1
      - >VAR2

- R Chart. The variable has raw data values, there are multiple measurements in a sample experiment, multiple experiments are run, and the range of the collected data is of interest.
  - Short Tip: Control R Chart depicting and measuring upper and lower control levels using repeated defective unit measurements.
  - Model Input: Data Type C. Multiple variables of measurements of defective units required.
    - Defective Units Measurement Variables:
      - >VAR1; VAR2; VAR3; …
- U Chart. The variable is an attribute (e.g., defective or nondefective), the data collected are in the total number of defects (actual count in units), and there are multiple measurements in a sample experiment; when multiple experiments are run and the average number of defects of the collected data is of interest; and with a different number of samples collected in each experiment.
  - Short Tip: Control U Chart depicting and measuring upper and lower control levels on the total units of defects.
  - Model Input: Data Type A. Only one input variable is required, and a second manual numerical input of the sample size.
    - Defective Units, Sample Size:
      - >VAR1
      - >20
- X Chart. The variable has raw data values, there are multiple measurements in a sample experiment, multiple experiments are run, and the range of the collected data is of interest.
  - Short Tip: Control X Chart depicting and measuring upper and lower control levels using multiple repeated defective unit measurements.
  - Model Input: Data Type C. Multiple variables of measurements of defective units required.
    - Defective Units Measurement Variables:
      - >VAR1; VAR2; VAR3; …
- XMR Chart. The variable has raw data values, there is a single measurement taken in each sample experiment, multiple experiments are run, and the actual value of the collected data is of interest.

- - Short Tip: Control XMR Chart depicting and measuring upper and lower control levels on the total units of defects.
  - Model Input: Data Type A. Only one input variable is required, and a second manual numerical input of the sample size.
    - Defective Units:
      - >VAR1
- Convolution Simulation. Runs a simulation that convolutes discrete risk event frequencies (e.g., discrete normal and Poisson distributions) and sums its continuous impact severities (e.g., lognormal, Frechet, Gumbel max, normal, Pareto, and Weibull distributions). The simulated distribution has the same expected values as the static multiplication of the first moments and the multiplication of two simulated probability distributions. However, the second-moment distributional width is lower and more conservative, as compared to a simple multiplication of two independent simulated probability distributions. This convolution method is useful for modeling operational risk losses.

  - Discrete Normal with Lognormal Arithmetic Scale
  - Discrete Normal with Lognormal Logarithmic Scale
  - Poisson with Frechet
  - Poisson with Gumbel Max
  - Poisson with Lognormal Arithmetic Scale
  - Poisson with Lognormal Log Scale
  - Poisson with Normal
  - Poisson with Pareto
  - Poisson with Weibull

  - Short Tip: Runs a simulation that convolutes discrete risk event frequencies and sums its continuous impact severities.
  - Model Input: Data Type A. Multiple manual input parameters.

    - Lambda, Mean, Stdev, Deductible (Optional), Trials (Optional), Seed (Optional):
      - >6
      - >2
      - >0.8
      - >0
      - >1000
      - >123

- Correlation Matrix (Linear and Nonlinear). Computes the Pearson's linear product-moment correlations (commonly referred to as the Pearson's R) as well as the nonlinear Spearman rank-based correlation between variable pairs and returns them as a correlation matrix. The correlation coefficient ranges between -1.0 and $+1.0$, inclusive. The sign indicates the direction of association between the variables, while the coefficient indicates the magnitude or strength of association.
    - Short Tip: Runs the linear Pearson and nonlinear nonparametric Pearson correlations as well as significant p-values (H_0: each correlation is equal to zero).
    - Model Input: Data Type C. Two or more input variables are required. Different variables are arranged in columns and all variables must have at least 3 data points each, with the same number of data points for all variables.
        - Variables:
            - >VAR1; VAR2; VAR3; …
- Covariance Matrix. Runs the variance-covariance matrix for a sample and population as well as Pearson's linear correlation matrix. For additional details on correlations, run the Correlation Matrix method instead for Pearson's linear, nonparametric Spearman rank nonlinear, and significant p-values on correlations.
    - Short Tip: Generates variance-covariance and correlation matrices.
    - Model Input: Data Type C. Two or more input variables are required. Different variables are arranged in columns and all variables must have the same number of data points or rows.
        - Variables:
            - >VAR1; VAR2; VAR3…
- Cox Regression. Runs Cox's proportional hazards model for survival time and tests the effect of several variables upon the time a specified event takes to happen.
    - Short Tip: Runs a Cox Regression proportional hazards model.
    - Model Input: Data Type C. Multiple input variables are required. Different variables are arranged in columns and all variables must have the same number of data points or rows.
        - Survived, Dead, Independent Variables:
            - >VAR1
            - >VAR2
            - >VAR3, VAR4; VAR5; …

- **Cubic Spline.** Interpolates missing values of a time-series dataset and extrapolates values of future forecast periods using nonlinear curves. Spline curves can also be used to forecast or extrapolate values of future time periods beyond the time period of available data and the data can be linear or nonlinear.
  - o Short Tip: Interpolates and extrapolates a data series with missing values.
  - o Model Input: Data Type B. Two input variables are required. Different variables are arranged in columns and all variables must have at least 5 data points each, with the same number of total data points or rows per variable.
    - ▪ Known X Values, Known Y Values, Starting Period, Ending Period, Step Size:
      - >VAR1
      - >VAR2
      - >3
      - >8
      - >0.5
- **Custom Econometric Model.** Applicable for forecasting time-series and cross-sectional data and for modeling relationships among variables and allows you to create custom multiple regression models. Econometrics refers to a branch of business analytics, modeling, and forecasting techniques for modeling the behavior of or forecasting certain business, financial, economic, physical science, and other variables. Running the Basic Econometrics models is like regular regression analysis except that the dependent and independent variables can be modified before a regression is run.
  - o Short Tip: Customizes your linear and nonlinear regression model using custom independent variables.
  - o Model Input: Data Type C. One dependent variable and multiple independent variables are required.
    - ▪ Dependent Variable, Independent Variables:
      - >VAR1
      - >VAR2; LN(VAR3); (VAR4)^2; LAG(VAR5,1); (VAR6*VAR7)
- **Data Analysis: Cross Tabulation.** Used to find alphanumeric values (number and word combinations) and to find unique values and then perform a cross tabulation.
  - o Short Tip: Runs Cross Tabulation on unique alphanumeric values or text.
  - o Model Input: Data Type B. Two input variables are required. Both variables can be numerical, alphabetical, or alphanumeric.

- Variable 1 (Alphanumeric), Variable 2 (Alphanumeric):
  - >VAR1
  - >VAR2
- **Data Analysis: New Values Only.** Used to find new values in the Main Variable that do not exist in the Reference Variables, and to find the values that already exist in the Reference Variable as well as values that are Duplicates if both variables are combined.
  - Short Tip: Finds alphanumeric data in the main variable that either exists or doesn't exist in the reference variable, as well as identifies duplicates if both variables are combined.
  - Model Input: Data Type B. Two input variables are required. Different variables are arranged in columns and all variables must have at least 3 data points each, with the same number of total data points or rows per variable.
    - Main Variable (Alphanumeric), Reference Variable (Alphanumeric), Number of Characters (Optional, default set to all characters):
      - >VAR1
      - >VAR2
      - >5
- **Data Analysis: Subtotal by Category.** Used to find value subtotals based on unique categories.
  - Short Tip: Computes subtotals based on unique categories.
  - Model Input: Data Type B. Two input variables are required: Category can be alphanumeric whereas Values must be numerical.
    - Category (Alphanumeric), Values (Numeric):
      - >VAR1
      - >VAR2
- **Data Analysis: Unique Values Only.** Identifies the values that are unique in each variable. Data can be alphanumeric, and the first N characters can optionally be used to determine uniqueness.
  - Short Tip: Finds unique alphanumeric values in each variable.
  - Model Input: Data Types B and C. Two or more input variables are required. Different variables are arranged in columns and all variables must have at least 3 data points each, with the same number of total data points or rows per variable.

- Main Variables (Alphanumeric), Number of Characters:
  - >VAR1; >VAR2; VAR3; …
  - >5

- **Data Descriptive Statistics.** Almost all distributions can be described within four moments (some distributions require one moment, while others require two moments, and so forth). This tool computes the four moments and associated descriptive statistics.
  - Short Tip: Computes various moments and descriptive statistics.
  - Model Input: Data Type A. One input variable is required.
    - Variable:
      - >VAR1

- **Deseasonalize.** This model deseasonalizes and detrends your original data to take out any seasonal and trending components. In forecasting models, the process eliminates the effects of accumulating datasets from seasonality and trend to show only the absolute changes in values and to allow potential cyclical patterns to be identified by removing the general drift, tendency, twists, bends, and effects of seasonal cycles of a set of time-series data.
  - Short Tip: Deseasonalizes a time-series dataset.
  - Model Input: Data Type A. One input variable is required, and the number of periods per season.
    - Variable, Periodicity:
      - >VAR1
      - >4

- **Discriminate Analysis (Linear).** LDA (Linear Discriminant Analysis) is related to ANOVA and multivariate regression analysis, which attempt to model one dependent variable as a linear combination of other independent variables. Discriminant Analysis has continuous independent variables and a categorical dependent variable.
  - Short Tip: Continuous independent variables are used to linearly explain and model a categorical dependent variable.
  - Model Input: Data Type C. One dependent variable (categorical data) and one or multiple independent variables are required.
    - Categorical Dependent Variable, Independent Variables:
      - >VAR1
      - >VAR2; VAR3; …

- **Discriminate Analysis (Quadratic).** QDA (Quadratic Discriminant Analysis) is related to ANOVA and multivariate regression analysis, which attempt to model one dependent variable as a nonlinear combination of other independent variables. Discriminant Analysis has continuous independent variables and a categorical dependent variable. This QDA is a nonlinear version of the LDA (Linear Discriminant Analysis).
  - Short Tip: Continuous independent variables are used to nonlinearly explain and model a categorical dependent variable.
  - Model Input: Data Type C. One dependent variable (categorical data) and one or multiple independent variables are required.
    - Categorical Dependent Variable, Independent Variables:
      - >VAR1
      - >VAR2; VAR3; …
- **Distributional Fitting.** Which distribution does an analyst or engineer use for an input variable in a model? What are the relevant distributional parameters? The null hypothesis tested is that the fitted distribution is the same distribution as the population from which the sample data to be fitted comes.
  - Short Tip: Performs various distributional fitting methods to identify the best-fitting distribution.
  - Model Input: Data Type A. One variable is required.
    - Variable:
      - >VAR1
  - **Akaike Information Criterion (AIC).** Rewards goodness-of-fit but also includes a penalty that is an increasing function of the number of estimated parameters (although AIC penalizes the number of parameters less strongly than other methods).
  - **Anderson–Darling (AD).** When applied to testing if a normal distribution adequately describes a set of data, it is one of the most powerful statistical tools for detecting departures from normality and is powerful for testing normal tails. However, in non-normal distributions, this test lacks power compared to others.
  - **Kolmogorov–Smirnov (KS).** A nonparametric test for the equality of continuous probability distributions can be used to compare a sample with a reference probability distribution, making it useful for testing abnormally-shaped distributions and non-normal distributions.

o   **Kuiper's Statistic (K).** Related to the KS test making it as sensitive in the tails as at the median and is invariant under cyclic transformations of the independent variable. This test is invaluable when testing for cyclic variations over time. In comparison, the AD provides equal sensitivity at the tails as the median, but it does not provide for cyclic invariance.

o   **Schwarz/Bayes Information Criterion (SC/BIC).** The SC/BIC introduces a penalty term for the number of parameters in the model with a larger penalty than AIC.

o   **Discrete (Chi-Square).** The Chi-Square test is used to perform distributional fitting on discrete data.

- **Diversity Index (Shannon, Brillouin, Simpson).** Diversity measures the probability distribution of observations or frequencies among different categories and computes the probability that any two items randomly selected will belong to the same category. Three indices are computed: Shannon's Diversity Index for a sample of categorical data (frequencies of occurrence among different categories), Brillouin's Diversity Index for when the entire population is present, and Simpson's Diversity Index for sampling with replacement within a large population. The closer the diversity indices to the maximum, the higher the level of diversity.

    o   Short Tip: Measures the diversity of a dataset using frequencies of various categories as inputs. The closer the diversity indices to the maximum, the higher the level of diversity.

    o   Model Input: One input variable is required with at least 3 rows of data.

        ▪   Frequency:
            •   >VAR1

- **Eigenvalues and Eigenvectors.** Runs and calculates the Eigenvalues and Eigenvectors of your data matrix.

    o   Short Tip: Calculates the Eigenvalues and Eigenvectors of your data matrix.

    o   Model Input: Two or more input variables are required. Different variables are arranged in columns and all variables must have at least 3 data points each, with the same number of total data points or rows per variable. The total number of variables must match the number of rows, i.e., the data entered should be in an $N \times N$ matrix.

        ▪   Variables:
            •   >VAR1; VAR2; VAR3; …

- **Endogeneity Test with Two-Stage Least Squares (Durbin–Wu–Hausman).** Tests if a regressor is endogenous using the two-stage least squares method and applying the Durbin–Wu–Hausman test. A Structural Model and a (2SLS) Reduced Model are both computed in a 2SLS paradigm, and a Hausman test is administered to test if one of the variables is endogenous.
  - Short Tip: Tests if a regressor is endogenous using the two-stage least squares method and applying the Durbin–Wu–Hausman test.
  - Model Input: Data Type C.
    - Structural Dependent Variable, Test Variable, Structural Independent Variables, Reduced Equation Independent Variables:
      - VAR1
      - VAR2
      - VAR3
      - VAR4; VAR5; VAR6; VAR7
- **Endogenous Model (Instrumental Variables with Two-Stage Least Squares).** Runs a two-stage least squares with instrumental variables on a bivariate model for slope estimation.
  - Short Tip: Runs a two-stage least squares with instrumental variables on a bivariate model for slope estimation.
  - Model Input: Data Type C.
    - Dependent Variable, Endogenous Variable, Instrumental Variables:
      - VAR1
      - VAR2
      - VAR3; VAR4; VAR5; VAR6; VAR7

- **Error Correction Model (Engle–Granger).** Runs an error correction model assuming the variables exhibit cointegration. If two time-series variables are nonstationary in the first order, $I(1)$, and when both variables are cointegrated, we can run an error correction model for estimating the short-term and long-term effects of a time series on another. The error correction comes from previous periods' deviation from a long-run equilibrium, where the error influences its short-run dynamics.
  - Short Tip: Runs an error correction model assuming the variables exhibit cointegration.
  - Model Input: Data Type B. Exactly two input variables are required. Variables are arranged in columns and both variables must have at least 3 data points each, with the same number of total data points or rows per variable.

- Dependent Variable, Independent Variable:
    - \>VAR1
    - \>VAR2
- **Exponential J-Curve.** This method generates an exponential growth where the value of the next period depends on the current period's level and the increase is exponential. Over time, the values will increase significantly from one period to another. This model is typically used in forecasting biological growth and chemical reactions over time.
    - Short Tip: Generates a time-series forecast using Exponential J-curve.
    - Model Input: Data Type A. Requires three simple manual inputs: starting value of the forecast, the periodic growth rate in percent, and the total number of periods to forecast.
        - Starting Value, Growth Rate (%), Forecast Periods:
            - \>400
            - \>3
            - \>100
- **Factor Analysis.** Runs Factor Analysis to analyze interrelationships within large numbers of variables and simplifies said factors into a smaller number of common factors. The method condenses information contained in the original set of variables into a smaller set of implicit factor variables with minimal loss of information. The analysis is related to the Principal Component Analysis (PCA) by using the correlation matrix and applying PCA coupled with a Varimax matrix rotation to simplify the factors.
    - Short Tip: Runs Factor Analysis to analyze interrelationships within large numbers of variables and simplifies said factors into a smaller number of common factors.
    - Model Input: Data Type C. Requires at least three or more variables with an equal number of rows.
        - Variables:
            - \>VAR1; VAR2; VAR3; …
- **Forecast Accuracy: All Goodness of Fit Measures.** Runs various forecast accuracy and forecast error measurements using actual and forecast values. Models to run include multiple R, R-squared, standard error of estimates, Akaike, Bayes, Log-Likelihood, Hannan–Quinn, SSE (sums of squared errors), MAD (mean absolute deviation), MAPE (mean absolute percentage error), MSE (mean squared error), RMSE (root mean squared error), MdAE (median absolute error), MdAPE (median absolute percentage error), RMSLE (root mean square log error), RMSPE (root mean square percentage error loss), RMdSPE (root median

square percentage error loss), sMAPE (symmetrical mean absolute percentage error), Theil's U1 (Theil's measure for accuracy), and Theil's U2 (Theil's measure for quality).

- o Short Tip: Runs various forecast accuracy and forecast error measurements using your forecast errors.
- o Data Input: Data Type B. Actual data variable, forecast data variable, and manual input of the number of regressors used to generate your forecast and subsequent errors.
  - Actuals, Forecasts, Total Number of Variables (Dep. + Indep.):
    - \>VAR1
    - \>VAR2
    - \>6

- **Forecast Accuracy: Akaike, Bayes, Schwarz, MAD, MSE, RMSE.** Runs various forecast accuracy and forecast error measurements using your forecast errors. Models to run include the Akaike Information Criterion (AIC), Bayes and Schwarz Criterion (BSC), AIC Correction (Augmented AIC), BSC Correlation (Augmented BSC), Mean Absolute Deviation (MAD), Mean Squared Errors (MSE), and Root Mean Squared Error (RMSE).
  - o Short Tip: Runs various forecast accuracy and forecast error measurements using your forecast errors.
  - o Data Input: Data Type A. One input variable of the forecast errors is required, as is manual input of the number of regressors used to generate your forecast and subsequent errors.
    - Forecast Errors, Total Number of Variables (Dep. + Indep.):
      - \>VAR1
      - \>6

- **Forecast Accuracy: Diebold–Mariano (Dual Competing Forecasts).** Runs the Diebold–Mariano test and Harvey–Leybourne–Newbold test comparing two forecasts to see if there is a difference. The null hypothesis tested is that there is no significant difference between the two forecasts.
  - o Short Tip: Tests if two forecasts are similarly valid (H_0: no difference between the two forecasts).
  - o Model Input: Data Type C. Three variables are required: Actual Data, First Forecasted Data, and Second Forecasted Data, with at least 5 rows of data for each variable. Each variable must have the same number of rows.

- Actual (=1), Forecast 1; Forecast 2:
    - \>VAR1
    - \>VAR2; VAR3

- **Forecast Accuracy: Pesaran–Timmermann (Single Directional Forecast).** Runs the Pesaran–Timmermann test to see if the forecast can adequately track directional changes in the data. The null hypothesis tested is that the forecast does not track directional changes in the data.
    - Short Tip: Tests if the forecast adequately tracked directional changes in the data (H_0: forecast does not track directional changes).
    - Model Input: Data Type B. Two variables are required: Actual Data and Forecast, with at least 5 rows of data for each variable. Each variable must have the same number of rows.
        - Actual, Forecast:
            - \>VAR1
            - \>VAR2

- **Generalized Linear Models (Logit with Binary Outcomes).** Limited dependent variables techniques are used to forecast the probability of something occurring given some independent variables (e.g., predicting if a credit line will default given the obligor's characteristics such as age, salary, credit card debt levels; or the probability a patient will have lung cancer based on age and number of cigarettes smoked monthly, and so forth). The dependent variable is limited (i.e., binary 1 and 0 for default/cancer, or limited to integer values 1, 2, 3, etc.). Traditional regression analysis will not work as the predicted probability is usually less than zero or greater than one, and many of the required regression assumptions are violated (e.g., independence and normality of the errors). We also have a vector of independent variable regressors, X, which are assumed to influence the outcome, Y. A typical ordinary least squares regression approach is invalid because the regression errors are heteroskedastic and non-normal, and the resulting estimated probability estimates will return nonsensical values of above 1 or below 0. This analysis handles these problems using an iterative optimization routine to maximize a log-likelihood function when the dependent variables are limited.
    - Short Tip: Runs a Binary Logistic Regression model with one binary (0/1) dependent variable and multiple independent variables.
    - Model Input: Data Type C. One binary dependent variable with 0 and 1 values and multiple continuous or categorical independent variables are required.

- Dependent Variable, Independent Variables:
  - >VAR1
  - >VAR2; VAR3; …
- **Generalized Linear Models (Logit with Bivariate Outcomes).** Runs the Multivariate Logistic Regression or Logit Model with two dependent bivariate variables (Number of Successes and Failures) that are dependent on one or more independent variables. Instead of the standard Logit Model that requires raw data of 0 and 1 as a single variable, we can use this Generalized Linear Model (GLM) Logit with Binary Outcomes model with successes and failures (frequency counts) as two separate variables.
  - o Short Tip: Runs the General Linear Model Logit Regression with two dependent variables (counts of successes and failures).
  - o Model Input: Data Type C. Two dependent variables are required (Number of Successes and Failures), and one or more independent variables are allowed, with the same number of total data points or rows per variable.
    - Independent Variables, Successes, Failures:
      - >VAR1; VAR2: …
      - >VAR3
      - >VAR4
- **Generalized Linear Models (Probit with Binary Outcomes).** A Probit model (sometimes also known as a Normit model) is a popular alternative specification for a binary response model. It employs a Probit function estimated using maximum likelihood estimation and is called Probit regression. The Probit and logistic regression models tend to produce very similar predictions where the parameter estimates in a logistic regression tend to be 1.6 to 1.8 times higher than they are in a corresponding Probit model. The choice of using a Probit or Logit is entirely up to convenience, and the main distinction is that the logistic distribution has a higher kurtosis (fatter tails) to account for extreme values. For example, suppose that house ownership is the decision to be modeled, and this response variable is binary (home purchase or no home purchase) and depends on a series of independent variables X_i such as income, age, and so forth, such that $I_i = \beta_0 + \beta_1 X_1 + … + \beta_n X_n$, where the larger the value of I_i, the higher the probability of home ownership. For each family, a critical I^* threshold exists, where if exceeded, the house is purchased, otherwise, no home is purchased, and the outcome probability (P) is assumed to be normally distributed, such that $P_i = CDF(I)$ using a standard-normal cumulative distribution function (CDF). Therefore, use the estimated coefficients exactly like that of a regression

model and, using the estimated Y, apply a standard-normal distribution to compute the probability.

- o Short Tip: Runs a Binary Probit Regression model with one binary (0/1) dependent variable and multiple independent variables.
- o Model Input: Data Type C. One binary dependent variable with 0 and 1 values and multiple continuous or categorical independent variables are required.
  - Dependent Variable, Independent Variables:
    - \>VAR1
    - \>VAR2; VAR3; …

- **Generalized Linear Models (Probit with Bivariate Outcomes).** Runs the Multivariate Probit Regression or Probit Model with two dependent bivariate variables (Number of Successes and Failures) that are dependent on one or more independent variables. Instead of the standard Probit Model that requires raw data of 0 and 1, we can use this Generalized Linear Model (GLM) Probit with Binary Outcomes model where successes and failures are frequency counts.
  - o Short Tip: Runs the General Linear Model Probit Regression with two dependent variables (counts of successes and failures).
  - o Model Input: Data Type C. Two Dependent Variables are required (Number of Successes and Failures), and one or more Independent Variables are allowed, with the same number of total data points or rows per variable.
    - Independent Variables, Successes, Failures:
      - \>VAR1; VAR2: …
      - \>VAR3
      - \>VAR4

- **Generalized Linear Models (Tobit with Censored Data).** The Tobit model (Censored Tobit) is an econometric and biometric modeling method used to describe the relationship between a non-negative dependent variable Y_i and one or more independent variables X_i. A Tobit model is an econometric model in which the dependent variable is censored; that is, the dependent variable is censored because values below zero are not observed. The Tobit model assumes that there is a latent unobservable variable Y^*. This variable is linearly dependent on the X_i variables via a vector of β_i coefficients that determine their interrelationships. In addition, there is a normally distributed error term U_i to capture random influences on this relationship. The observable variable Y_i is defined to be equal to the latent variables whenever the latent variables are above zero, and Y_i is assumed to be zero otherwise. That is, $Y_i = Y^*$ if $Y^* > 0$ and $Y_i = 0$ if $Y^* = 0$. If the relationship parameter β_i is estimated by using ordinary least squares regression of the observed Y_i on X_i, the resulting regression estimators are inconsistent and yield downward-biased slope coefficients and an upward-biased intercept.

- o Short Tip: Runs a Tobit Regression model with one limited or censored dependent variable and multiple independent variables.
- o Model Input: Data Type C. One censored dependent variable and multiple continuous or categorical independent variables are required.
  - Dependent Variable, Independent Variables:
    - \>VAR1
    - \>VAR2; VAR3; …

- **Granger Causality.** Tests if one variable Granger causes another variable and vice versa, using restricted autoregressive lags and unrestricted distributive lag models. Predictive causality in finance and economics is tested by measuring the ability to predict the future values of a time series using prior values of another time series. A simpler definition might be that a time-series variable X Granger causes another time-series variable Y if predictions of the value of Y based solely on its own prior values and on the prior values of X are comparatively better than predictions of Y based solely on its own past values.
  - o Short Tip: Tests if one variable Granger causes another variable and vice versa, using restricted autoregressive lags and unrestricted distributive lag models.
  - o Model Input: Data Type B. Exactly two input variables are required. Variables are arranged in columns and both variables must have at least 3 data points each, with the same number of total data points or rows per variable.
    - Variables, Maximum Lags:
      - \>VAR1; VAR2
      - \>3

- **Grubbs Test for Outliers.** Runs the Grubbs test for outliers to test the null hypothesis if all the values are from the same normal population without outliers.
  - o Short Tip: Tests for outliers in your data (H_0: there are no outliers).
  - o Model Input: Data Type A. One input variable is required with at least 3 rows of data.
    - Variable:
      - \>VAR1

- **Heteroskedasticity Test (Breusch–Pagan–Godfrey).** Runs the Breusch–Pagan–Godfrey test for heteroskedasticity. It uses the main model to obtain error estimates and, using squared estimates, a restricted model is run, and the Breusch–Pagan–Godfrey test is computed. The null hypothesis is that the time series is homoskedastic.
  - o Short Tip: Tests for heteroskedasticity (H_0: time series is homoskedastic).
  - o Data Input: Data Type C. One dependent variable and one or multiple independent variables are required.
    - Dependent Variable, Independent Variables:
      - \>VAR1
      - \>VAR2; VAR3; VAR4; …
- **Heteroskedasticity Test (Lagrange Multiplier).** Runs the Lagrange Multiplier Test for Heteroskedasticity. It uses the main model to obtain error estimates and, using squared estimates, a restricted model is run, and the Lagrange multiplier test is computed. The null hypothesis is that the time series is homoskedastic.
  - o Short Tip: Tests for heteroskedasticity (H_0: time series is homoskedastic).
  - o Data Input: Data Type C. One dependent variable and one or multiple independent variables are required.
    - Dependent Variable, Independent Variables:
      - \>VAR1
      - \>VAR2; VAR3; VAR4; …
- **Heteroskedasticity Test (Wald–Glejser).** Runs the Wald–Glejser Test for Heteroskedasticity. It uses the main model to obtain error estimates and, using squared estimates, a restricted model is run, and the Wald–Glejser test is computed. The null hypothesis is that the time series is homoskedastic.
  - o Short Tip: Tests for heteroskedasticity (H_0: time series is homoskedastic).
  - o Data Input: Data Type C. One dependent variable and one or multiple independent variables are required.
    - Dependent Variable, Independent Variables:
      - \>VAR1
      - \>VAR2; VAR3; VAR4; …
- **Heteroskedasticity (Wald's on Individual Variables).** Several tests exist to test for the presence of heteroskedasticity, that is, volatilities or uncertainties (standard deviation or variance of a variable is nonconstant over time). Applicable only to time-series data, these tests can also be used for testing misspecifications and nonlinearities. The test is based on the null hypothesis of no heteroskedasticity.

- o Short Tip: Runs Wald's test for heteroskedasticity on each of the independent variables (H_0: each independent variable is homoskedastic).
- o Model Input: Data Type C. One dependent variable and multiple continuous or categorical independent variables are required.
  - ▪ Dependent Variable, Independent Variables:
    - • >VAR1
    - • >VAR2; VAR3; …

- **Hodrick–Prescott Filter.** The Hodrick–Prescott filter helps to reduce data noise and stochastic variation of a time-series variable while maintaining the data's fluctuations and cycles. The filtered data are typically more predictable due to the random noise reduction. The lambda smoothing parameter can be calibrated to increase or reduce the noise filter. Typically, lambda is set to 100 for yearly data, 1,600 for quarterly data, and 14,400 for monthly data.

  - o Short Tip: Runs the Hodrick–Prescott filter to reduce data noise and stochastic variation of a time-series variable.
  - o Model Input: Data Type A. A single variable and a manual input parameter.
    - ▪ Time Series Data, Lambda:
      - • >VAR1
      - • >100

- **Hotelling T-Square: 1 VAR with Related Measures.** Runs the Hotelling T-Square test for one sample set of multiple related features (variables). For example, features such as usefulness, attractiveness, durability, and interest level on a single new product are collected and listed as column variables. The null hypothesis tested is that there is zero difference between all the related features (variables) against their respective goals. The Hotelling T-Square for One Variable with Related Measures is an extension of the T-test for independent variables and Bonferroni adjustments are applied simultaneously to multiple variables.
  - o Short Tip: Simultaneously tests multiple features of one group of multiple variables (H_0: no difference between the feature variables against their goals).
  - o Model Input: Data Type C. Two or more input variables are required. Different variables are arranged in columns and all variables (features) must have at least 5 data points each, with the same number of total data points or rows per variable. The number of Goals entered must match the number of variables.

- Data, Goals:
  - \>VAR1; VAR2; VAR3; …
  - \>7
  - \>8
- **Hotelling T-Square: 2 VAR Dependent Pair with Related Measures.** Runs the Hotelling T-Square Two Paired Group test for two sample sets of multiple related features (variables). For example, features such as usefulness, attractiveness, durability, and interest level on two new products are collected and listed as column variables. The null hypothesis tested is that there is zero difference between all the related features (variables) compared across the two groups against their respective goals. The Hotelling T-Square for Two Dependent Variables with Related Measures is an extension of the T-test for dependent variables and Bonferroni adjustments are applied simultaneously to multiple paired variables.
  - o Short Tip: Simultaneously tests multiple features of two groups of paired variables (H_0: no difference between the feature variables of the two groups against their respective goals).
  - o Model Input: Data Type D. Exactly two groups are required. Two or more input variables are required in each group. Different variables are arranged in columns and all variables (features) must have at least 5 data points each. All variables in both groups must have an equal number of data rows. The number of Group 2 Variables needs to be equal to the number of Group 1 Variables. The number of Goals must match the number of variables in Group 1 and are optional inputs (the default setting is that all goals are equal to 0).
    - Group 1 Variables, Group 2 Variables, Goals:
      - \>VAR1; VAR2; VAR3; …
      - \>VAR6; VAR7; VAR8; …
      - \>7
      - \>8
- **Hotelling T-Square: 2 VAR Indep. Equal Variance with Related Measures.** Runs the Hotelling T-Square Two Independent Groups with Equal Variance Related Measures test for two sample sets of multiple related features (variables). For example, features such as usefulness, attractiveness, durability, and interest level on two new products are collected and listed as column variables. The null hypothesis tested is that there is zero difference between all the related features (variables) compared across the two groups. The Hotelling T-Square Two Independent Groups with Equal Variance Related Measures test is an extension

of the T-test for independent variables with equal variance and Bonferroni adjustments are applied simultaneously to multiple independent variables.

- o Short Tip: Simultaneously tests multiple features of two groups of multiple variables with equal variance (H_0: no difference between the feature variables of the two groups).
- o Model Input: Data Type D. Exactly two groups are required. Two or more input variables are required in each group. Different variables are arranged in columns and all variables (features) must have at least 5 data points each. All variables in each group must have an equal number of rows, but the number of rows in Group 1 and Group 2 can be different. The number of Group 2 Variables needs to be equal to the number of Group 1 Variables.
  - Group 1 Variables, Group 2 Variables:
    - >VAR1; VAR2; VAR3; ...
    - >VAR6; VAR7; VAR8; ...

- **Hotelling T-Square: 2 VAR indep. Unequal Variance with Related Measures.** Runs the Hotelling T-Square Two Independent Groups with Unequal Variance Related Measures test for two sample sets of multiple related features (variables). For example, features such as usefulness, attractiveness, durability, and interest level on two new products are collected and listed as column variables. The null hypothesis tested is that there is zero difference between all the related features (variables) compared across the two groups. The Hotelling T-Square Two Independent Groups with Unequal Variance Related Measures is an extension of the t-test for independent variables with equal variance and Bonferroni adjustments are applied simultaneously to multiple independent variables.

  - o Short Tip: Simultaneously tests multiple features of two groups of multiple variables with unequal variance (H_0: no feature variable differences between the two groups).
  - o Model Input: Data Type D. Exactly two groups are required. Two or more variables are required in each group, with more than 5 rows of data in each variable. All variables in each group must have an equal number of rows, but the number of rows in Group 1 and Group 2 can be different. The number of Group 2 Variables needs to be equal to the number of Group 1 Variables.
    - Group 1 Variables, Group 2 Variables:
      - >VAR1; VAR2; VAR3; ...
      - >VAR6; VAR7; VAR8; ...

- **Internal Consistency Reliability: Cronbach's Alpha (Dichotomous Data).** Cronbach's Alpha measures the internal consistency and reliability for continuous and non-dichotomous data including questionnaire and Likert scale data. A high alpha (> 0.7) implies strong reliability versus the null hypothesis tested for alpha equals zero where there is no internal consistency and no reliability among the raters. Each question is set up as different column variables versus the rows of data, which are different raters' assessments or answers.
    - o Short Tip: Checks for internal consistency and reliability of different peoples' responses to the same questions (H_0: there is zero alpha reliability and no internal consistency).
    - o Model Input: Data Type C. Two or more input variables are required. Different variables are arranged in columns and all variables must have at least 5 data points each, with the same number of total data points or rows per variable.
        - Variables: >VAR1; VAR2; VAR3; …
- **Internal Consistency Reliability: Guttman's Lambda and Split Half Model.** Internal consistency and reliability imply that the measurements of an experiment will be consistent over repeated tests of the same subject under identical conditions. The Guttman's test and Split Half test take an existing dataset and divide it into multiple replicable internal tests. These tests measure the consistency and reliability of different responses to the same question where low correlations and lambda scores mean low reliability and low consistency, and higher lambda and correlation scores (>0.7) imply a higher level of reliability.
    - o Short Tip: Measures consistency and reliability of different responses to the same questions where low correlations and lambda scores mean low reliability and low consistency.
    - o Model Input: Data Type C. Two or more input variables are required. Different variables are arranged in columns and all variables must have at least 3 data points each, with the same number of total data points or rows per variable. The total number of variables must be even.
        - Variables: >VAR1; VAR2; VAR3; …
- **Internal Consistency Reliability: Kuder–Richardson Statistic (Dichotomous Data).** Kuder–Richardson 20 and 21 Statistics measure the internal consistency of measurements of dichotomous and binary responses, and are typically between 0 and 1. The higher the value, the higher the level of consistency,

and the method is similar to Cronbach's Alpha. The KR 20 and KR 21 statistics measure the internal consistency and reliability for dichotomous data. A high KR statistic (> 0.7) implies strong reliability.

- o Short Tip: Checks for internal consistency and reliability of different peoples' responses to the same questions.
- o Model Input: Data Type C. Two or more input variables are required. Different variables are arranged in columns and all variables must have at least 5 data points, with an identical number of total data points/rows per variable.
  - Variables: >VAR1; VAR2; VAR3; ...

- **Inter-rater Reliability: Cohen's Kappa.** Cohen's Kappa test measures the reliability of two independent raters by measuring their agreement levels and accounting for random chances of disagreement. The null hypothesis tested is that the two independent researchers' judgments are reliable or have no significant difference. Enter the data as an $N \times N$ matrix (rows as one judge's responses to various questions and columns as the second judge's responses to the same questions).
  - o Short Tip: Measures the reliability of two independent raters and their agreement levels (H_0: both sets of judgments agree and are reliable compared to one another).
  - o Model Input: Data Type C. Two or more input variables are required. Different variables are arranged in columns and all variables must have at least 5 data points each, with the same number of total data points or rows per variable. The number of columns must equal the number of rows ($N \times N$ matrix).
    - Variables: >VAR1; VAR2; VAR3; ...

- **Inter-rater Reliability: Inter-Class Correlation (ICC).** The Interclass Correlation (ICC) Reliability tests the reliability of ratings by comparing the variability of various ratings of the same subject to the total variation across all ratings and all subjects simultaneously. A high ICC indicates a high level of reliability, and the analysis can be applied to Likert scales and any other quantitative scales. The variable columns are each judge's responses to different subjects (rows).
  - o Short Tip: Measures the reliability of different judges' responses to the same subjects where low correlations mean low reliability and low consistency.
  - o Model Input: Data Type C. Two or more input variables are required. Different variables are arranged in columns and all variables must have at least 5 data points each, with the same number of total data points or rows per variable.

- Variables: >VAR1; VAR2; VAR3; …

- **Inter-rater Reliability: Kendall's W (No Ties).** Runs the Kendall's W Measure of Concordance between raters. Each column is a different item, and each row is a judge's or rater's value. The null hypothesis tested is that there is no agreement among different judges (W = 0), indicating no reliability among raters.
  - Short Tip: Measures inter-rater concordance (H_0: there is zero concordance among different raters, indicating W = 0 or no inter-rater reliability).
  - Model Input: Data Type C. Two or more input variables are required. Different variables are arranged in columns and all variables must have at least 3 data points each, with the same number of total data points or rows per variable.
    - Variables: >VAR1; VAR2; VAR3; …

- **Inter-rater Reliability: Kendall's W (with Ties).** Runs the Kendall's W Measure of Concordance between raters after adjusting for ties. Each column is a different item, and each row is a judge's or rater's value. The null hypothesis tested is that there is no agreement among different judges (W = 0), indicating no reliability among raters.
  - Short Tip: Measures inter-rater concordance adjusted for ties (H_0: there is zero concordance among different raters, indicating W = 0 or no inter-rater reliability).
  - Model Input: Data Type C. Two or more input variables are required. Different variables are arranged in columns and all variables must have at least 3 data points each, with the same number of total data points or rows per variable.
    - Variables: >VAR1; VAR2; VAR3; …

- **Kendall's Tau Correlation (No Ties).** Kendall's Tau is a nonparametric correlation coefficient, considering concordance or discordance of pairwise combinations of ranked *ordinal* data. The null hypothesis tested is that there is zero correlation.
  - Short Tip: Nonparametric Kendall's Tau concordance correlation (H_0: there is zero correlation between the two variables).
  - Model Input: Data Type B. Two input variables are required. Different variables are arranged in columns and all variables must have at least 3 data points each, with the same number of total data points or rows per variable.
    - Variables: >VAR1; VAR2

- **Kendall's Tau Correlation (with Ties).** Kendall's Tau with Ties is a nonparametric correlation coefficient, considering concordance or discordance, and correcting for ties, using pairwise combinations of ranked *ordinal* data. The null hypothesis tested is that there is zero correlation between the two variables.
    - Short Tip: Nonparametric Kendall's Tau concordance correlation corrected for ties (H_0: there is zero correlation between the two variables).
    - Model Input: Data Type B. Two input variables are required. Different variables are arranged in columns and all variables must have at least 3 data points each, with the same number of total data points or rows per variable.
        - Variables: >VAR1; VAR2
- **Linear Interpolation.** Sometimes interest rates or any type of time-dependent rates may have missing values. For instance, the Treasury rates for Years 1, 2, and 3 exist, and then jump to Year 5, skipping Year 4. We can, using linear interpolation (i.e., we assume the rates during the missing periods are linearly related), determine and "fill in" or interpolate their values.
    - Short Tip: Fills in the missing points in a data series.
    - Model Input: Data Type B. Two input variables are required. Different variables are arranged in columns and all variables must have at least 3 data points each, with the same number of total data points or rows per variable.
        - Periods, Values, Required Value for Period:
            - >VAR1
            - >VAR2
            - 5
- **Logistic S-Curve.** The S-curve, or logistic growth curve, starts off like a J-curve, with exponential growth rates. Over time, the environment becomes saturated (e.g., market saturation, competition, overcrowding), the growth slows, and the forecast value eventually ends up at a saturation or maximum level. The S-curve model is typically used in forecasting market share or sales growth of a new product from market introduction until maturity and decline, population dynamics, growth of bacterial cultures, and other naturally occurring variables.
    - Short Tip: Generates a time-series forecast using the Logistic S-curve.
    - Model Input: Data Type A. Requires four simple manual inputs: assumed growth rates (%), starting value of the forecast, maximum capacity value, and the total number of periods to forecast.

- Assumed Growth Rate (%), Initial Starting Value, Max Capacity Value, Forecast Periods:
  - \>10
  - \>10
  - \>1200
  - \>120

- **Mahalanobis Distance.** The Mahalanobis distance measures the distance between point X and a distribution Y, based on multidimensional generalizations of the number of standard deviations X is away from the average of Y. This multidimensional Mahalanobis distance is equivalent to standard Euclidean distance. The null hypothesis tested is that there are no outliers in each of the data rows.
  - Short Tip: Checks for outliers in each row of data.
  - Model Input: Data Type C. Two or more input variables are required. Different variables are arranged in columns and all variables must have at least 5 data points each, with the same number of total data points or rows per variable.
    - Variables:
      - \>VAR1; VAR2; VAR3; …

- **Markov Chain.** The Markov Chain models the probability of a future state that depends on a previous state (a mathematical system that undergoes transitions from one state to another), forming a chain when linked together (a random process characterized as memoryless, i.e., the next state depends only on the current state and not on the sequence of events that preceded it) that reverts to a long-run steady-state level. Used to forecast the market share of two competitors.
  - Short Tip: Generates a time series of a two-state Markov Chain of alternating states.
  - Model Input: Data Type A. Requires two simple manual inputs, State 1 Probability and State 2 Probability.
    - State 1, State 2:
      - \>10
      - \>10

- **Markov Chain Transition Risk Matrix.** The Markov Chain Transition Matrix models the probability of future states using a mathematical system that undergoes transitions from one state to another. It is an extension of the two-state Markov Chain.
    o Short Tip: Generates a time series of a multiple-state Markov Chain of alternating states as a risk transition matrix.
    o Model Input: Data Type A. Requires one variable of historical data and a simple manual input of the number of states to model.
        ▪ Variable, Number of States:
            • >VAR1
            • >5
- **Multiple Poisson Regression (Population and Frequency).** The Poisson regression is like the logit regression in that the dependent variables can only take on non-negative values, but also that the underlying distribution of the data is a Poisson distribution, drawn from a known population.
    o Short Tip: Runs Poisson regression with non-negative dependent variables where all variables follow a Poisson distribution with some known population size.
    o Model Input: Data Type C. One Dependent Variable, one Population Size or Frequency variable, and one or more Independent Variables are allowed, with the same number of total data points or rows per variable.
        ▪ Dependent Variable, Population or Frequency, Independent Variables:
            • >VAR1
            • >VAR2
            • >VAR3; VAR4; VAR5
- **Multiple Regression (Deming Regression with Known Variance).** In regular multivariate regressions, the dependent variable Y is modeled and predicted by independent variables X_i with some error ε. However, in a Deming regression, we further assume that the data collected for Y and X have additional uncertainties and errors, or variances, that are used to provide a more relaxed fit in a Deming model.
    o Short Tip: Runs a bivariate regression assuming the variables have additional uncertainties or variances.
    o Model Input: Data Type B. Two variables are required with at least 5 rows of data each, the Dependent Variable, and the Independent Variable. Also, the variances of these two variables are required.

- Dependent Variable, Independent Variable, Dependent Variable's Variance, Independent Variable's Variance:
  - VAR1
  - VAR2
  - 0.09
  - 0.02
- **Multiple Regression (Linear).** Multivariate linear regression is used to model the relationship structure and characteristics of a certain dependent variable as it depends on other independent exogenous variables. Using the modeled relationship, we can forecast the future values of the dependent variable. The accuracy and goodness-of-fit for this model can also be determined. Linear and nonlinear models can be fitted in multiple regression.
  - Short Tip: Runs a multiple linear regression.
  - Model Input: Data Type C. Two sets of variables are required: one dependent variable and one or multiple independent variables, with at least 5 rows of data in each variable, with the same number of total data points or rows per variable.
    - Dependent Variable, Independent Variables:
      - >VAR1
      - >VAR2; VAR3; …
- **Multiple Regression (Nonlinear).** Multivariate nonlinear regression is used to model the relationship structure and characteristics of a certain dependent variable as it depends on other independent exogenous variables. Using the modeled relationship, we can forecast the future values of the dependent variable. The accuracy and goodness-of-fit for this model can also be determined. Linear and nonlinear models can be fitted in the multiple regression analysis.
  - Short Tip: Runs a multiple nonlinear regression.
  - Model Input: Data Type C. Two sets of variables are required: one dependent variable and one or multiple independent variables, with at least 5 rows of data in each variable, with the same number of total data points or rows per variable.
    - Dependent Variable, Independent Variables:
      - >VAR1
      - >VAR2; VAR3; …
- **Multiple Regression (Ordinal Logistic Regression).** Runs a multivariate ordinal logistic regression with two dependent variables and multiple independent variables.
  - Short Tip: Runs a multivariate ordinal logistic regression with two dependent variables and multiple independent

variables. The independent variables can be ordinal variables and data points are counts. For instance, the two dependent variables can be categories of Age (1-5) and Sex (0/1), with five independent variables filled with the number or frequencies of people who responded Strongly Agree, Agree, Neutral, Disagree, or Strongly Disagree.

- o Model Input: Data Type C. Two sets of variables are required: two dependent variables and one or multiple independent variables, with at least 5 rows of data in each variable, with the same number of total data points or rows per variable.
  - Dependent Variables, Independent Variables:
    - >VAR1; VAR2
    - >VAR3; VAR4; VAR5; …

- **Multiple Regression (Through Origin).** Runs a multiple linear regression but without an intercept.
  - o Short Tip: Runs a multiple linear regression but without an intercept.
  - o Model Input: Data Type C. Two sets of variables are required: one dependent variable and one or multiple independent variables, with at least 5 rows of data in each variable, with the same number of total data points or rows per variable.
    - Dependent Variable, Independent Variables:
      - >VAR1
      - >VAR2; VAR3; …

- **Multiple Regression (Two-Variable Functional Form Tests).** Runs a bivariate regression test on multiple functional forms including Linear, Linear Log, Reciprocal, Quadratic, Log-Linear, Log Reciprocal, Log Quadratic, Double Log, Logistic.
  - o Short Tip: Runs a bivariate regression test on multiple functional forms.
  - o Model Input: Data Type B. Two variables are required: one dependent variable and one independent variable, with at least 5 rows of data in each variable, with the same number of total data points or rows per variable.
    - Dependent Variable, Independent Variable:
      - >VAR1
      - >VAR2

- **Multiple Ridge Regression (Low Variance, High Bias, High VIF).** A ridge regression comes with a higher bias than an ordinary least squares multiple regression but has less variance. It is more suitable in situations with high variance inflation factors and multicollinearity or when there is a high number of variables compared to data points.

- o Short Tip: Multiple regression adjusted for high VIF multicollinearity or when there is a high number of independent variables compared to available data points.
- o Model Input: Data Type C. One dependent variable is required, and one or more independent variables are allowed, with the same number of total data points or rows per variable. Lambda is an optional input.
  - Dependent Variable, Independent Variables, Lambda (Optional, default is 0.1):
    - VAR1
    - VAR2
    - 0.09
    - 0.02

- **Multiple Weighted Regression (Regression Method for Fixing Heteroskedasticity).** Runs a multivariate regression on weighted variables to correct for heteroskedasticity in all the variables. The weights used to adjust these variables are the user input standard deviations.
  - o Short Tip: Multiple regression modeling on weight-adjusted variables to correct for heteroskedasticity.
  - o Model Input: Data Type C. One dependent variable is required, and one or more independent variables are allowed, with the same number of total data points or rows per variable. Finally, a weight input variable is required, which is a series of standard deviations.
    - Dependent Variable, Independent Variable, Weights in Stdev:
      - VAR1
      - VAR2; VAR3; VAR4; …
      - VAR5

- **Neural Network.** Commonly used to refer to a network or circuit of biological neurons, modern usage of the term *neural network* often refers to artificial neural networks that consist of artificial neurons, or nodes, recreated in a software environment. Such networks attempt to mimic the neurons in the human brain in ways of thinking and identifying patterns and, in our situation, identifying patterns for the purposes of forecasting time-series data.
  - o **Linear.** Applies a linear function.
  - o **Nonlinear Logistic.** Applies a nonlinear logistic function.

- o **Nonlinear Cosine with Hyperbolic Tangent.** Applies a nonlinear cosine with hyperbolic tangent function.
- o **Nonlinear Hyperbolic Tangent.** Applies a nonlinear hyperbolic tangent function.
  - Short Tip: Runs a time-series neural network forecast through pattern recognition algorithms (linear, logistic, cosine, hyperbolic).
  - Model Input: Data Type A. Data Variable, Layers, Testing Set, Forecast Periods, and Apply Multiphased Optimization (Optional, default set to 0 or no optimization)
    - Data Variable, Layers, Testing Set, Forecast Periods:
      - >VAR1
      - >3
      - >20
      - >5
      - >1

- **Nominal Data Contingency Analysis (McNemar's Marginal Homogeneity).** Runs the McNemar's test on a pair of alphanumeric nominal data and creates 2 × 2 contingency tables with dichotomous traits. The test determines if the row and column variables' marginal probabilities are equal, that is, if there is marginal homogeneity. The null hypothesis is marginal homogeneity where the two marginal probabilities for each outcome are the same.
  - o Short Tip: Runs the McNemar's test on a pair of alphanumeric nominal data and creates 2 × 2 contingency tables with dichotomous traits.
  - o Model Input: Data Type B. Two alphanumeric variables are required, with the same number of total data points or rows per variable.
    - Variable 1, Variable 2
      - VAR1; VAR2

Nonparametric techniques make no assumptions about the specific shape or distribution from which the sample is drawn. This lack of assumptions is different from the other hypotheses tests such as ANOVA or t-tests (parametric tests) where the sample is assumed to be drawn from a population that is normally or approximately normally distributed. If normality is assumed, the power of the test is higher due to this normality restriction. However, if flexibility on distributional requirements is needed, then nonparametric techniques are superior. In general, nonparametric methodologies provide the following advantages over parametric tests:

- o Normality or approximate normality does not have to be assumed.
- o Fewer assumptions about the population are required and nonparametric tests don't require population assumption of any specific distribution.
- o Smaller sample sizes can be analyzed.
- o Compared to parametric tests, nonparametric tests use data less efficiently.
- o The power of the test is lower than that of the parametric tests.
- o Samples with nominal and ordinal scales of measurement can be tested.
- o Sample variances do not have to be equal (required in parametric tests).

- **Nonparametric Chi-Square Goodness-of-Fit for Normality (Grouped Data).** The chi-square test for goodness-of-fit is used to examine if a sample dataset could have been drawn from a population having a specified probability distribution. The probability distribution tested here is the normal distribution. The null hypothesis tested is such that the sample is randomly drawn from the normal distribution.
  - o Short Tip: Nonparametric test on normality (H_0: the dataset is normally distributed).
  - o Model Input: Data Type B. Two input variables are required with at least 3 rows of data each.
    - Upper Limit of Data Category, Frequency within that Category, Mean, Standard Deviation:
      - \>VAR1
      - \>VAR2
      - \>945
      - \>145

- **Nonparametric Chi-Square Independence.** The chi-square test for independence examines two variables to see if there is some statistical relationship between them. This test is not used to find the exact nature of the relationship between the two variables, but to simply test if the variables could be independent of each other. The null hypothesis tested is such that the variables are independent of each other.
    - o Short Tip: Nonparametric test on independence between two variables (H_0: the variables are independent and have no effects on one another).
    - o Model Input: Data Type B. Two input variables are required with at least 3 rows of data each.
        - ▪ Variables:
            - • >VAR1; VAR2
- **Nonparametric Chi-Square Population Variance.** The chi-square test for population variance is used for hypothesis testing and confidence interval estimation for population variance. The population variance of a sample is typically unknown, and hence the need for quantifying this confidence interval. The population is assumed to be normally distributed.
    - o Short Tip: Nonparametric test on the sample variance compared to a hypothesized variance (H_0: sample variance equals hypothesized variance).
    - o Model Input: Data Type A. Manually entered input variables are required.
        - ▪ Hypothesized Variance, Sample Variance, Sample Size:
            - • >4
            - • >5
            - • >20
- **Nonparametric: Cochran's Q (Binary Repeated Measures).** Runs the Cochran's test, which is the nonparametric equivalent of an ANOVA with repeated measures but where the values are binary 0 and 1. The null hypothesis tested is that the proportions of 1s and 0s for all variables are equivalent.
    - o Short Tip: Nonparametric equivalent of ANOVA with multiple treatments (H_0: the binary proportions are equivalent for all variables).
    - o Model Input: Data Type C. Two or more input variables are required. Different variables are arranged in columns and all variables must have at least 5 data points each, with the same number of total data points or rows per variable. Data must be 0 or 1 binary values only.
        - ▪ Variables: >VAR1; VAR2; VAR3; …

- **Nonparametric: D'Agostino–Pearson Normality Test.** Runs the D'Agostino–Pearson test for normality to test the null hypothesis if the data are normally distributed.
  - o Short Tip: Tests for normality of your data (H_0: the data are normally distributed).
  - o Model Input: Data Type A. One input variable is required with at least 5 rows of data.
    - ▪ Variable: >VAR1
- **Nonparametric Friedman's Test.** The Friedman test is the extension of the Wilcoxon Signed-Rank test for paired samples. The corresponding parametric test is the Randomized Block Multiple Treatment ANOVA, but, unlike the ANOVA, the Friedman test does not require that the dataset be randomly sampled from normally distributed populations with equal variances. The Friedman test uses a two-tailed hypothesis test where the null hypothesis is such that the population medians of each treatment are statistically identical to the rest of the group; that is, there is no effect among the different treatment groups.
  - o Short Tip: Runs the nonparametric Freidman's test, an equivalent of ANOVA with blocking variables.
  - o Model Input: Data Type C. Two or more input variables are required. Different variables are arranged in columns and all variables must have at least 3 data points each, with the same number of total data points or rows per variable.
    - ▪ Variable: >VAR1; VAR2; VAR3; …
- **Nonparametric Kruskal–Wallis Test.** The Kruskal–Wallis test is the extension of the Wilcoxon Signed-Rank test by comparing more than two independent samples. The corresponding parametric test is the One-Way ANOVA, but unlike the ANOVA, the Kruskal–Wallis does not require that the dataset be randomly sampled from normally distributed populations with equal variances. The Kruskal–Wallis test is a two-tailed hypothesis test where the null hypothesis is such that the population medians of each treatment are statistically identical to the rest of the group; that is, there is no effect among the different treatment groups.
  - o Short Tip: Runs the nonparametric Kruskal–Wallis test, an equivalent of ANOVA with Multiple Treatments.
  - o Model Input: Data Type C. Two or more input variables are required. Different variables are arranged in columns and all variables must have at least 3 data points each, with the same number of total data points or rows per variable.
    - ▪ Variables: >VAR1; VAR2; VAR3; …

- **Nonparametric Lilliefors Test for Normality.** The Lilliefors test evaluates the null hypothesis of whether the data sample was drawn from a normally distributed population, versus an alternate hypothesis that the data sample is not normally distributed. If the calculated p-value is less than or equal to the alpha significance value, then reject the null hypothesis and accept the alternate hypothesis. Otherwise, if the p-value is higher than the alpha significance value, do not reject the null hypothesis. This test relies on two cumulative frequencies: one derived from the sample dataset and one from a theoretical distribution based on the mean and standard deviation of the sample data. An alternative to this test is the chi-square test for normality. The chi-square test requires more data points to run compared to the Lilliefors test.
    - o Short Tip: Runs nonparametric Lilliefors test for normality of your data (H_0: the data is assumed to be normally distributed).
    - o Model Input: Data Type A. One input variable is required with at least 5 data points or rows of data.
        - Variable:
            - >VAR1
- **Nonparametric: Mann–Whitney Test (Two Var).** Runs the nonparametric Mann–Whitney test for two independent samples (related to Wilcoxon Signed-Rank test) and is the nonparametric equivalent of the two sample T-test for independent variables. The null hypothesis tested is that there is zero difference between the two variables.
    - o Short Tip: Nonparametric test on two variables (H_0: no difference between the two medians).
    - o Model Input: Data Type B. Two input variables are required with at least 3 rows of data each. The two variables do not need to have the same number of rows.
        - Variables:
            - >VAR1; VAR2
- **Nonparametric: Mood's Multivariate Median Test.** Runs the nonparametric Mood's test for medians of multiple variables simultaneously. It is an extension of the nonparametric Wilcoxon Signed-Rank test for two variables extended to multiple variables. Mood's test is related to the parametric ANOVA with Multiple Treatments and its nonparametric Kruskal–Wallis test equivalence.
    - o Short Tip: Nonparametrically tests if the medians from various variables are similar (H_0: all medians are equal or homogeneous), related to Wilcoxon and Kruskal–Wallis tests.

- Model Input: Data Type C. Two or more input variables are required. Different variables are arranged in columns and all variables must have at least 3 data points each. Different numbers of total data points or rows per variable are allowed.
  - Variables:
    - >VAR1; VAR2; VAR3; ...
- **Nonparametric Runs Test for Randomness.** The Runs test evaluates the randomness of a series of observations by analyzing the number of runs it contains. A run is a consecutive appearance of one or more observations that are similar. The null hypothesis tested is whether the data sequence is random, versus the alternate hypothesis that the data sequence is not random.
  - Short Tip: Runs nonparametric Runs test for randomness of the data (H_0: the data is random).
  - Model Input: Data Type A. One input variable is required with at least 5 data points or rows of data.
    - Variable:
      - >VAR1
- **Nonparametric: Shapiro–Wilk–Royston Normality Test.** Runs the Shapiro–Wilk test for normality using the Royston algorithm to test the null hypothesis if the data is normally distributed.
  - Short Tip: Tests for normality of your data (H_0: the data is assumed to be normally distributed).
  - Model Input: Data Type A. One input variable is required with at least 3 rows of data.
    - Variable:
      - >VAR1
- **Nonparametric Wilcoxon Signed-Rank Test (One Var).** The single-variable Wilcoxon Signed-Rank test looks at whether a sample dataset could have been randomly drawn from a population whose median is being hypothesized. The corresponding parametric test is the one-sample t-test, which should be used if the underlying population is assumed to be normal, providing a higher power on the test.
  - Short Tip: Runs a nonparametric Wilcoxon test for one variable (H_0: the median is equivalent to zero).
  - Model Input: Data Type A. One input variable is required with at least 3 rows of data.
    - Variable:
      - >VAR1

- **Nonparametric Wilcoxon Signed-Rank Test (Two Var).** The Wilcoxon Signed-Rank test for paired variables looks at whether the median of the differences between the two paired variables are equal. This test is specifically formulated for testing the same or similar samples before and after an event (e.g., measurements taken before a medical treatment are compared against those measurements taken after the treatment to see if there is a difference). The corresponding parametric test is the two-sample t-test with dependent means, which should be used if the underlying population is assumed to be normal, providing a higher power on the test.
  - Short Tip: Nonparametric test on equality of medians (H_0: the two variables have equal medians).
  - Model Input: Data Type B. Two input variables are required with at least 3 rows of data each.
    - Variable 1, Variable 2, Hypothesized Median Difference
      - >VAR1; VAR2
      - >0

- **Parametric One Variable (T) Mean.** The one-variable t-test of means is appropriate when the population standard deviation is not known but the sampling distribution is assumed to be approximately normal (the t-test is used when the sample size is less than 30). This t-test can be applied to three types of hypothesis tests—a two-tailed test, a right-tailed test, and a left-tailed test—to examine if the population mean is equal to, less than, or greater than the hypothesized mean based on the sample dataset.
    - Short Tip: Runs a one-variable t-test for means (H_0: the population mean is statistically equal to the hypothesized mean).
    - Model Input: Data Type A. One input variable is required with at least 5 rows of data.
        - Variable:
            - >VAR1
- **Parametric One Variable (Z) Mean.** The one-variable z-test is appropriate when the population standard deviation is known, and the sampling distribution is assumed to be approximately normal (this applies when the number of data points exceeds 30).
    - Short Tip: Runs a one variable z-test for means (H_0: the population mean is statistically equal to the hypothesized mean).
    - Model Input: Data Type A. One input variable is required with at least 5 rows of data.
        - Variable:
            - >VAR1
- **Parametric One-Variable (Z) Proportion.** The one-variable z-test for proportions is appropriate when the sampling distribution is assumed to be approximately normal (this applies when the number of data points exceeds 30, and when the number of data points, N, multiplied by the hypothesized population proportion mean, P, is greater than or equal to 5, $NP \geq 5$). The data used in the analysis must be proportions and be between 0 and 1.
    - Short Tip: Runs a one variable z-test for proportions (H_0: the population proportion is statistically equal to the hypothesized mean).
    - Model Input: Data Type A. One input variable is required with at least 5 rows of data.
        - Variable:
            - >VAR1

- **Parametric: Power Curve for T-Test.** Beta is the acceptable level of Type II error (the probability that the null hypothesis is not rejected when it is false) and power is 1 – Beta.
    - Short Tip: Computes the Beta and power of a single variable test.
    - Model Input: Data Type A. One input variable is required with at least 5 rows of data. Hypothesized mean can be any numerical value, and the Alpha level must be a positive input (typically 0.01, 0.05, or 0.10).
        - Data Variable, Hypothesized Mean, Alpha:
            - >VAR1
            - >50
            - >0.05
- **Parametric Two-Variable (F) Variances.** The two-variable F-test analyzes the variances from two samples (the population variance of Sample 1 is tested with the population variance of Sample 2 to see if they are equal) and is appropriate when the population standard deviation is not known but the sampling distribution is assumed to be approximately normal.
    - Short Tip: Tests if the variances of two variables are equal (H_0: the two variables' variances are equal).
    - Model Input: Data Type B. Two input variables are required with at least 5 rows of data each.
        - Variable 1, Variable 2:
            - >VAR1; VAR2
- **Parametric Two-Variable (T) Dependent Mean.** The two-variable dependent t-test is appropriate when the population standard deviation is not known but the sampling distribution is assumed to be approximately normal (the t-test is used when the sample size is less than 30). In addition, this test is specifically formulated for testing the same or similar samples before and after an event (e.g., measurements taken before a medical treatment are compared against those measurements taken after the treatment to see if there is a difference).
    - Short Tip: Tests if the means of two variables are equal when the variables are dependent (H_0: the two variables' means are equal).
    - Model Input: Data Type B. Two input variables are required with at least 5 rows of data each.
        - Variable 1, Variable 2:
            - >VAR1; VAR2
- **Parametric Two-Variable (T) Independent Equal Variance.** The two-variable t-test with equal variances is appropriate when the population standard deviation is not known but the sampling distribution is assumed to be approximately normal

(the t-test is used when the sample size is less than 30). In addition, the two independent samples are assumed to have similar variances.

- o Short Tip: Tests if the means are equal for two independent equal variance variables (H_0: the two variables' means are equal).
- o Model Input: Data Type B. Two input variables are required with at least 5 rows of data each.
  - Variable 1, Variable 2:
    - >VAR1; VAR2

- **Parametric Two-Variable (T) Independent Unequal Variance.** The two-variable t-test with unequal variances (the population variance of sample 1 is expected to be different from the population variance of sample 2) is appropriate when the population standard deviation is not known but the sampling distribution is assumed to be approximately normal (the t-test is used when the sample size is less than 30). Also, the two independent samples are assumed to have similar variances.
  - o Short Tip: Tests if the means are equal for two independent unequal variance variables (H_0: the two variables' means are equal).
  - o Model Input: Data Type B. Two input variables are required with at least 5 rows of data each.
    - Variable 1, Variable 2
      - >VAR1; VAR2

- **Parametric Two-Variable (Z) Independent Means.** The two-variable z-test is appropriate when the population standard deviations are known for the two samples and the sampling distribution of each variable is assumed to be approximately normal (when the number of data points of each variable exceeds 30).
  - o Short Tip: Tests if the means are equal for two independent variables with known variances (H_0: the two variables' means are equal).
  - o Model Input: Data Type B. Two input variables are required with at least 5 rows of data each.
    - Variable 1, Variable 2, Hypothesized Mean Difference, Stdev 1, Stdev 2
      - >VAR1; VAR2
      - >5
      - >123.45
      - >87.6

- **Parametric Two-Variable (Z) Independent Proportions.** The two-variable Z-test on proportions is appropriate when the sampling distribution is assumed to be approximately normal (this applies when the number of data points of both samples exceeds 30). Further, the data should all be proportions and be between 0 and 1.
  - Short Tip: Tests if the proportions are equal for two independent variables (H_0: the two variables' proportions are equal).
  - Model Input: Data Type B. Two input variables are required with at least 5 rows of data each.
    - Variable 1, Variable 2, Hypothesized Mean Difference:
      - >VAR1; VAR2
      - >5

CONTINUED LIST OF ANALYTICAL METHODS

- **Partial Correlations (Using Correlation Matrix).** Runs and computes the partial correlation matrix using your existing $N \times N$ full correlation matrix.
  - Short Tip: Computes the partial correlation matrix using an existing $N \times N$ full square correlation matrix.
  - Model Input: Data Type C. Two or more input variables are required. Different variables are arranged in columns and all variables must have at least 2 data points each, with the same number of total data points or rows per variable. The total number of variables must match the number of rows, i.e., the data entered should be in an $N \times N$ matrix.
    - Variables:
      - >VAR1; VAR2; VAR3; …
- **Partial Correlations (Using Raw Data).** Runs and computes the partial correlation matrix using raw data of multiple columns.
  - Short Tip: Computes the partial correlation matrix using raw data.
  - Model Input: Data Type C. Two or more input variables are required. Different variables are arranged in columns and all variables must have at least 5 data points each, with the same number of total data points or rows per variable.
    - Variables:
      - >VAR1; VAR2; VAR3; …

- **Principal Component Analysis.** Principal component analysis, or PCA, makes multivariate data easier to model and summarize. To understand PCA, suppose we start with N variables that are unlikely to be independent of one another, such that changing the value of one variable will change another variable. PCA modeling will replace the original N variables with a new set of M variables that are less than N but are uncorrelated to one another, while at the same time, each of these M variables is a linear combination of the original N variables so that most of the variation can be accounted for just using fewer explanatory variables.
  - Short Tip: Runs a principal component analysis on multiple variables.
  - Model Input: Data Type C. Three or more input variables are required. Different variables are arranged in columns and all variables must have at least 5 data points each, with the same number of total data points or rows per variable.
    - Variables:
      - >VAR1; VAR2; VAR3; …
- **Process Capability.** Given the user inputs of the process mean, sigma, as well as upper and lower specification limits, the model returns the various process capability measures (CP, CPK, PP), defective proportion units (DPU), defects per million opportunities (DPMO), output yield (%), and overall process sigma.
  - Short Tip: Process capability is used to calculate projected manufacturing process output yield and defects.
  - Model Input: Data Type A. Process Mean, Process Sigma, Upper Specification Limit USL, Lower Specification Limit LSL
    - Variables:
      - >2.2500
      - >0.0500
      - >2.1375
      - >2.8125

- **Quick Statistic.** Absolute Values (ABS), Average (AVG), Count, Difference, LAG, Lead, LN, LOG, Max, Median, Min, Mode, Power, Rank Ascending, Rank Descending, Relative LN Returns, Relative Returns, Semi-Standard Deviation (Lower), Semi-Standard Deviation (Upper), Standard Deviation Population, Standard Deviation Sample, Sum, Variance (Population), Variance (Sample). Various basic statistics such as average, standard deviation, ranking, sum, and others are computed using a single variable dataset.

- o Short Tip: Runs various basic statistics such as average, standard deviation, ranking, sum, etc.
- o Model Input: Data Type A. One input variable is required with at least 3 data points or rows of data.
  - Variable:
    - >VAR1

- ROC Curves, AUC, and Classification Tables. Runs the ROC and Classification Tables for numbers of failures and successes. The area under the curve (AUC) is computed using rectangular mode (R) and trapezoidal mode (T).
  - o Short Tip: Runs ROC and Classification Tables for failures and successes and computes the area under the curve (AUC).
  - o Model Input: Data Type B. Two input variables are required: Failures and Successes, with at least 3 rows of data for each variable. Each variable needs to have the same number of data rows. A final input required is the Cutoff value.
    - Failures, Successes, Cutoff:
      - >VAR1
      - >VAR2
      - >5

- Seasonality. Many time-series data exhibit seasonality where certain events repeat themselves after some time period or seasonality period (e.g., ski resorts' revenues are higher in winter than in summer, and this cycle will repeat itself every winter). The method tests for multiple periods of seasonalities (number of periods in one seasonal cycle).
  - o Short Tip: Runs various seasonality models to determine the best seasonality fit.
  - o Model Input: Data Type A. One input variable is required with at least 3 data points or rows of data and the maximum seasonality to test.
    - Variable:
      - >VAR1
      - >4

- Segmentation Clustering. Taking the original dataset, we run some internal algorithms (a combination or k-means hierarchical clustering and other methods of moments in order to find the best-fitting groups or natural statistical clusters) to statistically divide or segment the original dataset into multiple groups.

- o Short Tip: Runs segmentation clustering of an existing dataset and segregates the data into various statistical groups.
- o Model Input: Data Type A. One input variable is required with at least 3 data points or rows of data.
  - ▪ Variable:
    - • >VAR1
- **Skew and Kurtosis: Shapiro–Wilk and D'Agostino–Pearson.** Runs the Skew and Kurtosis tests to see if the data has both statistics equal to zero (normality), and the D'Agostino–Pearson test if skew and kurtosis are simultaneously zero. The null hypothesis is the data has zero skew and kurtosis, approximating normality.
  - o Short Tip: Tests if both skew and kurtosis are equal to zero and therefore approximating normality (H_0: skew and kurtosis are zero and data approximates normality).
  - o Model Input: Data Type A. One input variable is required with at least 5 rows of data.
    - ▪ Variable:
      - • >VAR1
- **Specifications Cubed Test (Ramsey's RESET).** Ramsey's regression specification error test (RESET) tests for general misspecification of your model using an F-test variation and cubed predictions. Rejecting the null hypothesis indicates some sort of misspecification in the model. The null hypothesis tested is that the current model is correctly specified.
  - o Short Tip: Ramsey's regression specification error test (RESET) tests for general misspecification of your model using an F-test variation and cubed predictions.
  - o Model Input: Data Type C. One dependent variable and one or more independent variables with custom modifications are required.
    - ▪ Variable:
      - • >VAR1
      - • >VAR2; LN(VAR3); (VAR4)^2
- **Specifications Squared Test (Ramsey's RESET).** Ramsey's regression specification error test (RESET) tests for general misspecification of your model using an F-test variation and squared predictions. Rejecting the null hypothesis indicates some sort of misspecification in the model. The null hypothesis tested is that the current model is correctly specified.
  - o Short Tip: Ramsey's regression specification error test (RESET) tests for general misspecification of your model using an F-test variation and squared predictions.

- o Model Input: Data Type C. One dependent variable and one or more independent variables with custom modifications are required.
  - ▪ Variable:
    - • >VAR1
    - • >VAR2; LN(VAR3); (VAR4)^2
- • **Stationarity: Augmented Dickey-Fuller.** Runs the unit root test for stationarity with no constant intercept and no linear trend using a multi-order autoregressive AR(p) process. The null hypothesis tested is that there is a unit root, and the time series is not stationary.
  - o Short Tip: Unit root test with a constant and trend (H_0: data exhibit unit root and the time series is a nonstationary AR(p) series).
  - o Model Input: Data Type A. One input variable is required with at least 10 rows of data.
    - ▪ Variable:
      - • >VAR1
- • **Stationarity: Dickey-Fuller (Constant and Trend).** Runs the unit root test for stationarity with a constant intercept and a linear trend using a first-order autoregressive AR(1) process. The null hypothesis tested is that there is a unit root, and the time series is not stationary.
  - o Short Tip: Unit root test with constant and trend (H_0: data exhibit unit root and the time series is a nonstationary AR(1) series).
  - o Model Input: Data Type A. One input variable is required with at least 10 rows of data.
    - ▪ Variable:
      - • >VAR1
- • **Stationarity: Dickey-Fuller (Constant No Trend).** Runs the unit root test for stationarity with a constant intercept and no linear trend using a first-order autoregressive AR(1) process. The null hypothesis tested is that there is a unit root, and the time series is not stationary.
  - o Short Tip: Unit root test with a constant but no trend (H_0: data exhibit unit root and the time series is a nonstationary AR(1) series).
  - o Model Input: Data Type A. One input variable is required with at least 10 rows of data.
    - ▪ Variable:
      - • >VAR1

- **Stationarity: Dickey-Fuller (No Constant No Trend).** Runs the unit root test for stationarity with no constant intercept and no linear trend using a first-order autoregressive AR(1) process. The null hypothesis tested is that there is a unit root, and the time series is not stationary.
  - Short Tip: Unit root test without constant or trend (H_0: data exhibit unit root and the time series is a nonstationary AR(1) series).
  - Model Input: Data Type A. One input variable is required with at least 10 rows of data.
    - Variable:
      - >VAR1
- **Stepwise Regression.**
  - Short Tip: Runs various multiple stepwise linear regression models.
  - Model Input: Data Type C. Two sets of variables are required: one dependent variable and one or multiple independent variables, with at least 5 rows of data in each variable, with the same number of total data points or rows per variable.
    - Dependent Variable, Independent Variables:
      - >VAR1
      - >VAR2; VAR3; …
  - **Stepwise Regression (Backward).** In the backward method, we run a regression with Y on all X variables and, reviewing each variable's p-value, systematically eliminate the variable with the largest p-value. Then run a regression again, repeating each time until all p-values are statistically significant.
  - **Stepwise Regression (Correlation).** In the correlation method, the dependent variable Y is correlated to all the independent variables X, and starting with the X variable with the highest absolute correlation value, a regression is run. Then subsequent X variables are added until the p-values indicate that the new X variable is no longer statistically significant. This approach is quick and simple but does not account for interactions among variables, and an X variable, when added, will statistically overshadow other variables.
  - **Stepwise Regression (Forward).** In the forward method, we first correlate Y with all X variables, run a regression for Y on the highest absolute value correlation of X, and obtain the fitting errors. Then, correlate these errors with the remaining X variables and choose the highest absolute value correlation among this remaining

set and run another regression. Repeat the process until the p-value for the latest X variable coefficient is no longer statistically significant and then stop the process.

- o Stepwise Regression (Forward-Backward). In the forward and backward method, apply the forward method to obtain three X variables, and then apply the backward approach to see if one of them needs to be eliminated because it is statistically insignificant. Repeat the forward method and then the backward method until all remaining X variables are considered.

- **Stochastic Processes.** Sometimes variables cannot be readily predicted using traditional means, and these variables are said to be stochastic. Nonetheless, most financial, economic, and naturally occurring phenomena (e.g., the motion of molecules through the air) follow a known mathematical law or relationship. Although the resulting values are uncertain, the underlying mathematical structure is known and can be simulated using Monte Carlo risk simulation.

  - o Short Tip: Generates various time-series stochastic process forecasts.
  - o Model Input: Data Type A. Multiple manual inputs are required. The specific input requirements depend on the stochastic process selected.
    - ▪ Initial Value, Drift Rate, Volatility, Horizon, Steps, Random Seed, Iterations
      - • >100
      - • >0.05
      - • >0.25
      - • >10
      - • >100
      - • >123456
  - o Brownian Motion Random Walk Process. The Brownian motion random walk process takes the form of $\frac{\delta S}{S} = \mu(\delta t) + \sigma \varepsilon \sqrt{\delta t}$ or a more generic version takes the form of $\frac{\delta S}{S} = (\mu - \sigma^2/2)\delta t + \sigma \varepsilon \sqrt{\delta t}$ for a geometric process. For an exponential version, we simply take the exponentials, and, as an example, we have $\frac{\delta S}{S} = exp[\mu(\delta t) + \sigma \varepsilon \sqrt{\delta t}]$, where we define S as the variable's previous value, δS as the change in the variable's value from one step to the next, μ as the annualized growth or drift rate, and σ as the annualized volatility.
  - o Mean-Reversion Process. The following describes the mathematical structure of a mean-reverting

process with drift: $\frac{\delta S}{S} = \eta(\bar{S}e^{\mu(\delta t)} - S)\delta t + \mu(\delta t) + \sigma\varepsilon\sqrt{\delta t}$. Here we define η as the rate of reversion to the mean and $\bar{S}$ as the long-term value to which the process reverts.

- o Jump-Diffusion Process. A jump-diffusion process is like a random walk process but includes a probability of a jump at any point in time. The occurrences of such jumps are completely random, but their probability and magnitude are governed by the process itself. We have the structure $\frac{\delta S}{S} = \eta(\bar{S}e^{\mu(\delta t)} - S)\delta t + \mu(\delta t) + \sigma\varepsilon\sqrt{\delta t} + \theta F(\lambda)(\delta t)$ for a jump-diffusion where we define θ as the jump size of S, $F(\lambda)$ as the inverse of the Poisson cumulative probability distribution, and λ as the jump rate of S.
  - o Jump-Diffusion Process with Mean Reversion. This model is essentially a combination of all three models discussed above (geometric Brownian motion with mean-reversion process and a jump-diffusion process).

- Structural Break. Tests if the coefficients in different datasets are equal and the method is most commonly used in time-series analysis to test for the presence of a structural break. A time-series dataset can be divided into two subsets and each subset is tested on the other and on the entire dataset to statistically determine if, indeed, there is a break starting at a particular time period. A one-tailed hypothesis test is performed on the null hypothesis such that the two data subsets are statistically similar to one another; that is, there is no statistically significant structural break.
  - o Short Tip: Runs a structural break test at specified break points using a dependent variable and one or more independent variables.
  - o Model Input: Data Type C. Two sets of variables are required: one dependent variable and one or multiple independent variables, with at least 5 rows of data in each variable, with the same number of total data points or rows per variable.
    - ▪ Dependent Variable, Independent Variables, Structural Break Points:
      - >VAR1
      - >VAR2; VAR3; …
      - 6; 8

- **Structural Equation Model: Path Estimation (Partial Least Squares).** Structural Equation Model (SEM) is typically used to solve path-dependent structures with endogenous variables. In a standard multivariate regression, we have one dependent variable (Y) and multiple independent variables (X_i), where the latter are independent of each other. However, in situations where the independent variables are related (e.g., endogenous variables), then SEM is needed. For instance, if X3 is impacted by X1 and X2, and X4 is impacted by X1 and X3, these need to be modeled in a simultaneous structure and solved using partial least squares.

  o Short Tip: Runs a Path Estimation model using sequential and simultaneous models (path analysis using Partial Least Squares method in Structural Equation Modeling).
  o Model Input: Data Type C. One or Multiple Independent Variables, and One Dependent Variable, with at least 5 rows of data in each variable, with the same number of total data points or rows per variable.

    ▪ Independent Variables, Dependent Variable (repeat for all the paths, starting with the longest to the shortest, and make sure the last variable is the dependent variable)

      • >VAR1; VAR2; VAR3; VAR4; VAR5
      • >VAR1; VAR2; VAR3; VAR4
      • >VAR1; VAR3; VAR4
      • >VAR1; VAR2

- **Survival and Hazard Tables (Kaplan–Meier).** The Kaplan–Meier method, the most commonly used life-table method in medical practice, does permit comparisons between patient groups or between different therapies.
  o Short Tip: Runs a Kaplan–Meier survival and hazard tables.
  o Model Input: Data Type C. Three variables are required: Starting Points of Interval, At Risk at the End of Interval, and Died at End of Interval, with at least 3 rows of data in each variable, with the same number of total data points or rows per variable.

    ▪ Starting Points of Interval, At Risk at the End of Interval, Died at End of Interval:
      • >VAR1
      • >VAR2
      • >VAR3

- **Time-Series Analysis.** In well-behaved time-series data (e.g., sales revenues and cost structures of large corporations), the values tend to have up to three elements: a base value, trend, and seasonality. Time-series analysis uses these historical data and decomposes them into these three elements and recomposes them into future forecasts. In other words, this forecasting method, like some of the others described, first performs a backfitting (backcast) of historical data before it provides estimates of future values (forecasts).
  - Short Tip: Runs various time-series forecasts with optimization using historical data, accounting for history, trend, and seasonality, and selects the best-fitting model.
  - Model Input: Data Type A. One input variable is required with at least 5 data points or rows of data, followed by simple manual inputs depending on the model selected:
    - Variable:
      - >VAR1
      - 4
      - 4
  - **Time-Series Analysis (Auto).** Selecting this automatic approach will allow the user to initiate an automated process in methodically selecting the best input parameters in each model and ranking the forecast models from best to worst by looking at their goodness-of-fit results and error measurements.
  - **Time-Series Analysis (DES).** The double exponential-smoothing (DES) approach is used when the data exhibit a trend but no seasonality.
  - **Time-Series Analysis (DMA).** The double moving average (DMA) method is used when the data exhibit a trend but no seasonality.
  - **Time-Series Analysis (HWA).** The Holt–Winters additive (HWA) approach is used when the data exhibit both seasonality and trend.
  - **Time-Series Analysis (HWM).** The Holt–Winters multiplicative (HWM) approach is used when the data exhibit both seasonality and trend.
  - **Time-Series Analysis (SA).** The seasonal additive (SA) approach is used when the data exhibit seasonality but no trend.
  - **Time-Series Analysis (SM).** The seasonal multiplicative (SM) approach is used when the data exhibit seasonality but no trend.

- o Time-Series Analysis (SES). The single exponential smoothing (SES) approach is used when the data exhibit no trend and no seasonality.
- o Time-Series Analysis (SMA). The single moving average (SMA) approach is used when the data exhibit no trend and no seasonality.
- Trending and Detrending. The typical methods for trending and detrending data are difference, exponential, linear, logarithmic, moving average, polynomial, power, rate, static mean, and static median. This function detrends your original data to take out any trending components. In forecasting models, the process removes the effects of accumulating datasets from seasonality and trend to show only the absolute changes in values and to allow potential cyclical patterns to be identified after removing the general drift, tendency, twists, bends, and effects of seasonal cycles of a set of time-series data. For example, a detrended dataset may be necessary to discover a company's true financial health—one may detrend increased sales around Christmas time to see a more accurate account of a company's sales in a given year more clearly by shifting the entire dataset from a slope to a flat surface to better see the underlying cycles and fluctuations. The resulting charts show the effects of the detrended data against the original dataset, the percentage of the trend that was removed based on each detrending method employed, and the detrended dataset.
  - o Short Tip: Runs various time-series trend lines and forecasts using historical data, accounting for history, trend, and seasonality.
  - o Model Input: Data Type A. One input variable is required with at least 5 data points or rows of data, followed by simple manual inputs depending on the model selected:
    - Variable:
      - >VAR1
      - 4
- Value at Risk (VaR and CVaR). Given a return's mean and standard deviation, as well as degrees of freedom, this model computes the Value at Risk (VaR) and Conditional Value at Risk (CVaR) of the returns using standardized normal and t distributions.
  - o Short Tip: Returns Value at Risk and Conditional Value at Risk based on distributions of returns using normal and t distributions.
  - o Model Input: Data Type A. Mean of Returns, Sigma of Returns, Degrees of Freedom

- Variables:
  - \>100
  - \>20
  - \>8
- **Variances Homogeneity Bartlett's Test.** Returns the sample variance calculations for each of the input variables and uses a pooled logarithmic Bartlett's test. The null hypothesis tested is that the variances are homogeneous and statistically similar.
  - o Short Tip: Tests if the variances from various variables are similar (H_0: all variances are equal or homogeneous).
  - o Model Input: Data Type C. Two or more input variables are required. Different variables are arranged in columns and all variables must have at least 3 data points each. Different numbers of total data points or rows per variable are allowed.
    - Variables: >VAR1; VAR2; VAR3; ...
- **Volatility: GARCH Models.** The Generalized Autoregressive Conditional Heteroskedasticity model is used to model historical and forecast future volatility levels of a time series of raw price levels of a marketable security (e.g., stock prices, commodity prices, and oil prices). GARCH first converts the prices into relative returns and then runs an internal optimization to fit the historical data to a mean-reverting volatility term structure, while assuming that the volatility is heteroskedastic in nature (changes over time according to some econometric characteristics). Several variations of this methodology are available in Risk Simulator, including EGARCH, EGARCH-T, GARCH-M, GJR-GARCH, GJR-GARCH-T, IGARCH, and T-GARCH. The dataset must be a time series of raw price levels.
  - o Short Tip: Generates various time-series volatility forecasts using GARCH model variations.
  - o Model Input: Data Type A. One data variable is required, followed by multiple manual inputs. The specific input requirements depend on the GARCH model selected.
    - Stock Prices, Periodicity, Predictive Base, Forecast Periods, Variance Targeting, P, Q:
      - \>VAR1
      - \>250
      - \>12
      - \>12
      - \>1
      - \>1
      - \>1

- **Volatility: Log Returns Approach.** Calculates the volatility using the individual future cash flow estimates, comparable cash flow estimates, or historical prices, computing the annualized standard deviation of the corresponding log relative returns.
  - Short Tip: Generates time-series volatility using the log-returns approach.
  - Model Input: Data Type A. One data variable is required, followed by the periodicity (number of periods per season).
    - Data, Periodicity
      - >VAR1
      - >250
- **Yield Curve (Bliss).** Used for generating the term structure of interest rates and yield curve estimation with five beta and lambda estimated parameters. Some econometric modeling techniques are required to calibrate the values of several input parameters in this model. Virtually any yield curve shape can be interpolated using these models, which are widely used at banks around the world.
  - Short Tip: Generates a time-series interest yield Bliss curve.
  - Model Input: Data Type A. Multiple manual inputs are required.
    - Beta 0, Beta 1, Beta 2, Lambda 1, Lambda 2, Starting Year, Ending Year, Step Size:
      - >0.8
      - >0.8
      - >0.1
      - >0.1
      - >1.5
      - >1
      - >10
      - >0.5
      - >1
- **Yield Curve (Nelson–Siegel).** An interpolation model with four estimated parameters for generating the term structure of interest rates and yield curve estimation. Some econometric modeling techniques are required to calibrate the values of several input parameters in this model.
  - Short Tip: Generates a time-series interest yield curve using the Nelson–Siegel method.
  - Model Input: Data Type A. Multiple manual inputs are required.

- Beta 0, Beta 1, Beta 2, Lambda, Starting Year, Ending Year, Step Size:
  - >0.03
  - >0.04
  - >0.02
  - >0.25
  - >1
  - >15
  - >1

DATA TYPE A: ONE COLUMN VARIABLE, MULTIPLE ROWS OR SIMPLE INPUTS

One input column variable is required, typically with at least 5 rows of numerical data. There are some models requiring only 3 data points (e.g., some of the Quick Statistics). Some models require only simple inputs such as Exponential J-Curve (e.g., 400, 3, 100).

Row	VAR1
1	155
2	125
3	201
4	135
5	220
6	130
7	210
8	125
9	165
10	165

ARIMA
Auto ARIMA
Autocorrelation and Partial Autocorrelation
Box-Cox Normal Transformation
Charts: 2D Area, Bar, Line, Point, Scatter
Charts: 3D Area, Bar, Line, Point, Scatter
Charts: Box-Whisker
Charts: Q-Q Normal
Combinatorial Fuzzy Logic
Control Chart: C
Control Chart: NP
Control Chart: U
Control Chart: XMR
Data Descriptive Statistics
Deseasonalize
Distributional Fitting: ALL: Continuous
Distributional Fitting: Continuous (Akaike Information Criterion)
Distributional Fitting: Continuous (Anderson–Darling)
Distributional Fitting: Continuous (Kolmogorov–Smirnov)
Distributional Fitting: Continuous (Kuiper's Statistic)
Distributional Fitting: Continuous (Schwarz/Bayes Criterion)
Distributional Fitting: Discrete (Chi-Square)
Diversity Index (Shannon, Brillouin, Simpson)
Exponential J-Curve
Forecast Accuracy: Akaike, Bayes, Schwarz, MAD, MSE, RMSE

Grubbs Test for Outliers
Logistic S-Curve
Markov Chain
Markov Chain Transition Risk Matrix
Neural Network (Cosine with Hyperbolic Tangent)
Neural Network (Hyperbolic Tangent)
Neural Network (Linear)
Neural Network (Logistic)
Nonparametric: Chi-Square Population Variance
Nonparametric: D'Agostino–Pearson Normality Test
Nonparametric: Lilliefors Test for Normality
Nonparametric: Runs Test for Randomness
Nonparametric: Shapiro–Wilk–Royston Normality Test
Nonparametric: Wilcoxon Signed-Rank Test (One Var)
Parametric: One Variable (T) Mean
Parametric: One Variable (Z) Mean
Parametric: One Variable (Z) Proportion
Parametric: Power Curve for T Test
Quick Statistic: Absolute Values (ABS)
Quick Statistic: Average (AVG)
Quick Statistic: Count
Quick Statistic: Difference
Quick Statistic: LAG
Quick Statistic: Lead
Quick Statistic: LN
Quick Statistic: LOG
Quick Statistic: Max
Quick Statistic: Median
Quick Statistic: Min
Quick Statistic: Mode
Quick Statistic: Power
Quick Statistic: Rank Ascending
Quick Statistic: Rank Descending
Quick Statistic: Relative LN Returns
Quick Statistic: Relative Returns
Quick Statistic: Semi-Standard Deviation (Lower)
Quick Statistic: Semi-Standard Deviation (Upper)
Quick Statistic: Standard Deviation Population
Quick Statistic: Standard Deviation Sample
Quick Statistic: Sum
Quick Statistic: Variance (Population)
Quick Statistic: Variance (Sample)
Seasonality
Segmentation Clustering
Skew and Kurtosis: Shapiro–Wilk and D'Agostino–Pearson
Stationarity: Augmented Dickey Fuller

Stationarity: Dickey Fuller (Constant and Trend)
Stationarity: Dickey Fuller (Constant No Trend)
Stationarity: Dickey Fuller (No Constant No Trend)
Stochastic Process (Exponential Brownian Motion)
Stochastic Process (Geometric Brownian Motion)
Stochastic Process (Jump Diffusion)
Stochastic Process (Mean Reversion)
Stochastic Process (Mean Reverting and Jump Diffusion)
Structural Break
Time-Series Analysis (Auto)
Time-Series Analysis (Double Exponential Smoothing)
Time-Series Analysis (Double Moving Average Lag)
Time-Series Analysis (Double Moving Average)
Time-Series Analysis (Holt–Winters Additive)
Time-Series Analysis (Holt–Winters Multiplicative)
Time-Series Analysis (Seasonal Additive)
Time-Series Analysis (Seasonal Multiplicative)
Time-Series Analysis (Single Exponential Smoothing)
Time-Series Analysis (Single Moving Average)
Trend Line (Difference Detrended)
Trend Line (Exponential Detrended)
Trend Line (Exponential)
Trend Line (Linear Detrended)
Trend Line (Linear)
Trend Line (Logarithmic Detrended)
Trend Line (Logarithmic)
Trend Line (Moving Average Detrended)
Trend Line (Moving Average)
Trend Line (Polynomial Detrended)
Trend Line (Polynomial)
Trend Line (Power Detrended)
Trend Line (Power)
Trend Line (Rate Detrended)
Trend Line (Static Mean Detrended)
Trend Line (Static Median Detrended)
Volatility (EGARCH)
Volatility (EGARCH-T)
Volatility (GARCH)
Volatility (GARCH-M)
Volatility (GJR GARCH)
Volatility (GJR TGARCH)
Volatility (Log Returns)
Yield Curve (Bliss)
Yield Curve (Nelson–Siegel)

DATA TYPE B: TWO COLUMN VARIABLES, MULTIPLE ROWS

Two input column variables are required. Different variables are arranged in columns and all variables must have at least 3 data points each, typically with the same number of total data points or rows per variable.

All Tests Listed Below

	DEP Y	INDEP X
Row	VAR1	VAR2
1	5.1	5.4
2	5.6	5.6
3	6.8	6.3
4	5.9	6.1
5	4.0	4.7
6	5.6	5.1
7	6.6	6.6
8	6.7	6.8
...	...	...
N	4.5	4.1

***Wilcoxon, Independent T-Tests**

Row	VAR1	VAR2
1	78	4
2	78	23
3	60	25
4	53	48
5	85	17
6	84	8
7	73	4
8	78	26
...	78	
N	75	

* Unequal rows are acceptable

Charts: 2D Area
Charts: 2D Bar
Charts: 2D Line
Charts: 2D Point
Charts: 2D Scatter
Charts: 3D Area
Charts: 3D Bar
Charts: 3D Line
Charts: 3D Point
Cointegration Test (Engle–Granger)
Control Chart: P
Cubic Spline
Data Analysis: Cross Tabulation
Data Analysis: New Values Only
Data Analysis: Subtotal by Category
Data Analysis: Unique Values Only

Error Correction Model (Engle–Granger)
Forecast Accuracy: Pesaran–Timmermann (Single Directional Forecast)
Granger Causality
Kendall's Tau Correlation (No Ties)
Kendall's Tau Correlation (with Ties)
Linear Interpolation
Multiple Regression (Deming Regression with Known Variance)
Multiple Regression (Two Variable Functional Form Tests)
Nominal Data Contingency Analysis (McNemar's Marginal Homogeneity)
Nonparametric: Chi-Square GOF for Normality (Grouped Data)
Nonparametric: Chi-Square Independence
Nonparametric: Mann–Whitney Test (Two Var)
Nonparametric: Wilcoxon Signed-Rank Test (Two Var)
Parametric: Two Variable (F) Variances
Parametric: Two Variable (T) Dependent Mean
Parametric: Two Variable (T) Independent Unequal Variances
Parametric: Two Variable (T) Independent Equal Variances
Parametric: Two Variable (Z) Independent Proportions
Parametric: Two Variable (Z) Independent Means
ROC Curves, AUC, and Classification Tables

DATA TYPE C: MULTIPLE COLUMN VARIABLES, MULTIPLE ROWS

Two or more input column variables are required and typically start with three variables. Different variables are arranged in columns and all variables must have at least 3 to 5 data points each, typically with the same number of total data points or rows per variable. In the special cases for Eigenvalues and Eigenvectors, Inter-rater Reliability: Cohen's Kappa, and Partial Correlations (Using Correlation Matrix), the total number of variables must also match the number of rows, i.e., the data entered should be in an $N \times N$ matrix. Several examples with how certain variable types are set up follow.

Row	VAR1	VAR2	VAR3
1	2	6	-2
2	6	8	7
3	-2	7	3
N	...	...	...

ANOVA Randomized Block

	Method 1	Method 2	Method 3
Block 1	2	6	-2
Block 2	6	8	7
Block 3	-2	7	3

ANOVA Multiple Treatments

	Method 1	Method 2	Method 3
Person 1	2	6	-2
Person 2	6	8	7
Person 3	-2	7	3

Interclass Correlation

	Judge 1	Judge 2	Judge 3
Wine 1	10	4	1
Wine 2	6	16	2
Wine 3	0	3	8

Cohen's Kappa

Judge 1

Judge 2	Answer 1	Answer 2	Answer 3
Answer 1	10	4	1
Answer 2	6	16	2
Answer 3	0	3	8

ANOVA Two Way

	Factor B1	Factor B2	Factor B3
Factor A1	804	836	804
Factor A1	816	828	808
Factor A2	819	844	807
Factor A2	813	836	819
Factor A3	820	814	819
Factor A3	821	811	829
Factor A4	806	811	827
Factor A4	805	806	835

Cronbach's Alpha, Guttman's Lambda
Kendall's W, Split Half Method

	Question 1	Question 2	Question 3
Person 1	10	4	1
Person 2	6	16	2
Person 3	0	3	8

MANOVA

Row	VAR1	VAR2	VAR3	VAR4
1	loam	76.7	29.5	7.5
2	loam	60.5	32.1	6.3
3	loam	96.1	40.7	4.2
4	sandy	88.1	45.1	4.9
5	sandy	50.2	34.1	11.7
6	sandy	55.0	31.1	6.9
7	salty	65.4	21.6	4.3
8	salty	65.7	27.7	5.3
9	salty	67.3	48.3	5.5
N	...	...	...	...

Custom Econometrics, Multiple Regression

Row	VAR1	VAR2	VAR3	VAR4
1	804	76.7	29.5	7.5
2	816	60.5	32.1	6.3
3	819	96.1	40.7	4.2
4	813	88.1	45.1	4.9
5	820	50.2	34.1	11.7
6	821	55.0	31.1	6.9
7	806	65.4	21.6	4.3
8	805	65.7	27.7	5.3
9	884	67.3	48.3	5.5
N	...	...	...	...

ANOVA (MANOVA General Linear Model)
ANOVA (Randomized Blocks Multiple Treatments)
ANOVA (Single Factor Multiple Treatments)
ANOVA (Two-Way Analysis)
ARIMA
Auto ARIMA
Auto Econometrics (Detailed)
Auto Econometrics (Quick)
Autocorrelation Durbin-Watson AR(1) Test
Bonferroni Test (Single Variable with Repetition)
Charts: 2D Pareto
Charts: 3D Pareto
Coefficient of Variation Homogeneity Test
Control Chart: R
Control Chart: X
Correlation Matrix (Linear, Nonlinear)
Covariance Matrix
Cox Regression
Custom Econometric Model
Discriminate Analysis (Linear)
Discriminate Analysis (Quadratic)
Eigenvalues and Eigenvectors
Endogeneity Test with Two-Stage Least Squares (Durbin–Wu–Hausman)
Endogenous Model (Instrumental Variables with Two-Stage Least Squares)
Factor Analysis (PCA with Varimax Rotation)
Forecast Accuracy: Diebold–Mariano (Dual Competing Forecasts)
Generalized Linear Models (Logit with Binary Outcomes)
Generalized Linear Models (Logit with Bivariate Outcomes)
Generalized Linear Models (Probit with Binary Outcomes)
Generalized Linear Models (Probit with Bivariate Outcomes)
Generalized Linear Models (Tobit with Censored Data)
Heteroskedasticity Test (Breusch-Pagan-Godfrey)
Heteroskedasticity Test (Lagrange Multiplier)
Heteroskedasticity Test (Wald-Glejser)
Heteroskedasticity Test (Wald's on Individual Variables)
Hotelling T-Square: 1 VAR with Related Measures
Internal Consistency Reliability: Cronbach's Alpha (Dichotomous Data)
Internal Consistency Reliability: Guttman's Lambda and Split Half Model
Inter-rater Reliability: Cohen's Kappa
Inter-rater Reliability: Inter-Class Correlation (ICC)
Inter-rater Reliability: Kendall's W (No Ties)
Inter-rater Reliability: Kendall's W (with Ties)
Multiple Poisson Regression (Population and Frequency)
Multiple Regression (Linear)
Multiple Regression (Nonlinear)
Multiple Regression (Ordinal Logistic Regression)

Multiple Regression (Through Origin)
Multiple Ridge Regression (Low Variance, High Bias, High VIF)
Multiple Weighted Regression (Fixing Heteroskedasticity)
Nonparametric: Cochran's Q (Binary Repeated Measures)
Nonparametric: Friedman's Test
Nonparametric: Kruskal–Wallis Test
Nonparametric: Mood's Multivariate Median Test
Partial Correlations (Using Correlation Matrix)
Partial Correlations (Using Raw Data)
Principal Component Analysis
Specifications Cubed Test (Ramsey's RESET)
Specifications Squared Test (Ramsey's RESET)
Stepwise Regression (Backward)
Stepwise Regression (Correlation)
Stepwise Regression (Forward)
Stepwise Regression (Forward-Backward)
Survival and Hazard Tables (Kaplan–Meier)
Variances Homogeneity Bartlett's Test

DATA TYPE D: TWO GROUPS OF MULTIPLE COLUMN VARIABLES, MULTIPLE ROWS

For Type D data, two groups of variables are required. In each group, two or more column variables are required with at least 5 data points each and the same total number of data points or rows for all variables are required for the Hotelling Dependent Pair. The other tests allow an unequal number of rows between groups but must have the same number of rows within the same group.

GROUP 1   GROUP 2

Row	VAR1	VAR2	VAR3	VAR4	VAR5	VAR6	VAR7	VAR8	VAR9	VAR10
1	6	8	3	5	19	8	6	5	6	10
2	6	7	3	4	9	8	6	3	6	4
3	5	7	1	4	16	7	5	6	4	17
4	10	9	8	4	4	9	8	6	3	4
5	7	9	7	6	9	8	5	6	8	11
6	6	6	3	9	17	8	7	4	4	13
7	5	8	6	7	6	7	3	6	3	8
8	3	7	3	6	16	6	6	5	8	14
9	8	8	9	3	8	6	9	7	5	12
10	8	6	5	3	13	7	5	9	6	11
11	5	9	5	4	17	7	5	4	6	15
12	8	8	2	3	5	5	7	4	4	6
13	5	8	7	5	8	6	4	6	4	12
14	4	9	10	2	16	8	7	8	5	12
15	2	9	4	10	14	5	6	5	7	12
16	7	5	8	6	15	10	5	7	6	6
17	4	8	8	2	16	9	6	9	5	11
18	5	10	9	3	11	8	7	10	5	5
19	7	7	3	7	12	6	2	5	3	8
20	1	5	2	7	17	5	7	5	5	8
21	5	6	7	7	20	8	4	8	8	10
22	4	3	1	2	15	3	2	4	4	15
23	7	9	6	6	9	8	6	3	6	12
24	4	5	2	4	12	5	4	6	5	9
25	8	9	5	7	18	6	3	4	8	8

ANCOVA (Single Factor Multiple Treatments)
Bonferroni Test (Two Variables with Repetition)
Box's Test for Homogeneity of Covariance
Hotelling T-Square: 2 VAR Dependent Pair with Related Measures
Hotelling T-Square: 2 VAR Independent Equal Variance Related Measures
Hotelling T-Square: 2 VAR Independent Unequal Variance Related Measures

Partial Area Standard Normal (Z)

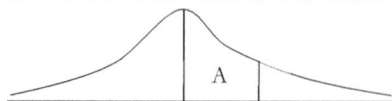

Z	0.00	0.01	0.02	0.03	0.04	0.05	0.06	0.07	0.08	0.09
0.0	0.0000	0.0040	0.0080	0.0120	0.0160	0.0199	0.0239	0.0279	0.0319	0.0359
0.1	0.0398	0.0438	0.0478	0.0517	0.0557	0.0596	0.0636	0.0675	0.0714	0.0753
0.2	0.0793	0.0832	0.0871	0.0910	0.0948	0.0987	0.1026	0.1064	0.1103	0.1141
0.3	0.1179	0.1217	0.1255	0.1293	0.1331	0.1368	0.1406	0.1443	0.1480	0.1517
0.4	0.1554	0.1591	0.1628	0.1664	0.1700	0.1736	0.1772	0.1808	0.1844	0.1879
0.5	0.1915	0.1950	0.1985	0.2019	0.2054	0.2088	0.2123	0.2157	0.2190	0.2224
0.6	0.2257	0.2291	0.2324	0.2357	0.2389	0.2422	0.2454	0.2486	0.2517	0.2549
0.7	0.2580	0.2611	0.2642	0.2673	0.2704	0.2734	0.2764	0.2794	0.2823	0.2852
0.8	0.2881	0.2910	0.2939	0.2967	0.2995	0.3023	0.3051	0.3078	0.3106	0.3133
0.9	0.3159	0.3186	0.3212	0.3238	0.3264	0.3289	0.3315	0.3340	0.3365	0.3389
1.0	0.3413	0.3438	0.3461	0.3485	0.3508	0.3531	0.3554	0.3577	0.3599	0.3621
1.1	0.3643	0.3665	0.3686	0.3708	0.3729	0.3749	0.3770	0.3790	0.3810	0.3830
1.2	0.3849	0.3869	0.3888	0.3907	0.3925	0.3944	0.3962	0.3980	0.3997	0.4015
1.3	0.4032	0.4049	0.4066	0.4082	0.4099	0.4115	0.4131	0.4147	0.4162	0.4177
1.4	0.4192	0.4207	0.4222	0.4236	0.4251	0.4265	0.4279	0.4292	0.4306	0.4319
1.5	0.4332	0.4345	0.4357	0.4370	0.4382	0.4394	0.4406	0.4418	0.4429	0.4441
1.6	0.4452	0.4463	0.4474	0.4484	0.4495	0.4505	0.4515	0.4525	0.4535	0.4545
1.7	0.4554	0.4564	0.4573	0.4582	0.4591	0.4599	0.4608	0.4616	0.4625	0.4633
1.8	0.4641	0.4649	0.4656	0.4664	0.4671	0.4678	0.4686	0.4693	0.4699	0.4706
1.9	0.4713	0.4719	0.4726	0.4732	0.4738	0.4744	0.4750	0.4756	0.4761	0.4767
2.0	0.4772	0.4778	0.4783	0.4788	0.4793	0.4798	0.4803	0.4808	0.4812	0.4817
2.1	0.4821	0.4826	0.4830	0.4834	0.4838	0.4842	0.4846	0.4850	0.4854	0.4857
2.2	0.4861	0.4864	0.4868	0.4871	0.4875	0.4878	0.4881	0.4884	0.4887	0.4890
2.3	0.4893	0.4896	0.4898	0.4901	0.4904	0.4906	0.4909	0.4911	0.4913	0.4916
2.4	0.4918	0.4920	0.4922	0.4925	0.4927	0.4929	0.4931	0.4932	0.4934	0.4936
2.5	0.4938	0.4940	0.4941	0.4943	0.4945	0.4946	0.4948	0.4949	0.4951	0.4952
2.6	0.4953	0.4955	0.4956	0.4957	0.4959	0.4960	0.4961	0.4962	0.4963	0.4964
2.7	0.4965	0.4966	0.4967	0.4968	0.4969	0.4970	0.4971	0.4972	0.4973	0.4974
2.8	0.4974	0.4975	0.4976	0.4977	0.4977	0.4978	0.4979	0.4979	0.4980	0.4981
2.9	0.4981	0.4982	0.4982	0.4983	0.4984	0.4984	0.4985	0.4985	0.4986	0.4986
3.0	0.4987	0.4987	0.4987	0.4988	0.4988	0.4989	0.4989	0.4989	0.4990	0.4990

Cumulative Standard Normal (Z)

Z	0.00	0.01	0.02	0.03	0.04	0.05	0.06	0.07	0.08	0.09
0.0	0.5000	0.5040	0.5080	0.5120	0.5160	0.5199	0.5239	0.5279	0.5319	0.5359
0.1	0.5398	0.5438	0.5478	0.5517	0.5557	0.5596	0.5636	0.5675	0.5714	0.5753
0.2	0.5793	0.5832	0.5871	0.5910	0.5948	0.5987	0.6026	0.6064	0.6103	0.6141
0.3	0.6179	0.6217	0.6255	0.6293	0.6331	0.6368	0.6406	0.6443	0.6480	0.6517
0.4	0.6554	0.6591	0.6628	0.6664	0.6700	0.6736	0.6772	0.6808	0.6844	0.6879
0.5	0.6915	0.6950	0.6985	0.7019	0.7054	0.7088	0.7123	0.7157	0.7190	0.7224
0.6	0.7257	0.7291	0.7324	0.7357	0.7389	0.7422	0.7454	0.7486	0.7517	0.7549
0.7	0.7580	0.7611	0.7642	0.7673	0.7704	0.7734	0.7764	0.7794	0.7823	0.7852
0.8	0.7881	0.7910	0.7939	0.7967	0.7995	0.8023	0.8051	0.8078	0.8106	0.8133
0.9	0.8159	0.8186	0.8212	0.8238	0.8264	0.8289	0.8315	0.8340	0.8365	0.8389
1.0	0.8413	0.8438	0.8461	0.8485	0.8508	0.8531	0.8554	0.8577	0.8599	0.8621
1.1	0.8643	0.8665	0.8686	0.8708	0.8729	0.8749	0.8770	0.8790	0.8810	0.8830
1.2	0.8849	0.8869	0.8888	0.8907	0.8925	0.8944	0.8962	0.8980	0.8997	0.9015
1.3	0.9032	0.9049	0.9066	0.9082	0.9099	0.9115	0.9131	0.9147	0.9162	0.9177
1.4	0.9192	0.9207	0.9222	0.9236	0.9251	0.9265	0.9279	0.9292	0.9306	0.9319
1.5	0.9332	0.9345	0.9357	0.9370	0.9382	0.9394	0.9406	0.9418	0.9429	0.9441
1.6	0.9452	0.9463	0.9474	0.9484	0.9495	0.9505	0.9515	0.9525	0.9535	0.9545
1.7	0.9554	0.9564	0.9573	0.9582	0.9591	0.9599	0.9608	0.9616	0.9625	0.9633
1.8	0.9641	0.9649	0.9656	0.9664	0.9671	0.9678	0.9686	0.9693	0.9699	0.9706
1.9	0.9713	0.9719	0.9726	0.9732	0.9738	0.9744	0.9750	0.9756	0.9761	0.9767
2.0	0.9772	0.9778	0.9783	0.9788	0.9793	0.9798	0.9803	0.9808	0.9812	0.9817
2.1	0.9821	0.9826	0.9830	0.9834	0.9838	0.9842	0.9846	0.9850	0.9854	0.9857
2.2	0.9861	0.9864	0.9868	0.9871	0.9875	0.9878	0.9881	0.9884	0.9887	0.9890
2.3	0.9893	0.9896	0.9898	0.9901	0.9904	0.9906	0.9909	0.9911	0.9913	0.9916
2.4	0.9918	0.9920	0.9922	0.9925	0.9927	0.9929	0.9931	0.9932	0.9934	0.9936
2.5	0.9938	0.9940	0.9941	0.9943	0.9945	0.9946	0.9948	0.9949	0.9951	0.9952
2.6	0.9953	0.9955	0.9956	0.9957	0.9959	0.9960	0.9961	0.9962	0.9963	0.9964
2.7	0.9965	0.9966	0.9967	0.9968	0.9969	0.9970	0.9971	0.9972	0.9973	0.9974
2.8	0.9974	0.9975	0.9976	0.9977	0.9977	0.9978	0.9979	0.9979	0.9980	0.9981
2.9	0.9981	0.9982	0.9982	0.9983	0.9984	0.9984	0.9985	0.9985	0.9986	0.9986
3.0	0.9987	0.9987	0.9987	0.9988	0.9988	0.9989	0.9989	0.9989	0.9990	0.9990

Student's T

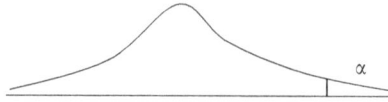

t df	0.10	0.05	0.01	0.005	df	0.10	0.05	0.01	0.005
1	3.0777	6.3138	31.8205	63.6567	31	1.3095	1.6955	2.4528	2.7440
2	1.8856	2.9200	6.9646	9.9248	32	1.3086	1.6939	2.4487	2.7385
3	1.6377	2.3534	4.5407	5.8409	33	1.3077	1.6924	2.4448	2.7333
4	1.5332	2.1318	3.7469	4.6041	34	1.3070	1.6909	2.4411	2.7284
5	1.4759	2.0150	3.3649	4.0321	35	1.3062	1.6896	2.4377	2.7238
6	1.4398	1.9432	3.1427	3.7074	36	1.3055	1.6883	2.4345	2.7195
7	1.4149	1.8946	2.9980	3.4995	37	1.3049	1.6871	2.4314	2.7154
8	1.3968	1.8595	2.8965	3.3554	38	1.3042	1.6860	2.4286	2.7116
9	1.3830	1.8331	2.8214	3.2498	39	1.3036	1.6849	2.4258	2.7079
10	1.3722	1.8125	2.7638	3.1693	40	1.3031	1.6839	2.4233	2.7045
11	1.3634	1.7959	2.7181	3.1058	41	1.3025	1.6829	2.4208	2.7012
12	1.3562	1.7823	2.6810	3.0545	42	1.3020	1.6820	2.4185	2.6981
13	1.3502	1.7709	2.6503	3.0123	43	1.3016	1.6811	2.4163	2.6951
14	1.3450	1.7613	2.6245	2.9768	44	1.3011	1.6802	2.4141	2.6923
15	1.3406	1.7531	2.6025	2.9467	45	1.3006	1.6794	2.4121	2.6896
16	1.3368	1.7459	2.5835	2.9208	46	1.3002	1.6787	2.4102	2.6870
17	1.3334	1.7396	2.5669	2.8982	47	1.2998	1.6779	2.4083	2.6846
18	1.3304	1.7341	2.5524	2.8784	48	1.2994	1.6772	2.4066	2.6822
19	1.3277	1.7291	2.5395	2.8609	49	1.2991	1.6766	2.4049	2.6800
20	1.3253	1.7247	2.5280	2.8453	50	1.2987	1.6759	2.4033	2.6778
21	1.3232	1.7207	2.5176	2.8314	51	1.2984	1.6753	2.4017	2.6757
22	1.3212	1.7171	2.5083	2.8188	52	1.2980	1.6747	2.4002	2.6737
23	1.3195	1.7139	2.4999	2.8073	53	1.2977	1.6741	2.3988	2.6718
24	1.3178	1.7109	2.4922	2.7969	54	1.2974	1.6736	2.3974	2.6700
25	1.3163	1.7081	2.4851	2.7874	55	1.2971	1.6730	2.3961	2.6682
26	1.3150	1.7056	2.4786	2.7787	56	1.2969	1.6725	2.3948	2.6665
27	1.3137	1.7033	2.4727	2.7707	57	1.2966	1.6720	2.3936	2.6649
28	1.3125	1.7011	2.4671	2.7633	58	1.2963	1.6716	2.3924	2.6633
29	1.3114	1.6991	2.4620	2.7564	59	1.2961	1.6711	2.3912	2.6618
30	1.3104	1.6973	2.4573	2.7500	60	1.2958	1.6706	2.3901	2.6603

SOFTWARE DOWNLOAD & INSTALL

As current versions of the software are continually updated, we highly recommend that you visit the Real Options Valuation, Inc., website and follow the instructions below to install the latest software applications.

- **Step 1**: Visit **www.realoptionsvaluation.com** and click on **Downloads** and **Download Software** (Figure A). You will be prompted to log in. Please first register if you are a first-time user (Figure B) and an automated e-mail will be sent to you within several minutes. (If you do not receive a registration e-mail after you register, then please send a note to support@realoptionsvaluation.com.) While waiting for the automated e-mail, browse this page and see the free getting started videos, case studies, and sample models you can download.

- **Step 2**: Return to this site and LOGIN using the login credentials you received via e-mail. Download and install the latest versions of **Risk Simulator** and **Real Options SLS** on this Web page. The download links, installation instructions, and Hardware ID information are also presented on this page (Figure C).

- **Step 3**: After installing the software, start Excel and you will see a Risk Simulator ribbon. Follow the instructions provided on the Web page to obtain and e-mail support@realoptionsvaluation.com your Hardware ID and mention the code "**MR3E 30 Days**" and you will be sent a free extended 30-day license to use both the Risk Simulator and Real Options SLS software.

www.realoptionsvaluation.com getting started and modeling videos

Testimonials | FAQ | Global Partners | Contact Us

🖥️ English   🇨🇳 Chinese (Simplified)   🇨🇳 Chinese (Traditional)   🇫🇷 French   🇩🇪 German   🇮🇹 Italian
● Japanese   🇰🇷 Korean   🇧🇷 Portuguese (Brazil)   🇷🇺 Russian   🇪🇸 Spanish

$0.00

CQRM CERTIFICATE | TRAINING | CONSULTING | SOFTWARE | BOOKS | DOWNLOADS | PURCHASE |

SOFTWARE DOWNLOADS

GETTING STARTED AND
MODELING VIDEOS

PRODUCT BROCHURES

SAMPLE MODELS

WHITEPAPERS AND CASE STUDIES

DOWNLOAD CENTER

You can also visit our mirror download site if you have problems downloading from this page

Welcome to Real Options Valuation, Inc.'s download center. Here you will be able to download versions of the software you have purchased (license information required to install these full versions), product brochures, case ple training videos to help you get started in using our software, as well as sample Excel models to use with Risk Simulator and Re............ftware.

GETTING STARTED AND MODELING VIDEOS

The following are some live-motion and voice narrated videos which are playable on your computer using Windows Media Player or other video players capable of WMV playback. You can simply click on any of these links below to view the streaming videos.

ROV SOFTWARE GETTING STARTED VIDEOS

We also have some more detailed Risk Analysis and Risk Simulator software getting started videos that you can download and watch. These videos total about 2 hours. For even more detailed training, please check out our set of 12 Training DVDs (over 30 hours) or our hands-on Certified in Risk Management seminars (4 days). The following are updated detailed getting started videos on Risk Simulator, featuring all the new tools such as Auto ARIMA, GARCH, JS Curves, Cubic Spline, Maximum Likelihood, Data Diagnostics, Statistical Analysis, Modeling Toolkit, and more...

Figure A: Step 1 – Software download site

DOWNLOAD CENTER

You can also visit our mirror download site if you have problems downloading from this page

Welcome to Real Options Valuation, Inc.'s download center. Here you will be able to download trial versions of our software, full versions of the software you have purchased (license information required to install these full versions), product brochures, case studies and white papers, and sample training videos to help you get started in using our software, as well as sample Excel models to use with Risk Simulator and Real Options Super Lattice Solver software.

YOU ARE REQUIRED TO LOGIN TO VIEW THIS PAGE.

Username

Password

LOG IN

REGISTER

Figure B: Register if you are a first-time visitor

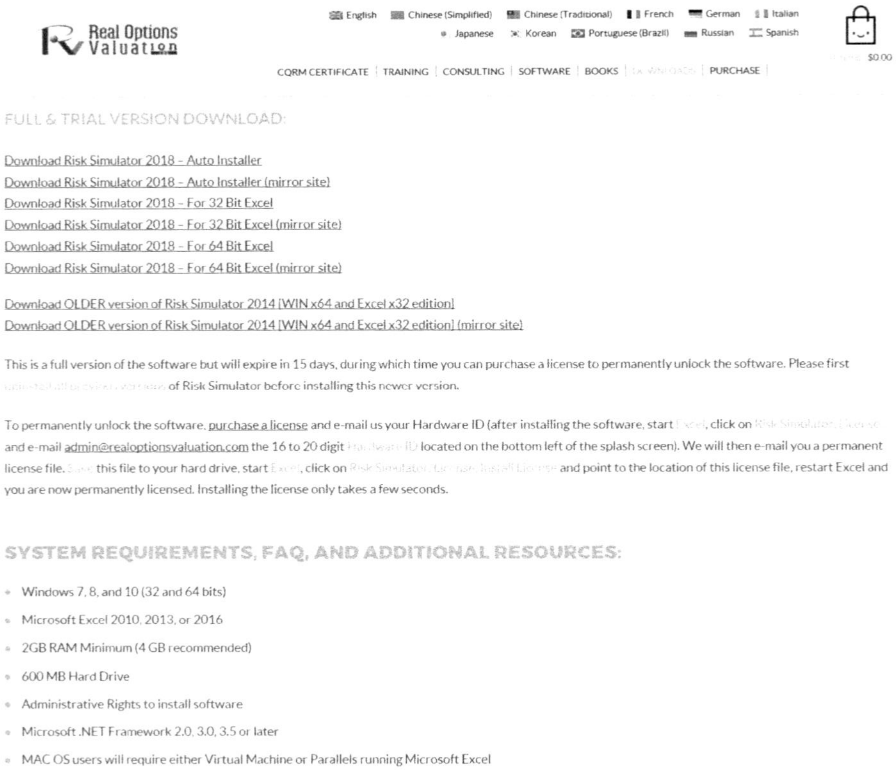

Real Options Valuation

English | Chinese (Simplified) | Chinese (Traditional) | French | German | Italian
Japanese | Korean | Portuguese (Brazil) | Russian | Spanish

CORM CERTIFICATE | TRAINING | CONSULTING | SOFTWARE | BOOKS | | PURCHASE |

$0.00

FULL & TRIAL VERSION DOWNLOAD

Download Risk Simulator 2018 – Auto Installer
Download Risk Simulator 2018 – Auto Installer (mirror site)
Download Risk Simulator 2018 – For 32 Bit Excel
Download Risk Simulator 2018 – For 32 Bit Excel (mirror site)
Download Risk Simulator 2018 – For 64 Bit Excel
Download Risk Simulator 2018 – For 64 Bit Excel (mirror site)

Download OLDER version of Risk Simulator 2014 (WIN x64 and Excel x32 edition)
Download OLDER version of Risk Simulator 2014 (WIN x64 and Excel x32 edition) (mirror site)

This is a full version of the software but will expire in 15 days, during which time you can purchase a license to permanently unlock the software. Please first uninstall any previous version of Risk Simulator before installing this newer version.

To permanently unlock the software, purchase a license and e-mail us your Hardware ID (after installing the software, start , click on Risk Simulator | License and e-mail admin@realoptionsvaluation.com the 16 to 20 digit Hardware ID located on the bottom left of the splash screen). We will then e-mail you a permanent license file. Save this file to your hard drive. start , click on Risk Simulator | License | Install License and point to the location of this license file, restart Excel and you are now permanently licensed. Installing the license only takes a few seconds.

SYSTEM REQUIREMENTS, FAQ, AND ADDITIONAL RESOURCES:

- Windows 7, 8, and 10 (32 and 64 bits)
- Microsoft Excel 2010, 2013, or 2016
- 2GB RAM Minimum (4 GB recommended)
- 600 MB Hard Drive
- Administrative Rights to install software
- Microsoft .NET Framework 2.0, 3.0, 3.5 or later
- MAC OS users will require either Virtual Machine or Parallels running Microsoft Excel

Figure C: Download links and hardware ID instructions

SAMPLE COMPREHENSIVE OR ORAL EXAM QUESTIONS

1. Provide an example of a problem statement. What are some of the required elements and characteristics of a well-written problem statement?

2. Provide an example of a research thesis or dissertation layout. Describe each of the sections or chapters involved.

3. Explain what Bayesian analysis is and how it works. You can use Bayes' Theorem as an illustration of the approach. What are some of the main requirements to run a Bayesian analysis?

4. What is conditional probability and how does it work? Are conditional probabilities important in situations where there is dependence or independence between events?

5. What is the difference between descriptive statistics used in deduction versus inferential statistics used for induction purposes? How do inferential statistics work in terms of using statistical samples?

6. Explain some basic sampling methods (e.g., stratified sampling, random sampling) and how one might control or block on intervening variables. What about proper population representation, spread, and diversity?

7. What is the definition of a hypothesis? What does it mean and how is it usually constructed?

8. Provide examples of directional vs. non-directional hypotheses. What happens to the alpha significance levels and the computed p-values when we change from a one-tail to a two-tailed test and vice versa?

9. What are the four levels of data measurement? Provide some examples. Under which levels of measurement would degrees Fahrenheit, binary conditional outcomes, placement in a race, kilograms, time, and stock prices fall?

10. What is the difference between a parameter and a statistic of distributional moments? How can you tell the difference? Which ones would have a larger uncertainty?

11. What is a standard deviation? What is a coefficient of variation? When is each used? Which is a relative measure, and which would be an absolute measure? Provide examples to support your response.

12. What are the differences among arithmetic average, geometric average, moving average, weighted average, and harmonic average? When do you use each?

13. What are the assumptions surrounding the use of a binomial distribution versus a Poisson distribution? Provide examples for each distribution.

14. Provide an example of how a hypergeometric distribution may be applied. Is this a discrete or continuous distribution? Does this distribution have event memory or is it considered memoryless? Why or why not?

15. What are the four distributional moments and what do they each measure? What are IQR, Beta, and VaR, and what moments are these?

16. What does a high kurtosis in your data imply? Does a triangular distribution have positive, negative, or zero kurtoses? What about a uniform distribution and normal distribution? Is high kurtosis a good thing or a concern for someone working in Six Sigma quality control?

17. What do you use to measure the spread and dispersion of a dataset? What information does dispersion provide? How is dispersion used in hypothesis tests?

18. What is the main difference between combinations and permutations? In determining the number of required pairwise correlations of a variable set, which would we use?

19. What do PDF, CDF, ICDF stand for and how are they used? Explain how you can identify the four moments from the shape of a CDF S-curve.

20. When is a Z-score used and when might it be appropriate? What are the required main assumptions for a Z-score model? Provide an example of how a Z-score model works.

21. What are the main characteristics of a normal distribution and why is normality so important in quantitative research methods?

22. What are Type I, Type II, Type III, and Type IV errors? Which can we control directly, and which ones of these errors might be a false positive or false negative?

23. What is the statistical power of a test and how is it computed? Which error types might statistical power be related to?

24. What is the difference between accuracy and precision, and which can you possibly exert control over and how? Explain the differences: accurate and precise, accurate but not precise, not accurate but precise, and not accurate and not precise.

25. Does risk lead to uncertainty or does uncertainty lead to risk? What are some measures of risk and uncertainty?

26. What is the central limit theorem, how does it work, and why is it important? Provide an example of statistical sampling as it pertains to the central limit theorem.

27. What is a sampling distribution and how does it work? Provide an example of a full-scale sample versus statistical sampling.

28. Explain what the following terms mean and how they might be tested: data reliability, consistency, and credibility. What is inter-rater versus intra-rater reliability?

29. How would you measure a model's internal validity and external validity? What are some of the statistical measures you can use?

30. What is predictive validity? How is that measured or quantified?

31. When and why are nonparametrics employed? How are the hypotheses different? What are the strengths and weaknesses of nonparametrics versus parametric methods?

32. Why do nonparametric methods use medians instead of means? Which has higher statistical power?

33. Does correlation imply causality? Does causality imply correlation? How do you test for causality?

34. What test do you apply to see if there is a statistically significant difference in an effect? Specifically, if you wanted to test a before and after

effect of a new vaccine or viral therapeutic treatment, what approach would you use and why?

35. How do you test if two variables are statistically independent of one another? Is correlation a good way to measure statistical dependence and statistical independence? If not, what other tests or approaches might you use and why?

36. What is the difference between a Spearman and Pearson correlation? How do you compute a Spearman correlation using the Pearson's approach?

37. Compare and contrast the various ANOVA models. Specifically, explain what each model is used for and under what conditions.

38. What do the Hotelling and Bonferroni methods do? Why could we not simply use multiple standard tests instead of these larger and bulkier tests?

39. Provide an example of how ANOVA with blocking variables might be used, and why we might run into data and modeling biases if this method is not used. What are these variable blocks?

40. What does a two-way ANOVA factorial model with replication look like? Can we test for interactions between factors using this method?

41. Multivariate regression has two main uses. What are they? What are the pros and cons of a multivariate linear regression?

42. What is a unit root and why might it be important? Is this applicable for time-series or cross-section data or both?

43. Do independent variables need to be independent of the dependent variable or from other independent variables? Why or why not? What happens if the requirement is violated?

44. Compare and contrast the following terms: binary, binomial, bivariate, bimodal.

45. What are some examples of bivariate regression model specifications?

46. Can you run a regular multivariate regression when the independent variable is binary or truncated? What about when the dependent variable is binary or truncated?

47. What are some of the assumptions required in running an ordinary least squares multivariate regression? What are some of the potential errors in a regression model?

48. What are autocorrelation, multicollinearity, and heteroskedasticity?

49. What are Logit and Probit models and when are they applicable? What are the differences and similarities between these two methods?

50. What are random walks, Brownian motion, mean reversion, and jump-diffusion processes? Are these dynamic or stochastic processes and what are they used for?

51. How do you measure the accuracy of a forecast model? What about the precision of a forecast model? Compare and contrast these two terms.

52. What is a Runs test used for and how does it work? Is it a powerful test? What are some alternatives to the Runs test?

53. What are the Cronbach's Alpha and Kendall's W tests used for? Provide an example of how these methods may be applicable.

54. Why is normality in the data such an important thing? How do you know if the data are normal? If not normal, what happens then? Are statistical results still valid? What do we do if the data are not normal?

55. What are the Lilliefors test, Shapiro–Wilk–Royston test, and D'Agostino–Pearson test used for? What about the Kuiper's model or Akaike models?

56. In a Kolmogorov–Smirnov distributional fitting routine, what is the null hypothesis tested, would you look for a low or high p-value, and why?

57. What are some examples of errors and biases in your data and in your model?

58. If your data are nonlinear and non-normal, how would you linearize or normalize them and why would you bother?

59. Explain what the following means: heteroskedasticity, multicollinearity, nonlinearity, outliers, micronumerosity, structural breaks.

60. What is data stationarity and why is it important to know? What issues might you encounter and how would you handle the issues if your data are stationary versus nonstationary?

61. What are inter-rater reliability and intra-rater reliability? How would you test these?

62. What is the Kruskal–Wallis test and what is the Friedman's test?

63. What is the Wilcoxon test used for?

64. How would you identify and model cause and effect? How do you identify and know if you run into a causality loop? How would Granger causality models help?

65. A hypothesis is usually an induction or inference to the population from a sample, as opposed to deduction with constructs and propositions. Can one truly with absolute confidence reject a hypothesis or accept a hypothesis? Which action is easier? Can you provide an example?

66. What are some examples of data and modeling biases? Provide details.

67. What do calculations such as the Akaike Information Criterion (AIC), Bayes and Schwarz Criterion (BSC), and Hannan–Quinn Criterion (HQC) measure?

68. Explain self-selection bias and survivorship bias. Provide examples.

69. Computational Monte Carlo simulations and stochastic models were performed to generate data from experiments or theoretical constructs. Provide some examples on where you might run into the need to do this in future research?

70. What is Granger causality? Explain leading, lagging, and coincident indicators. How would one use the results from the Granger model?

71. How does a statistical process control chart work? What are SPC charts used for? Can I use SPC to identify normality, outliers, and extreme events?

72. Describe some examples of potential data and modeling errors that may exist in a multivariate regression.

73. How do you test for randomness of data? Is the approach valid for time-series, cross-sectional, mixed panel data, or some combination thereof?

74. What is the difference between an ARIMA and a GARCH model? What are each used for, what types of data are most appropriate, and

why use these models as compared to other methods? What might be the limitations and advantages of these methods?

75. How would you model interactions among various independent variables? Are the same approaches applicable for time-series data as cross-sectional data?

76. If you find a high variance inflation factor in your model, is it a good thing or a bad thing? How would you solve any potential issues that might occur with a high VIF?

77. If asked to model a presidential election or some other national election results, describe the steps and methodology you would take.

78. What is a neural network model and how does it work?

79. Is heteroskedasticity critical in both time-series and cross-sectional models? Why or why not? How would you fix heteroskedasticity?

80. The Akaike Information Criterion and the Bayes Schwartz Criterion are used in a variety of models. What do these two methods actually do?

81. Name some of the various types of multivariate regression and when each one might be used and under what conditions?

82. When is a mean-reversion model most appropriately used?

83. What is the Kolmogorov–Smirnov test used for? Explain the idea behind this method.

84. What is the difference between precision and accuracy? Which can you control for in a computational Monte Carlo simulation model?

85. What is a seed value used for? How does it work and how will the results change?

86. All time-series data can be decomposed into three fundamental elements. What are these elements and how do they work in combination to help generate a forecast?

87. Compare and contrast among the following methods: tornado analysis, scenario analysis, dynamic sensitivity analysis, bootstrap simulation, computational Monte Carlo simulation, and spider analysis.

88. Explain the differences among static analysis, dynamic analysis, and stochastic analysis in terms of computational Monte Carlo simulation and nonlinear optimization.

89. What types of data and what data properties might be best suited for a Holt–Winters model? What is this model used for?

90. What is a dynamic model and what is a stochastic process model? How are they similar or different? When would you use each?

91. Under what circumstances would an exponential curve or a logistic curve be more appropriate to use?

92. Discuss the various types of stepwise regression and how they work (e.g., forward, backward, forward-backward, correlation, and others).

93. What are the four typical input parameters required to run a stochastic optimization? Provide examples of stochastic optimization and how you would obtain these inputs.

94. What is a two-stage least squares 2SLS model and how do you use instrumental variables to model it? What is endogeneity in this case?

95. Is seasonality or cyclicality in a dataset easier to model? Why? Are cross-sectional data susceptible to these changes? What about mixed panel data?

96. Explain factor analysis and principal component analysis. What does each do? Explain how you would use the computed eigenvalues and eigenvectors.

97. How does a Markov chain work? What would a multi-state Markov chain be used for?

98. What is a cubic spline? Provide an example of how this method would apply.

99. What is combinatorial fuzzy logic? What is fuzzy logic in general and why would someone use this method?

100. What is a simultaneous equations model or a structural equations model? Provide an example of when this method might be applicable.

INDEX